The Boundaries of the EU Internal Market

The book examines the twofold 'boundaries' of the concept of the European Union's internal market – the geographical and the substantive – through the prism of expanding the internal market to third countries without enlarging the Union. The book offers a comprehensive analysis of the conditions under which the internal market can effectively be extended to third countries by exporting EU acquis via international agreements without sacrificing its defining characteristics. Theoretical rather than empirical in approach, the book scrutinises and meticulously questions the required level of uniformity within flexible integration relating to the substantive scope of the internal market, the role of foundational principles in the European Union's market edifice and the institutional framework necessary for granting third country actors full participation in the internal market while safeguarding the autonomy of the Union's legal order.

Marja-Liisa Öberg is Senior Lecturer in European Union Law at the Faculty of Law, Lund University.

Cambridge Studies in European Law and Policy

The focus of this series is European law broadly understood. It aims to publish original monographs in all fields of European law, from work focusing on the institutions of the EU and the Council of Europe to books examining substantive fields of European law as well as examining the relationship between European law and domestic, regional and international legal orders. The series publishes works adopting a wide variety of methods: comparative, doctrinal, theoretical and inter-disciplinary approaches to European law are equally welcome, as are works looking at the historical and political facets of the development of European law and policy. The main criterion is excellence i.e. the publication of innovative work, which will help to shape the legal, political and scholarly debate on the future of European law.

Books in the Series

The Boundaries of the EU Internal Market: Participation Without Membership
Marja-Liisa Öberg

The Currency of Solidarity: Constitutional Transformation during the Euro Crisis
Vestert Borger

Empire of Law: Nazi Germany, Exile Scholars and the Battle for the Future of Europe
Kaius Tuori

*In the Court We Trust: Cooperation, Coordination and Collaboration between the
European Court of Justice and Supreme Administrative Courts*
Rob van Gestel and Jurgen de Poorter

*Beyond Minimum Harmonisation: Gold-Plating and Green-Plating of European
Environmental Law*
Lorenzo Squintani

The Politics of Justice in European Private Law: Social Justice, Access Justice, Societal Justice
Hans Micklitz

*The Transformation of EU Treaty Making: The Rise of Parliaments, Referendums and
Courts Since 1950*
Dermot Hodson and Imelda Maher

Redefining European Economic Integration
Dariusz Adamski

*Human Rights in the Council of Europe and the European Union: Achievements,
Trends and Challenges*
Steven Greer, Janneke Gerards and Rosie Slowe

Core Socio-Economic Rights and the European Court of Human Rights
Ingrid Leijten

*Green Trade and Fair Trade in and with the EU: Process-based Measures within the
EU Legal Order*
Laurens Ankersmit

New Labour Laws in Old Member States: Trade Union Responses to European Enlargement
Rebecca Zahn

The Governance of EU Fundamental Rights
Mark Dawson

*The International Responsibility of the European Union: From Competence
to Normative Control*
Andrés Delgado Casteleiro

The Boundaries of the EU Internal Market

Participation without Membership

Marja-Liisa Öberg

Lund University

CAMBRIDGE
UNIVERSITY PRESS

CAMBRIDGE
UNIVERSITY PRESS

University Printing House, Cambridge CB2 8BS, United Kingdom

One Liberty Plaza, 20th Floor, New York, NY 10006, USA

477 Williamstown Road, Port Melbourne, VIC 3207, Australia

314–321, 3rd Floor, Plot 3, Splendor Forum, Jasola District Centre,
New Delhi – 110025, India

79 Anson Road, #06–04/06, Singapore 079906

Cambridge University Press is part of the University of Cambridge.

It furthers the University's mission by disseminating knowledge in the pursuit of
education, learning, and research at the highest international levels of excellence.

www.cambridge.org
Information on this title: www.cambridge.org/9781108499729
DOI: 10.1017/9781108584531

© Marja-Liisa Öberg 2020

First published 2020

A catalogue record for this publication is available from the British Library.

Library of Congress Cataloging-in-Publication Data
Names: Öberg, Marja-Liisa, author.
Title: The boundaries of the EU internal market : participation without
membership / Marja-Liisa Öberg, Örebro University.
Other titles: Boundaries of the European Union internal market
Description: Cambridge, United Kingdom ; New York, NY : Cambridge University
Press, 2020. | Series: Cambridge studies in European law and policy | Includes
index.
Identifiers: LCCN 2020019432 (print) | LCCN 2020019433 (ebook) | ISBN
9781108499729 (hardback) | ISBN 9781108584531 (epub)
Subjects: LCSH: Trade regulation – European Union countries. | European Union
countries – Economic integration.
Classification: LCC KJE6569 .O24 2020 (print) | LCC KJE6569 (ebook) | DDC
343.2407–dc23
LC record available at https://lccn.loc.gov/2020019432
LC ebook record available at https://lccn.loc.gov/2020019433

ISBN 978-1-108-49972-9 Hardback

To Jacob, August and Teodor

Contents

Series Editors' Preface

This fascinating book seeks to conceptualise the extension of the European Union's internal market to third countries without membership of the EU and to provide a legal analysis of the twofold 'boundaries' of the concept of the internal market. These boundaries are principally geographical but also have a substantive dimension. The book offers a comprehensive analysis of the conditions under which the internal market can be effectively expanded by exporting the *acquis* to allow for the participation of third countries without sacrificing its defining characteristics. This work is most timely in view of Brexit and the negotiations on the future relationship between the European Union and the United Kingdom, but its canvas stretches way beyond Brexit issues to examine the substantive scope of the internal market, the required level of uniformity within flexible integration, the role of foundational principles in the EU's market edifice and the institutional framework and related concerns (such as the autonomy of the EU's legal order which is keenly guarded by the Court of Justice) of extending the internal market beyond the Union's borders. Instead of looking at the effectiveness of norms transport from the point of view of the third countries involved, the book discusses the limits of integration from the perspective of EU constitutional law.

Exporting the Union's *acquis* is scarcely a new idea; the European Economic Area (EEA) is the most celebrated instance of this working extremely well for many years. Öberg uses the EEA Agreement and three sectoral treaties: the Energy Community Treaty, the European Common Aviation Area Agreement and the Transport Community Treaty as case studies illustrating the challenges of setting up institutions and procedures which respect both the autonomy of the EU legal order and the sovereignty of the contracting parties, while seeking to achieve and maintain homogeneity in the expanded internal market. These four treaties in fact establish homogeneous markets within a wide region rather than between the EU and individual third countries. The extent of market integration envisaged and achieved, generally in the case of the EEA, and in specific sectors in the case of the others, involves the third countries engaging in extensive commitments to adhere to the EU *acquis*. Like the EU itself, they go much further than bilateral agreements. Accordingly, these multilateral case studies demonstrate feasible responses to the challenges of setting up elaborate institutions and procedures to support the achievement and maintenance of homogeneity in a legal space founded upon the EU *acquis*, while at the same time respecting the EU legal order's inherent limits to the EU's exportation of norms.

The analysis in this book is both dynamic and invigorating, and it deserves to be read widely; academics, postgraduate students and legal practitioners will find much wisdom over which to mull, and decision-makers and influencers will read it to their profit. Accordingly, we are very pleased indeed to welcome this latest addition to the series Cambridge Studies in European Law and Policy.

Mark Dawson
Laurence Gormley
Jo Shaw

Acknowledgements

This book is a revised version of the PhD thesis I defended at the European University Institute (EUI) in September 2015. Many people have contributed to the writing of this book, directly and indirectly, and to them I owe great gratitude. Professor Marise Cremona, my PhD supervisor, has provided many valuable insights and respectful guidance in shaping this work. Professor Loïc Azoulai has shown great enthusiasm for the research and acted as a truly inspiring academic. The valuable and challenging comments from Professor Christophe Hillion and Professor Stephen Weatherill and the fruitful discussion at the thesis defence have greatly contributed to the writing of this book.

I am very grateful to Tom Randall, Gemma Smith and Becky Jackaman at Cambridge University Press for their kind assistance and patience, and the Series Editors for their trust and encouragement. I also thank Kate McIntosh for compiling the index and Gayathri Tamilselvan and Akash Udayakumar for copy-editing the manuscript.

Some parts of this book are based on previously published material. Chapter 2 has been published as 'Internal Market Acquis as a Tool in EU External Relations: From Integration to Disintegration' (2020) 47 *Legal Issues of Economic Integration* 151; a part of Chapter 5, Section 5.3.1.3 in 'From EU Citizens to Third Country Nationals: The Legacy of *Polydor*' (2016) 22(1) *European Public Law* 97, republished in A Biondi and P Birkinshaw (eds.), *Britain Alone! The Implications and Consequences of United Kingdom Exit from the EU* (Kluwer Law International 2016) 199; and Chapter 6 as 'Autonomy of the EU Legal Order: A Concept in Need of Revision?' (2020) 26 *European Public Law*.

I have had the opportunity to work in several fantastic research environments, most recently at the EUI and at Lund University. The success of this project owes much to the wonderful staff at the EUI and to my supportive colleagues at the Faculty of Law at Lund University. During the writing of this book, I enjoyed the privilege of long uninterrupted research time owing to generous funding by the Ragnar Söderberg Foundation.

Many other EUI professors, fellow researchers and participants at workshops and conferences have during the years contributed to this book with helpful questions, comments, discussions and generous assistance with otherwise inaccessible materials. Jacqueline Breidlid, in particular, has provided me with crucial 'insider information' about the functioning of the EEA, and Ranyta Yusran with the nuances of public international law.

Lastly, my precious family have given me much love and support during the long writing process. Jacob has tirelessly cared for us all during the most intense periods, proofread the drafts and provided invaluable insights. August and Teodor have wonderfully been just who they are and a constant reminder of why academic work, however rewarding, cannot be everything.

Table of Cases

Court of Justice of the European Union

Court of Justice

Other International Courts and Arbitral Tribunals

National Courts

Germany

Norway

United Kingdom

Table of Legislation

European Union

Treaties

Treaty establishing the European Economic Community,
  25 March 1957, 298 UNTS 3, 4 Eur YB 412.
Consolidated version of the Treaty on European Union [1997] OJ
  C340/02
Treaty establishing the European Community (Consolidated version
  2002) [2002] OJ C325/33
Consolidated version of the Treaty on European Union [2016] OJ
  C202/13
Consolidated version of the Treaty on the Functioning of the European
  Union [2016] OJ C202/47
Charter of Fundamental Rights of the European Union [2016] OJ
  C202/389

Regulations

Regulation (EEC) No 1612/68 of the Council of 15 October 1968 on
  freedom of movement for workers within the Community [1968] OJ
  L257/2
Council Regulation (EC) No 2062/94 of 18 July 1994 establishing
  a European Agency for Safety and Health at Work [1994] OJ L216/1 as
  amended by Council Regulations (EC) No 1643/95, 1654/2003 and
  1112/2005
Council Regulation (EC) No 2894/94 of 28 November 1994 concerning
  arrangements for implementing the Agreement on the European
  Economic Area [1994] OJ L305/6

Regulation (EC) No 549/2004 of the European Parliament and of the
   Council of 10 March 2004 laying down the framework for the creation
   of the single European sky [2004] OJ L96/1
Regulation (EU) No 182/2011 of the European Parliament and of the
   Council of 16 February 2011 laying down the rules and general
   principles concerning mechanisms for control by Member States of
   the Commission's exercise of implementing powers [2011] OJ L55/13
Regulation (EU) No 211/2011 of the European Parliament and of the
   Council of 16 February 2011 on the citizens' initiative [2011] OJ L65/1
Regulation (EU) 2018/1806 of the European Parliament and of the
   Council of 14 November 2018 listing the third countries whose
   nationals must be in possession of visas when crossing the external
   borders and whose nationals are exempt from that requirement
   [2018] OJ L303/39

Directives

Council Directive 89/104/EEC of 21 December 1988 to approximate the
   laws of the Member States relating to trade marks [1989] OJ L40/1
Council Directive 90/364/EEC of 28 June 1990 on the right of residence
   [1990] OJ L180/26
Council Directive 90/365/EEC of 28 June 1990 on the right of residence
   for employees and self-employed persons who have ceased their
   occupational activity [1990] OJ L180/28
Council Directive 93/13/EEC of 5 April 1993 on unfair terms in
   consumer contracts [1993] OJ L95/29
Council Directive 93/96/EEC of 29 October 1993 on the right of residence
   for students [1993] OJ L317/59
Council Directive 96/34/EC of 3 June 1996 on the framework agreement
   on parental leave concluded by the Union des Confédérations de
   l'Industrie et des Employeurs d'Europe (UNICE), the Centre Européen
   de l'Entreprise Publique (CEEP) and the Confédération Européenne
   des Syndicats (ETUC) [1996] OJ L145/4
Directive 96/92/EC of the European Parliament and of the Council of
   19 December 1996 concerning common rules for the internal market
   in electricity [1997] OJ L27/20
Directive 97/67/EC of the European Parliament and of the Council of
   15 December 1997 on common rules for the development of the
   internal market of Community postal services and the improvement
   of quality of service [1998] OJ L15/14

Directive 98/30/EC of the European Parliament and of the Council of 22 June 1998 concerning common rules for the internal market in natural gas [1998] OJ L204/1

Directive 2002/22/EC of the European Parliament and of the Council of 7 March 2002 on universal service and users' rights relating to electronic communications networks and services [2002] OJ L108/51

Directive 2003/54/EC of the European Parliament and of the Council of 26 June 2003 concerning common rules for the internal market in electricity and repealing Directive 96/92/EC [2003] OJ L176/37

Directive 2003/55/EC of the European Parliament and of the Council of 26 June 2003 concerning common rules for the internal market in natural gas and repealing Directive 98/30/EC [2003] OJ L176/57

Directive 2004/38/EC of the European Parliament and of the Council of 29 April 2004 on the right of citizens of the Union and their family members to move and reside freely within the territory of the Member States [2004] OJ L158/77

Directive 2006/123/EC of the European Parliament and of the Council of 12 December 2006 on services in the internal market [2006] OJ L367/36

Directive 2009/72/EC of the European Parliament and of the Council of 13 July 2009 concerning common rules for the internal market in electricity [2009] OJ L211/55

Directive 2013/36/EU of the European Parliament and of the Council of 26 June 2013 on access to the activity of credit institutions and the prudential supervision of credit institutions and investment firms [2013] OJ L176/338

Council Decisions

Council Decision of 22 December 1994 amending the Protocol on the Statute of the Court of Justice of the European Community (94/993/ EC) [1994] OJ L379/1

Decision No 884/2004/EC of the European Parliament and of the Council of 29 April 2004 amending Decision No 1692/96/EC on Community guidelines for the development of the trans-European transport network [2004] OJ L167/1

Council Decision (EU) 2017/1937 of 11 July 2017 on the signing, on behalf of the European Union, and provisional application of the Treaty establishing the Transport Community [2017] OJ L278/1

Agreement on the withdrawal of the United Kingdom of Great Britain and Northern Ireland from the European Union and the European Atomic Energy Community [2020] OJ L29/7

Accession Documents

Joint Declaration on Common Foreign and Security Policy attached to the Treaty concerning the accession of the Kingdom of Norway, the Republic of Austria, the Republic of Finland and the Kingdom of Sweden to the European Union [1994] OJ C241/381

Act concerning the conditions of accession of the Republic of Croatia and the adjustments to the Treaty on European Union, the Treaty on the Functioning of the European Union and to the Treaty establishing the European Atomic Energy Community [2012] OJ L112/21

European Council

European Council, 'Conclusions of the Presidency – Edinburgh, 12 December 1992, Annex I Overall approach to the application by the Council of the subsidiarity principle and Article 3b of the Treaty on European Union' SN 456/92

European Council, 'Conclusions of the Presidency – Copenhagen, 21–22 June 1993' SN 180/1/93 REV 1

European Council, 'Conclusions of the Presidency – Corfu, 24–25 June 1994' SN 150/94

European Council, 'Conclusions of the Presidency – Essen, 9–10 December 1994' SN 300/94

European Council, 'Conclusions of the Presidency – Lisbon, 23–24 March 2000' SN 100/00

European Council, 'Conclusions of the Presidency – Feira, 19–20 June 2000' SN 200/00

European Council, 'Conclusions of the Presidency – Stockholm, 23–24 March 2001' SN 100/01

European Council, 'Conclusions – Brussels, 4 February 2011' EUCO 2/1/11 REV 1

European Council, Art. 50 Guidelines, EUCO XT 20001/18, 23 March 2018

European Commission

Commission, 'Conclusions of the first Summit Conference of the enlarged Community – Paris, 19–20 October 1972' Bulletin of the European Communities 10–1972

'Conclusions of the 8th Union for the Mediterranean Trade Ministerial
Conference – 9 December 2009' (Press Release) MEMO/09/547,
9 December 2009

Council, 'Joint Statement on the Partnership for Modernisation – 25th
EU-Russia Summit, Rostov-on-Don, 31 May–1 June 2010' (Press
Release) 10546/10, 1 June 2010

EEAS, 'New agreement signed between the European Union and
Armenia set to bring tangible benefits to citizens' (Press Release)
24 November 2017 https://eeas.europa.eu/headquarters/headquar
ters-homepage/36141/new-agreement-signed-between-european-
union-and-armenia-set-bring-tangible-benefits-citizens_en accessed
10 February 2020

'Council conclusions on enlargement and stabilisation and association
process' (Press Release) 479/19, 18 June 2019

Speeches

De Clercq W, speech held at the EC-EFTA ministerial meeting,
Interlaken, 20 May 1987, SPEECH/87/32

Prodi R, 'A Wider Europe – A Proximity Policy as the key to stability',
speech held at the Sixth ECSA-World Conference 'Peace, Security And
Stability International Dialogue and the Role of the EU', Brussels,
5–6 December 2002, SPEECH/02/619

International Legal Acts and Policy Documents

United Nations

Statute of the International Court of Justice, San Francisco, 1945, UKTS
67 (1946) UKTS 67 (1946) Cmd 7015

Vienna Convention on the Law of Treaties, 23 May 1969, 1155 UNTS 331,
8 ILM 679

Declaration of the United Nations Conference on the Human
Environment, Report of the United Nations Conference on the
Human Environment (1972) A/CONF.48/14/Rev.1, 3

Articles on Responsibility of States for Internationally Wrongful Acts,
General Assembly Resolution 56/83 of 12 December 2001, A/RES/56/83

International Law Commission

Draft Articles on the Law of Treaties with commentaries (1966) II
Yearbook of the International Law Commission

Draft Articles on the Responsibility of International Organizations (2011) II Yearbook of the International Law Commission Part II

European Economic Area

Decision of the EEA Joint Committee No 158/2007 of 7 December 2007 amending Annex V (Free movement of workers) and Annex VIII (Right of establishment) to the EEA Agreement that incorporated the Citizenship Directive into the EEA Agreement [2008] OJ L124/20

Joint Declaration by the Contracting Parties to Decision of the EEA Joint Committee No 158/2007 incorporating Directive 2004/38/EC of the European Parliament and of the Council into the Agreement [2008] OJ L124/20

Decision of the EEA Joint Committee No 160/2009 of 4 December 2009 amending Protocol 31 to the EEA Agreement, on cooperation in specific fields outside the four freedoms [2010] OJ L62/67

EEA Joint Parliamentary Committee, 'EC comitology and the EEA' (Report and Resolution) M/20/R/029, 21 June 2011

Council of Europe

Convention for the Protection of Human Rights and Fundamental Freedoms, ETS No.005

Treaty Bodies

Decision 1/95 of the EC-Turkey Association Council of 22 December 1995 on implementing the final phase of the Customs Union [1996] OJ L35/1

Memorandum of Understanding on the Regional Electricity Market in South East Europe and its Integration into the European Union Internal Electricity Market, 2002

Memorandum of Understanding on the Regional Energy Market in South East Europe and its Integration into the European Community Internal Energy Market, 2003, 15548/03/bis

Ministerial Council Decision 2008/03/MC-EnC implementing certain provisions of the Treaty and creating Energy Community Oil Forum

Decision of the Ministerial Council of the Energy Community D/2013/03/MC-EnC on extending the duration of the Energy Community Treaty [2013] OJ L320/81

National Legal Acts

United States of America: Constitution

Abbreviations

AA	Association Agreement
AC	Appeal Cases
ACER	Agency for the Cooperation of Energy Regulators
ACP	African, Caribbean and Pacific
AETR Agreement	European Agreement concerning the Work of Crews of Vehicles Engaged in International Road Transport
AFSJ	Area of Freedom, Security and Justice
AG	Advocate General
ARSIWA	Articles on the Responsibility of States for Internationally Wrongful Acts
ATM	Air Traffic Management
BIT	Bilateral Investment Treaty
BUSINESSEUROPE	Confederation of European Business
BVerfGE	Bundesverfassungsgericht
CAA	Common Aviation Area
CAP	Common Agricultural Policy
CCP	Common Commercial Policy
CEC	European Confederation of Executives and Managerial Staff
CEECs	Central and Eastern European Countries
CEEP	European Centre of Employers and Enterprises providing Public Services
CETA	EU-Canada Comprehensive Economic and Trade Agreement
CFI	Court of First Instance
CFSP	Common Foreign and Security Policy

Cm	command paper
CSDP	Common Security and Defence Policy
CTP	Common Transport Policy
DCFTA	Deep and Comprehensive Free Trade Area
EA	Europe Agreement
EASA	European Union Aviation Safety Agency
EC	European Community
ECAA	European Common Aviation Area
ECHR	European Convention on Human Rights
ECSC	European Coal and Steel Community
ECtHR	European Court of Human Rights
EEA	European Economic Area
EEAS	European External Action Service
EEC	European Economic Community
EESC	European Economic and Social Committee
EFTA	European Free Trade Association
EFTA Ct Rep	Report of the EFTA Court
Eionet	European Environment Information and Observation Network
EMAA	Euro-Mediterranean Association Agreement
EMU	Economic and Monetary Union
EnCT	Energy Community Treaty
ENP	European Neighbourhood Policy
ESA	EFTA Surveillance Authority
ETS	European Treaty Series
ETUC	European Trade Union Confederation
EU	European Union
Eurocadres	Council of European Professional and Managerial Staff
Eur YB	European Yearbook
FTA	Free Trade Area/Agreement
GATT	General Agreement on Tariffs and Trade
HC	House of Commons
HL	House of Lords
ICJ	International Court of Justice
IGO	Inter-governmental Organisation
ILC	International Law Commission
ITLOS	International Tribunal for the Law of the Sea
MoU	Memorandum of Understanding
NEPIs	New Environmental Policy Instruments

OECD	Organisation for Economic Co-operation and Development
OJ	Official Journal
OMC	Open Method of Co-ordination
P4M	Partnership for Modernisation
PCA	Partnership and Cooperation Agreement
PCIJ	Permanent Court of International Justice
PEC	Pan-European Corridors
PHLG	Permanent High Level Group
RIAA	Reports of International Arbitral Awards
RSC	Regional Steering Committee
SAA	Stabilisation and Association Agreement
SAP	Stabilisation and Association Process
SCA	Surveillance and Court Agreement
SEA	Single European Act
SEE	South East Europe
SEETO	South East Europe Transport Observatory
SES	Single European Sky
SESAR ATM	Single European Sky Air Traffic Management Research
SGEIs	Services of General Economic Interest
SMEunited	European Association of Craft, Small and Medium-Sized Enterprises
SNE	Seconded National Expert
SSC	Single Sky Committee
TCT	Transport Community Treaty
TEN-T	Trans-European Transport Network
TEU	Treaty on European Union
TFEU	Treaty on the Functioning of the European Union
TRIPs	Agreement on Trade-Related Aspects of Intellectual Property Rights
UEAPME	European Association of Craft, Small and Medium-Sized Enterprises
UfM	Union for the Mediterranean
UN	United Nations
UNMIK	United Nations Interim Administration Mission in Kosovo
VCLT	Vienna Convention on the Law of Treaties
WTO	World Trade Organization

1   Introduction

The competitive position of the European Union (EU) in the world depends not only on pure economic (trade) power but also on the Union's ever-increasing regulatory impact. The latter includes both participation in multilateral bodies that create global rules, standards and practices and exporting its own norms and values in exchange for access to the internal market.[1] The latter phenomenon of integration through EU acquis is most visible in the Union's neighbourhood and exemplified by an array of regulatory tools varying in form and intensity.

Exporting the EU acquis to third countries has a variety of objectives, ranging from economic development in the Union and the neighbouring regions to coordinated responses to mutual threats and challenges. Regulatory approximation between the EU and the third countries' legal orders increases political and economic stability in the EU's immediate neighbourhood while assisting the non-EU Member States to reach internal policy goals, which are equally beneficial for the EU.[2] The latter holds true especially for states in a modernisation or transitional phase, such as the countries of the former Soviet Union. Furthermore, providing third countries an alternative to membership in the form of access to the internal market coupled with financial and technical aid instead of a broad enlargement strategy is a possible means of dealing with the Union's accession capacity.[3]

---

[1] See further M Cremona, 'The Union as a Global Actor: Roles, Models and Identity' (2004) 41 *Common Market Law Review* 553. On the external dimension of the internal market see also Commission, 'The External Dimension of the Single Market Review' (Staff Working Document) SEC (2007) 1519; Commission, 'A single market for 21st century Europe' (Communication) COM (2007) 724 final.

[2] S Lavenex, 'EU External Governance in "Wider Europe"' (2004) 11 *Journal of European Public Policy* 680, 694.

[3] The former President of the European Commission Romano Prodi suggested as a solution the creation of a Common European Economic Space based on 'sharing everything with the Union but institutions': R Prodi, 'A Wider Europe – A Proximity

Certain categories of agreements concluded between the Union and the neighbourhood countries share the common feature of exporting to the non-Member States the EU's norms, policies and institutions. The scope of the acquis and the depth of integration envisaged in each agreement vary to a large extent depending on factors such as the broader political aims of the general framework or programme into which the agreement belongs, the specific aim of the particular agreement, the geographical proximity of the contracting parties, the economic situation of the third country and the latter's prospect of and attitude towards EU membership.

Differently from the enlargement process, agreements that envisage legal approximation[4] between the EU and neighbouring countries on the basis of EU acquis do not aim for total regulatory convergence encompassing the entire body of EU acquis. Most often, the norms export only concerns the acquis of the internal market and is, thus, directly connected to granting third countries access to the European market.[5] Furthermore, in some instances, the process of regulatory approximation is based primarily on international or bilateral norms,[6] whereas in other cases, complete legal homogeneity on the basis of internal market acquis is sought between the EU and the third countries. The evolution of the role of the internal market acquis in the EU's external relations is one of deepening and broadening towards a common set of rules, featuring a variety of policy frameworks, types of agreements and objectives in terms of future EU membership.

Exporting the internal market acquis to third countries and, especially, the aim of thereby expanding the internal market is a significant

---

Policy as the Key to Stability', speech held at the Sixth ECSA-World Conference 'Peace, Security And Stability International Dialogue and the Role of the EU', Brussels, 5–6 December 2002, SPEECH/02/619.

[4] In the context of EU external relations the term refers to alignment with EU law rather than legislative harmonisation involving the participation of the Member States. See M Cremona, 'The New Associations: Substantive Issues of the Europe Agreements with the Central and Eastern European States' in SV Konstadinidis (ed.), *The Legal Regulation of the European Community's External Relations after the Completion of the Internal Market* (Dartmouth 1996) 141, 154.

[5] For the purposes of this study, the internal market acquis, which is a concept of variable content, is defined broadly to include all primary and secondary law, political instruments, and case law of the EU judiciary pertaining to the establishment and functioning of the internal market, including the fundamental freedoms and competition law as well horizontal provisions and fundamental rights.

[6] E Barbé and others, 'Drawing the Neighbours Closer . . . to What?' (2009) 44 *Cooperation and Conflict* 378.

part of the EU's external action and the most prominent example of third countries' legal approximation to the EU. It questions the correlation between the twofold boundaries of the internal market – the geographical and the substantive. From the perspective of EU constitutional law, the blurring of the boundaries of the internal market raises a set of questions pertaining to the nature of the internal market and the EU legal order as well as the overall 'expandability' of the internal market separate from the enlargement process.

Certain multilateral agreements, in particular, have in common the ambitious objective of exporting a significant share of EU acquis to non-EU Member States to, thereby, extend the internal market. These agreements aim to create 'homogeneous' internal market spaces operating on the basis of EU acquis also outside the Union's borders. Exporting part of the EU's regulatory framework outside the Union will not, however, perforce result in a legal space that is homogeneous with the internal market. The European Communities set out to create a multi-state market in which the factors of production can move freely to create maximum efficiency. The question of whether the internal market is 'expandable' to non-EU Member States requires a close look at the concept of the internal market, the required level of compliance with the common rules and the role of the foundational principles therein. The internal market acquis has been designed to function in a supranational legal order with supranational principles and an institutional system to ensure uniform interpretation and application and effective enforcement of the common rules. When extracted from the Union's legal order, the framework in which the acquis is applied changes to a legal order governed by the principles of public international law. Beyond the EU borders, the internal market acquis does not, therefore, enjoy the same guarantees for homogeneity in substance, interpretation, application and enforcement as within the Union.

In broad terms, legal homogeneity can be achieved by legislative, administrative and judicial means.[7] Legislative means encompass the mechanisms for participation in the decision-making processes, the procedures for duly updating the acquis and the status of EU law in the third countries' legal orders; administrative means include the

---

[7] See A Lazowski, 'Box of Chocolates Integration: The European Economic Area and the Swiss Models Revisited' in S Blockmans and S Prechal (eds.), *Reconciling the Deepening and Widening of the European Union* (T.M.C. Asser Press 2007) 87.

surveillance and enforcement mechanisms; and judicial means comprise infringement procedures and the possibility to give (binding) interpretations of the acquis. The contracting parties to the agreements that export the acquis are not, however, entirely free to choose an appropriate institutional design to achieve and maintain homogeneity between EU acquis and the acquis contained in the international agreements.

The main conflict lies in the need to preserve the autonomy of the European legal order – a concept keenly protected by the Court of Justice of the EU (the Court). The question of autonomy vis-à-vis international agreements concluded by the EU has been in the focus of a strand of case law of the Court.[8] A set of conditions has been distilled, which the institutional and procedural framework of an international agreement must conform to, in order to be regarded as compatible with the principle of autonomy.

The central question that hereby arises is to what extent it is feasible to extend the substantive boundaries of the internal market beyond the geographical borders of the Union. In other words, to what extent can either the entire internal market or a policy sector thereof be expanded by exporting the internal market acquis to third countries outside the enlargement process? An answer to the question necessitates an analysis of two broad issues: first, the constitutional limitations inherent to the concept of the internal market and, second, the institutional constraints to exporting the acquis outside the EU and maintaining its homogeneity while preserving the autonomy of the EU legal order. The first category comprises the concept of the EU internal market in the broadest sense: its substantive content, the perception of the EU legal order and the internal market as uniform constellations, and the effect of the uniform rules in the common legal order. The second category pertains to the requisite institutional structures to support the aim of extending the internal market to third countries in a homogeneous manner, including institutions for ensuring the dynamic export and updating of the acquis as well as the surveillance, enforcement, interpretation and application of the exported rules. The possibilities to set up any institutional structures by an international

---

[8] Opinion 1/76 *European laying-up fund for inland waterway vessels* EU:C:1977:63; Opinion 1/91 *EEA I* EU:C:1991:490; Opinion 1/92 *EEA II* EU:C:1992:189; Opinion 1/00 *ECAA* EU:C:2002:231; Opinion 1/09 *Patents Court* EU:C:2011:123; Opinion 2/13 *ECHR II* EU:C:2014:2454; Case C-284/16 *Achmea* EU:C:2018:158; Opinion 1/17 *CETA* EU:C:2019:341.

agreement concluded by the EU are restricted by the limitations deriving from the concept of autonomy.

This book aims to provide a legal analysis of the 'boundaries' of the concept of the internal market, which can also be understood as its 'exportability' to non-EU Member States. It highlights the possible effects of such norms export on the EU's legal order and the potential challenges for the third countries' legal orders. The book adopts the perspective of EU constitutional law rather than of the third countries' legal systems and provides a theoretical rather than practical or empirical account of the subject matter. The analysis does not, therefore, consider the practical difficulties associated with the exporting of the EU acquis or examine empirical data on the adoption and transposition of EU acquis in the multilateral frameworks and the national legal orders.

Four case studies are used in the analysis to illustrate the challenges of setting up institutions and procedures to respect both the autonomy of the EU legal order and the sovereignty of the contracting parties while achieving and maintaining homogeneity in the expanded internal market: the Agreement on the European Economic Area (EEA Agreement),[9] the Treaty establishing the Energy Community (EnCT),[10] the Agreement on the Establishment of a Common Aviation Area (ECAA Agreement)[11] and the Treaty establishing the Transport Community (TCT).[12] Agreements by which the Union exerts normative influence globally and in the neighbourhood region are many and prominently include the new generation free trade agreements concluded with, for example, Canada, Japan, Singapore, South Korea and Vietnam, as well as the Deep and Comprehensive Free Trade Areas (DCFTAs) combined with association agreements (AAs) concluded to date with Georgia, Moldova and Ukraine. However, the aims of the four multilateral agreements that are analysed in detail in the book go well beyond the objectives of the bilateral free trade agreements including those coupled with AAs, both in terms of creating homogeneous market spaces within a region rather than between the EU and individual third countries, as well as envisaging deep integration into the EU internal market or a sector thereof through extensive commitments assumed on behalf of third countries to adhere to the EU acquis. Similarly to the EU not

---

[9] [1994] OJ L1/3.
[10] [2006] OJ L198/18.
[11] [2006] OJ L285/3.
[12] [2017] OJ L278/3.

being constituted by a web of bilateral agreements, the multilateral case studies best illustrate the challenges of setting up elaborate institutions and procedures to support the achievement and maintenance of homogeneity in a legal space constructed upon EU acquis while respecting the limits to the EU's norms export inherent to the EU legal order.

The EEA Agreement, which is comprehensive in scope, provides the example of a 'best case scenario' of extending the internal market to third countries. The EEA Agreement allows for an analysis of the general expandability of the internal market in depth as well as breadth. The EnCT, the ECAA Agreement and the TCT that are sectoral in scope provide, on the other hand, a basis for a study into whether, and if so, how can the sectoral scope of the acquis export that pertains to the depth of integration rather than the breadth affect the possibilities of expanding the EU internal market in a homogeneous manner.

The book consists of two main parts. Following Chapter 2 which situates the practice of exporting the internal market acquis to third countries in the context of the EU's external relations, the first part of the book deals with the constitutional limitations to expanding the internal market by international agreements deriving from the specificities of the concept of the internal market and the legal framework in which it operates. The second part of the book addresses the institutional limitations to achieving and maintaining homogeneity in the expanded internal market that arise from the need to preserve the autonomy of the EU legal order and the sovereignty of the non-EU Member State parties to the multilateral agreements.

Chapter 2 conceptualises the phenomenon of exporting the internal market acquis and thereby expanding the internal market to non-EU Member States without membership in the Union. The Chapter explores the evolving role of the internal market acquis in the EU's external relations by analysing the dynamics between the aims of various international instruments and the character and scope of the internal market acquis contained therein. The various functions of the acquis are identified and presented in a progression in time and across various country groups in the EU's neighbourhood.

Chapter 3 identifies the defining features of the internal market – the characteristics that distinguish the internal market from any single market constellation and serve as a possible benchmark for determining the degree of homogeneity in the expanded internal market. The Chapter focuses on the principles that constitute the economic core of the internal market, such as the four fundamental freedoms and competition policy, and their interaction with horizontal provisions, fundamental rights and EU citizenship. In addition to looking at the internal market as a whole, the Chapter also explores whether the specific sectors of the internal market feature distinctive cores.

Chapter 4 scrutinises the notion of unity as an essential characteristic of the EU legal order and the internal market, and the aims of the multilateral agreements to achieve 'homogeneity' in the expanded internal market. The Chapter provides an examination of the notions of 'unity' and 'homogeneity' and the nature of the homogeneity provision in the acquis-exporting agreements. The Chapter seeks to establish the level of legislative commonality – as opposed to flexibility and differentiation – necessary in the extended internal market to be able to consider the position of the third country market participants equal to that of their EU counterparts.

Chapter 5 addresses the role of the foundational principles of EU law – primacy, direct effect, consistent interpretation and state liability – in ensuring the proper functioning of the internal market. The EU-specific principles are juxtaposed with their equivalents in public international law and in the EEA, the Energy Community, the ECAA and the Transport Community legal orders. The analysis helps to determine the implications of a possible absence of the supranational principles in the agreements exporting the acquis on the effectiveness of the acquis transferred to third countries by means of agreements operating under public international law.

Chapter 6 defines the concept of the autonomy of the EU legal order and examines its implications for the choice of the most effective institutional framework for achieving and maintaining homogeneity in the expanded internal market. The Chapter scrutinises the concept of autonomy from the perspectives of domestic law and public international law, analyses its content and application by the Court of Justice as well as its ramifications for the acquis-exporting agreements concluded by the Union.

Chapter 7 scrutinises the institutional and procedural structures necessary for achieving homogeneity in the process of exporting the acquis to third countries. The first part of the analysis addresses the necessary institutional and procedural frameworks for dynamically updating the multilateral agreements to reflect changes in the internal market acquis. The second part considers the procedures for defining the key elements of the internal market acquis and the modalities of third country participation in the process of defining the acquis on the

EU level. This includes an examination of the implications of the increasing use of new governance methods in the EU policy-making on the third country actors' possibilities to influence the content of the internal market acquis and to, thereby, increase the effectiveness of the norms transfer.

Chapter 8 explores the essential institutional characteristics for maintaining homogeneity in the expanded internal market in the stages of the application and the implementation of the acquis. The analysis focuses on the institutional and procedural frameworks in the EU and in the multilateral agreements, respectively, that are vested with the task of the uniform enforcement and application of the acquis in and outside the Union. The analysis is divided into two parts dealing with the centralising and decentralising dynamics, respectively. The former pertains to the centralised institutions and procedures for surveillance, enforcement and judicial protection in the EU and the multilateral agreements; and the latter to the procedural links between the international or supranational institutions, on the one hand, and national authorities and individuals, on the other.

The final Chapter 9 addresses both the substantive and institutional aspects of the process of expanding the internal market to third countries without enlarging the Union and provides a conclusion on the viability of the ambition to truly extend the internal market to third countries, either in a comprehensive or a sectoral manner, by means of exporting internal market acquis by international agreements.

2 Expanding the Internal Market
The Phenomenon

Close regulatory cooperation between the EU and its neighbouring countries dates back to the early days of the European Communities. The European Economic Community (EEC) signed the first Association Agreements with Greece and Turkey in 1961 and 1963, respectively.[1] During the next 50 years, the EU has concluded numerous association, cooperation and partnership agreements with its closer and more distant neighbours. To date, almost every country in the EU's neighbourhood[2] has entered into formalised relations with the EU through one or more bilateral or multilateral agreements. The agreements in question vary according to the broader political context in which they are situated, their pronounced aims and the scope of the EU acquis contained therein. Yet, the central element in the rapprochement between the EU and the third countries concerned is the acquis of the EU's internal market.

The acquis-exporting agreements concluded that the neighbourhood countries fall within three broad categories based on the depth of integration with the EU thereby envisaged: Partnership and Cooperation Agreements (PCAs) and other agreements belonging to the European Neighbourhood Policy (ENP); AAs, including those establishing DCFTAs; and multilateral agreements, either sectoral or comprehensive in scope. In turn, the majority of association and partnership agreements form part of broader policy frameworks, such as the Europe Agreements (EAs) or the Stabilisation and Association Process (SAP).

---

[1] Agreement establishing an association between the European Economic Community and Greece [1963] OJ L26/294; Agreement establishing an association between the European Economic Community and Turkey [1964] OJ L217/3685 (EEC-Turkey AA, 'Ankara Agreement').

[2] A notional area that exceeds the geographical borders of Europe and includes the Mediterranean and the Caucasus regions.

Next to these 'macro-policies', regulatory approximation also takes place on the level of 'meso-policies' that represent the external dimension of developments within the internal market,[3] which are especially relevant with regard to multilateral sectoral agreements.

On the basis of the aims and scope of the agreements concerning legal approximation with the internal market one can distil five principal functions of the internal market acquis. These include the gradual integration of non-member countries into the wider area of cooperation in Europe; liberalisation of trade in the form of establishing a free trade area (FTA) or customs union; preparing potential candidate countries for membership in the EU; integrating third countries into the internal market; and, as a limited version of the latter, integrating non-member countries into a sector of the internal market. A currently hypothetical sixth function pertains to the managing of a relationship between the EU and a former member or associated state. Different functions of the acquis can overlap within a single agreement and within several agreements concluded with one country.

2.1 Gradual Integration of Third Countries into the Wider Area of Cooperation in Europe

The loosest connection between a third country and the internal market acquis is represented by the model of cooperation between the EU and non-Member States without directly integrating the latter into the internal market. Such cooperation mainly takes place in the framework of PCAs and Euro-Mediterranean Association Agreements (EMAAs)[4] but also includes the ENP, the EU-Russia Common Spaces, the Eastern Partnership and the Union for the Mediterranean (UfM). The latter four programmes do not impose specific obligations of approximation

---

[3] S Lavenex, D Lehmkuhl and N Wichmann, 'Modes of External Governance: A Cross-national and Cross-sectoral Comparison' (2009) 16 *Journal of European Public Policy* 813, 814.

[4] The EU-Israel relationship is exceptional in this regard. Free trade between the EU and Israel in industrial products has been in place since the 1975 Agreement between the EEC and the State of Israel [1975] OJ L136/3. Article 6(1) of the Euro-Mediterranean Agreement establishing an association between the European Communities and their Member States, of the one part, and the State of Israel, of the other part [2000] OJ L147/3 (EC-Israel EMAA) aims to 'reinforce' the existing FTA. Pursuant to Article 1(2) of the EC-Israel EMAA, the specific aim of the agreement is the setting up of political dialogue and the expansion of trade in goods and services, the liberalisation of the right of establishment and of public procurement, the free movement of capital and the intensification of cooperation in science and technology.

with EU acquis but instead endeavour to intensify cooperation already started by the conclusion of the PCAs and the EMAAs. In all of these frameworks, approximation frequently takes place on the basis of international conventions[5] and World Trade Organisation (WTO) law[6] instead of EU acquis. Speaking of a function of internal market acquis is, therefore, only notional.

The majority of the PCAs were concluded in the late 1990s with the former Soviet Union countries, except for the Baltic States. The PCAs aim at setting up a partnership without further association or accession of the respective third country to the EU. For example, some of the explicit objectives of the EC-Russia PCA include the provision of an 'appropriate framework for the gradual integration between Russia and a wider area of cooperation in Europe', and the creation of necessary conditions for the future establishment of an FTA including all of the four internal market freedoms except for the most sensitive, the free movement of persons.[7] The Court of Justice limited the objective of the PCA to setting up a partnership without further association or accession of the Russian Federation to the EU.[8] More specifically, the EC-Russia PCA was 'not intended to establish an association with a view to the gradual integration of that non-member country into the European Communities'.[9] By separating the area of wider cooperation from integration into the Communities, the Court also preordained the PCA countries' feeble prospects of approaching membership within the framework at hand.

The PCA does not grant Russia access to the internal market, nor does it establish an FTA. The PCAs contain some EU acquis which in certain situations grants to third country nationals equal treatment with EU citizens but contrary to AAs, the competition and state aid clauses in the PCAs do not foresee any harmonisation whatsoever.[10] Moreover, the predominantly soft nature of the obligations arising from the PCAs provides evidence both of their flexibility and of the absence of a deep integration perspective between the EU and the contracting parties.

---

[5] Article 2 of Annex 10 to the Agreement on partnership and cooperation establishing a partnership between the European Communities and their Member States, of one part, and the Russian Federation, of the other part [1997] OJ L327/3 (EC-Russia PCA).
[6] See, for example, Articles 10(1), 28(1) and 36 EC-Russia PCA.
[7] Article 1 EC-Russia PCA.
[8] Case C-265/03 *Simutenkov* EU:C:2005:213, paras. 27–28.
[9] Ibid., para. 35.
[10] See, for example, Article 53(1) EC-Russia PCA.

To replace the outdated PCAs, new generation AA/DCFTAs discussed in Section 2.2 are being concluded with the more ambitious of the countries in question, with 'lighter' agreements remaining as an option for the others.[11]

The ENP was launched in 2004 as a broader framework for governing the relations between the EU and the southern and eastern neighbourhood countries. Implicitly, the ENP provides an alternative to EU membership for those neighbourhood countries that lack a viable membership prospect aiming to avoid new demarcation lines between an integrated Europe and the more distant neighbours.[12] The ENP set out to offer third countries 'the prospect of a stake in the EU's internal market' and the promotion of the four freedoms for the purpose of achieving the primary objective of the ENP – security coupled with stability and prosperity.[13] It is based on a differentiation approach. The priorities for each participating country are specified in action plans, which are soft law instruments covering inter alia political dialogue and reform, trade and measures for gradually obtaining a stake in the EU's internal market.[14] For the achievement of the latter, legislative and regulatory approximation is to take place on the basis of mutually agreed priorities, which are defined in bilateral agreements such as the PCAs or the EMAAs.

Russia does not participate in the ENP. In addition to the 1997 PCA and a number of sectoral agreements, EU-Russia relations are instead governed by the Four EU-Russia Common Spaces on economic affairs, Area of Freedom, Security and Justice (AFSJ), external security, and research, education and culture; and the EU-Russia Partnership for Modernisation (P4M), which builds on the Four Common Spaces.[15] The aim of the Common Economic Space, in particular, is to create an 'open and integrated market' between the EU and Russia without any hard legal obligations regarding approximation with the EU acquis.[16]

---

[11] Commission and High Representative, 'Review of the European Neighbourhood Policy' (Joint Communication) JOIN(2015) 50 final, 6–7.

[12] See Commission, 'Wider Europe – Neighbourhood: A New Framework for Relations with our Eastern and Southern Neighbours' (Communication) COM (2003) 104 final, 4.

[13] Ibid.

[14] Commission 'European Neighbourhood Policy Strategy Paper' (Communication) COM (2004) 373 final, 3.

[15] Council, 'Joint Statement on the Partnership for Modernisation – 25th EU-Russia Summit, Rostov-on-Don, 31 May–1 June 2010' (Press Release) 10546/10, 1 June 2010.

[16] Commission, '"Common Economic Space" with Russia: Vice-President Verheugen and Russian Industry Minister agree on permanent framework for dialogue' (Press Release) IP/05/1547, 7 December 2005.

Similar to the ENP, therefore, the Common Spaces mainly serve as platforms for intensifying cooperation, which is laid out in greater detail in a separate regulatory framework.

In 2009, the EU launched the Eastern Partnership as a special eastern dimension of the ENP to support the political and socio-economic reforms of the partner countries and to facilitate approximation with the EU acquis. The Eastern Partnership restates the objectives of the ENP: the shared commitment to the stability, security and prosperity of the European Union, the partner countries and the entire European continent.[17] Overtime, the Union has recognised the need for more differentiation as not all ENP countries wish to integrate to the internal market and 'not all partners aspire to EU rules and standards'.[18] The new direction calls for more individually designed partnerships.[19] The multilateral framework enables the participating countries to share information and best practices with each other while allowing the EU to observe these processes.[20] The Eastern Partnership builds on AAs that outline the reform agendas and where applicable comprise DCFTAs as their integral part. The partnership does not create binding obligations on behalf of the participating states but recognises the importance of legislative and regulatory approximation and undertakes to disseminate information about EU law and standards.[21] Its ultimate aim is to create a Neighbourhood Economic Community based on a 'common regulatory framework and improved market access for goods and services', possibly leading to access to the 'non-regulated area of the Internal Market for goods' conditional upon proven 'political and legal reliability'.[22]

The Lisbon Treaty introduced a new legal basis for concluding agreements with the neighbourhood countries in Article 8 of the Treaty on European Union (TEU).[23] It introduces specific, value-based conditionality on the neighbourhood relations[24] and provides a basis for the ENP in

[17] Council, 'Joint Declaration of the Prague Eastern Partnership Summit' (Press Release) 8435/09, 7 May 2009, 6.
[18] Commission and High Representative, 'Review of the European Neighbourhood Policy' (n 11) 2.
[19] Ibid., 4.
[20] Council, 'Joint Declaration of the Prague Eastern Partnership Summit' (n 17) 8.
[21] Ibid.
[22] Commission, 'Strengthening the European Neighbourhood Policy' (Communication) COM (2006) 726 final, 5; High Representative and Commission, 'A new response to a changing Neighbourhood' (Joint Communication) COM (2011) 303 final, 9.
[23] Consolidated version of the Treaty on European Union [2016] OJ C202/13.
[24] See D Hanf, 'The ENP in the Light of the New "Neighbourhood Clause" (Article 8 TEU)' (2011) College of Europe Research Papers in Law 2/2011, 9.

the Treaties.[25] The practical value of the new provision is yet to be seen as the development of the Eastern Partnership shows that AAs maintain their role as the preferred legal form of governing the relations with the countries in the eastern neighbourhood.[26]

Cooperation between the EU and the southern Mediterranean countries is primarily based on the Euro-Mediterranean Partnership ('Barcelona Process') launched in 1995.[27] The EU has concluded EMAAs with all of the Euro-Mediterranean Partnership countries except for Syria and Libya. In spite of being FTAs, the level of 'association' envisaged by the EMAAs does not differ considerably from the PCAs. The fact that the EMAAs were concluded as AAs suggests diversity among the latter category rather than the greater depth of the EU's relations with the southern Mediterranean countries as compared to PCAs. Contrary to other AAs, EMAAs do not endeavour to integrate the southern Mediterranean countries into the Union. The objectives of the EC-Algeria EMAA, for example, include the promotion of trade and the establishment of conditions for the gradual liberalisation of trade in goods, services and capital.[28] Trade liberalisation is to be based on WTO rules,[29] although in standardisation and conformity assessment the use of EU standards is encouraged.[30] The lack of a membership perspective due to the geographical location of the participating countries combined with the poor economic and turbulent political situations in most of the countries in the region leads to very limited alignment with EU acquis.

---

[25] P Van Elsuwege and R Petrov, 'Article 8 TEU: Towards a New Generation of Agreements with the Neighbouring Countries of the European Union?' (2011) 36 *European Law Review* 688, 701–703; C Hillion, 'Anatomy of EU Norm Export towards the Neighbourhood: The impact of Article 8 TEU', in P Van Elsuwege and R Petrov, *Legislative Approximation and Application of EU Law in the Eastern Neighbourhood of the European Union* (Routledge 2014) 13, 17.

[26] References have been made to Article 8 TEU in the negotiation process of AAs with the European micro-states Andorra, Monaco and San Marino, yet not as a legal basis, see P Van Elsuwege and M Chamon, 'The Meaning of "Association" under EU Law' (2019) *Study commissioned by the European Parliament's Policy Department for Citizens' Rights and Constitutional Affairs*, 13–14, www.europarl.europa.eu/thinktank/en/document.html?reference=IPOL_STU%282019%29608861 accessed 10 February 2020.

[27] Barcelona Declaration adopted at the Euro-Mediterranean Conference, Barcelona, 27–28 November 1995. The founding members were the EC, Algeria, Egypt, Israel, Jordan, Lebanon, Morocco, the Palestinian Authority, Syria, Tunisia and Turkey.

[28] Article 1(2) of the Euro-Mediterranean Agreement establishing an Association between the European Community and its Member States, of the one part, and the People's Democratic Republic of Algeria, of the other part [2005] OJ L265/2 (EC-Algeria EMAA). For the exceptional case of the EC-Israel EMAA, see n 4.

[29] For example, Articles 6, 11, 30(1) and 42 EC-Algeria EMAA.

[30] Article 55 EC-Algeria EMAA.

The state of affairs may, however, change with the adoption of the new DCFTAs. In 2008, similar to the Eastern Partnership, the UfM was initiated to complement the existing bilateral EMAAs.[31] The specific objective of the UfM is to liberalise trade in two dimensions – bilaterally between the EU and the Mediterranean countries and multilaterally among the latter. Its long-term perspective was proclaimed in the Euro-Mediterranean Trade Roadmap beyond 2010, according to which the existing AAs and South-South Agreements shall be replaced with DCFTAs.[32] Negotiations on DCFTAs with Morocco and Tunisia are currently underway, aiming to complement the existing EMAAs.

2.2 Trade Liberalisation through Establishing an FTA or a Customs Union

In addition to gradual integration of third countries into a broader area of cooperation in Europe, the internal market acquis also plays a role in liberalising trade by means of an FTA or a customs union. Some examples include the EEC-Turkey AA, the EAs and Stabilisation and Association Agreements (SAAs) – instruments of the SAP, as well as the new AA/DCFTAs concluded in the framework of the Eastern Partnership.

Association agreements, concluded under Article 217 of the Treaty on the Functioning of the European Union (TFEU),[33] constitute the main vehicle for trade liberalisation with the neighbourhood countries. The objectives of AAs may include preparing countries for membership in the EU; offering an alternative to membership; development cooperation; and inter-regional assistance.[34] The common feature of the AAs is reciprocity, although the scope of rights and obligations may vary from one agreement to another. According to the Court, 'an association agreement creat[es] special, privileged links with a non-member

---

[31] Council, 'Joint Declaration of the Paris Summit for the Mediterranean – 13 July 2008' (Press Release) 11887/08, 15 July 2008, para. 13. The founding members were the EU27 and Albania, Algeria, Bosnia and Herzegovina, Croatia, Egypt, Israel, Jordan, Lebanon, Mauritania, Monaco, Montenegro, Morocco, the Palestinian Authority, Syria, Tunisia and Turkey.

[32] Commission, 'Conclusions of the 8th Union for the Mediterranean Trade Ministerial Conference – Brussels, 9 December 2009' (Press Release) MEMO/09/547, 9 December 2009.

[33] Consolidated version of the Treaty on the Functioning of the European Union [2016] OJ C202/47.

[34] D Hanf and P Dengler, 'Accords d'association' *College of Europe Research Papers in Law* 2004/1, 10–14.

country which must, at least to a certain extent, take part in the Community system'.[35] The precise character of the special, privileged links was, however, not clarified in the judgment. In practice, the reciprocal rights and obligations in the AAs regularly include the third countries' adoption of EU acquis or accession to international conventions in exchange for financial and technical assistance and, to varying degrees, access to the internal market.

One of the earliest association agreements, the 1963 EEC-Turkey AA, does not belong to any other overarching policy agendas. Its objective is to promote trade and economic relations between the EU and Turkey and, subsequently, to create a customs union covering all trade in goods.[36] The specific acquis to be adopted by Turkey is identified in the decisions of the Association Council,[37] which together with the Agreement form the 'law of association'.[38] Legal convergence with EU acquis is, however, only to take place 'as far as possible',[39] not aiming at complete regulatory harmonisation. The EU-Turkey law of association comprises extensive parts of internal market acquis but falls short of all four free movement rights. Pursuant to the programmatic Article 12 of the EEC-Turkey AA,[40] for example, the parties are to progressively secure the free movement of workers; yet to this date, the free movement of workers between the EU and Turkey has 'not at all' been realised.[41]

In the 1990s, the European Community (EC) concluded almost identical bilateral association agreements – the EAs – with ten Central and Eastern European Countries (CEECs) that joined the EU during the two

---

[35] Case 12/86 *Demirel* EU:C:1987:400, para. 9.

[36] Article 2 EEC-Turkey AA.

[37] Most importantly, Decision 1/95 of the EC-Turkey Association Council of 22 December 1995 on implementing the final phase of the Customs Union [1996] OJ L35/1 (Decision 1/95); and a number of subsequent decisions of the EC-Turkey Customs Cooperation Committee laying down the detailed rules for the application of Decision 1/95.

[38] E Lenski, 'Turkey (including Northern Cyprus)' in S Blockmans and A Lazowski (eds.), *The European Union and Its Neighbours: A Legal Appraisal of the EU's Policies of Stabilisation, Partnership and Integration* (T.M.C. Asser Press 2006) 283, 289.

[39] Article 54(1) Decision 1/95 (n 37).

[40] Case 12/86 *Demirel* (n 35) para. 23.

[41] Commission, 'Proposal for a Council Decision on the position to be taken on behalf of the European Union within the EEC-Turkey Association Council with regard to the provisions on the coordination of social security systems' COM (2012) 152 final, 6; Case C-81/13 *United Kingdom v Council* EU:C:2014:2449, para. 57. Moreover, the opening of labour markets has been stalled on both sides and restrictions are in place also for EU citizens to undertake labour activities in Turkey: Lenski (n 38) 294–296.

consecutive enlargements of 2004 and 2007. The explicit objective of the EAs was to gradually establish an FTA.[42] The agreements provided for the abolishment of quantitative restrictions and, gradually, customs duties,[43] liberalisation of trade in most areas except for agriculture and fisheries, and provisions on the movement of workers, capital and services. Eliminating unfair competition in the CEECs prior to their integration into the internal market was of crucial importance.[44] Yet, the intensity of legal approximation in the EAs was very different from one provision to another. Whereas the rules on trade in goods and on competition and state aid of the EAs reflected the EC Treaty[45] quite precisely, there were substantial differences in the rules pertaining to the free movement of persons, services, capital and the right of establishment.[46] Compared to the EEC-Turkey AA, the EAs were much more oriented towards integration into the internal market.

Between 2000 and 2005, the EU concluded SAAs with six Western Balkan countries: Albania, Bosnia and Herzegovina, Croatia, North Macedonia, Montenegro and Serbia. SAA with Kosovo was concluded in 2015. Similar to the EAs, the SAAs are virtually identical in content and envisage the creation of an FTA. In order to avoid distortions to the internal market that the SAA countries will gradually be gaining access to, competition provisions play an important role in the agreements.[47] The SAAs provide for approximation with the fundamental elements of the internal market acquis and other key policy areas including

[42] For example Article 7(1) of the Europe Agreement establishing an association between the EC and their Member States, and Poland [1993] OJ L348/1 (EC-Poland EA).

[43] Article 13 EC-Poland EA.

[44] Commission, 'The Europe Agreements and beyond: A Strategy for the countries of Central and Eastern Europe for Accession' (Communication) COM (94) 320 final, 5.

[45] Treaty establishing the European Community (Consolidated version 2002) [2002] OJ C325/33.

[46] PC Müller-Graff, 'Legal Framework for Relations between the European Union and Central and Eastern Europe: General Aspects' in M Maresceau (ed.), *Enlarging the European Union* (Longman 1997) 27, 34. An indication of the more restricted scope of the fundamental freedoms in the EAs is provided in the agreements that do not speak of the 'free' movement of persons and 'freedom of establishment' but merely the movement of workers, establishment, and the supply of services: M Cremona, 'The New Associations: Substantive Issues of the Europe Agreements with the Central and Eastern European States' in SV Konstadinidis (ed.), *The Legal Regulation of the European Community's External Relations after the Completion of the Internal Market* (Dartmouth 1996) 141, 145.

[47] For example Article 40 of the Stabilisation and Association Agreement between the EC and their Member States, of the one part, and the Republic of Albania, of the other part [2009] OJ L107/166 (EC-Albania SAA) on state monopolies, Article 71 on competition law and Article 72 on public undertakings.

provisions on the free movement of workers, services and capital and the freedom of establishment,[48] albeit subject to restrictions.[49]

The EU's new integration approach towards the neighbourhood is two-dimensional. The AAs coupled with DCFTAs envisage multilateral cooperation through the approximation of the third countries' legal systems with EU acquis, provide for the third countries' entry into the EU's internal market and expect to lead to increased competition within the neighbourhood. The new AA/DCFTAs have been concluded with Georgia, Moldova and Ukraine. Negotiations with Azerbaijan on a DCFTA, but excluding an AA, are currently ongoing. Negotiations with Armenia on a DCFTA were finalised in 2013, but since Armenia's membership in the Eurasian Economic Union proved incompatible with the provisions of the DCFTA, a different agreement narrower in scope and more modest in terms of access to the internal market – the EU-Armenia Comprehensive and Enhanced Partnership Agreement (CEPA) – was instead signed in November 2017.[50] The CEPA's aim is to establish legislative cooperation between EU acquis and Armenian law without establishing an association.[51] The scope of EU acquis in the CEPA is largely limited to the field of energy in which increased market integration and gradual regulatory approximation with 'the key elements of EU acquis' are envisaged.[52]

The high ambitions of the AA/DCFTAs are reflected in their aims to 'gradually'[53] bring the third countries as close as possible to the internal

---

[48] Title V EC-Albania SAA.

[49] These restrictions primarily concern the free movement of workers. See, for example, Article 47 EC-Albania SAA.

[50] EEAS, 'New agreement signed between the European Union and Armenia set to bring tangible benefits to citizens' (Press Release), 24 November 2017, https://eeas.europa.eu/headquarters/headquarters-homepage/36141/new-agreement-signed-between-european-union-and-armenia-set-bring-tangible-benefits-citizens_en accessed 10 February 2020.

[51] Commission and High Representative, 'Joint Proposal for a Council Decision on the conclusion, on behalf of the European Union, of the Comprehensive and Enhanced Partnership Agreement between the European Union and the European Atomic Energy Community and their Member States, of the one part, and the Republic of Armenia, of the other part' JOIN(2017) 37 final, 3.

[52] Recital 20, Preamble to the Comprehensive and Enhanced Partnership Agreement between the European Union and the Republic of Armenia [2018] OJ L23/4.

[53] Article 1(2)(d) of the Association Agreement between the European Union and its Member States, of the one part, and Ukraine, of the other part [2014] OJ L161/3 (EU-Ukraine AA/DCFTA); Article 1(2)(h) of the Association Agreement between the European Union and the European Atomic Energy Community and their Member States, of the one part, and Georgia, of the other part [2014] OJ L261/4 (EU-Georgia AA/DCFTA); Article 1(2)(g) of the Association Agreement between the European Union and the European

market by providing far-reaching market access and comprehensive regulatory approximation[54] without, however, offering a membership perspective.[55] Several sectors of the internal market are covered, such as energy, transport, services and agriculture, and all four fundamental freedoms incorporated albeit with substantial exceptions from the free movement of persons.[56] Differently from other FTAs, in the AA/DCFTAs, integration on the basis of EU acquis is a legal obligation,[57] subject to strict, ENP and pre-accession type of conditionality.[58] The scope of the AA/DCFTAs and the level of integration envisaged therein are significant: in the fields of services, establishment and public procurement, for example, the EU-Ukraine AA/DCFTA reaches close to the level of integration envisaged in the EEA Agreement.[59] They, moreover, build on the third countries' participation in the Energy Community and the Common Aviation Area through which the relevant acquis is already being adopted.

2.3 (Pre-) Pre-accession

The third function of EU acquis in international agreements is to prepare potential candidate countries for future EU candidacy status. This category is made up of essentially the same frameworks as discussed in the previous section with the exception of the AA/DCFTAs.

The aims and content of the EEC-Turkey AA together with the subsequent political developments demonstrate most explicitly that while

Atomic Energy Community and their Member States, of the one part, and the Republic of Moldova, of the other part [2014] OJ L260/4 (EU-Moldova AA/DCFTA).

[54] Recital 16, preamble to the EU-Ukraine AA/DCFTA; Article 1(2)(h) EU-Georgia AA/DCFTA; Article 1(2)(g) EU-Moldova AA/DCFTA.

[55] See further G Van der Loo, 'The EU's Association Agreements and DCFTAs with Ukraine, Moldova and Georgia: A Comparative Study' (2017) *CEPS Special Report*, 4.

[56] The aim of the parties is visa liberalisation, see Recital 22, preamble and Article 19(3) EU-Ukraine AA/DCFTA; Recital 18, preamble and Article 15(2) EU-Moldova AA/DCFTA; Recital 21, preamble and Article 16(2) EU-Georgia AA/DCFTA. Visa facilitation for short-stay travel to the EU has been implemented by Regulation (EU) 2018/1806 of the European Parliament and of the Council of 14 November 2018 listing the third countries whose nationals must be in possession of visas when crossing the external borders and whose nationals are exempt from that requirement [2018] OJ L303/39.

[57] G Van der Loo, *The EU-Ukraine Association Agreement and Deep and Comprehensive Free Trade Area* (Brill 2016) 362.

[58] G Van der Loo, P Van Elsuwege and R Petrov, 'The EU-Ukraine Association Agreement: Assessment of an Innovative Legal Instrument', *EUI Working Papers LAW* 2014/09, 16 and 28.

[59] G Van der Loo (n 57) 304–308; European Commission, 'EU-Ukraine Deep and Comprehensive Free Trade Area', 5–6, https://eeas.europa.eu/sites/eeas/files/tra doc_150981.pdf accessed 10 February 2020.

AAs are a starting point for approximating third countries' legal systems with the EU acquis, their conclusion is not strictly connected to future membership in the EU. Article 28 of the AA makes a reference to Turkey's possible future accession to the EU.[60] At the 1999 Helsinki Summit, Turkey obtained the status of a candidate country. Accession negotiations were started in 2005, following which Turkey has been adopting EU acquis as part of the pre-accession strategy.[61] Following a significant deterioration of the rule of law in Turkey, the accession negotiations have effectively come to a halt.[62]

The EAs, on the other hand, were initially not considered part of the pre-accession strategy but rather as a means of modernisation and integration without an imminent membership perspective.[63] Their example proves that the role of the internal market acquis can change overtime within the same instrument. While the EAs had more ambitious objectives of integrating the CEECs into the internal market than the EEC-Turkey AA, the preambles of the first EAs did not contain but a slight indication of the associated countries' membership aspirations.[64]

The EU's initial careful approach changed after the 1993 Copenhagen European Council where EU membership was declared to be available for the associated CEECs who so desire after satisfying the relevant economic and political criteria.[65] The 1994 European Council at Corfu included the EAs into the pre-accession strategy by stating that the full potential of the EAs and the decisions taken in Copenhagen in 1993

---

[60] The provision reads as follows: 'As soon as the operation of this Agreement has advanced far enough to justify envisaging full acceptance by Turkey of the obligations arising out of the Treaty establishing the Community, the Contracting Parties shall examine the possibility of the accession of Turkey to the Community.'

[61] Maresceau defines, despite admitting the difficulty thereof, pre-accession strategies as 'EU initiatives whereby candidate countries for EU membership are brought closer to the EU in political, economic, and legal terms so that, in the end, accession is not too abrupt for both the candidate countries *and* the EU to absorb': M Maresceau, 'Pre-accession' in M Cremona (ed.), *The Enlargement of the European Union* (Oxford University Press 2003) 9, 10.

[62] 'Council conclusions on enlargement and stabilisation and association process' (Press Release) 479/19, 18 June 2019, para. 37.

[63] This was made explicit by the Commission: '[Eventual membership] is not among the objectives of the [EAs] ... [which] have a special value in themselves and should be distinguished from the possibility of accession to the Community ... ': Commission, 'Association Agreements with the countries of central and eastern Europe: a general outline' (Communication) COM (90) 398, 3.

[64] See, for example, Recital 15, preamble to the EC-Poland EA.

[65] European Council, 'Conclusions of the Presidency – Copenhagen, 21–22 June 1993' SN 180/1/93 REV 1, 13.

must be 'exploited with a view to preparing for accession'.[66] The following European Council in Essen, furthermore, recognised the preparation of the CEECs for integration into the internal market as the key
element of the pre-accession strategy.[67] The post-1994 EAs already
contained explicit references to the associated countries' membership
perspectives.[68]

Transforming the EAs into pre-accession instruments was not
a difficult task. They did not contain the entire accession acquis
but their far-reaching substantive content set a good basis for the
application of the four freedoms and legislative approximation and
established a suitable institutional framework.[69] In the 1995 White
Paper, the Commission sketched out the pre-accession strategy of
integrating the CEECs into the internal market, hence filling out
the remaining gaps.[70] With the exception of the free movement of
persons, the voluntary approximation framework of the White Paper
was content-wise equivalent to the EEA Agreement.[71] The aim of the
EAs themselves had never been to fully integrate the CEECs into the
internal market as that stage was envisaged and accomplished by
the EEA Agreement.

The EAs and the SAAs have operated in similar political contexts, and
neither has explicitly proclaimed EU membership as their imminent
goal. The SAAs, nevertheless, recognise the non-EU contracting parties
as potential candidates for EU membership,[72] and mention their 'gradual
rapprochement with the European Union'[73] despite its limited effect on

---

[66] European Council, 'Conclusions of the Presidency – Corfu, 24–25 June 1994' SN 150/94.
[67] European Council, 'Conclusions of the Presidency – Essen, 9–10 December 1994' SN
300/94.
[68] See, for example, Recital 23, preamble to the Europe Agreement establishing an association between the European Communities and their Member States, of the one part,
and the Republic of Estonia, of the other part [1998] OJ L68/3.
[69] M Maresceau (n 61) 16–17. In fact, only after 1994 has the EU engaged in genuine pre-
accession strategies: Ibid., 9.
[70] Commission, 'White Paper – Preparation of the associated countries of Central and
Eastern Europe for integration into the internal market of the Union' COM (95) 163 final
(CEEC White Paper).
[71] M Maresceau and E Montaguti, 'The Relations between the European Union and Central
and Eastern Europe: A Legal Appraisal' (1995) 32 Common Market Law Review 1327, 1336.
For a contrasting view of the EEA and the CEEC White Paper see MA Gaudissart and
A Sinnaeve, 'The Role of the White Paper in the Preparation of the Eastern
Enlargement' in M Maresceau (ed.), Enlarging the European Union (Longman 1997) 41,
66–71.
[72] Recital 17, preamble to the EC-Albania SAA.
[73] Article 8(2)(1) EC-Albania SAA.

the content of the agreements. The SAAs' function in the pre-pre-accession process is to prepare future candidate countries for a subsequent accession process. The potential candidate status of the SAP countries was recognised in 2000.[74] Among the SAA countries, Croatia joined the EU in 2013, Bosnia and Herzegovina and Kosovo are currently potential candidate countries, North Macedonia and Albania enjoy official candidate status, and Montenegro and Serbia have started accession negotiations.

2.4 Expanding the Internal Market

The final category of the current functions of the internal market acquis in the EU's external relations is that of integrating third countries into the internal market independently of the non-EU contracting parties' membership aspirations. This integration may either cover the entire internal market or be limited to one or more specific policy sectors. In spite of differences in the breadth of the cooperation across policy areas, both categories share roughly the same depth of integration in terms of the free movement provisions as far as applicable to the policy sector in question.

2.4.1 Comprehensive Integration into the Internal Market

The only genuine example of an agreement exporting EU acquis for the purpose of extending the internal market outside the Union in a comprehensive manner without explicit membership aspirations is the Agreement establishing the EEA. It was signed in 1992 as a multilateral AA between the EC, its Member States and the countries of the European Free Trade Association (EFTA) except for Switzerland, and entered into force in 1994. Most of the former EEA EFTA countries have by now joined the EU,[75] rendering Iceland, Liechtenstein and Norway the only non-EU participants in the EEA. There are no indications, however, that the EEA would cease to exist in the foreseeable future.[76]

---

[74] European Council, 'Conclusions of the Presidency – Feira, 19–20 June 2000' SN 200/00.

[75] Austria, Denmark, Portugal, Sweden, United Kingdom, Finland.

[76] Norway's possible accession to the EU was rejected at referenda both in 1972 and 1994. In July 2009, Iceland submitted an application for EU membership and started accession negotiations in 2010 but negotiations were suspended in 2013 and in March 2015, Iceland withdrew the application. Liechtenstein's EU membership has not been subject to genuine discussion.

The objective of the EEA Agreement is to create a 'homogeneous European Economic Area' based on equal conditions of competition and respect for the same rules.[77] This explicit aim of homogeneity distinguishes the EEA Agreement from all other neighbourhood agreements discussed earlier. The EEA Agreement covers almost the entire spectrum of internal market acquis making the EEA EFTA States fully fledged participants in the internal market while excluding the customs union and the Common Commercial Policy (CCP) as well as the common agricultural and fisheries policies.[78]

The annexes to the EEA Agreement containing 'EEA-relevant provisions' are updated on a continuous basis by a decision of the Joint Committee for the purpose of guaranteeing legal security and homogeneity within the EEA.[79] An elaborate institutional framework, too, has been set up for the purpose of ensuring a uniform application of the acquis. In contrast to the AAs discussed earlier, which mainly establish an association council, the EEA agreement features a Joint Committee, parliamentary cooperation, and the EFTA Court as the body adjudicating disputes between the EFTA countries arising from the interpretation of the EEA Agreement. The system established by the EEA agreement thus goes well beyond exporting the internal market acquis, having become a legal system of its own.[80]

Switzerland, albeit a member of the EFTA, is not party to the EEA Agreement. Switzerland participated in the negotiations together with the other EFTA members but following a negative referendum in 1992 did not proceed to conclude the EEA Agreement. The EU-Switzerland relationship is instead governed by over a hundred bilateral agreements. These agreements notably include the two packages of 'Bilateral I' and 'Bilateral II' signed in 1999 and 2004 and containing seven and nine agreements, respectively. The policy areas covered by the agreements include, for example, the free movement of persons, air transport, rail and road transport, trade in agricultural products, public procurement, mutual recognition of conformity assessment, processed agricultural products and the environment.

The two series of agreements feature some noticeable differences. The Bilateral I agreements were concluded as AAs as a single package. The termination of a single agreement in the package is not possible due

---

[77] Article 1(1) EEA Agreement.
[78] Article 8(3) EEA Agreement.
[79] Article 102(1) EEA Agreement.
[80] Case E-9/97 *Sveinbjörnsdóttir* [1998] EFTA Ct Rep 95, para. 59.

to the 'guillotine clause', which requires that all seven agreements enter into force together and that none of them can be terminated individually.[81] The guillotine clause binds together some of the pieces of acquis in the jigsaw puzzle of the EU-Switzerland relationship and helps maintain its uniformity.[82] The Bilateral II agreements are not AAs and do not contain a guillotine clause because their subject matters are not as closely interconnected as those included in Bilateral I.

The objective of the EU-Switzerland bilateral agreements is to enhance deep sectoral cooperation but not to offer full participation in the internal market on equal terms with the EU Member States like the EEA. Similar to the latter, the annexes to the bilateral agreements list applicable EU legislative acts and strive towards homogeneity between EU acquis and the pre-signature acquis in the agreements, leaving the effect of post-signature acquis to be decided on an ad hoc basis.[83] The fact that the provisions of the bilateral agreements are to be interpreted and applied in the light of the case law of the Court confirms that the nature of the EU-Swiss relationship is to some extent comparable to the sui generis character of the EU and the EEA legal orders.[84]

Echoing the negative result of the Swiss referendum to participate in the EEA, the cooperation is rightfully referred to as 'differentiated integration' resting somewhere between cooperation and integration.[85] On the one hand, the EU-Swiss bilateral agreements envisage much deeper integration with the EU internal market than the EAs and SAAs requiring Switzerland to adopt all EU acquis in the fields covered by the bilateral agreements. On the other hand, not all of the four freedoms of the internal market operating in the EU and the EEA apply to the bilateral agreements, notably excluding to varying degrees the free movement of capital and services and the freedom of establishment. Yet differently from multilateral sectoral agreements, the EEA

---

[81] See, for example, Article 25 of the Agreement between the European Community and its Member States, of the one part, and the Swiss Confederation, of the other, on the free movement of persons [2002] OJ L114/6. The Bilateral I agreements entered into force simultaneously on 1 July 2002.

[82] See R Schwok, *Switzerland–European Union: An impossible membership?* (P.I.E. Peter Lang 2009) 39.

[83] For example, Article 1(2) of the Agreement between the European Community and the Swiss Confederation on Air Transport [2002] OJ L114/73.

[84] S Breitenmoser, 'Sectoral Agreements between the EC and Switzerland: Contents and Context' (2003) 40 *Common Market Law Review* 1137, 1144.

[85] Ibid., 1185.

Agreement and the EU-Swiss bilateral cooperation provide comprehensive frameworks for the respective third countries' participation in the internal market.

2.4.2 Sectoral Integration into the Internal Market

The new form of sectoral cooperation between the EU and the countries in its neighbourhood – 'legally binding sectoral multilateralism'[86] – is providing a successful alternative to bilateral agreements such as those concluded between the EU and Switzerland. It is a means of exporting the internal market acquis in individual policy areas thereby creating 'homogeneous' regulatory spaces that comprise the EU as well as a group of third countries.

The function of the internal market acquis in sectoral integration differs significantly from those discussed earlier. In the previous categories, acquis is used mainly as a tool of the EU's external policy[87] and a platform for political and economic cooperation between the EU and individual third countries or regional groups. Deep sectoral cooperation, however, builds on the foundation of the ENP, SAP and Euro-Mediterranean cooperation that have gradually prepared the neighbourhood countries for adopting EU acquis while fulfilling the EU's internal policy purposes. On the one hand, sectoral integration contributes to the overarching policy frameworks by further integrating the energy markets of the Eastern Partnership,[88] or deepening cooperation in the aviation sector of the Euro-Mediterranean framework.[89] On the other hand, it complements the EU's internal policies with a structured external dimension.[90]

The EU has currently concluded three multilateral sectoral agreements – the EnCT, the ECAA Agreement and the TCT.

---

[86] S Blockmans and B Van Vooren, 'Revitalizing the European "Neighbourhood Economic Community": The Case for Legally Binding Sectoral Multilateralism' (2012) 17 *European Foreign Affairs Review* 577.

[87] See, for example, M Cremona, 'Enlargement: A Successful Instrument of Foreign Policy?' in T Tridimas and P Nebbia (eds.), *European Union Law for the Twenty-First Century: Volume 1: Rethinking the New Legal Order* (Hart Publishing 2004) 397.

[88] Council, 'Joint Declaration of the Eastern Partnership Summit – Warsaw, 29–30 September 2011' 14983/11, para. 13.

[89] In 2006, the first Euro-Mediterranean aviation agreement between the European Community and its Member States, of the one part and the Kingdom of Morocco, of the other part was concluded in 2006: [2006] OJ L386/57.

[90] See, for example, Commission, 'Common Aviation Area with the Neighbouring Countries by 2010 – Progress Report' (Communication) COM (2008) 596 final.

2.4.2.1 Energy Community Treaty

The majority of energy resources consumed in the EU, in particular oil and gas, come from producers outside the Union, making coordinated external action indispensable for the creation of an internal energy sector.[91] Whereas constructing the external dimension of the EU's energy market on bilateral relations carries the risk of fragmenting the market, jeopardising the security of supply and leaving the Union politically vulnerable, a multilateral approach has been preferred both within the EU and in cooperation with third countries.[92]

Setting up the EU's internal energy market has not been an easy task. In 1996, Directive 96/92/EC on common rules for the internal market in electricity was adopted with the objective of creating an open internal electricity market; two years later, the internal energy market was extended to trade in gas.[93] The internal market for energy and gas was intended to be completed by the year 2014,[94] but further action is still required.[95]

In 1995, the Commission pointed to the effect of trans-European energy networks on the neighbouring countries.[96] Action in the external dimension was taken further and in 2002, the EU signed together with nine South East European (SEE) countries the Athens Memorandum – a political document in which the parties agreed to work towards establishing an integrated regional energy market in electricity in South-East Europe by 2005.[97] A year later, a similar

---

[91] Commission, 'White Paper – An Energy Policy for the European Union' COM (95) 682 final (1995 White Paper), 8.

[92] The sensitivities surrounding energy policy do not, in themselves, support a move from bilateralism to multilateralism: see K Westphal, 'Energy Policy between Multilateral Governance and Geopolitics: Whither Europe?' (2006) 4 *Internationale Politik und Gesellschaft* 44, 58–60.

[93] Directive 96/92/EC of the European Parliament and of the Council of 19 December 1996 concerning common rules for the internal market in electricity [1997] OJ L27/20; Directive 98/30/EC of the European Parliament and of the Council of 22 June 1998 concerning common rules for the internal market in natural gas [1998] OJ L204/1. In 2003, the two directives were replaced by Directives 2003/54/EC and 2003/55/EC, respectively.

[94] European Council, 'Conclusions – Brussels, 4 February 2011' EUCO 2/1/11 REV 1, para. 4.

[95] Commission, 'A Framework Strategy for a Resilient Energy Union with a Forward-Looking Climate Change Policy' (Communication) COM (2015) 80 final, 7–8; Commission, 'Fourth report on the State of the Energy Union' COM (2019) 175 final, 7.

[96] 1995 White Paper (n 91) 29–30.

[97] Memorandum of Understanding on the Regional Electricity Market in South East Europe and its Integration into the European Union Internal Electricity Market, 2002 (The Athens Memorandum 2002).

Memorandum of Understanding (MoU) was signed in Athens on the gas market.[98] It was recognised from early on[99] and made explicit in 2003[100] that the Athens Process should be given a legally binding form.

In 2005, the EnCT was signed between the EC, of the one part, and Albania, Bulgaria, Bosnia and Herzegovina, Croatia, North Macedonia, Montenegro, Romania, Serbia and Kosovo (United Nations Interim Administration Mission (UNMIK)), of the other part.[101] The Treaty entered into force in 2006. Moldova joined the Energy Community in 2010, followed by Ukraine in 2011 and Georgia in 2017. Initially concluded for a period of ten years, the EnCT was extended for another ten-year period in 2013.[102]

The specific aims of the EnCT include, among others, the creation of a stable regulatory and market framework for ensuring steady and continuous energy supply; the creation of a 'single regulatory space' for trade in Network Energy including the electricity and gas sectors; and establishing conditions for trade in energy.[103] These objectives are, according to Article 3 EnCT, to be attained via extending the relevant EU acquis to all contracting parties, setting up a mechanism for the operation of the Network Energy Markets and establishing a single market in electricity and gas. Included is the acquis on energy, environment, competition and renewables. The Energy 2020 strategy followed up on the provision and set the objective of extending the EnCT both substantially and geographically.[104]

2.4.2.2 European Common Aviation Area Agreement

The logic underpinning the creation of the ECAA is similar to that of the Energy Community. The EU's single market for aviation was created in

---

[98] Memorandum of Understanding on the Regional Energy Market in South East Europe and its Integration into the European Community Internal Energy Market, 2003, 15548/03/bis (The Athens Memorandum 2003).

[99] The Athens Memorandum 2002 (n 97) para. 9.

[100] 'The Participants will seek to replace this Memorandum of Understanding with a legally binding agreement as soon as possible.' The Athens Memorandum 2003 (n 98) para. 9.

[101] Treaty establishing the Energy Community [2006] OJ L198/18. The EnCT was concluded on the legal bases of Articles 47, 55, 83, 89, 95, 133 and 175 EC Treaty.

[102] Article 97 EnCT; Decision of the Ministerial Council of the Energy Community D/2013/03/MC-EnC on extending the duration of the Energy Community Treaty [2013] OJ L320/81.

[103] Article 2 EnCT.

[104] Commission, 'Energy 2020 A strategy for competitive, sustainable and secure energy' (Communication) COM (2010) 639 final, 18. The new Energy Union strategy calls for further strengthening of the EnCT: Commission, 'A Framework Strategy for a Resilient Energy Union' (n 95) 7.

the 1990s by liberalising the air transport sector.[105] In 1999, the European Commission launched the Single European Sky (SES) initiative on air traffic management (ATM) and regulation to reduce delays and congestion in the European airspace and to bring ATM under the common transport policy.[106] The initiative was followed by two legislative packages, which came into force in 2004[107] and 2009,[108] respectively.

Traditionally, the EU's external aviation policy had been based on bilateral cooperation between the Member States and third countries. The 2002 Open Skies judgments marked a revolutionary departure from the prevailing practice. In the sequence of judgments, the Court declared that computerised reservation systems, intra-Community tariffs and time slots forming part of the Open Skies Agreements fall within the EU's exclusive competence.[109] As a result, around 2000 bilateral agreements concluded by the Member States had to be renegotiated in order to be brought in line with EU law.

The judicial momentum was followed by political initiatives by the Commission, which declared that the development and competitiveness of the internal aviation market demanded further action in the external sphere.[110] Deep multilateral cooperation was first undertaken with the SEE countries whose aviation markets were already

---

[105] This was achieved by the three market liberalisation packages of 1987, 1990 and 1992: L Butcher, 'Aviation: European Liberalisation, 1986–2002' (2010) House of Commons Library Standard Note SN/BT/182.

[106] Commission, 'The creation of the single European sky' (Communication) COM (1999) 614 final.

[107] Commission, 'First Report on the implementation of the Single Sky Legislation: achievements and the way forward' (Communication) COM (2007) 845 final. The 'SES I' package included regulations setting out the general framework, common requirements for the provision of air navigation services, rules on the organisation and use of airspace, and interoperability of the Air Traffic Management Network.

[108] Commission, 'Single European Sky II: towards more sustainable and better performing aviation' (Communication) COM (2008) 389 final. The 'SES II' package comprised updates to the 2004 legislation, technological regulation of SESAR ATM (Single European Sky Air Traffic Management Research), rules on safety and an action plan for airport capacity. An Interim update of SES II is envisaged by SES 2+: Commission, 'Accelerating the implementation of the Single European Sky' (Communication) COM (2013) 408 final.

[109] Case C-467/98 Commission v. Denmark EU:C:2002:625; Case C-468/98 Commission v. Sweden EU:C:2002:626; Case C-469/98 Commission v. Finland EU:C:2002:627; Case C-471/98 Commission v. Belgium EU:C:2002:628; Case C-472/98 Commission v. Luxembourg EU: C:2002:629; Case C-475/98 Commission v. Austria EU:C:2002:630; Case C-476/98 Commission v. Germany EU:C:2002:631.

[110] Commission, 'Developing the agenda for the Community's external aviation policy' (Communication) COM (2005) 79 final, 4.

inclining towards the EU and were considered to deliver greater operational efficiency, security and safety than other possible markets, as well as to provide sectoral impetus to the EU's neighbourhood policy.[111]

The Agreement on the Establishment of a Common Aviation Area was signed in 2006 between the EC and its Member States, of the one part, and Albania, Bosnia and Herzegovina, Bulgaria, Croatia, North Macedonia, Iceland, Montenegro, Norway, Romania, Serbia and Kosovo (UNMIK), of the other part,[112] and entered into force in 2017. Pursuant to Article 1(1) of the Agreement, the ECAA is based on 'free market access, freedom of establishment, equal conditions of competition, and common rules including in the areas of safety, security, ATM, social and environment'. The relevant acquis to be adopted by the non-EU contracting parties comprises among others access to the aviation market, aviation safety, aviation security, ATM, environment, social aspects and consumer protection.[113]

The more recent Common Aviation Area (CAA) Agreements, similar in content but bilateral in form and somewhat less ambitious than the ECAA Agreement,[114] are part of the process of developing a wider CAA in the EU's neighbourhood, complementing the EU's aviation policy as well as the ENP.[115] The CAAs have been concluded with Georgia in 2010 and Moldova in 2012, essentially serving as an ante-chamber before joining the ECAA.[116] Analogous agreements with Ukraine and Armenia are pending signature whereas negotiations on a CAA with Azerbaijan are currently ongoing. In the southern neighbourhood, the EU has signed Euro-Mediterranean Aviation Agreements with Morocco in 2006, Jordan in 2010 and Israel in 2013. Negotiations with Tunisia have been completed and await signature while the negotiations started

---

[111] Ibid., 8.

[112] [2006] OJ L285/3.

[113] Article 3 ECAA Agreement.

[114] The ECAA Agreement, for example, envisages the direct application of the judgments of the Court which does not apply to the bilateral agreements: see Commission, 'The EU and its neighbouring regions: A renewed approach to transport cooperation' (Communication) COM (2011) 415 final, 4.

[115] Commission, 'Common Aviation Area with the Neighbouring Countries by 2010 – Progress Report' (n 90) 2.

[116] Article 25(2) of the Common Aviation Area Agreement between the European Union and its Member States and Georgia [2012] OJ L321/3; Article 25(2) of the Common Aviation Area Agreement between the European Union and its Member States and the Republic of Moldova [2012] OJ L292/3.

with Lebanon in 2009 are not currently active.[117] The conclusion of a similar agreement with Algeria is envisaged.[118]

External action in the aviation sector including the exporting of the EU's aviation acquis is thereby not constrained to the multilateral model but features a variety of instruments that take into consideration the development of the aviation market, the ambitions of the third countries including their readiness to adapt to EU regulations and standards and the interests of the EU and its Member States.[119] This is notwithstanding the Union's ultimate aim of creating a 'single ECAA' with two multilateral agreements, one for the eastern and one for the southern neighbourhood countries to be striven for as an intermediate goal.[120]

2.4.2.3 Transport Community Treaty

Road, rail, inland waterway and maritime transport are further key areas of cooperation between the EU and its neighbouring countries. The focus of the EU's common transport policy is on integrating transport networks for the benefit of greater cohesion in the internal market as a whole.[121] The ambitious Trans-European Transport Network (TEN-T) policy seeks to enhance transport connectivity within the EU to overcome existing bottlenecks and technical barriers.[122]

The neighbourhood countries have been integrated into the EU's transport networks since ten Pan-European Corridors (PEC) and Transport Areas were identified at the Ministerial Conferences on Crete (1994)[123] and in Helsinki (1997).[124] Following the subsequent enlargement rounds, most of the PECs are now part of the TEN-T

---

[117] Commission, 'International Aviation: Lebanon', https://ec.europa.eu/transport/modes/air/international_aviation/country_index/lebanon_en accessed 10 February 2020.

[118] Commission, 'Creation of a Common Aviation Area with Algeria' (Communication) COM (2008) 682 final.

[119] Commission, 'Common Aviation Area with the Neighbouring Countries by 2010 – Progress Report' (n 90) 6.

[120] Commission, 'The EU and its neighbouring regions' (n 114) 4.

[121] Commission, 'Extension of the major trans-European transport axes to the neighbouring countries' (Communication) COM (2007) 32 final, 4.

[122] Revised in 2004 by Decision No 884/2004/EC of the European Parliament and of the Council of 29 April 2004 amending Decision No 1692/96/EC on Community guidelines for the development of the trans-European transport network [2004] OJ L167/1.

[123] Crete Declaration adopted at the Second Pan-European Transport Conference, Crete, 16 March 1994.

[124] Helsinki Declaration 'Towards a European Wide Transport Policy: A Set of Common Principles' adopted at the Third Pan-European Transport Conference, Helsinki, 25 June 1997.

network. The Pan-European Transport Areas focus on specific regions and include, for example, the South East Europe Transport Observatory (SEETO) in the Western Balkans, operational since 2005; the Euro-Mediterranean Transport Forum in the Mediterranean region, created in 1998; and the TRACECA corridor connecting the EU with Turkey, the Southern Caucasus and Central Asia, set up in 1993.[125] The extension of EU transport networks to the neighbouring countries has been closely connected with the implementation of the ENP and the enlargement strategy and enjoys a prominent place in the new DCFTAs.[126]

The SEETO was launched in 2004 with the signing of the MoU for the development of the Core Regional Transport Network between the EU and Albania, Bosnia and Herzegovina, Croatia, North Macedonia, Montenegro, Serbia and Kosovo (UNMIK). The MoU established a transport strategy for the region, including infrastructure pro-grammes and policy cooperation to enhance investment capacity. In order to give transport cooperation in the SEE region a legally binding form and to improve the regulatory and investment environment,[127] the TCT was concluded in 2017 between the EU and the six South East European Parties.[128] The agreement has not yet entered into force but is being applied provisionally.[129]

The TCT builds on the ECAA Agreement and aims at fully integrating the SEE region into the EU's internal transport market. Similar to the EnCT and the ECAA Agreement, the TCT is based on the alignment of third country legal systems with the EU acquis in the field of transport, including in the areas of technical standards, interoperability, safety, security, traffic management, social policy, public procurement and environment.[130] Similar to the ECAA Agreement, integration into the internal market in transport takes place in stages with transitional periods, subject to alignment with the EU acquis, which is assessed by the Commission.[131] The future plans of the TCT include further

---

[125] Commission, 'Extension of the major trans-European transport axes' (n 121) 5.

[126] Commission, 'The EU and its neighbouring regions' (n 114) 3.

[127] SEETO Comprehensive Network Development Plan 2014, 58 www.seetoint.org/librar y/multi-annual-plans/.

[128] [2017] OJ L278/3. On the negotiating history and the difficulties surrounding the conclusion of the Treaty, see S Blockmans and B Van Vooren (n 86) 597–598.

[129] Council Decision (EU) 2017/1937 of 11 July 2017 on the signing, on behalf of the European Union, and provisional application of the Treaty establishing the Transport Community [2017] OJ L278/1.

[130] Article 1(1) TCT.

[131] Article 27 ECAA; Article 40 TCT.

integration of the eastern neighbourhood into the EU's transport stand-ards and networks but no satellite bilateral agreements of the CAA-type are currently envisaged.[132]

2.5 Managing the Relationship between the Union and a Former Member or Associated State

In addition to gradual rapprochement with the EU, it may be necessary to employ the internal market acquis also for the purposes of maintain-ing a link between the EU and a state that is not moving closer but rather further away from an enhanced level of cooperation with the EU and its internal market. Brexit, in particular, designating the United Kingdom's withdrawal from the EU on 31 January 2020 is a case in point.[133] In such scenarios, the internal market acquis may play a crucial role as a lifeline to be held on to in the continuing relationship between the Union and the countries concerned.

Brexit is currently the sole example of 'differentiated disintegration' by an EU Member State.[134] It entails complete withdrawal from the Union whereby, according to the most radical of scenarios, all ties between the and the supranational legal order of the EU will be cut after the expiry of the transition period on 31 December 2020. In spite of losing its immediate compulsory character, however, the EU internal market acquis is unlikely to become entirely redundant in the United Kingdom. Some segments of the acquis will probably remain in force as the 'sensible' rules approved by the national government[135] despite becoming extracted from the EU's constitutional system. Other ties may be (re-)established with the conclusion of the agreement governing the United Kingdom's future relationship with the Union.

During the long period of negotiations following the notification in March 2017 of the United Kingdom's intention to withdraw from the Union, a 'no deal' and 'hard' Brexit proved to be the least attractive of

---

[132] See Commission, 'The EU and its neighbouring regions' (n 114).

[133] References have also been made to 'Turkxit' – a possible reorganisation of the EU-Turkey partnership in the future: see, for example, T Ash, 'Turkey's EU accession: the way forward' *Financial Times* (20 September 2017) www.ft.com/content/81b92208-9d50-11e7-9a86-4d5a475ba4c5 accessed 10 February 2020.

[134] And, in fact, the sole example of 'differentiated disintegration' by an EU member state: F Schimmelfennig, 'Brexit: Differentiated Disintegration in the European Union' (2018) 25 *Journal of European Public Policy* 1154.

[135] As opposed to 'stupid' and 'amendable': C Barnard, 'The Practicalities of Leaving the EU' (2016) 41 *European Law Review* 484, 485.

the solutions available. In order to avoid significant disruptions in the economy, the repeatedly renegotiated Agreement on the withdrawal of the United Kingdom from the EU (Withdrawal Agreement) predominantly retains the *status quo* of the application of EU acquis for the transition period,[136] while excluding the United Kingdom's influence from the making of the acquis.[137] Article 50(2) TEU provides that the Union, when negotiating the arrangements for the withdrawal of a Member State shall '[take] account of the framework for its future relationship with the Union'. Whereas the withdrawal agreement is incapable of predicting the precise contents of the future agreement, subject to separate negotiations, it could be expected to include internal market acquis, which in turn will assume a wholly new function in the Union's relations with a neighbouring country.

Any country in the EU's neighbourhood, especially one sharing a common border with the EU is dependent on maintaining a well-functioning trade relationship with the Union whose Member States combined typically constitute its largest trade partner. Constructing a trade partnership on WTO rules alone is hardly sufficient for the withdrawing state,[138] nor would a customs union or an FTA be void of shortcomings.[139] An EEA or Switzerland type of a solution would also be possible in theory, but despite allowing for access to the internal market, it is an option unlikely to be resorted to in practice.[140] The EEA, for example, is unappealing to the United Kingdom due to its inflexibility whereas the EEA EFTA States fear disruption to the balance between the current participants.[141]

---

[136] Agreement on the withdrawal of the United Kingdom of Great Britain and Northern Ireland from the European Union and the European Atomic Energy Community [2020] OJ L29/7. For a detailed account, see M Dougan, 'An Airbag for the Crash Test Dummies? EU-UK Negotiations for a Post-Withdrawal "Status Quo" Transitional Regime under Article 50 TEU' (2018) 55 *Common Market Law Review* 57, 62.

[137] Article 7(1) Withdrawal Agreement.

[138] See F Baetens, '"No Deal Is Better Than a Bad Deal"? The Fallacy of the WTO Fall-back Option as a Post-Brexit Safety Net' (2018) 55 *Common Market Law Review* 133, 174.

[139] European Union Committee, *Brexit: the options for trade* (HL 2016–17 5) 73–75; G Sacerdoti, 'The Prospects: The UK Trade Regime with the EU and the World' in F Fabbrini (ed.), *The Law & Politics of Brexit* (Oxford University Press 2017) 71.

[140] See MJ Pérez Crespo, 'After Brexit ... The Best of Both Worlds? Rebutting the Norwegian and Swiss Models as Long-Term Options for the UK' (2017) 36 *Yearbook of European Law* 94.

[141] European Union Committee, *Brexit: The Options for Trade* (n 139) 21.

The EU has held a firm position in the negotiations insisting on a partnership 'as close as possible' while maintaining the 'balance of rights and obligations' and ensuring 'a level playing field' between the parties.[142] This partnership would preferably build on the idea of the indivisibility of the four fundamental freedoms that form the core of the internal market,[143] essentially rejecting a Swiss-style piecemeal solution deemed to 'undermine the integrity and proper functioning of the Single Market'.[144] The United Kingdom's approach, on the other hand, has been selective towards the internal market, welcoming continued internal market access for manufactured goods and agricultural products as well as profound cooperation in a number of priority areas such as energy and transport while excluding the continued application of the entire internal market acquis, especially the free movement of persons.[145] The negotiators' compromise on the future agreement at the time of the withdrawal was communicated in the Political declaration setting out the framework for the future relationship between the EU and the United Kingdom accompanying the Withdrawal Agreement (Political Declaration).[146] In the Political Declaration, the parties expressed their common intent to give the future 'ambitious, broad, deep and flexible' partnership the form of a comprehensive agreement – an FTA possibly coupled with an AA as an overarching framework – featuring deep integration also in other prioritised sectors; ambitious in scope and depth and mindful of the economic integration of the parties, their respective sizes and geographic proximity.[147] Despite proposing an AA/DCFTA, the post-Brexit model has objectives and is expected to fulfil a function very different from the AA/DCFTAs already concluded with the eastern neighbourhood countries. It is designed to decrease the level of integration between the EU and the United Kingdom which the existing agreements are rather aiming to achieve.

---

[142] European Council, Art. 50 Guidelines, EUCO XT 20001/18, 23 March 2018, para. 3.

[143] Ibid., The 'integrity of the Union's Single Market and the Customs Union' has been reiterated in the Political declaration setting out the framework for the future relationship between the European Union and the United Kingdom [2020] OJ C34/1, para. 4. Note, however, in the same paragraph a contradicting reference to '[...] respecting the result of the 2016 referendum including with regard to [...] the ending of free movement of people between the Union and the United Kingdom'.

[144] European Council, Art. 50 Guidelines (n 142) para. 7.

[145] United Kingdom Government, *The Future Relationship between the United Kingdom and the European Union* (White Paper, Cm 9593, 2018).

[146] Political declaration (n 143).

[147] Ibid., paras. 3, 5, 16, 17 and 120.

During the transitional period, the internal market acquis will serve to maintain the prevailing conditions for economic and personal exchange and, in fact, the continued participation of the United Kingdom in the internal market. In the post-Brexit agreement, the acquis will be confined to the quite particular role of maintaining close – but not too close – ties with the EU and the internal market. In practice, this cannot in the case of a withdrawing Member State mean but a significant downgrade from the membership level of integration. Anything else would question the very purpose of the withdrawal if not narrowly limited to the question of membership *per se*.[148]

The United Kingdom has previously declared an ambition of continued alignment with EU acquis in certain preferential areas[149] and has agreed with the EU that the post-Brexit relationship may evolve in the future.[150] The current experiences of the EU's integration with third countries outside the accession process have revealed that close cooperation with the Union in the realm of the internal market is generally expected to be both gradually deepening and entailing significant spill-over effects in other areas of collaboration. Placing a permanent constraint on the depth or, indeed, the breadth of a deeply integrated country's[151] future relationship with the EU is an onerous task. Furthermore, while it is unprecedented for the Union to enter into an agreement with a neighbourhood country that reverses integration in such a drastic manner, it would be equally unprecedented for any deep form of economic integration with a geographically close neighbour to the EU to take place on the basis of any rulebook other than the Union's. Underscored by the loss of bargaining power on behalf of the United Kingdom as a withdrawing state vis-à-vis the Union,[152] the EU may be expected to play a major role in deciding the regulatory menu. This, in turn, speaks for a high probability that the future partnership will be

---

[148] The United Kingdom's 2016 'new settlement' in the EU as compared to the post-Brexit arrangement is a case in point. For analysis, see E-M Poptcheva and D Eatock, 'The UK's "new settlement" in the European Union: Renegotiation and referendum' European Parliamentary Research Service PE 577.983 (2016).

[149] See United Kingdom Government White Paper (n 145) 12–14. Note, however, the later position of the UK Government aiming for an FTA similar to the EU-Canada Comprehensive Economic and Trade Agreement (CETA) as well as a number of sectoral agreements excluding, i.a. regulatory alignment and joint institutions: UK Government, 'The Future Relationship between the UK and the EU' Written statement to Parliament, 3 February 2020 www.gov.uk/government/speeches/the-future-relationship-between-the-uk-and-the-eu accessed 10 February 2020.

[150] Political declaration (n 143) para. 5.

[151] See ibid.

[152] See F Schimmelfennig (n 134).

constructed around the United Kingdom's continued application of the internal market acquis.

The EU has persistently rejected a piecemeal approach to the future partnership with the United Kingdom. Third countries in a forward-moving integration process are generally granted a step-by-step entry into the internal market conditional upon their implementation of the acquis, including both sectoral integration and partial access to the internal market that does not comprise all of the four fundamental freedoms. Sectoral integration such as in the fields of energy and transport is generally considered advantageous for the internal market and, indeed, an indispensable element thereof. In the same vein, participation in the internal market to the extent of some freedoms but not all is regarded as acceptable when the neighbouring country does not (yet) fulfil the Union's requirements for, in particular, the free movement of persons. It also applies when the third country has opted for a partial form of integration from the beginning, such as the EU-Swiss partnership, which excludes the free movement of services and establishment. The limited integration of third countries into the internal market is, thus, generally considered a success for the Union without concerns being raised as to its detrimental effect on the integrity and proper functioning of the EU internal market.[153] In the case of the withdrawal of a Member State, however, cherry-picking especially among the fundamental freedoms is regarded as a threat to the internal market. While inconsistent with previous practice, the EU's position may be motivated by the size and prominence of the United Kingdom as a (former) Member State as well as the inequality of their respective bargaining powers, but is essentially driven by a perceived existential threat of Brexit to the European project rather than the future functioning of the internal market.[154]

2.6 Conclusion

The various functions of the acquis identified in this chapter generally correlate to the 'concentric circles of EUropean integration'.[155] First, the

---

[153] Should the aim be the extension of the internal market to non-member countries one could merely ask whether an arrangement falling short of full membership could be regarded as equally effective or whether the institutional arrangements could possibly adversely affect the autonomy of the EU legal order.

[154] See, for example, M Wind, 'Brexit and Euroskepticism' in F Fabbrini (ed.), *The Law & Politics of Brexit* (Oxford University Press 2017) 221, 224–225.

[155] S Lavenex, 'Concentric Circles of Flexible "EUropean" Integration: A Typology of EU External Governance Relations' (2011) 9 *Comparative European Politics* 372, 387.

profundity of integration largely mirrors the third country's geographical proximity to the European Union and especially to the initial 'core' of European integration – the founding Member States. Multilateral sectoral cooperation which includes not only some of the EU's closest and economically most developed neighbours but also countries in the European periphery and beyond deviates from the prevailing trend. The second criterion that largely determines the extent to which non-members are willing to adopt EU acquis is their membership prospect. An outlook of future accession to the Union provides important incentives for third countries to align their national regulatory frameworks with the EU's acquis. Exceptions, however, include the non-European parties to the bilateral CAA agreements that serve as a preparatory stage for the ECAA and the EEA EFTA States and Switzerland that will not become members of the EU in the foreseeable future. The most far-reaching legal approximation projects in terms of aims and scope of the acquis have, paradoxically, been undertaken by countries that have chosen not to become members of the EU although accession would, at least from the perspective of fulfilling the membership criteria,[156] be predominantly a technical matter.

Bilateral and multilateral agreements are reinforcing mutually and vis-à-vis the internal market. Bilateralism has proven to be the EU's natural first choice for cooperation with third countries, allowing for individual approaches and tailor-made solutions, and catering for the interests and integration objectives of both the Union and the non-EU partners. Bilateral agreements, such as the PCAs, EMAAs, SAAs and the AA/DCFTAs, provide general political frameworks for the EU's relations with the neighbourhood countries. The internal market acquis included therein may act as a first step towards regulatory cooperation with the EU or, in the example of the AA/DCFTAs, a second stage in the move towards deeper forms of integration with the internal market. The comparably more inflexible multilateral agreements are few in number but have become the EU's preferred option for integrating into the internal market economically highly developed countries that are able to abide by EU standards, or for cooperating with less developed countries in policy sectors featuring a strong cross-border dimension. Multilateral frameworks are furthermore expected to facilitate the process of reaching

---

[156] 'Countries such as Switzerland and Norway already meet all of the membership criteria': 'Composite Paper on the Commission Reports 1999: Reports on progress towards accession by each of the candidate countries' 13 October 1999, 5.

the EU's internal policy goals by managing the indispensable external dimension of the EU's internal policies. Whereas bilateralism provides breadth in the integration of third countries to the Union's sphere of influence and to the internal market, multilateral frameworks offer depth. The EEA currently provides a satisfactory alternative to EU membership for the countries involved while multilateral sectoral cooperation is gaining ground due to the 'fast track' integration opportunities it provides in prioritised sectors. Multilateral agreements also enable the creation of a common market space outside the EU's borders, including among the third countries. This further facilitates trade, commitment to the EU project and the ultimate achievement of a pan-European market resembling a domestic market as closely as possible.

Part I

Expanding the Internal Market: The Concept

3 Internal Market Acquis
The Concept

Central to expanding the internal market is the concept of the latter – its special characteristics, substantive content in terms of the acquis and interoperability with the national legal orders. The internal market consists of a package of obligations to which the Member States must adhere as part of their membership in the EU and is, as a concept, dynamic and ambiguous. In order to be able to establish whether and to what extent exporting internal market acquis to third countries can result in a market space homogeneous with the EU internal market one must delimit, and therefore define the distinctive features of the latter.

This chapter explores both the 'old' and the 'new' elements of the internal market: the fundamental freedoms and competition policy, on the one hand, and non-economic policy considerations, on the other hand. It analyses the extent to which various non-economic elements affect the scope of the internal market and whether they can be considered an indispensable feature of the establishment and proper functioning of the internal market as envisaged by the contracting parties. In addition to exploring the core of the internal market as a whole, the chapter explores the core elements of two policy sectors: transport and energy.

3.1 Defining the Internal Market

The internal market is central to the European integration project. The EEC Treaty was concluded with the aim of enhancing economic prosperity through 'an ever closer union among the peoples of Europe'.[1] The creation of a common European market was not an objective in itself

---

[1] Recitals 1 and 2, preamble to the Treaty establishing the European Economic Community, 25 March 1957, 298 UNTS 3, 4 Eur YB 412.

but, indeed, a means to achieve the broader aims of the Union.[2] Over the decades of existence of the European Union and the Communities, different terms have been employed to denote the unified European market – 'common market', 'internal market' and 'single market'.[3]

3.1.1 Common Market

The origins of the 'common market' – the original term used in the EEC Treaty – can be found in international trade law. A common market features the removal of barriers to trade, the freedom of movement of people, services and capital, a system of competition law and a common external trade policy, which ensures undistorted competition for common market undertakings also in relation to trade with third countries.[4] The EEC Treaty envisaged the creation of a common market by removing customs duties and eliminating quantitative restrictions and measures of equivalent effect between Member States, setting up a common customs tariff and a common external commercial policy and abolishing restrictions to the free movement of persons, services and capital.[5] The Treaty also featured the common agricultural and transport policies, and a system of competition law. The transitional period for completing the common market was set to end on 1 January 1970. The Customs Union between the EEC Member States entered into force on 1 July 1968.

A definition of the common market was provided neither by the EEC Treaty nor by the subsequent amending treaties. In literature, it has been defined as 'a market in which every participant within the Community in question is free to invest, produce, work, buy and sell, to supply or obtain services under conditions of competition which have not been artificially distorted wherever economic conditions are most favourable.'[6] The definition includes the four fundamental

---

[2] Commission, 'White Paper – Preparation of the associated countries of Central and Eastern Europe for integration into the internal market of the Union' COM (95) 163 final, para. 2.1.

[3] A fourth term, 'European home market' is used in the meaning of 'a market with a homogeneous legal framework in which it is possible not only to move between Member States but also to operate within Member States as constituent parts of one market': K von Wogau, 'Completing the European Home Market by 2009' (2003) 38 *Intereconomics* 63, 64.

[4] PJG Kapteyn and P Ver Loren van Themaat, *The Law of the European Union and the European Communities* (Kluwer Law International 2008) 115, 127.

[5] Article 2 EEC Treaty.

[6] PJG Kapteyn and P VerLoren van Themaat (n 4) 127.

freedoms and undistorted competition but lacks the external aspect – the common external trade policy.

The Court, when defining the common market, has focused on its similarity to a national market. The objectives of the common market were elaborated in *Polydor* as follows:

... [T]he Treaty, by establishing a common market and progressively approximating the economic policies of the Member States, seeks to unite national markets into a single market having the characteristics of a domestic market.[7]

An almost identical definition was provided in *Gaston Schul*:

The concept of a common market ... involves the elimination of all obstacles to intra-Community trade in order to merge the national markets into a single market bringing about conditions as close as possible to those of a genuine internal market.[8]

Partial terminological change occurred in 1986 with the adoption of the Single European Act (SEA),[9] but the above definitions have retained their relevance insofar as they highlight the depth of market integration in the EU and compare the envisaged situation to that of a domestic market.

3.1.2 Internal Market

New momentum to the common market project was brought about by the SEA, which set a deadline for completing the 'internal market' by 31 December 1992.[10] A Commission White Paper identified the measures necessary to complete the internal market and outlined a precise timetable for meeting the deadline.[11] The White Paper was exceptionally detailed, containing 279 legislative initiatives for removing barriers to trade between Member States.

The SEA defined the internal market as 'compris[ing] an area without internal frontiers in which the free movement of goods, persons, services and capital is ensured in accordance with the provisions of this Treaty'.[12] This definition has remained virtually untouched by the subsequent treaty amendments and is replicated in essentially identical wording in Article 26(2) TFEU.

---

[7] Case 270/80 *Polydor* v. *Harlequin Records* EU:C:1982:43, para. 16.
[8] Case 15/81 *Gaston Schul* EU:C:1982:135, para. 33.
[9] The SEA entered into force on 1 July 1987.
[10] Article 8a EEC Treaty (SEA numbering).
[11] Commission, 'White Paper – Completing the Internal Market' COM (85) 310 final.
[12] Article 8a EEC, second paragraph (SEA numbering).

A major difference between the concepts of the common market and the internal market is the absence of internal frontiers in the latter. A borderless market was a novelty among the existing FTAs and customs unions and promised an achievement of truly free movement of persons and goods among the Member States.[13] The frontier-free market was accomplished by the creation of the Schengen Area: first by cooperation between EU Member States,[14] and since the entry into force of the Treaty of Amsterdam in 1999 within the framework of the EU. Schengen cooperation provides within the Schengen Area for the abolition of border controls, common rules for crossing the external borders, and common visa rules for third country citizens. The introduction of Schengen rules has altered the substance of the freedom of movement. The right to move freely within the internal market was originally vested with the economically active individuals: workers and the providers and receivers of services. Now the freedom of movement applies to all individuals in the Schengen Area, including EU citizens as well as non-citizens upon their entry into the area.[15] The changes in the concept of the internal market do not, however, apply to the Member States that have either opted out from[16] or not yet joined the Schengen framework.[17] In practice, as concerns the free movement of persons the EU's internal market does thus not correspond to an area without internal frontiers.

Notwithstanding the abolition of internal borders, a comparison between the definitions of the common market and the internal market reveals the strikingly narrower scope of the latter. The Court has called the objective of the common market to resemble a domestic market and identified its three fundamental characteristics: (1) the abolition of barriers to trade, (2) guarantees for undistorted competition and (3) unity of the market.[18] Only the first of the three elements is, however,

---

[13] In the areas of the free movement of goods and services and freedom of establishment, the removal of borders has taken place through the shift towards home state control.

[14] In 1985, five of the then ten Member States signed the Schengen Agreement, which was complemented by the Schengen Protocol in 1990.

[15] The notion of EU citizenship, too, has an impact on the freedom of movement of persons within the EU: see further in Section 3.5. See also S Carrera, 'What Does Free Movement Mean in Theory and Practice in an Enlarged EU?' (2005) 11 *European Law Journal* 699; N Reich, 'The Constitutional Relevance of Citizenship and Free Movement in an Enlarged Union' (2005) 11 *European Law Journal* 675; JD Mather, 'The Court of Justice and the Union Citizen' (2005) 11 *European Law Journal* 722.

[16] Ireland, previously also the United Kingdom.

[17] Bulgaria, Croatia, Cyprus, Romania.

[18] Case 32/65 *Italy* v. *Council and Commission* EU:C:1966:42; Case 14/68 *Walt Wilhelm* EU:C:1969:4, para. 5.

formally included in the definition of the internal market.[19] The definition given in Article 26(2) TFEU comprises the four fundamental freedoms but excludes competition policy, thus providing for the
establishment of the internal market but not for the conditions for its
functioning.[20] In practice, however, this peculiarity has not proven
decisive. The case law of the Court as well as legislation implementing
the internal market provision of Article 26(1) TFEU has recognised that
the approximation provision in Article 114(1) TFEU can be used for
adopting measures that aim at preventing distortions of competition.[21]
Article 114(1) TFEU furthermore requires that the approximating measures have the objective of 'establishment and functioning of the
internal market'. Since undistorted competition is indispensable for
the functioning of the market, the competition element continues to
be included in the internal market package despite the restrictive scope
of the definition.[22]

The use of terminology in post-SEA Treaties indicates that the internal
market had not wholly replaced the common market. Article 2 EC
Treaty, for instance, referred to the common market as a stage in
market integration alongside monetary and economic union rather
than a concept with a specific meaning in the EU context.[23] Other
provisions of the EC Treaty used the terminology in a more ambiguous
manner. Article 3(1) EC Treaty, for example, outlined the activities that
the Community must undertake in order to achieve the objectives of
Article 2. These activities included both 'a system ensuring that competition in the internal market is not distorted'[24] and 'the approximation
of the laws of Member States to the extent required for the functioning
of the common market'.[25] Several other provisions of the EC Treaty

---

[19] See P VerLoren van Themaat, 'The Contributions to the Establishment of the Internal
Market by the Case-Law of the Court of Justice of the European Communities' in
R Bieber and others (eds.), 1992: *One European Market?* (Nomos 1988) 109, 124.

[20] R Barents, 'The Internal Market Unlimited: Some Observations on the Legal Basis of
Community Legislation' (1993) 30 *Common Market Law Review* 85, 104.

[21] PJG Kapteyn and P VerLoren van Themaat (n 4) 127. For example, Case C-300/89
Commission v. Council (Titanium dioxide) EU:C:1991:244; Case C-376/98 *Germany v.
Parliament and Council (Tobacco Advertising)* EU:C:2000:544.

[22] As reinforced by Article 3(1)(b) TFEU which provides that the Union shall have exclusive
competence in the areas including: … '(b) the establishing of the competition rules
necessary for the functioning of the internal market'.

[23] 'The Community shall have as its task, by establishing a common market and an
economic and monetary union […].'

[24] Article 3(1)(g) EC Treaty.

[25] Article 3(1)(h) EC Treaty.

mirrored the continued terminological plurality. The two paragraphs of Article 15 EC Treaty (now Article 27 TFEU), for example, referred to both the 'establishment of the internal market' and the 'functioning of the common market'. Articles 94 and 95 EC Treaty (now Articles 115 and 114 TFEU) concerned the approximation of Member States' laws, regulations and administrative provisions, which 'directly affect the establishment or functioning of the common market' and 'which have as their object the establishment and functioning of the internal market', respectively.

For the purposes of delimiting the scope of Articles 94 and 95 EC Treaty, it became necessary to define the terms 'internal market' and 'common market'. In the Opinion given in the *Titanium Dioxide* case, Advocate General (AG) Tesauro argued for a broad definition of the 'area without internal frontiers' provided in Article 8a EC Treaty (SEA numbering), as 'a truly integrated area where the prevailing conditions are as close as possible to those of a single internal market' including the harmonisation of rules concerning products as well as competition between undertakings.[26] The AG further clarified that the two market concepts 'differ in breadth in that the 'common market' extends to areas which are not part of the 'internal market', but not in depth, in that both concepts relate to the same level of integration'.[27] This reasoning suggests that the three elements of the common market – the abolition of barriers to trade, guarantees for undistorted competition and unity of the market – are equally represented in the internal market. In order to discern the real difference between the 'common' and the 'internal' market recourse must be had to the areas to which the common market extends, but the single market does not. The AG did not specify these areas but having established that the prevention of distortions to competition is in fact included in the internal market concept, they might include common policies such as the environment, energy and transport, or the harmonisation of the Member States' legislation for reasons other than the elimination of barriers to trade.[28]

Despite the high ambitions and partial success, the internal market could not be completed by the 1993 deadline. Efforts in that regard continued whereas the Commission emphasised that the legal framework of the Single Market essentially required the addition of other

---

[26] Case C-300/89 *Commission v. Council (Titanium dioxide)* EU:C:1991:115, Opinion of AG Tesauro, para. 10.

[27] Ibid.

[28] P VerLoren van Themaat (n 19) 111.

policy instruments, 'first and foremost, a single currency',[29] marking a move from a common market to a monetary union. Subsequently, in 1997, the Commission published an Action plan for the single market focusing on four strategic targets: (1) increasing the effectiveness of existing rules by improving implementation, enforcement and problem-solving; (2) addressing key market distortions in the fields of taxation and competition; (3) removing sectoral obstacles to market integration; and (4) enhancing the role of the citizens through eliminating internal borders as well as reinforcing the social dimension of the single market.[30]

The Commission hence no longer strives for its original goal of a 'finalised' or 'complete' internal market. In the communication 'A Single Market for 21st Century', the Commission instead emphasised the dynamic character of the internal market and its need to adapt to the changes in time.[31] The new perspective takes the internal market beyond the idea of eliminating obstacles to cross-border trade and endorses the need to take into account the consequences for the functioning of the internal market of globalisation and increased competition, new economic, environmental and social challenges, and the enlarged Union.[32] While the principles of the single market remain relevant, their application needs to adapt to new realities, and right balance must be struck between a market without frontiers, on the one hand, and labour law, health, safety and environmental standards, on the other.[33] The

---

[29] Commission, 'The impact and effectiveness of the Single Market' (Communication) COM (96) 520 final, para. 5.4.

[30] Commission, 'Action Plan for the Single Market' (Communication) CSE (97) 1 final.

[31] Commission, 'A single market for 21st century Europe' (Communication) COM (2007) 724 final, 3.

[32] Ibid. Already the 4 June 1997 Communication from the Commission to the European Council stated that the internal market was not 'simply an economic structure' but set 'basic standards of health and safety, equal opportunities and labour law': Commission, 'Action Plan for the Single Market' (n 30) 1. As one of the four strategic targets to be pursued, the Action Plan included 'a single market for the benefit of all citizens' comprising social, labour and consumer rights as well as health and environment issues. In addition, a number of European Councils, such as Lisbon March 2000, Feira June 2000, Nice December 2000 and Stockholm March 2001 addressed the non-economic dimension of European integration and its effects on the internal market: see, for example, European Council, 'Conclusions of the Presidency – Lisbon, 23–24 March 2000' SN 100/00; European Council, 'Conclusions of the Presidency – Stockholm, 23–24 March 2001' SN 100/01.

[33] Commission, 'A single market for 21st century Europe' (n 31) 7. Later reports and communications have further elaborated on the non-economic aspects of the internal

fact that the common policies will never be 'finalised'[34] insofar as they affect the internal market also means that the internal market concept will never lose its dynamic outline.

In 2009, the Lisbon Treaty finally replaced the common market terminology with that of the internal market, and the common/internal market distinction has thus lost its relevance in today's discourse. Nevertheless, the historical definitional perplexity has demonstrated that establishing the European single market is not a straightforward endeavour.

3.1.3 Single Market

The third term often used in the context of the unified European market is 'single market'. The notion does not appear in the EU Treaties but is frequently used in the EU's policy documents. The 'single market' arguably dates back to the SEA which brought together in a single amending act amendments to the EC Treaty and provisions on European Political Cooperation, the predecessor of the Common Foreign and Security Policy (CFSP).

Since the early days of the case law of the Court, 'single market' has served as a generic term denoting a commonly organised economic space without barriers and with fair competition between undertakings,[35] featuring conditions similar to a domestic market.[36] The single market does not have specific content nor does it refer to any particular degree of integration.

In literature, the three terms are often used interchangeably and many do not regard the terminological question as decisive.[37] One observer notes, though, that 'common market' is mainly used in economic context, 'single market' in political discourse and 'internal market' in EU documentation and legislation.[38] In the context of exporting the acquis to third countries, however, the terminological distinction continues to be relevant. The creation of a homogeneous EU single market requires

---

market: see M Monti 'A New Strategy for the Single Market at the Service of Europe's Economy and Society' report to the President of the European Commission, 9 May 2010; Commission, 'Single Market Act: Twelve levers to boost growth and strengthen confidence; Working together to create new growth' (Communication) COM (2011) 206 final.

[34] PJG Kapteyn and P VerLoren van Themaat (n 4) 137.

[35] Case 32/65 *Italy* v. *Council and Commission* (n 18) 405; Case 270/80 *Polydor* v. *Harlequin Records* (n 7); Case 15/81 *Gaston Schul* (n 8).

[36] Case 26/76 *Metro* v. *Commission* EU:C:1977:167, para. 20.

[37] K Mortelmans, 'The Common Market, the Internal Market and the Single Market, What's in a Market?' (1998) 35 *Common Market Law Review* 101, 107–108.

[38] P Craig, 'The Evolution of the Single Market' in C Barnard and J Scott (eds.), *The Law of the Single European Market* (Hart Publishing 2002) 1, 40.

that a similar level of integration as in the EU's internal market is transferred to the participating non-EU Member States. The visible differences between the acquis applied in the EU and the acquis exported to third countries are the precise reason for creating a borderless area. In the EU, the nature and scope of the internal market are inseparable from the objective of ever-deeper integration, hence the gradual establishment and expansion of the Schengen area that now belongs to the 'package deal' of the internal market. The multilateral agreements exporting the acquis do not share the general objective of ever-deeper integration in Europe but are directly connected to the concept of the internal market in the specific areas covered by the agreements. The export excludes Schengen acquis, which means that the objective of the agreements cannot strictly be seen as the extension of the EU's internal market but the creation of a single market on the basis of a selection of the internal market acquis. For the sake of clarity and simplicity, in this book the term 'internal market acquis' is used to denote the export of EU internal market acquis to non-member countries notwithstanding the more limited scope of the acquis and the lower degree of market integration than applicable to the EU.

3.2 Defining the Acquis

In the EU, the term 'acquis' is a 'notion of variable content' – its scope and functions vary according to the specific context.[39] One speaks of the *acquis communautaire*, EU acquis, internal market acquis, accession acquis, EEA acquis and many others. The term is frequently used in the EU's internal as well as external contexts.

Magen sees the internal and external dimensions of the acquis as its two personalities: one, an inward-looking character representing the EU patrimony and the unique features of European integration, the other, an outward-looking 'transformative engagement' or 'governance export' personality that advances the EU's norms and interests outside the Union without the aim of integrating future members into the EU.[40]

---

[39] C Jarrosson, *La notion d'arbitrage* (Librairie Générale de Droit et de Jurisprudence 1987) 225. Also S Weatherill, 'Safeguarding the *Acquis Communautaire*' in T Heukels, N Blokker and M Brus (eds.), *The European Union after Amsterdam* (Kluwer Law International 1998) 153, 161. 'Unitary in language but binary in function': A Magen, 'Transformative Engagement through Law: The Acquis Communautaire as an Instrument of EU External Influence' (2007) 9 *European Journal of Law Reform* 361, 362.

[40] A Magen (n 39) 392.

Insofar as it is debatable whether accession policy can be considered an external policy in a truly EU-external sense,[41] it is reasonable to agree with Magen in his claim that accession acquis is an example of the internal rather than external dimension of the EU acquis.[42]

One of the functions of the acquis, however – integrating non-member countries into the EU's internal market without membership in the EU by exporting EU acquis[43] – does not fit squarely into either the internal or the external dimension. On the one hand, the countries to which the internal market acquis is exported are not necessarily in the process of accession. This would suggest the 'governance export' personality of the exported acquis. On the other hand, however, the objective of such norm transfer is to expand the internal market to include third countries or to integrate non-EU Member States into the EU's internal market. The acquis, therefore, serves the purpose of maintaining homogeneity both within the expanded internal market and between that and the EU internal market while preserving the key features of the latter.

3.2.1 Acquis within the EU

The origin and content of the term 'acquis' have been profusely discussed in literature.[44] The notion, albeit not defined anywhere in the Treaties, signifies the accumulation of rights and obligations that the Member States and their individuals derive from the EU Treaties, whether legally binding or not. Until recently, the most common use of the term was the '*acquis communautaire*' which makes a reference to its Community origin. The terminological choice does not, however, define the scope of the notion. In the accession process, in which the term is most frequently used, the *acquis communautaire* has absorbed the obligations deriving from the former non-Community pillars.[45] The

---

[41] Temporally limited and aimed at internalising something external, enlargement is an unusual form of foreign policy: Ibid., 377.

[42] Ibid.

[43] See further Section 3.2.3.

[44] For a comprehensive overview of the origins of the term see KE Jørgensen, 'The Social Construction of the Acquis Communautaire: A Cornerstone of the European Edifice' (1999) 3 *European Integration online Papers*, 8–10, http://eiop.or.at/eiop/texte/1999-005a.htm accessed 10 February 2020. For the history of the use of the term in the Treaties see C Delcourt, 'The Acquis Communautaire: Has the Concept Had Its Day?' (2001) 38 *Common Market Law Review* 829, 829–831; R Petrov, *Exporting the Acquis Communautaire through European Union External Agreements* (Nomos 2011) 29–32.

[45] For example, the Joint Declaration on CFSP attached to the Treaty concerning the accession of the Kingdom of Norway, the Republic of Austria, the Republic of Finland and the Kingdom of Sweden to the EU refers to the *acquis communautaire* as the 'content,

'Union acquis', which has been used in parallel and often interchangeably with 'acquis communautaire', denotes the rights and obligations conferred by the TEU, which contains provisions of the former second and third pillars. Whereas the continued use of 'acquis communautaire' in the meaning of a timeless 'fundamental acquis'[46] or the EU's 'genetic code' or 'genetic inheritance' has been argued for,[47] the present study does not necessitate such terminological distinction. When referring to the acquis as it appears within the EU as well as in the accession process, therefore, the term 'EU acquis' is used.

Neither the Treaties nor literature has ever provided a single definition for the acquis, the 'holiest cow of all'.[48] Since the entry into force of the Lisbon Treaty, references to the acquis can only be found in two Treaty provisions. Article 20(4) TEU provides that acts adopted in the framework of enhanced cooperation do not form part of the accession acquis whereas Article 87(3) TFEU makes a reference to Schengen acquis.

The EU acquis is a flexible and constantly evolving concept. Its elements can be classified into those of legislative, political and jurisprudential origin pursuant to their function and institutional origin.[49] Legislative acquis[50] includes the body of legally binding and non-binding acts: the Treaties on which the EU is founded and their subsequent amendments; secondary legislative acts including regulations, directives, decisions, recommendations and opinions; internal acts of the EU institutions and inter-institutional agreements; international agreements concluded by the EU, mixed agreements and agreements concluded by the Member States in the areas of exclusive EU competence; and possibly also the acts of the representatives of the Member States meeting within the Council and measures adopted within the framework of enhanced cooperation.

principles and political objectives of the Treaties, including those of the Treaty on European Union': [1994] OJ C241/381, para. 1. For further examples see C Delcourt (n 44) 832. According to Curti Gialdino, 'acquis communautaire' goes 'beyond the concept of Community law strictu sensu' to include measures adopted in the field of external relations and justice and home affairs: C Curti Gialdino, 'Some Reflections on the Acquis Communautaire' (1995) 32 Common Market Law Review 1089, 1092–1093.

[46] P Pescatore, 'Aspects judiciaires de l'«acquis communautaire»' (1981) 20 Revue trimestrielle de droit européen 617, 620.

[47] C Delcourt (n 44) 835ff.

[48] JHH Weiler, 'The Reformation of European Constitutionalism' (1997) 35 Journal of Common Market Studies 97, 98.

[49] P Pescatore, 'Aspects judiciaires de l'«acquis communautaire»' (n 46) 619.

[50] Also referred to as normative acquis: C Curti Gialdino (n 45) 1092.

Political acquis generally comprises legally non-binding acts such as the political objectives of the Treaties as well as various resolutions, declarations, positions, guidelines and principles, including certain decisions and agreements adopted by the European Council and the Council. Although deficient of legal enforceability, the political aspects of the acquis have some legal implications. Article 3(3) of the Act of Accession of Croatia to the EU, for example, specifies that the principles and guidelines originating from declarations, resolutions and other positions of the European Council and the Council as well as positions 'concerning the Union adopted by common agreement of the Member States' must be observed and properly implemented by the Member States as well as the acceding state.[51]

The third category, jurisprudential acquis, consists of the case law of the EU's judiciary. On the one hand, the case law of the Court of Justice and the General Court can be regarded as acts of an EU institution – the Court of Justice of the EU.[52] On the other hand, the case law of the Court is a source of a number of fundamental principles such as direct effect, primacy, efficiency and unity of EU law. These principles can be regarded as more than merely the production of the Court, the latter operating as a mediator who expresses the *communis opinio* of the whole body of the EU.[53]

An inspection of the diverse sources of the acts belonging to the acquis and their legal force reveals that not all elements of the acquis are equally influential. Some legislative acts and parts of jurisprudence pertain to the fundamentals of the Union, its institutional structure and legal order as well as its economic and social organisation,[54] whereas the effect of others is not pivotal in establishing the EU's existence and identity. In order to distinguish between the privileged and unprivileged types of jurisprudential acquis, Pescatore introduced the categories of 'ordinary acquis' and 'fundamental acquis', dividing the latter further into 'structural acquis' concerning the general characteristics of the EU legal order and 'material acquis' relating to the choices made with respect to the Union's economic and social order such as the elimination of

---

[51] Act concerning the conditions of accession of the Republic of Croatia and the adjustments to the Treaty on European Union, the Treaty on the Functioning of the European Union and the Treaty establishing the European Atomic Energy Community [2012] OJ L112/21.

[52] Not, however, enlisted in Article 263 TFEU: C Curti Gialdino (n 45) 1098.

[53] P Pescatore, 'Aspects judiciaires de l'«acquis communautaire»' (n 46) 619.

[54] Ibid., 620.

obstacles to intra-Community free trade.[55] As a result of a direct link between the Treaties and the foundational principles mentioned in the section, fundamental acquis assumes a constitutional rank in the European edifice.[56] In case of a conflict between the 'fundamental' and 'ordinary' acquis, the legislative and political acquis including even primary law will have to recede. Only the hard core of the EU's constitutional framework can, therefore, be considered 'the Holy of Holies'.[57]

The Court has on a number of occasions ruled on conflicts between fundamental acquis and acquis of lesser, unconstitutional rank.[58] In Opinion 1/76, for example, the Court was called upon to examine the compatibility of the Draft Agreement establishing a European laying-up fund for inland waterway vessels with the provisions of the Treaties.[59] The Court found that the structure of the Supervisory Board, which envisaged an 'extremely limited' participation of the Community institutions, and the decision-making procedure in which the Community enjoyed no right to vote were impeding with the Community's independent external action as well as altered the prerogatives of the institutions and the Member States vis-à-vis one another. These consequences, in turn, would affect the 'internal constitution of the Community' and were, therefore, ruled to be contrary to the requirements of unity and solidarity.[60]

In addition to structural acquis, material acquis, too, has been subject to the Court's scrutiny. In Joined Cases 80 and 81/77, the Court found that the powers conferred upon the Community in the field of Common Agricultural Policy (CAP) must be exercised with due consideration given to the unity of the market. Any action incompatible with the objective of the unity of the market would create a risk of 'opening the way to mechanisms which would lead to disintegration contrary to the objectives of progressive approximation of the economic policies

---

[55] Ibid., 620–621.
[56] Ibid., 620.
[57] JHH Weiler (n 48) 98.
[58] The protection of the institutional aspects of the fundamental acquis, in particular, has been the subject of a number of cases discussed in Chapter 6 Section 6.2.
[59] Opinion 1/76 *European laying-up fund for inland waterway vessels* EU:C:1977:63.
[60] Ibid., para. 12. Not only the composition, structure and powers of the Supervisory Board but also of the Fund Tribunal were considered incompatible with the Treaties: paras. 17–22. See in detail in Chapter 6, Section 6.2.1.

of the Member States',[61] and thus violate an important principle of EU law.[62]

In addition to the general concept of EU acquis, frequent references are made to its subdivisions – the sectoral acquis, which mark out a fragment thereof. Sectoral acquis is often used in terms of policy sectors, such as 'consumer acquis', 'energy acquis' or 'Schengen acquis'. The 'internal market acquis' forms part of the overall EU acquis and can be divided into subsections such as, for example, the 'acquis in the area of free movement of workers' or 'competition acquis'. In the absence of a clear definition, 'sectoral acquis', too, can be regarded as a notion of variable content.

If the full EU acquis consists of the substantive rules, principles and objectives of the Treaties, secondary legislation, various non-binding acts adopted by the EU's political institutions, as well as case law of the EU's judiciary, then what makes 'sectoral acquis'? Given that all of the above elements contribute to establishing the scope and application of a sector of the acquis as well as one sector's interaction with the others, sectoral acquis cannot be limited to the primary and secondary law only. The composition of a sector of the acquis should be regarded as a cross-section of the entire EU acquis comprising all elements relevant to the application of the substantive acquis in the specific policy area.

Taking account of the definition of the internal market provided above, the internal market acquis should be regarded as including all primary and secondary law, political instruments and case law of the Court of Justice of the EU pertaining to the establishment and functioning of the internal market, including the four freedoms as well as horizontal provisions on, for example, competition, environment, social policies and consumer protection, and fundamental rights. Both the internal market and the acquis being broad and undefined concepts,[63] it is very difficult to determine with precision which instruments belong to the internal market acquis, but their number is expectedly vast.

---

[61] Joined Cases 80/77 and 81/77 *Commissionnaires Réunis* v. *Receveur des Douanes* EU: C:1978:87, paras. 35–36.

[62] W Sauter, 'The Economic Constitution of the European Union' (1998) 4 *Columbia Journal of European Law* 27, 42.

[63] See also S Weatherill, 'The Several Internal Markets' (2017) 36 *Yearbook of European Law* 125.

3.2.2 Acquis Outside the EU

In the course of the Union's acquis having become an exportable policy vehicle, the term frequently occurs in EU-external settings. This pertains both to the 'internal' acquis exported outside the Union and the acquis of a particular EU external policy such as, for example, trade policy acquis. Two out of the four categories of acquis identified by Curti Gialdino in the pre-Maastricht setting[64] – the Lomé acquis and the EEA acquis – denote a set of norms of EU origin placed outside the Union.

The Lomé acquis constitutes a body of shared objectives and principles coupled with provisions on trade preferences, which have governed the relationship between the EU and the African, Caribbean and Pacific (ACP) Countries across the four Lomé Conventions[65] and their successor, the Cotonou Agreement. The existing structure and essential components of the Lomé Conventions have been carried on throughout the renegotiations. An example of path dependence from a social science perspective,[66] the preservation of the previous political and legal choices translates into the maintenance of an acquis in legal terms. The foundation on which the Lomé acquis is constructed is a specific part of EU acquis – the acquis of the EU's external relations towards the ACP countries.

Just as the Lomé acquis, the EEA acquis relates to the relationship between the EU and the EEA EFTA countries. Differently from its Lomé counterpart, though, the EEA acquis comprises the core of the EU acquis – the internal market acquis. It includes all instruments relevant to the establishment and functioning of the EEA including the EEA Agreement together with annexes and protocols, acts referred to or contained in the annexes, decisions taken by the bodies established by the EEA Agreement and case law of the EFTA Court and the Court of Justice. Since only the first two of the four categories of elements constituting the EEA acquis feature a direct link to the EU acquis,[67] the EEA acquis as a whole should be considered as a separate entity rather than a limited section of the EU acquis replicated in the EEA.

---

[64] 'Accession' acquis, 'institutional' acquis, 'Lomé' acquis, 'EEA' acquis: C Curti Gialdino (n 45) 1090.

[65] Signed in 1975, 1979, 1985 and 1989, respectively.

[66] G Forwood, 'The Road to Cotonou: Negotiating a Successor to Lomé' (2001) 39 *Journal of Common Market Studies* 423, 438.

[67] The term 'acquis' is not mentioned in the EEA Agreement.

3.2.3 Acquis Expanding the Internal Market

Every international agreement concluded by the EU, which establishes a political and legal framework for the Union's relations with a third country, potentially creates a new type of acquis. The multilateral agreements that export entire sectors of EU acquis to non-member countries establish the EEA acquis discussed above, the Energy Community acquis, the ECAA acquis and the Transport Community acquis. The common feature of these agreements is the objective of establishing and maintaining a homogeneous legal space based on EU acquis which is absent in other agreements, such as the Lomé and Cotonou conventions or the EU-Switzerland bilateral agreements. This homogeneity-based process can be referred to as integrating the EEA EFTA countries' economies into the EU internal market,[68] or 'extending the full rights and obligations of the EU's internal market' to the respective countries.[69]

From the EU's perspective, exporting the internal market acquis by multilateral agreements is not merely a question of foreign policy towards third states. It is equally a matter of expanding the internal market, albeit incompletely or partially, as a result of which third countries become participants, at least to a limited extent, in the EU internal market. The very aim of the multilateral agreements is to integrate third countries into the EU internal market rather than to create a separate legal order constructed upon norms different from those that apply within the EU. The quest for homogeneity builds a bridge between the EU acquis and the acquis of the legal order created by the agreement, as well as between the internal and the external acquis.

3.3 Economic Principles of the Internal Market

The underlying economic ideal of the EU has been the creation of 'integrated economy in which the factors of production, as well as the fruits of production, may move freely and without distortion, thus bringing about a more efficient allocation of resources and a more

---

[68] Council, 'Conclusions on EU relations with EFTA countries' 3060th General Affairs Council meeting, Brussels, 14 December 2010, paras. 3 and 7.
[69] M Damen and F Garcés de los Fayos, 'The European Economic Area (EEA), Switzerland and the North' (2019) Factsheets of the European Union www.europarl.europa.eu/fact sheets/en/sheet/169/the-european-economic-area-eea-switzerland-and-the-north accessed 10 February 2020.

perfect division of labour'.[70] Within the scope of these broad principles, ample room is left for both the Member States and the Court to carve out the exact shape of the internal market and to, thereby, determine the breadth and depth of market integration in the EU.

The concept of the internal market consists primarily of rights and principles. The definition of the internal market provided in Article 26 (2) TFEU focuses on the four fundamental freedoms – the free movement of goods, persons, services and capital.[71] Recital 1 of the preamble to Protocol No 27 on internal market and competition annexed to the Treaties and Article 3(3) TEU also refer to equal conditions of competition between undertakings. These elements, in turn, are substantiated by two principles that prescribe the rules governing the relationships between market participants – the principles of non-discrimination and equality, enshrined in Articles 2 and 3(3) TEU as well as in Articles 8 and 10 TFEU as horizontal provisions.

In literature, the principles of non-discrimination and equality are often used interchangeably in spite of some noticeable differences. The principle of non-discrimination, on the one hand, is an expression of the principle of equality. In the context of the internal market, it refers specifically to the prohibition of discrimination on the basis of nationality. Provided in Article 18 TFEU and Article 21(2) of the Charter of Fundamental Rights of the European Union (the Charter),[72] the prohibition of discrimination on grounds of nationality, furthermore, has a strong connection to the concept of EU citizenship, applying to all EU citizens regardless of their status as a participant in the internal market.

The principle of equality, on the other hand, is a general principle of EU law and applies to two kinds of situations. First, it pertains to the idea of competitive equality between undertakings operating in the internal market and provides a justification for the EU's competition policy. Second, as a horizontal provision and as one of the fundamental freedoms protected by the EU, it operates in the context of equality between the sexes as well as age and race.

---

[70] Joined Cases C-92/92 and C-326/92 *Phil Collins* EU:C:1993:276, Opinion of AG Jacobs, para. 10.

[71] The Commission has proposed to promote the free movement of knowledge and innovation as a 'fifth freedom': 'A single market for 21st century Europe' (n 31) 9.

[72] [2016] OJ C202/389.

3.3.1 Non-discrimination

According to AG Jacobs, non-discrimination is a fundamental principle that underlies European integration. It plays more than a formal role:

[n]o other aspect of Community law touches the individual more directly or does more to foster that sense of common identity and shared destiny without which the 'ever closer union among the peoples of Europe', proclaimed by the preamble to the Treaty, would be an empty slogan.[73]

As a principle of national treatment, the principle of non-discrimination has a broad scope of application. It applies 'in every respect and in all circumstances governed by [EU] law to any person established in a Member State'.[74] The general prohibition of discrimination on grounds of nationality enables the nationals of a Member State to undertake economic activities in another Member State on equal terms with the nationals of the host Member State.[75] Due to its residual character, the concrete application of Article 18 TFEU in particular policy areas is specified in other provisions of the TFEU.[76] In some instances, such as intellectual property or the right to adequate judicial remedies for assisting a person to exercise or enforce his or her fundamental freedoms, Article 18 TFEU is applied directly.[77] The principle of non-discrimination has direct effect[78] and can even be enforced in disputes between individuals.[79]

   The Court of Justice has granted the principle of non-discrimination broad interpretation. In *Luisi* and *Carbone*, for example, the Court recognised that the freedom to provide services also has a passive dimension – the freedom of persons, including tourists, students and persons receiving medical services, 'to go to another Member State in order to receive a

---

[73] Joined Cases C-92/92 and C-326/92 *Phil Collins*, Opinion of AG Jacobs (n 70) paras. 10–11.
[74] Case 137/84 *Mutsch* EU:C:1985:335, para. 12.
[75] Joined Cases C-92/92 and C-326/92 *Phil Collins* EU:C:1993:847, para. 32.
[76] Case C-176/96 *Lehtonen and Castors Braine* EU:C:2000:201, para. 37. The policy areas to which the principle of non-discrimination applies include the free movement of goods (Article 36 TFEU), state monopolies (Article 37(1) TFEU), the common agricultural policy (Article 40(2) TFEU), the free movement of workers (Article 45(2) TFEU), the free movement of services (Article 61 TFEU), the free movement of capital (Article 65 (3) TFEU), transport policy (Article 95(1) TFEU), competition policy (Article 172(2)(a) TFEU), approximation of laws (Article 107(6) TFEU), association of overseas countries and territories (Article 200(5) TFEU), humanitarian aid (Article 214(2) TFEU) and enhanced cooperation (Article 326 TFEU).
[77] Case C-398/92 *Mund & Fester v. Hatrex* EU:C:1994:52, paras. 14–15.
[78] Joined Cases C-92/92 and C-326/92 *Phil Collins* (n 75) para. 35.
[79] Case C-413/93 *Bosman* EU:C:1995:463; Case C-281/98 *Angonese* EU:C:2000:296.

service there, without being obstructed by restrictions'.[80] In *Cowan*, the passive receivers of services were placed under the protection of the principle of national treatment.[81] Within the internal market, the application of the principle of non-discrimination is furthermore not restricted to grounds of nationality. It applies equally to cases that feature a cross-border element but where the nationality of the freely moving individual becomes irrelevant.[82]

The non-discrimination model is strongly present in the design of the free movement of workers and services, including the freedom of establishment. The principle of free movement of persons gives right to both employed workers[83] and the self-employed[84] to look for and undertake employment and establish themselves, respectively, in another EU Member State. Workers as well as service providers[85] from other Member States are not to be treated in a manner discriminatory as compared to their host country counterparts. Nevertheless, the non-discrimination approach is incapable of breaking down the barriers which apply to all workers and service providers equally, irrespective of their nationality but that do, in fact, impede the movement of labour or services within the internal market.

In sum, the principle of non-discrimination on grounds of nationality provides that all market actors, irrespective of their nationality, or whether or not they have exercised their free movement rights have free access to enter another Member State in order to trade in goods, provide or receive services, establish an undertaking, take up employment and transfer capital.

3.3.2 Equality

The functions of the principle of equal treatment in EU law include the unification and regulation of the market as well as the provision of constitutional protection.[86] The principle's market unification role pertains mainly to the non-discrimination of market participants on

---

[80] Joined Cases 286/82 and 26/83 *Luisi and Carbone* EU:C:1984:35, para. 16.
[81] Case 186/87 *Cowan* EU:C:1989:47, para. 17.
[82] See, for example, Case C-224/01 *Köbler* EU:C:2003:513; Case C-224/98 *D'Hoop* EU:C:2002:432, paras. 30–31.
[83] Articles 45–48 TFEU.
[84] Articles 49–55 TFEU.
[85] Articles 56 and 62 TFEU stipulate the free movement of services.
[86] G More, 'The Principle of Equal Treatment: From Market Unifier to Fundamental Right?' in P Craig and G de Búrca (eds.), *The Evolution of EU Law* (Oxford University Press 1999) 517, 518.

grounds of nationality. The market regulation role, on the other hand, concerns equal conditions of competition. The third, constitutional role of equal treatment, refers to EU law provisions on gender equality (Article 8 TFEU) and anti-discrimination on grounds of sex, racial or ethnic origin, religion or belief, disability, age or sexual orientation (Article 19 TFEU) for the sake of protecting individual rights affected by market integration. The equality principle is also firmly vested in Article 20 of the Charter as equality before the law, and in Article 23 of the Charter as equality between women and men.

As a 'key to the breaking down of protectionist barriers between Member State markets',[87] the principle of equality aims to ensure the elimination of distortions to competition in the internal market.[88] Equal competition is essential to ensure the efficient functioning of the market,[89] as well as the protection of public interest, individual undertakings and consumers and, ultimately, safeguarding the general economic well-being of the EU.[90] Conversely, harmonisation in the field of competition policy in the EU is limited by the objective of maintaining in the Union a 'harmonious development of economic activities'.[91]

Competition law is an example of how individuals who, on the one hand, are empowered as the enforcers of EU law may, on the other hand, impair the functioning of the internal market. Whereas the non-discrimination principles are addressed primarily to the Member States, rules on competition law target private undertakings. Without any regulation of competition, private actors would be capable of erecting barriers with a comparably detrimental effect on the functioning of the market as obstacles set up by states.[92] Hence, in the sphere of competition law, individual actors have become the subjects of the principle of equal treatment.[93]

---

[87] Ibid., 522.

[88] Case 6/64 *Costa* v. *ENEL* EU:C:1964:66.

[89] Case 6/72 *Continental Can* EU:C:1973:22, para. 24; Case C-126/97 *Eco Swiss* EU:C:1999:269, para. 36; Case C-453/99 *Courage and Crehan* EU:C:2001:465, para. 20.

[90] Joined Cases 46/87 and 227/88 *Hoechst* v. *Commission* EU:C:1989:337, para. 25; Case C-94/00 *Roquette Frères* EU:C:2002:603, para. 42; Case C-52/09 *TeliaSonera* EU:C:2011:83, para. 22.

[91] Case 6/72 *Continental Can* (n 89) para. 24.

[92] P Pescatore, 'Public and Private Aspects of European Community Competition Law' (1986) 10 *Fordham International Law Journal* 373, 383.

[93] R Lane, 'The Internal Market and the Individual' in N Nic Shuibhne (ed.), *Regulating the Internal Market* (Edward Elgar Publishing 2006) 245, 252.

3.4 Non-economic Considerations in the Internal Market

The internal market is but one – albeit the most significant – means of achieving the broader aims of the Union. The 'barriers which divide Europe' are not only physical or limited to tariffs and other direct barriers to trade.[94] They are increasingly of a social nature, or challenge the legitimacy of the EU legal order. The 'ever closer union among the peoples of Europe' proclaimed in Article 1 TEU[95] inevitably includes cooperation between Member States in non-economic policy areas in addition to the creation of the internal market.

The pre-Lisbon Article 2 TEU recognised the social and environmental aspects of European integration but in terms of 'promotion' rather than an imperative for the Union.[96] The Treaty of Lisbon challenged the fundamental position of the four fundamental freedoms by placing them, albeit as first, among all other EU policies.[97]

Gradual changes in the context in which the internal market operates have, in turn, led to a transformation of the original concept of the internal market. Specifically, in order to safeguard the political viability of the Union, the EU legislator and judiciary are commended to heed to the non-economic policies that shape the economies and societies of the Member States when defining and implementing EU policies.

A necessity to balance between the economic and the non-economic interests in the internal market is enshrined in the EU Treaties as well as the Charter. The non-economic dimension of the internal market is explicit in Article 3(3) TEU which outlines the objectives of the Union. The provision mirrors the deepening integration in the EU as well as the changing needs of the society. It asserts that the aims of the EU go beyond the mere abolition of barriers to the free movement of factors of production and amount to the creation of a 'highly competitive social market economy'. In addition to economic efficiency, the social market economy pursues a number of social and environmental objectives including, for example, full employment and social progress and a high level of protection and improvement of the quality of the environment.

---

[94] Recital 2, preamble to the TFEU.

[95] Initially in the preamble to the EEC Treaty.

[96] Cf 'shall work for' in Article 3(3) TEU (post-Lisbon). I Govaere, 'The Future Direction of the EU Internal Market: On Vested Values and Fashionable Modernism' (2009) 16 *Columbia Journal of European Law* 67, 70. Article 114(3) TFEU sets high level of protection as the basis for approximation measures in the fields of health, safety, environmental protection and consumer protection.

[97] R Lane (n 93) 258.

Non-economic policies play a twofold role in the EU. First, the EU pursues a number of non-economic policies in addition to the internal market project – employment, social policy, education and vocational training, culture, public health, consumer protection and environment, to name but some. Second, non-economic considerations affect the establishment and the functioning of the internal market.

In the internal market context, non-economic principles shape the nature and scope of application of the market freedoms. Non-economic policies exert influence on the level of rulemaking[98] via horizontal provisions, which require that the relevant policy considerations be taken into account in the definition and implementation of all EU policies and activities, including the internal market; and derogations, which allow the Member States to deviate from the fundamental freedoms and rules on competition. The changing character of the internal market is moreover accommodated in the case law of the Court of Justice,[99] with emphasis on the importance of balancing free movement rights against social policy objectives with respect to the social as well as the economic purposes of the Union.[100]

The horizontal and flanking policies, which complement the four freedoms and competition policy, are located in other parts of the TFEU.[101] Horizontal provisions such as environmental protection must, first, be taken into consideration by the EU institutions in the exercise of the powers entrusted to them; second, the measures of environmental protection may also be adopted on other legal bases than those specifically concerning the environment,[102] in particular, in the exercise of powers relating to the attainment of the internal market.[103] Internal market harmonisation measures may also take into account other policies in which the Union enjoys no general competence, such as public health, but the measures may not be taken solely on the purpose of protecting such objectives.[104]

---

[98] B de Witte, 'Non-Market Values in Internal Market Legislation' in N Nic Shuibhne (ed.), *Regulating the Internal Market* (Edward Elgar Publishing 2006) 61, 76.

[99] See I Govaere (n 96) 72.

[100] Case C-438/05 *Viking* EU:C:2007:772, para. 79.

[101] Article 8 on equal treatment, Article 9 on social policy, Article 10 on anti-discrimination, Article 11 on environment, Article 12 on consumer protection, and Article 13 on animal welfare.

[102] Articles 191–193 TFEU.

[103] Case C-300/89 *Titanium dioxide* (n 21) paras. 11–24.

[104] See, however, Case C-210/03 *Swedish Match* EU:C:2004:802 where the Court accepted a measure with a clear public health objective on the internal market legal basis of Article 114 TFEU.

Horizontal provisions may belong to the same fields as flanking policies, which denote cooperation outside the internal market. Examples include the environmental and social policy – areas in which the EU enjoys competence but the objectives of which must also be integrated into other EU policies, including the internal market. Other flanking policies are common policies in their own right, such as, for example, energy, transport, agriculture and fisheries, consumer policy, education and cultural policy. The rules of the internal market do not apply to flanking policies unless the latter feature an economic dimension.[105] Conversely, the fact that an economic activity – for example, offering goods or services on a given market – has a relation with a non-economic activity such as sports does not preclude the application of internal market rules.[106]

Since debate on the internal market almost inevitably concerns matters falling outside the four freedoms, it has been suggested that the internal market has two meanings: a narrow and a broad one. The narrow meaning comprises only the economic whereas the broad meaning covers the economic as well as the non-economic aspects of integrated Europe.[107] The emergence of a broader internal market is not, however, unproblematic. A number of tensions arise between the economic and social policies as exemplified prominently by *Viking* and *Laval*.[108]

3.4.1 Emergence of Non-economic Policies

The internal market was originally constructed around the legal principles laying out its economic core whereas the non-economic aspects of trade fell within the Member States' sphere of competence. In due course, the EU gradually gained additional competences in a number of areas previously governed by the Member States. From that point on, it fell on the Union to address the non-economic issues closely linked to the exercise of the market freedoms.[109]

3.4.1.1 Environment

Not included in the original Treaties, the first step towards a European environmental policy was taken by the 1972 Stockholm Declaration,

---

[105] I Govaere (n 96) 74–75.
[106] Case C-49/07 *MOTOE* EU:C:2008:376, para. 22.
[107] P Craig (n 38) 1 and 37–38.
[108] Case C-341/05 *Laval* EU:C:2007:809.
[109] S Weatherill, 'On the Depth and Breadth of European Integration' (1997) 17 *Oxford Journal of Legal Studies* 537, 546.

which recognised that the interconnection between the rational management of resources, and the objective of improving the environment require a coordination of national environmental policies.[110] The first European Environmental Action Programme adopted in 1973 acknowledged that the natural environment and its conservation are important for 'the organisation and promotion of human progress' and that environmental concerns must be integrated into the planning and execution of EU and national policies.[111] The Action Programme further identified the environmental aspect as a necessary corollary to the aims of the EEC regarding the 'harmonious development of economic activities and a continuous and balanced expansion'.[112] Appreciation was thus given to the importance of integrating environmental policy objectives into the EEC's economic policies.

In 1979, the Court made an important assertion that provisions on the environment may, indeed, be adopted on the basis of Article 100 EEC Treaty (now Article 115 TFEU) due to the potential adverse effects of diverging environmental standards on competition within the internal market.[113] Exceptions from the harmonisation provision of the then Article 100a EC Treaty only appeared in the Maastricht Treaty.

The 1987 SEA first granted the Union legislative powers in the field of environment and introduced the horizontal provision – the integration principle – of environmental policy.[114] In the following Maastricht Treaty,[115] the provision was reworded to avoid direct effect,[116] allegedly due to its undetermined scope and nature.[117] The Maastricht Treaty

---

[110] Principle 13, Declaration of the United Nations Conference on the Human Environment, Report of the United Nations Conference on the Human Environment (1972) A/CONF.48/14/Rev.1, 3.

[111] Declaration of the Council of the European Communities and of the Representatives of the Governments of the Member States Meeting in the Council of 22 November 1973 on the Programme of Action of the European Communities on the Environment [1973] OJ C112/1.

[112] Article 2 EEC Treaty.

[113] Case 91/79 *Commission* v. *Italy* EU:C:1980:85, para. 8.

[114] Article 130r EEC Treaty (SEA numbering).

[115] Article 130r(2) EC Treaty (Maastricht numbering): 'Environmental protection requirements must be integrated into the definition and implementation of other Community policies.'

[116] L Krämer, 'Giving a Voice to the Environment by Challenging the Practice of Integrating Environmental Requirements into Other EU policies' in S Kingston (ed.), *European Perspectives on Environmental Law and Governance* (Routledge 2013) 83, 86–87.

[117] M Hession and R Macrory, 'Balancing Trade Freedom with the Requirements of Sustainable Development' in N Emilou and D O'Keeffe (eds.), *The European Union and World Trade Law: After the GATT Uruguay Round* (John Wiley & Sons 1996) 181, reproduced

further demanded that sustainable growth and respect for the environment be promoted across the Community.[118] Subsequently, in the Treaty of Amsterdam, 'sustainable growth' was replaced by the principle of 'sustainable development', to the content of those concerned about the role of environmental policy in the EU.[119] The principle of sustainable development is now included in Articles 3(3) and 21 TEU.

The Amsterdam Treaty amendments moved the environmental integration principle from the chapter on environmental policy to the 'Principles' section of the EC Treaty. Since the Treaty of Lisbon, a significant number of horizontal provisions[120] have been recognised by EU primary law that must be integrated into other EU policies, in addition to the general principle of consistency between all Union policies and activities provided in Article 7 TFEU. Paradoxically, the increase in the number of horizontal provisions has led to environmental policy losing its special status as the first and, for a period of time, the only integration principle.[121] The curtailing of the importance and status of the environmental integration principle has been feared to lead to a so-called minestrone-effect of 'reversed integration' in which many aspects must be considered but none to a sufficient degree, especially vis-à-vis one another.[122]

3.4.1.2 Social Policy

Despite emerging after the environmental integration provision, there is little doubt that social policy has in the design of the internal market assumed a role comparable to environmental policy.[123] Initially, social policy considerations played a very modest role in the regulation of the internal market. It was primarily the task of the Court to balance the growing interest in social policy with market integration. More

---

in R Macrory, *Regulation, Enforcement and Governance in Environmental Law* (Oxford University Press 2014) 473, 477–478.

[118] Article 2 TEU (Maastricht numbering).

[119] JH Jans, 'Stop the Integration Principle?' (2009) 33 *Fordham International Law Journal* 1533, 1538.

[120] Enlisted in the 'Provisions of General Application' of Title II TFEU.

[121] JH Jans (n 119) 1545.

[122] Ibid., 1546–1547; O McIntyre, 'The integration challenge: Integrating Environmental Concerns into Other EU Policies' in S Kingston (ed.), *European Perspectives on Environmental Law and Governance* (Routledge 2013) 125, 137–138.

[123] S Weatherill, 'On the Depth and Breadth of European Integration' (n 109) 547; M Dewatripont and others, *Flexible Integration: Towards a More Effective and Democratic Europe* (Monitoring European Integration 1995) 93ff.

recently, developments in the EU social policy and, especially, its effects on the internal market have been firmly integrated into EU law, such as by the horizontal provision of Article 9 TFEU.

Initially, economic development and free competition were expected to lead to the most efficient division of resources and, subsequently, the best outcomes for both the economies and the participating individuals. The latter were primarily expected to benefit from the freedom to take up employment elsewhere in the Community. The EC social policy first comprised cooperation between Member States such as in the fields of employment, labour law and working conditions, equal pay for men and women, social security, vocational training, working hours and holiday pay.[124] Reliance on the Member States was further reflected in the 1956 Spaak Report as well as the ensuing wording of Article 117 EEC Treaty.[125] To this date, there is certain dualism between the market and social policy, reflected in Article 151 TFEU.[126] The tensions appear both in the delimitation of the respective competences of the EU and the Member States in social legislation as well as in the role of social policy in the development and functioning of the internal market.

In the famous report dating back to 1956, the Spaak Committee established that the efficiency of the common market depends on the free movement of labour to secure an optimal allocation of resources. In order to make labour move and, thus, achieve the desirable level of efficiency, two preconditions have to be fulfilled: first, the desire of workers to migrate and, second, the readiness of host states to receive them by incorporating the freedom of movement in their national legislation.[127]

---

[124] Articles 118–120 EEC Treaty.

[125] Article 117 EEC Treaty reads as follows: 'Member States agree upon the need to promote improved working conditions and an improved standard of living for workers, so as to make possible their harmonisation while the improvement is being maintained. They believe that such a development will ensue not only from the functioning of the common market, which will favour the harmonisation of social systems, but also from the procedures provided for in this Treaty and from the approximation of provisions laid down by law, regulation or administrative action.'

[126] 'The Union and the Member States [...] shall have as their objectives the promotion of employment, improved living and working conditions [...]. To this end the Union and the Member States shall implement measures which take account of the diverse forms of national practices [...].' See H Collins, *Employment Law* (Oxford University Press 2010) 20.

[127] S O'Leary, 'Free movement of persons and services' in P Craig and G de Búrca (eds.), *The Evolution of EU Law* (Oxford University Press 2011) 499, 502–503. The dual objectives of the free movement or workers were subsequently affirmed by the Court in Case 143/87

The social conditions under which labour migration in the EU takes place are scrutinised frequently.[128] The welfare of the free movers, and even of those who do not move, has been high on the agenda of both the founding fathers of the EU, the Court of Justice and the Member States. As explained by AG Jacobs in *Bettray*, '[L]abour is not, in Community law, to be regarded as a commodity and notably gives precedence to the fundamental rights of workers over satisfying the requirements of the economies of the Member States.'[129] AG Jacobs referred to the emphasis in secondary law implementing the free movement provisions on the instrumentality of the freedom of movement in allowing the workers to improve their and their families' quality of life and employment, and advance their social conditions.[130]

In 1999, a call for modernisation of the internal market was launched.[131] It was subsequently repeated in 2007[132] and in 2010.[133] The 2007 report put forward that the first step in the creation of the internal market – making the fundamental freedoms operational – was to be complemented by a second, '21st century' step geared towards enhancing the functioning of the internal market in the interest of, inter alia citizens, consumers and public confidence.[134] Sustainability, especially, as applicable both to the social and the environmental dimension of the internal market is the key goal in enhancing the future quality of life in the EU, thus broadening the understanding of the function of the internal market. It is inevitable for a healthy market to demonstrate respect for labour, health, safety and environmental standards.[135] The 2010 Report recognised that in order to consolidate support for the internal market project, there is a need to alleviate the

---

Stanton v. *Inasti* EU:C:1988:378, para. 13; Case C-370/90 *Surinder Singh* EU:C:1992:296, para. 16; and Case C-413/95 *Bosman* (n 79) para. 94.

[128] S O'Leary (n 127) 505.

[129] Case 344/87 *Bettray* EU:C:1989:113, Opinion of AG Jacobs, para. 29.

[130] Recital 3, preamble to Regulation (EEC) No 1612/68 of the Council of 15 October 1968 on freedom of movement for workers within the Community [1968] OJ L257/2.

[131] Commission, 'White Paper on Modernisation of the Rules Implementing Articles 85 and 86 of the EC Treaty' [1999] OJ C132/1.

[132] Commission, 'A single market for 21st century Europe' (n 31). Also Commission, 'Instruments for a modernised single market policy' (Staff Working Document) SEC (2007) 1518 final.

[133] M Monti (n 33).

[134] Commission, 'A vision for the single market of the 21st century' (Press Release) IP/07/214, 21 February 2007.

[135] Commission, 'A single market for 21st century Europe' (n 31) 7.

tensions between supranational market integration and national social protection policies. The problem needs to be tackled both by giving greater consideration in the internal market acquis to the Member States' social realities and by coordinating national regulatory systems in line with EU principles.[136]

3.4.1.3 Consumer Protection

Just as in the cases of environmental and social policy, the original Rome Treaty contained little in terms of consumer protection. References to consumer protection were limited to individual policies such as agriculture and competition. The need for a separate EEC consumer policy emerged in the 1970s. The EU consumer protection policy is considered to have been launched at the 1972 Paris Summit where the institutions were called upon to set up a plan for strengthening and coordinating consumer protection within the Communities.[137] A preliminary programme for consumer protection and information policy was adopted by the Council in 1975,[138] followed by a second programme in 1982.[139] The two initial action plans contained 'soft law' rather than hard legal obligations, the latter not emerging until much later.

The EEC Treaty lacked a separate legal basis for EU consumer protection law. Legislation in the field was thus adopted on the harmonisation legal basis of Article 100 EEC Treaty under the disguise of maintaining fair conditions for competition. From its very inception, consumer protection has therefore been intimately attached to the internal market. The SEA inserted consumer protection into Article 100a(3) EEC Treaty (now Article 114(3) TFEU), requiring a high level of protection of consumers but falling short of creating a separate EC consumer policy. The Maastricht Treaty finally included consumer protection among the Community's activities under Article 3(s) EC Treaty and introduced Article 129(a)(1) EC Treaty authorising the Community to pursue a high level of consumer protection. The latter provision enabled the Community to take separate action in the field to support and supplement the activities of the Member States in addition to

---

[136] M Monti (n 33) 68.

[137] 'Conclusions of the first Summit Conference of the enlarged Community – Paris, 19–20 October 1972' Bulletin of the European Communities 10–1972.

[138] Council Resolution of 25 April 1975 on a preliminary programme of the European Economic Community for a consumer protection and information policy [1975] OJ C92/1.

[139] Council Resolution of 19 May 1981 on a second programme of the European Economic Community for a consumer protection and information policy [1981] OJ C133/1.

engaging in consumer protection through the internal market legal basis of Article 100a EC Treaty. Amsterdam Treaty added a provision on consumer protection in Article 129a(2) (renumbered Article 153(2)) EC Treaty (now Article 169 TFEU). In practice, recourse to the separate consumer protection legal basis is still seldom sought.[140] Instead, internal market harmonisation has assumed the role of 'indirect consumer policy',[141] fostering integration with the internal market to the detriment of the development of an EU consumer protection policy independent of market integration.[142]

3.4.1.4 Fundamental Rights

Intrinsically, the question of balancing economic rights with those of a non-economic nature translates into an issue of empowering or limiting individual action.[143] The role of individuals in the construction of the European edifice and ensuring the effectiveness of the latter impinges on the development of the internal market. The higher the degree to which the activities of individuals are affected by the EU, the greater is the need for their protection. Since EU law binds not only the Member States but also individuals by virtue of the direct effect of some of its provisions, fundamental rights must adequately be safeguarded also on EU level.

The ever-stronger protection of fundamental rights in the EU owes greatly to the Member States' perception of a lack thereof. After the Member States' constitutional courts began to take the matter of ensuring the observance of fundamental rights in the field of application of EU law into their own hands, the EU became compelled to create an own catalogue of rights that applies to the implementation and application of EU acts. This was done to avoid the national courts undermining the autonomy of the EU legal order by relying on the fundamental rights protection accorded by national constitutions, and thereby challenging the primacy of EU law.[144] This, in turn, would undermine both the uniformity and efficacy of EU law.[145]

Prior to the Lisbon Treaty, fundamental rights enjoyed the status of general principles of law in the EU and bound both the Member States

---

[140] I Benöhr, *EU Consumer Law and Human Rights* (Oxford University Press 2013) 42.
[141] S Weatherill, *EU Consumer Law and Policy* (Edward Elgar Publishing 2013) 11.
[142] I Benöhr (n 140) 43.
[143] M Hession and R Macrory (n 117) 478–479.
[144] LFM Besselink, *A Composite European Constitution* (Europa Law Publishing 2007) 12. See, for example, Case 29/69 *Stauder* EU:C:1969:57; Case 11/70 *Internationale Handelsgesellschaft* EU:C:1970:114, para. 2.
[145] Case 11/70 *Internationale Handelsgesellschaft* (n 144) para. 3.

and the institutions. As general principles, fundamental rights were to be substantiated by the constitutional traditions common to the Member States as interpreted by the Court. Fundamental rights belonging to the Member States' legal orders were part of the catalogue of fundamental rights applying to EU law, yet only to the extent of broader recognition, that is when appearing in the legal orders of multiple Member States. In the meantime, the Member States' fundamental rights protection included their international commitments in the field, especially under the Convention for the Protection of Human Rights and Fundamental Freedoms (European Convention on Human Rights (ECHR)). The EU Charter of Fundamental Rights was proclaimed in 2000 and incorporated into EU primary law by the 2009 Lisbon Treaty, which also authorised the EU to join the ECHR.[146] The latter step pending, fundamental rights, originating both from the Member States' common constitutional traditions and from the ECHR are now recognised as general principles under Article 6(3) TEU. The fundamental rights protection accorded by the Charter has been applicable even to the United Kingdom and Poland that opted out from the Charter pursuant to Protocol No 30 to the Treaties insofar as the Charter mainly reiterates general principles of EU law that are already applicable by virtue of the case law of the Court.[147]

3.4.2 Effect of Non-economic Policies on the Internal Market: Policymaking

Non-economic policies shape the scope of the economic principles of the internal market most directly by their integration into internal market legislation, including by harmonisation measures. One of the most significant vehicles for that is the integration principle and the integration provisions, which give effect to it. The integration principle ensures that horizontal provisions are incorporated into free movement and competition policy legislation.[148]

The first environmental integration principle was deemed by the Court to be an 'essential objective' of the Union.[149] The importance of environmental protection in EU law is underscored by the strong language in Article 11 TFEU demanding that environmental protection requirements 'must be' integrated into EU policies and activities. Other horizontal provisions are referred to in softer language of 'shall aim' or 'shall be taken into account'. In addition to Article 11 TFEU, the

---

[146] Article 6 TEU.

[147] M Dougan, 'The Treaty of Lisbon 2007: Winning Minds, Not Hearts' (2008) 45 *Common Market Law Review* 617, 667–668.

[148] S de Vries, *Tensions within the Internal Market* (Europa Law Publishing 2006) 18.

[149] Case 240/83 *ADBHU* EU:C:1985:59, para. 13.

objectives of the EU's environmental policy are also stated in Title XX of the TFEU, specifically Article 191(1) TFEU; provisions on the EU social and employment policy in Titles IX and X of the TFEU; and consumer protection in Title XV TFEU.

The role of the EU's flanking policies in the internal market project is more ambiguous.[150] It is often difficult yet necessary to distinguish between the various legal bases for adopting legislation on flanking policies, such as the environment, as they may constitute EU policies of their own right as well as policies deeply embedded in the internal market.[151]

In addition to the dilemma of the legal bases, there is uncertainty surrounding the choice of environmental protection measures – the environmental policy objectives provided in Article 191(1) TFEU, the principles in Article 191(2) TFEU and the policy aspects in Article 191(3) TFEU.[152] Practice has shown that the integration principle allows only a partial integration of environmental policy considerations into the internal market, retaining the core of the economic activity.[153] The outcome is expected as the aim of the horizontal principle is, indeed, to provide a perspective of reviewing the fundamental freedoms through the prism of environmental and other non-economic concerns but not to replace the model of market economy envisaged by the Treaties by an environmental objective. The internal market is, therefore, a market project with certain characteristics – social, sustainable and so on.

The integration principle, which does not establish a hierarchical system, is not the root cause of conflicts between the internal market and other EU policies.[154] On the one hand, the integration principle requires that environmental concerns be incorporated in the legislation adopted in any field of EU law. Here, not only the horizontal provisions play a role but also the general principles of consistency in the Treaties, such as Article 7 TFEU. On the other hand, the integration principle requires that all EU law be interpreted in a manner consistent with the objectives of EU's environmental policy.[155] The objectives and principles of environmental protection under Article 191 TFEU can also

---

[150] S Weatherill, 'Safeguarding the *Acquis Communautaire*' (n 39) 163.

[151] S Weatherill, 'On the Depth and Breadth of European Integration' (n 109) 545.

[152] O McIntyre (n 122) 132.

[153] N Dhondt, *Integration of Environmental Protection into Other EC Policies* (Europa Law Publishing 2003) 482.

[154] JH Jans (n 119) 1543.

[155] Ibid., 1541. In the landmark judgment of EU environmental law *Waddenzee*, for example, the Court stated that secondary EU law must be interpreted in the light of the

serve as a ground for judicial review of the validity of an EU measure, but judicial review is limited to determining the existence of a 'manifest error of appraisal' of the conditions for applying the environmental policy objectives.[156] Regardless of the fact that the integration principle mainly addresses EU institutions and decision-making processes, it must also be observed by the Member States when implementing EU law.[157]

Insofar as different regulation of non-market values by the Member States can constitute a distortion of competition in the internal market or an obstacle to the fundamental freedoms, harmonising measures can be adopted. One of the landmark decisions analysing the interaction between the economic and non-economic policies in internal market legislation is *Titanium Dioxide*.[158] In the case, the Court considered the appropriate legal basis for adopting Directive 89/428/EEC on waste from the titanium dioxide industry. Although the envisaged directive pertained both to competition law and the protection of the environment, differences in the decision-making procedures rendered it impossible to adopt the directive on a dual legal basis. Article 100a(3) EEC Treaty did, however, provide for a possibility to adopt internal market harmonisation measures integrating health, safety, environmental protection and consumer protection objectives if they had as their predominant aim the establishment and functioning of the internal market. The Court considered the directive to have wrongly been adopted on the environmental policy legal basis and, subsequently, deemed the internal market harmonisation provision of Article 100a EEC Treaty to be the correct legal basis. The Court's decision was motivated by the threat of a distortion of competition between undertakings unless provisions stipulating environment and health considerations were harmonised.[159]

In *Tobacco Advertising*, the Court cast light on the extent to which non-economic considerations can be incorporated into internal market harmonising measures.[160] The Court affirmed that public health objectives may form part of other EU policies including those for which

precautionary principle, which is one of the guiding principles of EU environmental policy: Case C-127/02 *Waddenzee* EU:C:2004:482, para. 44.

[156] Case C-341/95 *Bettati* EU:C:1998:353, paras. 33–35.
[157] N Dhondt (n 153) 48ff.
[158] Case C-300/89 *Titanium dioxide* (n 21).
[159] Ibid., para. 23.
[160] Case C-376/98 *Tobacco Advertising* (n 21).

harmonisation measures are adopted. Insofar as the adoption of harmonisation measures in the field of public health is expressly prohibited by the Treaties, however, other Treaty articles, such as Article 100a EC Treaty (now Article 114 TFEU), may not be used to circumvent the absence of an authorisation for harmonisation in the field.[161] The Court however, underlined that Article 100a EC Treaty does not give the EU legislator a general power to regulate the internal market. Harmonisation measures may only be adopted under Article 100a EC Treaty if they are genuinely intended to facilitate the creation and functioning of the internal market or removing appreciable distortions to competition.[162]

The judgment in *Swedish Match* consolidated the Court's previous case law.[163] The case concerned the correct legal basis for adopting Directive 2001/37/EC concerning the manufacture, presentation and sale of tobacco products and pertained to the question of whether a public health measure can be adopted under Article 95 EC Treaty (Article 114 TFEU). Although the contested directive was primarily designed to deal with a public health problem, the Court nevertheless held that it could be adopted on the basis of Article 95 EC Treaty since the conditions for recourse to that provision were met. The Court confirmed that Article 152(1) EC Treaty (now Article 168(1) TFEU) provides that a high level of protection of human health should be ensured in the implementation of all Community policies, and that Article 95(3) EC Treaty expressly requires that a high level of protection of human health must be guaranteed during the harmonisation process.[164]

Article 114(4) TFEU notably includes a possibility for the Member States to refrain from a harmonisation measure if maintaining national regulations is necessary for protecting the environment or the working environment. This is subject to the condition of notifying the Commission according to Article 114(5) TFEU. The limits on the Union's legislative activity when prioritising non-economic concerns over the fundamental freedoms are essentially the same as apply for the Member States with respect to maintaining national legislation for the sake of public interest: the measures may not 'substantively impair'

---

[161] Ibid., paras. 78–79.
[162] Ibid., paras. 83–84 and 106–107.
[163] Case C-210/03 *Swedish Match* (n 104).
[164] Ibid., paras. 33 and 42.

the four freedoms, they must be necessary, proportional and non-discriminatory.[165]

The effect of the integration principle on internal market law has been substantial.[166] It restricts the Union's freedom to set up the internal market in the economically most efficient manner as exemplified by restrictions to offer preferential conditions to the producers of renewable energy,[167] and competitive advantages provided to tender participants on the basis of the level of environmental protection.[168] Horizontal provisions also influence the inherently efficiency-driven competition law. In this regard, competition law only confirms its position in the internal market project by integrating non-economic aspects just as the other market-defining factors – the fundamental freedoms.[169]

3.4.3 Effect of Non-economic Policies on the Internal Market: Derogations

In addition to being incorporated into the definition and implementation of the fundamental freedoms and competition policy, non-economic concerns also penetrate them as exceptions and justifications. Derogations from the free movement rights as well as mandatory requirements based on case law demonstrate the development of the internal market into a marketplace that encompasses a broader range of values than endorsed by the original economic constitution.[170]

3.4.3.1 Exceptions in Primary Law

Justifications on grounds of non-economic considerations allow the Member States to surpass the fundamental freedoms as provided in primary and secondary EU law as well as deviate from EU competition rules.

---

[165] Case 240/83 *ADBHU* (n 149) paras. 12–13.
[166] JH Jans (n 119) 1540.
[167] Case C-379/98 *PreussenElektra* EU:C:2001:160.
[168] Case C-513/99 *Concordia Bus Finland* EU:C:2002:495. Inevitably, a number of criteria need to be fulfilled: tender participants cannot be subjected to environmental requirements that are not linked to the subject-matter of the contract; the decision-maker cannot be given 'an unrestricted freedom of choice'; the environmental requirements must be notified expressly in the contract documents or the tender notice; and compliance must be ensured with the fundamental principles of EU law, especially the principle of non-discrimination: Ibid., para. 64.
[169] See J Nowag, *Environmental Integration in Competition and Free-Movement Laws* (Oxford University Press 2016).
[170] C Barnard, *The Substantive Law of the EU: The Four Freedoms* (Oxford University Press 2013) 166–168.

Each of the specific provisions on the free movement contains a clarification of their scope. While Articles 34 and 35 TFEU prohibit quantitative restrictions on imports and exports in trade between Member States and all measures having equivalent effect, Article 36 TFEU provides for exceptions. Notwithstanding the general principle of non-discrimination enshrined in Article 18 TFEU as well as Articles 34 and 35 TFEU, prohibitions or restrictions on imports, exports or goods in transit are *justified* on grounds of public morality, public policy or public security; the protection of health and life of humans, animals or plants; the protection of national treasures possessing artistic, historic or archaeological value; or the protection of industrial and commercial property. The exceptions to the general rule of national treatment may, nevertheless, not constitute arbitrary discrimination or a disguised restriction to inter-state trade.[171]

The same rule of justification applies to the free movement of workers by virtue of Article 45(3) TFEU, which provides for exceptions on the basis of public policy, public security or public health. Public service is, moreover, generally excluded from the general freedom of movement for workers by virtue of Article 45(4) TFEU. Article 48 TFEU adds an important qualification to the free movement of workers. The provision deems certain social security measures 'necessary' for the free movement of workers and authorises the EU to adopt social policy measures to enable the aggregation of all periods of employment under the laws of several Member States in order to grant to the moving worker the right to benefits and a proper calculation of the amount of the benefit. Due benefits must be paid also to those workers and their family members who are residents in the host Member State. However, should draft legislation implementing Article 48 TFEU affect important aspects of a Member State's social security system including its scope, cost or financial structure, or financial balance, the Member State may request the matter to be referred to the European Council for discussion. In individual cases, the non-economic considerations integrated in the free movement provisions may, thus, be limited by economic considerations.

Exceptions from the general principles of the freedom of establishment and the free movement of services provided in Article 52 TFEU essentially cover the same areas as above – public policy, public security and public health. Exceptions from the free movement of capital include taxation and supervision of financial institutions,

---

[171] Article 36 TFEU.

administrative or statistical information or reasons of public policy or public security.[172] The same rule applies as in the case of the free movement of goods: Article 65(3) TFEU provides that the measures and procedures adopted may not constitute a means of arbitrary discrimination or a disguised restriction to the free movement of capital and payments. Finally, Article 107(2)(a) TFEU provides an exception from the general rule prohibiting state aid by allowing social state assistance to individuals in need, provided that no discrimination occurs on the basis of the origin of the products that constitute the aid.

The above exceptions demonstrate the incorporation into the internal market of various non-economic concerns – primarily relating to the protection of public policy, public security and public health, and the social security system. The criteria for applying these exceptions are not stipulated by EU law but are, according to the Court, to be substantiated by the judiciaries of the Member States when interpreting the respective provisions of EU law. The Member States are free to decide on the requirements of public policy and public security according to their 'national needs', which may differ across the Member States and over the course of time.[173] The EU does not prescribe the values that the Member States must base their considerations on,[174] but the exceptions must be given strict interpretation and are subject to control by the institutions of the Union.[175] Invoking the exception of public policy, for example, requires that there exists not only a 'perturbation of the social order which any infringement of the law involves' but also 'a genuine, present and sufficiently serious threat to one of the fundamental interests of society'.[176]

The Court has also elaborated general rules to govern the application of these restrictions to the fundamental freedoms. Importantly, while 'obstacles to trade' are given broad interpretation, derogations must be interpreted restrictively. The restrictive interpretation of the Article 36 TFEU exceptions means, for example, that measures which are necessary for the protection of health and life of humans, animals or plants cannot be construed in a broad manner to incorporate general

---

[172] Article 65 TFEU.
[173] Case C-348/09 *P.I.* EU:C:2012:300, para. 23 and case law cited.
[174] Case C-268/99 *Jany and Others* EU:C:2001:616, para. 60; Ibid., para. 21.
[175] Case 36/75 *Rutili* EU:C:1975:137, paras. 26–27; Case C-36/02 *Omega* EU:C:2004:614, paras. 30–31.
[176] Case C-33/07 *Jipa* EU:C:2008:396, para. 23; Case C-434/10 *Aladzhov* EU:C:2011:750, para. 35.

environmental protection objectives.[177] Also, in order to deviate from the fundamental freedoms, Member States need to take into account the general principles of EU law that include fundamental rights,[178] demonstrate the proportionality of the national measure to the legitimate outcome[179] and endorse principles of good governance as part of the proportionality test.[180] Although the Member States enjoy relative freedom in determining the extent to which they provide exceptions from the free movement provisions, unity in the internal market is to be maintained by the conditions attached to the application of these exceptions, especially the control exercised by the Court.

3.4.3.2 Mandatory Requirements

In addition to the exceptions listed in primary law, the Court has developed a set of justifications for deviations from the fundamental freedoms in the form of 'mandatory requirements', also referred to as 'imperative requirements'[181] or 'overriding requirements in the public interest'.[182] The first four mandatory requirements were articulated in *Cassis de Dijon*, justifying deviations from the free movement of goods for the sake of effective fiscal supervision, protection of public health, fairness of commercial transactions and defence of the consumer.[183] Mandatory requirements provide certain flexibility in keeping up with the changes and needs of the modern society in situations where the exceptions from the fundamental freedoms enshrined in the Treaties are limited. *Cassis de Dijon* was followed by the recognition of a number of other significant public policy derogations, ranging from the protection of public health to the fight against crime.[184]

Apart from the free movement of goods, mandatory requirements also apply to other fundamental freedoms. The freedom to provide television services, for example, can be limited on considerations of

---

[177] J Scott, *EC Environmental Law* (Longman 1998) 68.
[178] Case C-260/89 *ERT v. DEP* EU:C:1991:254, para. 43.
[179] Case C-60/00 *Carpenter* EU:C:2002:434, para. 42; Case C-17/00 *De Coster* EU:C:2001:651, para. 37.
[180] Case C-19/92 *Kraus* EU:C:1993:125, paras. 37–41.
[181] Case C-524/07 *Commission v. Austria* EU:C:2008:717, para. 54.
[182] For example, Case C-244/04 *Commission v. Germany* EU:C:2006:49, para. 31; Case C-577/10 *Commission v. Belgium* EU:C:2012:814, para. 44.
[183] Case 120/78 *Rewe-Zentral AG v. Bundesmonopolverwaltung für Branntwein* (*Cassis de Dijon*) EU:C:1979:42.
[184] For example, Joined Cases C-1/90 and C-176/90 *Aragonesa* EU:C:1991:327, para. 13; Case C-265/06 *Commission v. Portugal* EU:C:2008:210, para. 38. For further examples see C Barnard, *The Substantive Law of the EU* (n 170) 172–173.

consumer protection or cultural policy.[185] Yet, the scope of the four fundamental freedoms differs both concerning primary law exceptions as well as mandatory requirements. The Court considers the scope of each free movement right individually and in its own context. Compared to the other three, for example, fewer restrictions are permitted on the free movement of persons.[186] Furthermore, the exceptions under Article 36 and other provisions of the TFEU as well as mandatory requirements are not unconditional. Recourse to mandatory requirements must be justified by the Member States as necessary, proportional and the least restrictive means to achieve the envisaged aim,[187] subject to the application of other conditions in specific cases.

Even though the possibilities of balancing between fundamental freedoms and non-economic policy considerations appear in primary and secondary law, neither is deemed to have absolute advantage over the other.[188] The Court, too, generally refrains from establishing predetermined and absolute hierarchies between different policy objectives.[189] Instead, the Court's balancing endorses the plurality of legal principles where coherence goes before primacy.[190]

Environmental protection was first recognised as one of the mandatory requirements that may be invoked to justify restrictions to trade brought about by indistinctly applicable measures, which the Member States have adopted in the absence of EU harmonisation, in *Danish Bottles*.[191] The recognition paved way for even deeper integration of environmental considerations into internal market legislation than what had been achieved by the integration principle.

The interplay between the economic and social policy objectives in the internal market was first explained in *Defrenne I*. In his Opinion, AG Dutheillet de Lamothe suggested that Article 119 EEC Treaty (now

---

[185] Case C-288/89 *Collectieve Antennevoorziening Gouda* EU:C:1991:323, para. 27; Case C-6/98 *ARD* EU:C:1999:532, para. 50; Case C-245/01 *RTL Television* EU:C:2003:580, para. 71.

[186] PJ Oliver (ed.), *Oliver on Free Movement of Goods in the European Union* (Hart Publishing 2010) 10–11.

[187] Case 120/78 *Cassis de Dijon* (n 183); Case 261/81 *Walter Rau Lebensmittelwerke v. De Smedt* EU:C:1982:382, para. 12.

[188] See, for example, Article 1(6) and (7) of Directive 2006/123/EC of the European Parliament and of the Council of 12 December 2006 on services in the internal market [2006] OJ L367/36, which provide that the Directive neither affects labour law nor the exercise of fundamental rights.

[189] See also Case C-438/05 *Viking* EU:C:2007:292, Opinion of AG Poiares Maduro, para. 23.

[190] A 'new type of "constitutionalisation"': L Azoulai, 'The Court of Justice and the Social Market Economy: The Emergence of an Ideal and the Conditions for its Realization' (2008) 45 *Common Market Law Review* 1335, 1336–1337.

[191] Case 302/86 *Commission v. Denmark (Danish Bottles)* EU:C:1988:421, para. 9.

Article 157 TFEU) on equal pay for men and women pursued a social as well as an economic objective.[192] The two are connected via the link between 'social dumping' and undistorted conditions for competition. The Court followed the AG's reasoning on the double aims of the equal pay provision in the follow-up case *Defrenne II*. In that judgment, the Court specifically referred to the nature of the Community being 'not merely an economic union, but [...] at the same time intended, by common action, to ensure social progress and seek the constant improvement of the living and working conditions of their peoples'.[193]

The dual purpose of the EU – economic as well as social – also extends to the realm of EU competition and state aid law. In *3F*, the Court ruled that the state aid and competition provisions must be balanced against the Union's social policy aims including those enshrined in Article 136 EC Treaty (now Article 151 TFEU).[194] A similar balancing exercise had previously been carried out in the context of the freedom of establishment and the freedom to provide services in the landmark cases *Viking*[195] and *Laval*.[196] In those cases, the fundamental social right under scrutiny was the right of collective action. The Court concluded that insofar as collective action restricts the fundamental freedoms, it can be justified to the extent that the following conditions are fulfilled: the exercise of the fundamental freedoms would adversely affect jobs or working conditions; collective action is a suitable means for achieving the objectives pursued; and collective action stays within the limits of what is necessary to achieve the objective.[197] It rests with the Member States to ensure that the above conditions are fulfilled before they permit derogations from any of the fundamental freedoms.[198] This outcome is in broad terms compatible with the initial rationale behind the creation of the internal market as expressed in the Spaak report, namely the convergence of economic and social standards across the EU, which will, eventually, lead to an overall beneficial situation for the citizens of both the economically further and less advanced Member States.[199]

---

[192] Case 80/70 *Defrenne I* EU:C:1971:43, Opinion of AG Dutheillet de Lamothe, 455.
[193] Case 43/75 *Defrenne II* EU:C:1976:56, para. 10.
[194] Case C-319/07 P *3F v. Commission* EU:C:2009:435, para. 58. Article 151 TFEU can, thus, be used to interpret other Treaty provisions. See F Lecomte, 'Embedding Employment Rights in Europe' (2010) 17 *Columbia Journal of European Law* 1, 13.
[195] Case C-438/05 *Viking* (n 100) paras. 78–79.
[196] Case C-341/05 *Laval* (n 108) paras. 104–105.
[197] Case C-438/05 *Viking* (n 100) para. 84; Case C-341/05 *Laval* (n 108) para. 101.
[198] Case C-265/95 *Commission v. France (Spanish Strawberries)* EU:C:1997:595, para. 32.
[199] C Barnard, 'Internal Market v. Labour Market: A Brief History' in M De Vos (ed.), *European Union Internal Market and Labour Law: Friends or Foes?* (Intersentia 2009) 19, 43.

In the balancing exercise, neither social policy nor consumer protection has been granted an overall higher position vis-à-vis fundamental market freedoms. Furthermore, while a high level of consumer protection has been recognised by the Court as one of the objectives of the EU alongside the functioning of the internal market, this does not necessitate that the EU should apply the highest level of consumer protection offered by any single Member State. The lowering of standards for the consumers in some Member States is not regarded by the Court as having a detrimental effect on the overall improvement of the protection of consumers in the EU.[200]

The need to protect public health, however, is exceptional in enjoying almost absolute precedence over fundamental freedoms. In *Artegodan*, the Court ruled that public health considerations 'must *unquestionably* take precedence over economic considerations'.[201] Using this firm wording, the Court relied on the precautionary principle enshrined in Article 174(2) EC Treaty (now Article 191(2) TFEU). The precautionary principle is universal in character. It applies not only in the field of environmental protection but also accords a high level of protection of human health and consumer protection across the whole spectrum of EU activities.[202] As a general principle of EU law, it demands that the EU and national authorities give precedence to the requirements related to the protection of public health, safety and the environment over economic interests,[203] hence establishing a hierarchy that is otherwise absent.

The balancing of economic interests against fundamental rights deserves special attention, especially as many of the cases where such balancing takes place concern fundamental social rights. Whereas it may have taken the EU legislator a long while to grant social policy a significant role in the internal market, the Court was swift to recognise the social dimension of the market. Fundamental rights apply both as general principles of EU law and by virtue of Article 51(1) of the Charter and affect not only the validity of the EU and national measures but also their interpretation.[204]

---

[200] Case C-233/94 *Deposit Guarantees* EU:C:1997:231, para. 48.
[201] Joined Cases T-74/00, T-76/00, T-83/00, T-85/00, T-132/00, T-137/00 and T-141/00 *Artegodan* EU:T:2002:283, para. 173 (emphasis added).
[202] Ibid., para. 183.
[203] Ibid., para. 184.
[204] When transposing and implementing EU law, national authorities and courts must avoid conflicts with both fundamental rights and general principles of EU law: Case C-275/06 *Promusicae* v. *Telefónica de España* EU:C:2008:54, para. 68.

Fundamental rights can be relied upon as mandatory requirements to justify derogations from the fundamental freedoms. In *Schmidberger*[205] and *Omega*,[206] the Court found that a Member State may have recourse to fundamental rights to justify derogation from the provisions on the free movement of goods and the freedom to provide services, respectively. However, despite being recognised as fundamental principles of EU law,[207] not even fundamental rights are absolute and enjoy automatic primacy over other EU law.[208] Fundamental rights must be viewed in light of their 'social function', that is, the objectives and general interest of the EU provided that the latter aims are proportionate and do not constitute 'intolerable interference' with the substance of the fundamental right in question.[209] Like other mandatory requirements, the application of fundamental rights must fall within the scope of the Treaty and, consequently, be balanced against other rights protected under the Treaty and be proportional to the aim pursued.[210]

In *Viking* and *Laval*, the fundamental right under scrutiny – the right of collective action – is also a social right. These cases illustrate how, eventually, the process of protecting fundamental rights is similar to the balancing undertaken vis-à-vis other mandatory requirements. The distinction lies in the fact that in the application of fundamental rights, the Court may also have recourse to the Member States' common constitutional traditions.[211] Whenever a horizontal provision is also deemed a social, environmental, and so on, fundamental right, its scope can, therefore, be broadened beyond the level of protection accorded to a comparable provision lacking a fundamental right dimension.

In *Lindqvist*, the Court dealt with a situation where the same legal measure pursues both the aims of the free movement of data between Member States and the protection of the fundamental rights of individuals.[212] The Court recognised that the two aims may be incompatible with one another. While the particular provision under scrutiny was found not to infringe fundamental rights, it was the task of the national authorities to ensure that in the application of the national

---

[205] Case C-112/00 *Schmidberger* EU:C:2003:333, para. 74.
[206] Case C-36/02 *Omega* (n 175) para. 35.
[207] Case C-200/96 *Metronome Musik* EU:C:1998:172, para. 21.
[208] Case C-438/05 *Viking* (n 100) para. 44; Case C-341/05 *Laval* (n 108) para. 91.
[209] Case 265/87 *Schraeder* EU:C:1989:303, para. 15.
[210] Case C-112/00 *Schmidberger* (n 205) para. 77; Case C-36/02 *Omega* (n 175) para. 36; Case C-438/05 *Viking* (n 100) para. 46; Case C-341/05 *Laval* (n 108) para. 94.
[211] Case 4/73 *Nold* EU:C:1974:51, para. 13.
[212] Case C-101/01 *Lindqvist* EU:C:2003:596, para. 79.

provisions implementing the directive a 'fair balance' is struck between the rights and interests at stake, including the fundamental freedoms.[213]

Fundamental rights can also in themselves pursue both economic and non-economic aims. In *Schröder*, the Court relied on its earlier affirmations that the principle of non-discrimination is a fundamental right observed by the Court.[214] As such, the Court deemed the economic aim of Article 119 EC Treaty (Maastricht numbering, now Article 157 TFEU) on equal pay for men and women to be secondary to the social aim pursued by the same provision as the latter constituted 'the expression of a fundamental human right'.[215]

It remains questionable, though, whether mandatory requirements constitute an exception from the fundamental freedoms or a clarification of the scope thereof. For example, it is uncertain whether collective action or, on the contrary, the practice of social dumping and other non-economic aspects form part of the concept of the internal market or whether they should be considered as restrictions thereof, albeit justifiable.[216] In the example of competition policy, the answer may lie in the assessment of the 'fairness' of competition, that is, whether fair competition is completely free of restrictions or whether the prevention of social dumping is an inherent characteristic of the concept of fair competition,[217] whereas the situation is more ambiguous with regard to the fundamental freedoms. Nevertheless, mandatory requirements play a vital role in clarifying the scope of the internal market in terms of the balance struck between economic and non-economic considerations, including fundamental rights.

3.5 EU Citizenship

The original range of the free movers in the EU – the importers and exporters of goods, services and capital, and the mobile labour force – has

---

[213] Ibid., para. 90. See also, for example, Case C-112/00 *Schmiedberger* (n 205); Case C-320/03 *Commission v. Austria* EU:C:2005:684; Case C-55/93 *van Schaik* EU:C:1994:363.

[214] Case 149/77 *Defrenne III* EU:C:1978:130, paras. 26–27; Joined Cases 75/82 and 117/82 *Razzouk and Beydoun v. Commission* EU:C:1984:116, para. 16; Case C-13/94 *P. v. S. and Cornwall County Council* EU:C:1996:170, para. 19.

[215] Case C-50/96 *Schröder* EU:C:2000:72, para. 57; Joined Cases C-270/97 and C-271/97 *Deutsche Post v. Sievers and Schrage* EU:C:2000:76, para. 57.

[216] B Bercusson, *European Labour Law* (Cambridge University Press 2009) 394–395.

[217] F Dorssemont, 'The Right to Take Collective Action v. Fundamental Economic Freedoms in the Aftermath of *Laval* and *Viking*' in M De Vos (ed.), *European Union Internal Market and Labour Law: Friends or Foes?* (Intersentia 2009) 45, 49.

been gradually widened to include family members, students, old-age pensioners and other economically non-active persons. Maastricht Treaty introduced the concept of EU citizenship. Prior to that, the free movement rights were extended to the non-economic movers mainly by secondary law and the case law of the Court of Justice.

The Court's judgment in *Lawrie-Blum*[218] has been considered to have introduced the concept of EU citizenship even before it appeared in the Treaties. The case was followed by judgments in *Reed*,[219] *Cowan*[220] and *Gravier*[221] – all dealing with question of discrimination on grounds of nationality of (unmarried) family members, tourists and students, respectively. In secondary law, the right of the economically non-active to move freely within the Union was first granted with the three residence directives adopted in 1990.[222] The directives provided retired persons, students and other non-workers the right to residence within the EU on the condition that they are covered by comprehensive medical insurance and in possession of sufficient resources so as not to become a burden on the social security system of the host Member State. In 2004, the three directives were replaced by a comprehensive Residence Directive.[223]

EU citizenship is the 'fundamental status of nationals of the Member States',[224] substantiated by the principle of equal treatment of Article 18 TFEU. In *Martínez Sala*, the Court, for the first time, tied Union citizenship to the non-discrimination provision of Article 6 EC Treaty (Maastricht numbering, now Article 18 TFEU) 'in all situations which fall within the scope *ratione materiae* of Community law'.[225] By virtue of EU citizenship, persons who are lawfully resident in the host Member State may invoke the principle of non-discrimination.[226] Pursuant to Article 21 TFEU, all

---

[218] Case 66/85 *Lawrie-Blum* EU:C:1986:284.

[219] Case 59/85 *Reed* EU:C:1986:157.

[220] Case 186/87 *Cowan* (n 81).

[221] Case 293/83 *Gravier* EU:C:1985:69, 593.

[222] Council Directive 90/364/EEC of 28 June 1990 on the right of residence [1990] OJ L180/26; Council Directive 90/365/EEC of 28 June 1990 on the right of residence for employees and self-employed persons who have ceased their occupational activity [1990] OJ L180/28; Council Directive 93/96/EEC of 29 October 1993 on the right of residence for students [1993] OJ L317/59.

[223] Directive 2004/38/EC of the European Parliament and of the Council of 29 April 2004 on the right of citizens of the Union and their family members to move and reside freely within the territory of the Member States [2004] OJ L158/77.

[224] Case C-184/99 *Grzelczyk* EU:C:2001:458, para. 31; Case C-413/99 *Baumbast* EU:C:2002:493, para. 82.

[225] Case C-85/96 *Martínez Sala* EU:C:1998:217, para. 63.

[226] Case C-184/99 *Grzelzcyk* (n 224) para. 32.

European citizens, thus not only those directly participating in the market as traders, workers, service providers or service receivers, are entitled to move and reside freely within the EU, yet subject to limits and conditions elaborated by the Treaties as well as implementing measures. Citizenship rights comprise a 'genuine enjoyment' of the right, including both the existing right of free movement and the protection of a future possibility of movement within the EU.[227] Moreover, a Union citizen cannot be expelled from a Member State if that would render the person without EU citizenship altogether.[228]

The core of the protection accorded by EU citizenship – the principle of non-discrimination – is substantiated identically in citizenship and free movement provisions, differences being limited to the personal scope of application of the principle.[229] EU citizenship does not, therefore, provide any rights additional to those granted under the internal market provisions to persons who derive rights from the Treaties by virtue of their participation in the internal market.[230] In the meantime, the contrary holds true – economic nature brings an activity into the scope of the free movement provisions and, thus, accords to persons involved therein all rights deriving from the Treaties.[231]

In wholly internal circumstances, the potential effect of EU citizenship on the establishment and functioning of the internal market is more limited than in cross-border situations. EU citizenship case law has had a certain 'cross-pollenisation' effect on free movement case law, particularly in the case of the free movement of workers.[232] For example, the requirement of a real or genuine link between a job seeker or worker and the host Member State in order to decide on the person's entitlement to social benefits in the host state first appeared in cases concerning EU citizenship.[233] It has thereafter been extended to cases involving the free movement of workers where the genuine link with the host Member State, which had previously been implied,[234] justifies

---

[227] Case C-34/09 *Ruiz Zambrano* EU:C:2011:124, para. 42.
[228] Case C-135/08 *Rottmann v. Freistaat Bayern* EU:C:2010:104, para. 54.
[229] G Davies, *Nationality Discrimination in the European Internal Market* (Kluwer Law International 2003) 188.
[230] Joined Cases C-64/96 and C-65/96 *Uecker and Jacquet* EU:C:1997:285, para. 23.
[231] Case C-519/04 P *Meca Medina* EU:C:2006:492, paras. 22–28.
[232] S O'Leary, 'Developing an Ever Closer Union between the Peoples of Europe? A Reappraisal of the Case Law of the Court of Justice on the Free Movement of Persons and EU Citizenship' (2008) 27 *Yearbook of European Law* 167.
[233] Case C-224/98 *D'Hoop* (n 82) para. 38.
[234] Case C-258/04 *Ioannidis* EU:C:2005:559, para. 33.

an extension of the host state social benefits to the non-national worker.[235]

Whereas EU citizenship shapes the rights of EU citizens within the EU legal order as well as the legal order itself, its effect on the scope of the fundamental freedoms and competition policy as well as the functioning of the internal market is limited. Consequently, EU citizenship has modest impact on the extendibility of the EU internal market beyond the EU. This is notwithstanding the fact that Citizenship Directive 2004/38/EC has been declared EEA relevant and is applied by the EFTA Court to the extent that its provisions are applicable to the free movement of persons within the EEA.[236]

3.6 Sectoral Internal Market

The internal market consists of several economic policy sectors. As a general rule, the fundamental freedoms, EU competition law, horizontal provisions and permissible derogations apply to the specific policy sectors unless limited by exceptions provided in the Treaties.

The EU internal market in energy has been extended to non-EU Member States by the EnCT. In principle, rules of the internal market apply to the energy sector – Article 194 TFEU explicitly states that the EU's energy policy is to be conducted 'in the context of the establishment and functioning of the internal market'. The four fundamental freedoms and rules on competition therefore apply to the energy sector without distinction, including horizontal provisions, derogations and exceptions. In particular, special focus in the internal market in energy is granted to environmental concerns. Article 194(1) TFEU accords special attention to the need to preserve and improve the environment.

---

[235] See, for example, ibid.; Case C-138/02 *Collins* EU:C:2004:172, para. 69.

[236] See, for example, Case E-15/12 *Wahl* [2013] EFTA Ct Rep 534; Case E-26/13 *Gunnarsson* [2014] EFTA Ct Rep 254. Not all parts of the Directive form part of the EEA acquis such as EU immigration law, political rights deriving from EU citizenship and the notion of EU citizenship itself. Recital 8 of the preamble to Decision of the EEA Joint Committee No 158/2007 of 7 December 2007 amending Annex V (Free movement of workers) and Annex VIII (Right of establishment) to the EEA Agreement that incorporated the Citizenship Directive into the EEA Agreement [2008] OJ L124/20; Joint Declaration by the Contracting Parties to Decision of the EEA Joint Committee No 158/2007 incorporating Directive 2004/38/EC of the European Parliament and of the Council into the Agreement [2008] OJ L124/20. See also H Haukeland Fredriksen and CNK Franklin, 'Of Pragmatism and Principles: The EEA Agreement 20 Years On' (2015) 52 *Common Market Law Review* 629, 639; J Breidlid and M Vahl, '20 Years on: Current and Future Challenges for the EEA' (2015) EFTA Bulletin 32, 36–37.

Article 192(2)(c) TFEU on EU environmental policy provides a possibility for the Member States to object to environmental policy instruments, which would 'significantly [affect] a Member State's choice between different energy sources and the general structure of its energy supply'. Furthermore, pursuant to Article 194(2) TFEU, Member States retain their right to determine how to exploit their own energy resources, which energy sources to use and how to ensure energy supply within their country.

The European common transport policy (CTP) is expanded to third countries by the ECAA Agreement in the aviation sector and the TCT in the field of land, rail, inland waterways and maritime transport. The CTP, the rail, road and inland waterway sectors of which are governed by Articles 90–100 TFEU, forms part of the internal market. Many particularities, however, concern the scope of the free movement rights in the transport sector, including exceptions from the provisions on the freedom to provide services[237] as well as competition law.

The question of the application of the free movement provisions to the transport sector is not straightforward. In the *French Seamen* case, the Court established that exceptions from the application of the fundamental freedoms must be provided expressly in the Treaties, such as Article 38(2) EEC Treaty (now Article 38(2) TFEU) on CAP.[238] Article 38(1) TFEU, moreover, explicitly states that the internal market extends to the field of agriculture. The TFEU contains no similar provisions on the CTP. Yet, the Court established that by virtue of Article 74 EEC Treaty (now Article 90 TFEU), which provides that the CTP incorporates the pursuit of the objectives of the Treaties as laid out in Articles 2 and 3 EEC Treaty (now Article 3 TEU) – 'for the attainment of which the fundamental provisions applicable to the whole complex of economic activity are of prime importance' – the fundamental freedoms also apply to the field of maritime transport.[239] Instead of considering the CTP as a departure from the fundamental freedoms, the Court interpreted the objective of common action in the CTP as complementary to the fundamental freedoms. The four fundamental freedoms are, thus, applicable insofar as they enable the achievement of the objectives of the CTP.[240] According to the Court, the rationale behind a separate transport policy is that being a service, a separate set of provisions allows due consideration to be given

---

[237] Article 58(1) TFEU.
[238] Case 167/73 *Commission* v. *France (French Seamen)* EU:C:1974:35, paras. 21–22.
[239] Ibid., para. 24.
[240] Ibid., paras. 25–26.

to its particularities; the common rules apply, however, to the extent that they are not explicitly excluded.[241] Sea and air transport are exempted from the general regulatory system of the Treaties by Article 100(2) TFEU. The aim of introducing the special provision was not to set up a special regulatory framework for these fields but rather to exempt sea and air transport from the specific rules laid down with respect to rail, road and inland waterways transport.[242] In *Nouvelles Frontières*, the Court confirmed that the findings with regard to maritime transport apply equally to air transport.[243]

An important aspect to consider with respect to the energy and transport sectors are the derogations accorded to many of the undertakings covered by the common policies by virtue of Articles 93, 106 and 107 TFEU. The latter provisions provide exceptions from the general rules on competition policy, especially state aid, to the commonly Member-State-defined[244] 'services of general economic interest' (SGEIs).[245] SGEIs are regulated by Article 14 TFEU and Protocol No 26 to the Treaties. They comprise services that must be provided due to public need irrespective of economic profitability.[246] Pursuant to Article 106(2) TFEU, SGEIs are subject to EU competition law to the

---

[241] Ibid., paras. 27–28.

[242] Ibid., para. 31.

[243] Joined Cases 209–213/84 *Nouvelles Frontières* EU:C:1986:188, paras. 42 and 45.

[244] Subject to a test of 'manifest error of assessment': see Case T-289/03 *BUPA* EU: T:2008:29, paras. 168–169. Exceptions include sectors which have been harmonised, for example telecommunications, postal and electricity sectors harmonised by Directive 2002/22/EC of the European Parliament and of the Council of 7 March 2002 on universal service and users' rights relating to electronic communications networks and services [2002] OJ L108/51; Directive 97/67/EC of the European Parliament and of the Council of 15 December 1997 on common rules for the development of the internal market of Community postal services and the improvement of quality of service [1998] OJ L15/14; Directive 2009/72/EC of the European Parliament and of the Council of 13 July 2009 concerning common rules for the internal market in electricity [2009] OJ L211/55.

[245] Article 14 TFEU reads as follows: '[...] given the place occupied by services of general economic interest in the shared values of the Union as well as their role in promoting social and territorial cohesion, the Union and the Member States, each within their respective powers and within the scope of application of the Treaties, shall take care that such services operate on the basis of principles and conditions, particularly economic and financial conditions, which enable them to fulfil their missions. [...]'

[246] H Schweitzer, 'Services of General Economic Interest: European Law's Impact on the Role of Markets and of the Member States' in M Cremona (ed.), *Market Integration and Public Services in the European Union* (Oxford University Press 2011) 11, 34. A definition of SGEIs is provided in Commission, 'A Quality Framework for Services of General Interest in Europe' (Communication) COM (2011) 900 final.

extent that they do not 'obstruct the performance, in law or in fact, of the particular task assigned to them'. In the energy and transport sectors, this provision specifically concerns the Member States' energy monopolies, transport networks and public transport.[247]

A similar discussion on exceptions from the internal market rules to the provision of public services has taken place in the context of Articles 45(4), 51 and 62 TFEU. It concerns exemptions from the rules on the free movement of persons and services granted to public service employees and activities in which the state exercises official authority. The exceptions are motivated by the idea of public service as an expression of state sovereignty.[248] The general scope of the public service exception was defined by the Court in *Sotgiu*,[249] and the concept of public service in *Commission* v. *Belgium*.[250] There has been considerable debate on the range of positions that fall under the exception. Representing vital sectors in a state's economy, the transport or energy sectors may include activities or positions that must be protected under the public service exception. The Court has given the exception a functional rather than institutional interpretation,[251] assessing whether the post in question 'involve[s] direct or indirect participation in the exercise of powers conferred by public law and duties designed to safeguard the general interests of the state or of other public authorities' and demanding proof of a 'special relationship of allegiance to the state and reciprocity of rights and duties which form the foundation of the bond of nationality'.[252] Excluded are positions in organisations governed by public law, which do not constitute public service 'properly so called'.[253] A number of positions in the national railways have, for example, not been considered to constitute employment in the public service.[254] The same applies to positions in public transport; water, gas and electricity supply; and airline and shipping

---

[247] A separate category among services of general interest are social services of general interest, which may include both economic and non-economic activities – those which are economic in nature are treated as SGEIs. See Commission, 'Implementing the Community Lisbon programme: Social services of general interest in the European Union' (Communication) COM (2006) 177 final; Commission, 'Services of general interest, including social services of general interest: a new European commitment' (Communication) COM (2007) 725 final.

[248] Case 307/84 *Commission* v. *France* EU:C:1986:150, Opinion of AG Mancini, para. 2.

[249] Case 152/73 *Sotgiu* EU:C:1974:13, para. 5.

[250] Case 149/79 *Commission* v. *Belgium* EU:C:1982:195, para. 10.

[251] Case 307/84 *Commission* v. *France* EU:C:1986:222, para. 12.

[252] Case 149/79 *Commission* v. *Belgium* (n 250) para. 10.

[253] Ibid., para. 11.

[254] Ibid.

companies.[255] Captains and first officers on ships may in some circumstances fall within the scope of the exception of Article 45(4) TFEU.[256]

The legal content of the sectors of the internal market, including exceptions granted under primary law, are easier to circumscribe in detail than the EU internal market as a whole because of the comparatively narrower scope of the former. However, the distinction between the substantive content of the comprehensive and sectoral internal markets is small, except for a limited number of sector-specific derogations. There is nothing to exempt from the cores of market sectors the application of horizontal provisions or mandatory requirements motivated by non-market concerns. It, therefore, makes little difference that in some sectors such as air transport a significant portion of the acquis is specified in secondary law. In the context of exporting the acquis, the distinction between primary and secondary law becomes irrelevant as all acquis, which is exported becomes part of an international agreement.

3.7 Conclusion

Pursuant to its definition, the internal market must warrant the free movement of goods, workers, services and capital while ensuring fair conditions for competition, the protection of fundamental rights and other non-economic interests of the market participants as laid out in the Treaties. Whereas the fundamental freedoms and competition policy have been in the centre of the internal market integration project from the beginning, fundamental rights and non-economic concerns have been introduced gradually over time. Embedded in horizontal provisions and various derogations from the fundamental freedoms and competition policy, non-economic consideration are assuming ever-greater relevance for the internal market. They influence the economic heart of the internal market from the policy-making stage to the implementation and application of the internal market rules.

Two main conclusions can be drawn from the developments in the internal market for the purposes of the possibility of extending the

---

[255] These areas, among others, were pointed out as generally exempted from the scope of Article 48(4) EEC Treaty (now Article 45(4) TFEU) in Commission, 'Freedom of workers and access to employment in the public service of Member States – Commission action in respect of the application of Article 48(4) of the EEC Treaty' [1988] OJ C72/2. It was confirmed by the Court in Case C-473/93 *Commission* v. *Luxemburg* EU:C:1996:263, para. 31.

[256] Case C-405/01 *Colegio de Oficiales de la Marina Mercante Española* EU:C:2003:515; Case C-47/02 *Anker* EU:C:2003:516; Case C-460/08 *Commission* v. *Greece* EU:C:2009:774.

internal market by exporting the acquis. First, although the Treaties provide a definition of the internal market, its scope remains just as ambiguous as that of the common market. A large part of the balancing between the economic and the non-economic concerns is conducted by the Court of Justice on a case-to-case basis, which renders the actual scope of the economic principles in the internal market difficult to circumscribe with precision. Second, the internal market is a constantly changing notion without a clear final destination. For third countries setting out to align their legal systems with that of the EU, the internal market is not a constant value that can easily be confined within the frames of an international agreement having more limited aims than the EU Treaties. It is demanding both to achieve a homogeneously expanded internal market reaching beyond the Union by exporting constantly changing internal market acquis with an ambiguous scope and to construct an institutional framework that is both capable of identifying the relevant internal market acquis among all EU acquis and incorporating the changes in the acquis to the international agreements without delay.

4   Internal Market
Unity

The broad objective of the European Union to achieve an ever closer union among the peoples of Europe by, among other means, creating a highly competitive market economy, not only affects the concept of the internal market in substantive terms but also prescribes a particular level of uniformity for the elements of the EU legal order generally and the internal market specifically. The concept of uniformity pertains specifically to the notion of acquis. It asks for the level of adherence required in relation to the entire body of the EU internal market acquis in order to be able to regard the exporting of EU acquis to third countries as a true extension of the internal market.

The general aim of the multilateral agreements exporting the acquis is homogeneity – a term comparable in meaning to uniformity and unity. The aim of homogeneity has two dimensions: homogeneity within the realm of the international agreement and homogeneity between the legal space created by the international agreement and the internal market acquis as applicable in the EU. In the former dimension, the question of homogeneity is unproblematic; in the latter context, it raises a number of questions and concerns. To determine the level of homogeneity within the expanded internal market, one must delimit the scope of the internal market with sufficient precision, both in terms of substance and unity. The necessary level of commonality within the internal market serves as a benchmark for establishing whether a set of acquis exported to third countries constitutes a mirror image of the internal market or whether the result is merely a type of a single market that operates on the basis of rules originating from the EU.

4.1 Integration in the Internal Market

Within the EU internal market, the level of conformity with the common rules is not absolute. Whereas unity and in some circumstances even uniformity are crucial elements of the internal market,[1] they also encompass numerous opt-outs and other types of derogations. The unity of the internal market furthermore appears in two contexts. The first concerns the unity of the EU legal order, part of which is the internal market. It denotes the unity of the parts that form the whole and draws largely on the application of the same legal rules across the geographical borders of the EU. The second context pertains to the unity of the market itself, referring to the orderly composition of the constituent elements of the market necessary for its optimal functioning. Both contexts are relevant for the purpose of establishing the essential commonality in the concept of the internal market.

4.1.1 Unity of the Internal Market

Unity in the internal market refers to the 'substance of [its] common and complete order'.[2] It constitutes a set of elements that define the rights and obligations of market participants across the Union territory. The internal market enjoys a degree of unity by virtue of the common rules that guide the activities of the market participants in the common market space.

Unity in the internal market is based on the unhindered movement of the factors of production and builds on the free movement of goods, services, people and capital, and rules on competition that support the establishment and the proper functioning of the market. In the most basic terms, the borderless internal market supposes that undertakings are able to operate and workers to take up employment in any of the Member States without discrimination based on their country of origin. Internal market legislation must eliminate any discrimination in a comprehensive and complete manner, leading to a result of unity by means of the application of a common set of rules that regulate all the relevant aspects of intra-EU trade. These rules are limited by the principle of conferral and do not, thus, apply to all fields of life. Neither does the internal market regulate differences in conditions of competition arising out of non-human factors such as natural phenomena, but deals

---

[1] On unity, see Case 14/68 *Walt Wilhelm* EU:C:1969:4, para. 5.
[2] R Barents, *The Autonomy of Community Law* (Kluwer Law International 2004) 208.

with 'differences in treatment arising from human activity, and especially from measures taken by public authorities'.[3]

Pursuant to the Court of Justice in *Walt Wilhelm*, the backbone of the internal market – the four fundamental freedoms and equal conditions of competition – is both the 'primary object' of the EU and a means of achieving it.[4] In the same vein is the creation of the internal market both a separate objective of the EU and a means of achieving the Union's broader aim of integration in Europe. A primary object of the Treaties is, in turn, also 'to confirm and safeguard the unity of that market'.[5] Consequently, the Court considers the unity of the market to constitute a value in itself – a 'fundamental principle'[6] or essential characteristic of the internal market that must be preserved by means of a single legislator and various actors implementing, applying[7] and interpreting[8] the acquis.[9]

The concept of the internal market, therefore, not only includes the four fundamental freedoms and rules on competition as provided in the Treaties and secondary legislation, interpreted by the Court and defined and circumscribed by a series of non-economic considerations, but also comprises the idea that these elements inherently belong together to form the 'EU internal market', which is distinct from any other inter-state single market formation.

4.1.2 Unity of the EU Legal Order

Intimately connected to the notion of unity of the internal market is the concept of unity of the EU legal order – the idea that EU law has the same effect in all Member States in all circumstances.[10] Differently from the unity of the internal market, the unity of the EU legal order does not look at its essential characteristics but rather at the similarity of its component elements. Distinct terms are used to denote the same set of rules applied across the Union and beyond, as in the case of international agreements seeking to extend the internal market to third

---

[3] Notwithstanding occasional compensation for natural inequalities: see Case 52/79 *Debauve* EU:C:1980:83, para. 21.
[4] Case 14/68 *Walt Wilhelm* (n 1) para. 5.
[5] Ibid.
[6] Case 193/80 *Commission* v. *Italy* EU:C:1981:298, para. 17.
[7] Case 314/85 *Foto-Frost* v. *Hauptzollamt Lübeck-Ost* EU:C:1987:452, para. 16; Case 61/79 *Denkavit II* EU:C:1980:100, para. 18.
[8] Case 299/84 *Neumann* EU:C:1985:463, para. 25.
[9] Case 40/70 *Sirena* v. *Eda* EU:C:1971:18, para. 10.
[10] Case 166/73 *Rheinmühlen I* EU:C:1974:3, para. 2.

countries. These notions include 'homogeneity', 'coherence', 'uniformity' and 'unity', each with a slightly different meaning.

'Homogeneity' is most frequently used in the context of the EEA.[11] Integration theorists define 'homogeneous integration' as normative and organisational convergence that leads to a uniform outcome across the Union,[12] but the term is otherwise seldom used in relation to EU law.[13] Instead, the comprehensiveness of the EU legal order is usually described using the notions of 'coherence', 'unity' and 'uniformity'.

'Coherence' generally implies a logical and orderly organisation of the constituent parts of a system, including a legal system.[14] An example of coherence within the EU legal order can be found in the EU's judicial system. In the latter, competences are allocated systematically between the EU and the Member State courts, whereas the procedures for reviewing the legality of the acts of EU institutions rest exclusively with the Union courts.[15] The 'fundamental mechanism' for maintaining coherence in the EU's judicial system is the preliminary reference procedure provided in Article 267 TFEU.[16] The procedure creates a necessary link between the Member States' national courts and the Court of Justice, safeguards the authoritative interpretation of EU law by the Court and ensures that the Court's interpretation of EU law is applied in the national legal orders by the referring national court. The expected outcome of the preliminary ruling procedure is the uniform interpretation and application of EU law throughout the EU.[17] It also serves to protect the autonomy of the EU legal order including

---

[11] 'Considering the objective of establishing a dynamic and homogeneous European Economic Area': Recital 4, preamble to the EEA Agreement, see Section 4.3.1. In this book, 'homogeneity' is used to refer to the objectives regarding unity of all of the four multilateral agreements under scrutiny.

[12] S Andersen and N Sitter, 'Differentiated Integration: What Is it and How Much Can the EU Accommodate?' (2006) 28 *European Integration* 313, 321.

[13] The term 'homogeneity' occurs predominantly in the field of competition law and is used to refer to homogeneous markets. Competition law is also regarded as the most 'homogeneous' among the EU's policy fields: see ibid., 321–322.

[14] Balkin distinguishes between logical, narrative and normative coherence, see JM Balkin, 'Understanding Legal Understanding: The Legal Subject and the Problem of Legal Coherence' (1993) 103 *Yale Law Journal* 105, 114. On whether or not a legal system as a whole can be coherent, see BB Levenbook, 'The Role of Coherence in Legal Reasoning' (1984) 3 *Law and Philosophy* 355.

[15] K Lenaerts, 'The Rule of Law and the Coherence of the Judicial System of the European Union' (2007) 44 *Common Market Law Review* 1625, 1631–1632.

[16] Court of Justice, 'Information Note on references from national courts for a preliminary ruling' [2005] OJ C143/01, para. 1.

[17] Case 166/73 *Rheinmühlen I* (n 10).

the role of the Court as the sole authoritative interpreter of EU law.[18] The uniform interpretation and application of EU law, on the one hand, and autonomy, on the other, are also strongly connected to the notions of uniformity and unity in the EU legal order. Coherence does not, however, demand the application of the same rules in each constituent part of the legal system such as in each and every EU Member State.

'Uniformity' refers specifically to identical quality. In the EU's legal order, the concept of uniformity manifests itself in the adoption of uniform rules and their subsequent application and interpretation across the Union in a uniform manner. The principal means of achieving uniformity is through positive integration in the form of harmonising laws. In the United States of America, the first step towards creating a 'more perfect Union' by the Constitution was to eliminate the principal barriers to trade between the states. After that had proven unsuccessful, recourse was had to the codification of state laws.[19] Integration in the EU's internal market has in broad terms followed the American example. Initially, market integration in the EU mainly took place by means of eliminating barriers to trade, predominantly through mutual recognition. Harmonisation did not pick up until negative integration had proven insufficient for reaching the established objectives, and in 1986, the SEA introduced qualified majority voting in the Council. Until the Treaty of Maastricht – the so-called market-building stage – harmonisation played a significant role in the European integration process.[20] Post-1992, however, the legislative ambition of the Union has been redirected towards less harmonisation coupled with 'better' laws and 'better' enforcement.[21]

The development of the EU's legal order in general and integration in the internal market in particular is, thus, not characterised by the uniformity of rules and procedures in the meaning of absolute identical quality or equivalence. The EU legal order strives for legal unity but not uniformity by definition. Moreover, rather than being a complete and fully comprehensive legal order of its own, the EU legal order builds upon those of the Member States. None of the Member States, especially

---

[18] See Chapter 6.

[19] JAC Grant, 'The Search for Uniformity of Law' (1938) 32 *The American Political Science Review* 1082, 1083–1085.

[20] S Weatherill, 'New Strategies for Managing the EC's Internal Market' (2000) 53 *Current Legal Problems* 595, 597–598.

[21] Ibid., 598.

the federal states, has completely uniform legal orders. Not more can, therefore, be demanded from a union comprising 27 states with distinct legal, political, economic, social and cultural backgrounds.

The unity and uniformity of EU law pertain both to the EU law dimension of the Member States' legal orders and to the institutional and procedural rules governing the Union's own functioning. The non-EU relevant areas of national legal orders, insofar as they do not give effect to EU law, fall outside the limits of the EU legal order. The unitary characteristics of those areas are, therefore, an expression of coherence in national legal traditions rather than EU membership. The boundaries of the EU legal order within the national legal order are drawn by the national courts, whereas the ultimate authority to determine the limits between national and EU law is vested with the Court of Justice.[22] Furthermore, the EU's legislative activity in its areas of competence is restricted by three factors:[23] (1) the nature of the competence – exclusive, shared or complementary; (2) the legal basis stipulating either the unification of laws through regulations, harmonisation through directives or coordination of the Member States' policies through recommendations and other soft law instruments; and (3) the principles of subsidiarity and proportionality. The latter two confine the EU's influence to areas where the goals of the Union cannot be reached by other means than concerted action and determine the choice of the legal instrument to be used. Lastly, complete harmonisation of the Member States' laws is seldom the preferred option for integration, leaving the Member States enough leeway to reconcile EU legislation with their national settings in terms of time, degree and substance. This renders the EU's legal system, as well as the legal systems of the Member States in EU-relevant areas, far from uniform.

The notion of 'unity' indicates harmony and accord between rules in a legal space without presenting a claim for identical quality as in the case of uniformity. A uniform legal order features unity but unity in a legal order does not require complete uniformity of rules, their application or interpretation. Minor differences between the constituent parts are generally not considered detrimental to the unity of a legal order whereas they would defeat the idea of uniformity. This reasoning

---

[22] N Walker, 'Sovereignty and Differentiated Integration in the European Union' (1998) 4 *European Law Journal* 355, 375.

[23] L Senden, 'Conceptual Convergence and Judicial Cooperation in Sex Equality Law' in S Prechal and G van Roermund (eds.), *The Coherence of EU Law: The Search for Unity in Divergent Concepts* (Oxford University Press 2008) 363, 366.

finds support in von Bogdandy's claims that 'coherence' is not a precondition for 'unity' in the EU legal order and that, to a certain extent, divergences in the application of EU law among the Member States do not play a decisive role in the process of identifying the EU legal system as a unitary legal system.[24] In this context, von Bogdandy uses 'coherence' in a meaning of 'uniformity'. Delving deeper into the concepts of 'unity' and 'uniformity', it appears that the unity of the EU legal order entails, indeed, a great deal of coherence but much less so of uniformity.

The concept of unity features a political as well as legal dimension. In the EU, legal unity enjoys the central position,[25] serving as an intermediary step on the path towards possible political unity in the future.[26] The gradual expansion and diversification of the initially small and homogeneous group of Member States, the increase in the Union's competences and the emergence of a number of alternative international legal fora[27] have called for a different approach as regards the level of legal and political integration of the Member States within and non-EU Member States to the Union. In the early decades, the ultimate aim of the Union was closer to the ideal situation of uniformity,[28] at least in the internal market.[29] This approach was subsequently deemed both impossible and unnecessary and, eventually, discarded. In the course of time, the EU has become much more diverse but also more fragmented.[30]

---

[24] A von Bogdandy, 'Founding Principles of EU Law: A Theoretical and Doctrinal Sketch' (2010) 16 *European Law Journal* 95, 109.

[25] A von Bogdandy, 'Doctrine of Principles' (2003) Jean Monnet Working Paper 9/03, 12; A von Bogdandy, 'The Legal Case for Unity: The European Union as a Single Organization with a Single Legal System' (1999) 36 *Common Market Law Review* 887, 889–890.

[26] L Senden (n 23) 364.

[27] G de Búrca and J Scott, 'Introduction' in G de Búrca and J Scott (eds.), *Constitutional Change in the EU: From Uniformity to Flexibility?* (Hart Publishing 2000) 1, 2.

[28] N Walker (n 22) 363.

[29] 'The general task of the Union to establish a common market and progressively to approximate the economic policies of the Member States creates a presumption in favour of uniformity – as a result a uniform rule cannot be considered discriminatory': CD Ehlermann, 'How Flexible is Community Law? An Unusual Approach to the Concept of "Two Speeds"' (1984) 82 *Michigan Law Review* 1274, 1288.

[30] G de Búrca and J Scott (n 27) 1. This fragmentation is characterised by notions such as 'differentiated integration', 'multi-speed', 'variable geometry', 'à la carte'. Within the multitude of terminology, 'differentiated integration' is the general term used to point at the lack of homogeneity within the EU: A Stubb, 'A Categorization of Differentiated Integration' (1996) 34 *Journal of Common Market Studies* 283, 283–284.

Legislative integration within the EU can be depicted as an inverted pyramid with unification/full harmonisation on top, followed by minimum harmonisation in the middle section and cooperation at the bottom. The inverted pyramid represents the different means of achieving unity in a legal system. Among those, unification (statutory uniformity or 'legal homogeneity') is the most intense yet not the only means of achieving unity nor its sine qua non.[31] Instead, the uniformity of laws has to be reconciled with the need for a legal system to retain a degree of flexibility for the sake of effectiveness. Contrary to Shaw who perceives flexibility as a proof of the Member States lacking an objective of unity,[32] the unity – in contrast to uniformity – of a legal order is not adversely affected by minor divergences among its constitutive elements. A legal order must demonstrate a degree of flexibility to accommodate differences as well as changes in the society.

As an evolving system, law should, however, retain certain fundamental common qualities.[33] The role of unification is primarily to avoid a mismatch between the parties' rights and obligations arising out of a multitude of rules regulating a single area.[34] As long as the principal components identifying the crucial rights and obligations[35] are in place, a legal order can accommodate some divergence in procedural rules, rule making and legal instruments without becoming fragmented.[36] The current legislative practice of the EU is geared towards differentiated integration, which corresponds more accurately with the reality of a heterogenic Europe.[37] In sum, despite the fact that diversification has clearly signalled the end of the idea of uniform Europe, it does not mark the end of unified Europe.

---

[31] See E Christodoulidis and R Dukes, 'On the Unity of European Labour Law' in S Prechal and B van Roermund (eds.), *The Coherence of EU Law: The Search for Unity in Divergent Concepts* (Oxford University Press 2008) 397, 398–399. On the lesser importance of uniformity as compared to unity see M Brand, 'Divergence, Discretion, and Unity' in S Prechal and B van Roermund (eds.), *The Coherence of EU Law: The Search for Unity in Divergent Concepts* (Oxford University Press 2008) 217, 231.

[32] J Shaw, 'Relating Constitutionalism and Flexibility in the European Union' in G de Búrca and J Scott (eds.), *Constitutional Change in the EU: From Uniformity to Flexibility?* (Hart Publishing 2000) 337, 341.

[33] E Christodoulidis and R Dukes (n 31) 397.

[34] R Sacco, 'Diversity and Uniformity in the Law' (2001) 49 *American Journal of Comparative Law* 171, 179.

[35] The 'fundamental acquis': P Pescatore, 'Aspects judiciaires de l'«acquis communautaire»' (1981) 20 *Revue trimestrielle de droit européen* 617, 620.

[36] A von Bogdandy, 'The Legal Case for Unity' (n 25) 908.

[37] A Stubb (n 30) 283.

4.2 Disintegration in the Internal Market

The above analysis demonstrates not only that the concepts of unified internal market and legal order differ but also that the level of uniformity in the two varies. This section aims to clarify the extent to which diversification can be accommodated within the internal market and the EU legal order, respectively, and the possible criteria that can help distinguish between permissible and impermissible divergences in the internal market.

4.2.1 Differentiation in the EU Legal Order

Differentiation in the EU takes different forms – temporal and substantive – and leads to divergent outcomes in terms of the depth of integration. Each of these outcomes is an expression of the nature of integration within the EU. Comprehensive analysis of the latter has been provided by Walker, in turn borrowing from Stubb[38] and Dewatripont and others.[39] Walker's five models of differentiated integration in the EU can be placed in a pyramid.[40] At the bottom of the pyramid is the ideal situation of uniformity, representing an EU with the most commonality, whereas Europe à la carte at the top of the pyramid characterises the extreme opposite. Between those two models of integration, moving upwards, one finds multi-speed Europe, Europe of concentric circles and Europe of flexible integration.

The model of multi-speed Europe is flexible but only in the temporal dimension. In substantive terms, the aim of a common level of integration is maintained.[41] Multi-speed Europe refers to a situation where one or more Member States are granted an extension for the deadline of implementation or entry into force of common EU standards if they are unable to fulfil the obligations in time, usually during the accession process. Postponed deadlines enable the Member States to whom the exceptions apply to enter a 'slow lane' while allowing other Member States to proceed with the implementation agenda. Additional substantive requirements may apply to the multi-speed model. For example, Article 27 TFEU allows for derogations from internal market legislation with a view of gradually preparing less developed economies for the entry into the internal

---

[38] Ibid.
[39] M Dewatripont and others, *Flexible integration: Towards a more effective and democratic Europe* (Monitoring European Integration 1995) 80.
[40] N Walker (n 22) 362–363.
[41] Ibid., 364–365.

market. The derogations are, however, restricted to temporary measures and those least disruptive to the functioning of the internal market. The derogations may, furthermore, be justified by economic and social but not political considerations.[42] The model of multi-speed Europe does not generally allow for permanent opt-outs from common rules.

The model of concentric circles represents a less intense model of integration than the former two. It allocates the Member States into spheres pursuant to their willingness and capability of integration. The core comprising the most progressive Member States that have not opted out from any of the common policies is located in the middle of the circle whereas the Member States with the most modest integration aims are placed at the outer edge. Differently from multi-speed integration, the model of concentric circles grants permanent exceptions to the Member States furthest from the centre.

The model of flexible integration is somewhat similar to the model of concentric circles but focuses on a substantive common base and voluntary areas of cooperation beyond the common base.[43] To this category belong, for example, the Member States that have entered a 'fast lane' of European integration by engaging in enhanced cooperation under Article 20 TEU.

The most liberal mode of integration in the EU is represented by the model of Europe à la carte. It imposes a framework of a few common objectives but leaves to the Member States freedom to 'pick-and-choose, as from a menu' the specific areas of cooperation.[44] Differently from flexible integration, Europe à la carte does not envisage a substantive common base, rendering the level of uniformity and even unity relatively low.

A further, rather unconventional mode of differentiation is known as 'structural variability'.[45] It has been exemplified by the EU's former pillar system in which the organisation of the EU's institutions and decision-making varied in accordance with the policy field and the nature of the EU competence in question. Yet despite the remaining lack of uniformity in the Union's institutional and procedural structure, the Lisbon Treaty amendments have by merging the former first and

---

[42] CD Ehlermann (n 29) 1289. As elaborated further, though, this restriction applies to derogations from secondary law that are approved by the EU institutions rather than to opt-outs from primary law.

[43] M Dewatripont and others (n 39).

[44] A Stubb (n 30) 288.

[45] N Walker (n 22) 363.

third pillars and articulating the overarching objectives of the Union contributed to increased unity within the EU.

4.2.1.1 Primary Law

The models of integration summarised in the previous section concern uniformity, flexibility and differentiation in various contexts – the adoption, implementation and interpretation of primary law and secondary law as well as procedural law. The uniformity of each features different dimensions. In the case of primary law, for example, the first dimension is that of common values. The common values are provided in Article 2 TEU and represent the'constitutional homogeneity' in the EU.[46] It is generally agreed that the actual level of homogeneity in the meaning of uniformity in the EU legal order is low,[47] owing largely to the factual diversity among the constitutions of the Member States.[48]

The second dimension of uniformity in primary law concerns the provisions of the Treaties. Here, the claim for uniformity has a stronger basis but is limited by different flexibility schemes and opt-outs. Ehlermann has provided a detailed categorisation of the diverse appearances of flexibility in primary law.[49] For example, a very common instance is the transitional period during which flexibility occurs with respect to both substantive and institutional provisions. Substantive uniformity is, however, programmed to be restored within a pre-determined timeframe. Another example of differentiation in primary law is of an ad hoc but permanent nature and concerns derogations from internal market harmonisation measures justified 'on grounds of major needs', such as public morality, public policy, public security, public health, protection of the natural environment and of the working environment, and a range of other grounds protected by public interest.[50] All of the above are subject to EU control measures. Yet another example concerns safeguard clauses – flexibility clauses 'par

---

[46] S Mangiameli, 'The Union's Homogeneity and Its Common Values in the Treaty on European Union' in H-J Blanke and S Mangiameli (eds.), *The European Union after Lisbon* (Springer 2012) 21, 21ff.

[47] Ibid., 25. Article 2 TEU reads as follows: 'The Union is founded on the values of respect for human dignity, freedom, democracy, equality, the rule of law and respect for human rights, including the rights of persons belonging to minorities. These values are common to the Member States in a society in which pluralism, non-discrimination, tolerance, justice, solidarity and equality between women and men prevail.'

[48] A von Bogdandy, 'Doctrine of Principles' (n 25) 39.

[49] CD Ehlermann (n 29) 1279–1281.

[50] Article 36 TFEU.

excellence' – which can be found in several Treaty provisions and allow the Member States to deviate from harmonisation measures in exceptional circumstances and temporarily, usually during the transitional period.[51]

Further differentiation in primary law appears in the form of procedural differentiation. It is reflected in the composition of the European Parliament and the number of votes allocated to the different Member States in the Council. The numbers of votes and voting majorities are further adjusted to the opt-outs from and the opt-ins to certain policies. In addition, general exceptions have been laid out in the protocols attached to the Treaties for disadvantaged regions as well as specific derogations from common policies accorded to particular Member States. Finally, Article 184 TFEU provides for supplementary research programmes in which a limited number of Member States may decide to participate and which are subsequently financed by the participating states only. Differentiation and flexibility are, thus, programmed into the very foundations of the EU.

True ad hoc differentiation from primary law, as opposed to derogations under Article 36 TFEU, are Member State opt-outs from entire policy fields for which no legal basis is provided in the Treaties and which are, therefore, negotiated separately between the Member States, usually in the course of negotiating Treaty amendments. Before the Maastricht Treaty, amendments to the EU Treaties seldom brought about serious deviations from the commonly agreed policies. The Treaties of Maastricht and Amsterdam, however, heralded a new era of opt-outs.[52] The Maastricht Treaty granted opt-outs to the United Kingdom and Denmark from the Social Policy Protocol and the third stage of the Economic and Monetary Union (EMU), respectively. These opt-outs have been regarded as examples of 'unreasoned differentiation'.[53] Criticism is directed towards them representing 'subjective' differentiation between the Member States that wish to participate in common policies and those who do not as opposed to the 'objective' differentiation between the Member States that have

---

[51] Articles 114(10) and 191(2) TFEU. D Hanf, 'Flexibility Clauses in the Founding Treaties, from Rome to Nice' in B De Witte, D Hanf and E Vos (eds.), *The Many Faces of Differentiation in EU Law* (Intersentia 2001) 3, 9.

[52] N Walker (n 22) 355.

[53] G de Búrca, 'Differentiation within the Core: The Case of the Common Market' in G de Búrca and J Scott (eds.), *Constitutional Change in the EU: From Uniformity to Flexibility?* (Hart Publishing 2000) 133, 148.

fulfilled the necessary economic criteria to participate in the EMU and those that have not.[54] This distinction also reflects the dichotomy between the derogations under Article 36 TFEU and the general ad hoc opt-outs mentioned above. Political reasons are generally not considered appropriate to justify derogations from the general EU policies. Yet the Maastricht opt-outs assumed great economic and symbolic significance.[55] The opt-outs from the Social Policy Protocol and the EMU represent divergence from an entire policy field, whereas other notable opt-outs, such as the protocols on the acquisition of secondary homes in Denmark and on abortions in Ireland are fairly specific and have little, if any, effect on other policies.[56] Developing further the differentiation process that started with the Maastricht Treaty, the Treaty of Amsterdam introduced enhanced cooperation in a number of first, second and third pillar policies as well as granted exceptions to the United Kingdom, Ireland and Denmark from the Schengen acquis. Other notable examples of general opt-outs include those granted to Denmark from the Common Security and Defence Policy (CSDP), Poland and the United Kingdom from the Charter of Fundamental Rights[57] and the United Kingdom from the EMU. Denmark, Ireland and the United Kingdom, furthermore, opted out from the AFSJ, although the flexible nature of the opt-outs of Ireland and the United Kingdom has allowed them to opt in to legislation.

Although the Maastricht and Amsterdam opt-outs covered large policy fields, they were not considered detrimental to the idea of unity in the EU as the opt-outs did not concern the Member States' core commitments towards the EU – the internal market.[58] The idea of the internal market as the 'core' of the EU is further expressed in the example of enhanced cooperation. Both the Treaty of Amsterdam[59] and the current TEU[60] and TFEU[61] require enhanced cooperation to maintain the unity of principle and the institutional framework of the EU; be used to 'further the objectives of the Union, protecting its interests and reinforcing its integration process'; and avoid disturbances to the internal

---

[54] D Hanf (n 51) 14–15.
[55] G de Búrca (n 53) 148.
[56] D Hanf (n 51) 16–17.
[57] See also Chapter 3, Section 3.4.1.4.
[58] G de Búrca (n 53) 149.
[59] Article 43 of the Consolidated version of the Treaty on European Union [1997] OJ C340/02.
[60] Article 20 TEU.
[61] Articles 326–334 TFEU.

market. The Member States are generally free to cooperate outside the framework of the EU but are restricted from doing so in areas of exclusive EU competence, as well as areas of non-exclusive EU competence unless absolutely indispensable.[62]

4.2.1.2 Secondary Law

In substantive terms, secondary EU law together with all implementing legislation and administrative acts demonstrate an even lower degree of uniformity than primary EU law. On the one hand, the Member States have claimed many more opt-outs from secondary law, not least because of the significantly larger quantity of secondary law as compared to primary law. On the other hand, whereas harmonisation is the principal tool for achieving uniformity in the EU legal system and the internal market, not all harmonisation measures envisage maximum harmonisation. Maximum harmonisation is a means of legislative harmonisation – harmonisation occurring as a result of EU legislation in contrast to judicial harmonisation where the Court declares national legislation incompatible with EU law, or mutual recognition. Minimum harmonisation establishes a common European minimum for national legislation but does not aim at full uniformity.[63] Generally, 'positive' harmonisation by means of EU legislation – regulations and directives – is the most effective method for establishing a uniform legal order. 'Negative' or 'judicial' harmonisation by which national barriers to trade are removed by the Court,[64] are more of an ad hoc nature. Yet, one must also question the true uniformity of the otherwise uniform rules in the light of their implementation and application.[65] Ineffective implementation and application of uniform rules lead to divergent outcomes. An example to the contrary is the practice of voluntary harmonisation whereby the Member States adhere to non-compulsory EU standards such as recommendations and, thereby, establish a level of uniformity through the actual implementation and application of legally binding rules.

---

[62] Article 20(1),(2) TEU; G Edwards and E Philippart, *Flexibility and the Treaty of Amsterdam: Europe's New Byzantium?* (1997) CELS Occasional Paper No. 3, 13.

[63] See S Weatherill, 'Supply of and Demand for Internal Market Regulation: Strategies, Preferences and Interpretation' in N Nic Shuibhne (ed.), *Regulating the Internal Market* (Edward Elgar Publishing 2006) 29, 46.

[64] A McGee and S Weatherill, 'The Evolution of the Single Market – Harmonisation or Liberalisation' (1990) 53 *The Modern Law Review* 578, 580.

[65] S Weatherill, 'New Strategies for Managing the EC's Internal Market' (n 20) 606.

Factors other than legislation, too, play a role in the creation and, especially, the management[66] of the EU legal order and the internal market. Neither regulations that lay down minimum requirements nor directives lead to a strictly uniform result in the EU legal order. Directives, which are by definition less efficient in creating uniformity than regulations, as well as decisions and recommendations, which are directed towards a single Member State, are ill-suited for achieving absolute uniformity. Recommendations that are directed to all Member States may, however, in spite of their soft law nature provide an EU policy field with a common direction with the help of a sufficient amount of self-regulation. In line with the principle of proportionality, the EU institutions should prefer, where the objective and the effectiveness of the outcome allow minimum harmonisation, recourse to measures with a more limited harmonising effect and soft law instruments rather than binding legislation.[67] Similar to primary EU law, secondary law, too, features various methods for differentiation in time and substance, safeguard clauses, quotas and compensation that differ from one Member State to another.[68] This kind of differentiation is, nevertheless, limited by the requirement of objectivity of criteria in order to 'ensure a proportionate distribution of advantages and disadvantages' within the territory of the internal market.[69]

4.2.1.3 Interpretation, Procedure and Implementation

The third large category of divergences in EU law pertains to the interpretation of common rules. Threats to the uniform interpretation of EU law are twofold. First, divergences in the interpretation of EU law provided by national courts appear in two dimensions: from one Member State to another and between the authoritative interpretations provided by the Court of Justice and the interpretations of the Member State courts. Second, similar and even identical legal concepts often assume different meanings in the different national legal systems. This phenomenon, known as the 'keyword trap',[70] affects the accurate and

---

[66] Ibid., 595.
[67] European Council, 'Conclusions of the Presidency – Edinburgh, 12 December 1992, Annex I Overall approach to the application by the Council of the subsidiarity principle and Article 3b of the Treaty on European Union' SN 456/92, 20–21.
[68] For examples, see CD Ehlermann (n 29) 1282–1285.
[69] Case 106/83 Sermide v. Cassa Conguaglio Zucchero EU:C:1984:394, para. 28.
[70] F Chirico and P Larouche, 'Conceptual Divergence, Functionalism, and the Economics of Convergence' in S Prechal and B van Roermund (eds.), The Coherence of EU Law: The Search for Unity in Divergent Concepts (Oxford University Press 2008) 463, 472–473.

uniform interpretation of EU law, which occasionally employs the same concepts as the national legal systems.[71]

It is important to note that no distinction can be made between the unity and uniformity of the interpretation of EU law. Uniform interpretation leads, inevitably, to the more realistic situation of unity in a legal order. Regarding the importance of uniform interpretation of law in the EU legal order, the Court has stated that '[...] it is manifestly in the interest of the Community legal order that, in order to forestall differences of interpretation, every Community provision should be given a uniform interpretation, irrespective of the circumstances in which it is to be applied'.[72] Contrary to legislative exceptions, which are approved and endorsed by the EU institutions, divergences in the interpretation and application of EU law are mostly unwelcome and difficult for the Union to exercise complete control over. Empirically, the difficulty of enforcing the requirement of uniform interpretation of EU law in the Member States renders the EU legal system inherently non-uniform.[73]

The fourth category of structural divergences in EU law concerns the uniformity of procedure. On the one hand, diverging national procedural rules may hamper both the uniformity and the effective implementation of EU law.[74] On the other hand, it is necessary that the application and interpretation of procedural and institutional provisions in the Member States mirror the application and interpretation of corresponding EU law.[75] The uniformity of procedure in the EU is crucial, setting the foundation for the 'European substantive supremacy'.[76]

Finally, divergences in the application of EU law may be caused by the Member States' unsatisfactory implementation efforts. Although there is no longer an intention to 'finalise' the internal market, the Member States still often fail to properly transpose and implement the EU

---

[71] See Case 283/81 *CILFIT* EU:C:1982:335, para. 19.

[72] Case C-126/97 *Eco Swiss* EU:C:1999:269, para. 40.

[73] While the preliminary ruling procedure in Article 267 TFEU has been designed to ensure uniformity in the interpretation and application of EU law, it is intrinsically difficult to safeguard this function if the national courts fail to refer questions to the Court. For discussion, see Chapter 8, Section 8.2.2.1.

[74] Case 130/79 *Express Dairy Foods* EU:C:1980:155; Case 54/81 *Fromme* EU:C:1982:142.

[75] S Magnusson, 'Procedural Homogeneity v. Inconsistency of European Courts – Comments on Order of the EFTA Court President of 15 June 2012 in Case E-16/11 EFTA Surveillance Authority V. Iceland' (2012), 2, http://papers.ssrn.com/sol3/papers.cfm?abstract_id=2140717 accessed 10 February 2020.

[76] JS Delicostopoulos, 'Towards European Procedural Primacy in National Legal Systems' (2003) 9 *European Law Journal* 599, 609.

measures. Paper transposition continues to be a problem as well as the non-uniform application of the common rules.[77] The inclusion of new Member States into the Union through the enlargement process,[78] as well as technical innovations that require legislative plans to be updated on a continuous basis,[79] makes uniformity even more difficult to achieve in practice.

4.2.1.4 From Uniformity to Unity: Permissible Differentiation

The lack in the EU legal order of uniformity in the meaning of identical interpretation and application of identical laws in all Member States calls for the question of what makes the EU legal system a unified one in terms of 'unity' of the system. According to von Bogdandy, principles, specifically those outlined in Article 3 TEU, create unity as well as necessary flexibility within the EU.[80] Moreover, the principle of rule of law acts as a creator of unity between the Member States' legal orders in the dimensions of both legal and procedural unity.[81] Sacco refers to the concept of cultural unity – the commonality of language, history, traditions and so on – which lays a foundation for uniting peoples by virtue of a uniform body of rules.[82] The level of cultural unity among the EU member States, especially in a Union composed of 27 nation states, can neither be presumed to reach a level high enough to sustain uniformity nor is it intended to assimilate the Member States into a group of culturally homogeneous states.[83] Whereas certain commonality of values and mutual cultural understanding is necessary for the proper functioning of an economic union, which might develop into a political union, there is economic value in specialisation and decentralisation.[84] The effects of cultural diversity in the EU lead in the legal sphere to the need to ensure judicial homogeneity, such as through the preliminary reference procedure.

[77] S Weatherill, 'New Strategies for Managing the EC's Internal Market' (n 20) 606.
[78] European Union Committee, *The Single Market: Wallflower or Dancing Partner?* (HL 2007-08, 5-I) paras. 29ff.
[79] Commission, 'The Internal Market for Goods: a cornerstone of Europe's competitiveness' (Communication) COM (2007) 35 final, 6.
[80] A von Bogdandy, 'Doctrine of Principles' (n 25) 36-38.
[81] A von Bogdandy, 'Founding Principles' in A von Bogdandy and J Bast (eds.), *Principles of European Constitutional Law* (Hart Publishing 2009) 11, 28-38.
[82] R Sacco (n 34) 172.
[83] This is reflected in the Union's motto 'United in diversity'.
[84] L Bovenberg, 'Unity produces diversity: The economics of Europe's social capital' in W Arts, J Hagenaars and L Halman (eds.), *The Cultural Diversity of European Identity* (Brill 2003) 403, 412-413.

Within the EU legal order, the foundation of unity is laid by the broad commitments shared by the Member States.[85] The sine qua non elements of its legal order or the 'hard core'[86] of the Member States' commitments towards the Union form the nucleus of European integration and are the key in maintaining the identity of the Union in the myriad of different models of flexible integration. In the context of the EU as a whole, defining the core of obligations of membership is necessary mainly in order to identify the range of acceptable differentiation.

The concept of a 'hard core' of the EU accommodates well the tension between uniformity and unity examined above by limiting flexible differentiation in the EU to the peripheral policy areas.[87] What exactly belongs to the hard core of the EU is in the light of the ever-expanding Union subject to continuous debate, yet the general opinion agrees on awarding this status to the norms and policies constituting the internal market.[88] The elevated position of the internal market is underpinned by the fact that its essential features have never been significantly altered by treaty amendments.[89]

According to Grabitz and Langeheine, a 'two-tier system' of flexible integration along the lines of a multi-speed model is acceptable in objectively justifiable circumstances insofar as appropriate instruments are employed for pursuing a 'high degree of conformity with the aims of integration'.[90] The authors suggest a three-level formula to determine whether or not their proposed two-tier system can be rendered admissible within the EU legal system. The formula includes tests on compatibility with the basic principles of EU law, primary EU law and specific policy fields including the internal market.[91] The definition

---

[85] G de Búrca and J Scott (n 27) 7.

[86] A Stubb (n 30); S Weatherill, 'On the Depth and Breadth of European Integration' (1997) 17 *Oxford Journal of Legal Studies* 537; N Walker (n 22); A von Bogdandy, 'The European Union as a Human Rights Organization? Human Rights and the Core of the European Union' (2000) 37 *Common Market Law Review* 1307; G de Búrca (n 53); W Sauter, 'The Economic Constitution of the European Union' (1998) 4 *Columbia Journal of European Law* 27; L Azoulai, 'The *Acquis* of the European Union and International Organisations' (2005) 11 *European Law Journal* 196.

[87] G de Búrca (n 53) 135.

[88] Ibid., 133.

[89] J Wouters, 'Constitutional Limits of Differentiation: The Principle of Equality' in B De Witte, D Hanf and E Vos (eds.), *The Many Faces of Differentiation in EU Law* (Intersentia 2001) 301, 327.

[90] B Grabitz and E Langeheine, 'Legal Problems Related to a Proposed "Two-Tier System" of Integration within the European Community' (1981) 18 *Common Market Law Review* 33, 38.

[91] Ibid., 39.

of what is acceptable as differentiation – an agreement on the common aim and the 'preliminary status of differentiation'[92] – is more questionable. The latter is mainly subject to political agreement and thereby likely to render subjective any objective criteria for the common aim.

4.2.2 Differentiation in the Internal Market

Enjoying the status of the hard core of the EU, the internal market consists of a package of obligations to which the Member States must adhere within the limits of their membership. In the case of the expanded internal market, the membership aspect obviously becomes redundant. Instead, identifying the core of the internal market becomes indispensable for assessing the unity of the expanded internal market vis-à-vis the EU internal market. Clearly, in order to be considered equivalent to the internal market, the expanded market needs to feature the same key elements as the internal market within the EU.

There is, as of now, no commonly accepted set of criteria for what constitutes the core of the internal market. The core of the internal market can, however, be scrutinised from both empirical and functionalist perspectives. The former focuses on legislation relevant to the internal market currently applicable to the Member States. Subsequently, the hard core should be constructed on the basis of the highest common denominator of elements empirically applied by all Member States.[93] Leaving aside the components from which one or more Member States have opted out, the remaining core reflects a fragmentary yet strong common commitment to the internal market. The weakness of the empirical method lies in the constant changes to the hard core of the market. Neither can the empirical method do entirely without a functionalist understanding of which parts of the legislation are relevant for the functioning of the internal market, that is, which legal acts pertain to its fundamentals. Better suited for identifying the core of the internal market is, therefore, the second, functionalist approach. This method draws on the objectives of the EU concerning the internal market and distils the defining features of the internal market from their purpose.[94]

The analysis in Chapter 3 demonstrated that in addition to the elements found in the definition of the internal market – the fundamental

---

[92] Ibid., 40.
[93] de Búrca has used the empirical approach: see G de Búrca (n 53) 141.
[94] See B Grabitz and E Langeheine (n 90) 41.

freedoms and equal conditions of competition – the concept of the internal market is interwoven with a number of other, non-economic policies and concepts. From a formal perspective, the economic foundation of the internal market as expressed in its definition should also be considered its hard core. Observing the broader aims of the internal market beyond unhindered trade between Member States, however, the limits of permissible differentiation cannot be based on the overly narrow and purely economic understanding of the internal market. Whereas the fundamental freedoms and equal conditions of competition form the non-derogable core of the internal market, the limits of permissible differentiation must be found in the broader concept of the internal market, which also includes the relevant non-economic aspects.

The establishment of the internal market is the most central aspect of the commitment of the Member States to 'ensure the economic and social progress of their States by common action to eliminate the barriers which divide Europe'[95] but being the core of the EU legal order does not mean that no flexibility is permitted from the internal market provisions. Distinction, however, must be made between the essential principles of the internal market – such as the fundamental freedoms, the principles of equality and non-discrimination – and the specific provisions laid down in primary and secondary legislation in which differentiation may occur without necessarily defeating the object and purpose of the internal market. According to de Búrca, the core of the internal market should pertain both to the substance of the specific policies and the 'specific legal and constitutional characteristics of such measures'.[96] Viewing the internal market as a collection of principles brought into effect by secondary law rather than specific policy measures, the substance of the particular policy fields should only play a role in the case of individual sectoral markets and not with respect to the internal market generally.

Pursuant to the philosophy underpinning its creation, for the internal market to function properly, not all relevant legislation in all Member States needs to be perfectly identical. Instead, the functionalist approach accommodates well the conclusion reached above that the idea of 'common rules for a common market' has been outlived and deemed an unnecessary restriction to the integration process.[97] Some

---

[95] Recital 2, preamble to the TFEU.
[96] G de Búrca (n 53) 135.
[97] S Weatherill, 'On the Depth and Breadth of European Integration' (n 86) 537.

barriers to trade are considered permissible whereas others, notably those that impede with the functioning of the internal market, are deemed incompatible with EU law.[98] Often, the necessary flexibility of the market can be guaranteed by minimum harmonisation, which abolishes the most detrimental barriers to trade while allowing the market to adjust itself to the changing economic and technological conditions.[99]

Apart from the legislative means of creating flexibility, most of the differentiation in the internal market occurs in the form of fairly specific opt-outs from secondary law. Like secondary law itself,[100] the opt-outs must conform to the objectives and tasks of the Union, the general principles of EU law and fundamental rights as well as be proportional as to the perceived aims.

The general principles of EU law include, among others, the respect of fundamental rights, proportionality, legal certainty, equality and non-discrimination, and effectiveness. In the context of flexibility within the internal market, the principles of equality and non-discrimination are of greatest relevance. The principle of equality is linked to the principle of solidarity[101] on the basis of the assumption that the Treaties lay out a balanced account of benefits and obligations for the Member States thereby leading to equality. A disruption of the equilibrium not only distorts equality but also solidarity between Member States.[102] However, the absoluteness of the principles of equality and solidarity depends on whether one adopts a strict or flexible understanding of the objectives of the EU.[103] Equality and solidarity between Member States are endangered primarily by a 'unilateral [breach]' by a Member State 'according to its own conception of national interest'.[104] Wherever a flexible approach has been chosen and is implemented with the approval of the EU and the other Member States, one cannot consider such a unilateral breach to have occurred. This includes derogations explicitly permitted by the Treaties. It follows that differentiation in the internal market is compatible with the principles of equality and

---

[98] A McGee and S Weatherill (n 64) 578.
[99] S Weatherill, 'New Strategies for Managing the EC's Internal Market' (n 20) 601–602.
[100] Case 11/70 *Internationale Handelsgesellschaft* EU:C:1970:114.
[101] Laid out in detail with references to case law in J Wouters (n 89) 317.
[102] Case 39/72 *Commission v. Italy* EU:C:1973:13, paras. 24–25; Case 128/78 *Commission v. United Kingdom* EU:C:1979:32, para. 12.
[103] B Grabitz and E Langeheine (n 90) 42.
[104] Case 39/72 *Commission v. Italy* (n 102) para. 24; Case 128/78 *Commission v. United Kingdom* (n 102) para. 12.

solidarity insofar as the deviations meet general approval and do not dilute the commonly agreed core as unilateral breaches. Whether primary law opt-outs, which result from political bargaining and fall outside the scope of review of the Court of Justice, can be justified in the light of the principles mentioned above is questionable,[105] even if the existence of political approval is beyond doubt.

In the same vein, the main question concerning permissible differentiation from the internal market acquis is whether one can ascertain a common set of rules that constitute the hard core of the internal market or whether the determination is entirely in the hands of the political actors. The requirement of cohesion in the internal market is qualified by the functionalist claim for establishing a well-functioning market and, as established above, unity is part of the very concept of the internal market. The unity of the internal market finds expression in its 'common and complete order'.[106] This common and complete order is precisely the objective core from which no derogations can be allowed without the EU internal market losing its distinct character. In practice, the limits of permissible differentiation to the internal market rules are often elaborated in the political process on the basis of a subjective perception of the Member States as to what level of differentiation can be accepted. This does not, however, render all differentiation compatible with the purposes of the internal market as laid out in the Treaties. The core elements include the main principles of the internal market as well as the concept of its unity. This conclusion about the internal market applies equally to the cores of the specific sectors of the internal market: any divergences from the common core must be justified in the light of the specific purpose of that policy sector to fit within the concept of a unified internal market.

4.3 Integration and Disintegration in the Expanded Internal Market

Just as the paradigm of the internal market has changed from a project to be completed to one in a constant process of development and adaptation, the discourse on European integration, too, has re-oriented to

---

[105] F Tuytschaever, *Differentiation in European Union Law* (Hart Publishing 1999) 113; G de Búrca (n 53) 143.

[106] R Barents (n 2) 208.

flexibility and differentiation.[107] The extension of the internal market to non-EU Member States by exporting the acquis is an example of limited integration into the EU without formal accession to the Union and, undoubtedly, proof of such flexibility. The question that remains is what kind of 'different Europes' can the internal market accommodate in the course of integrating third countries.[108]

While the extension of the acquis to third countries constitutes a type of flexible integration into the EU, the exported acquis and the expanded internal market do not necessarily enjoy more flexibility and differentiation than the same acquis within the EU. All four of the multilateral agreements seek to extend the EU's internal market or a sector thereof to the neighbouring countries by exporting relevant parts of the EU acquis, thus sharing both a common objective and the general means for doing so. The concrete objectives of each of the agreements, however, are worded in a slightly different manner. The following analysis focuses on the stated objectives of the four multilateral agreements as to upholding the unity inherent to the internal market with the aim of establishing the intended scope of uniformity, unity and permissible differentiation in the expanded internal market.

4.3.1 European Economic Area

The EEA EFTA countries are linked to the EU by the legal rules and principles provided in the EEA Agreement. The objective of the latter is to create a 'common economic space' between the EU Member States and the EEA EFTA countries.[109] The common economic space of the EU is the internal market, yet the EEA was not intended to become a literal extension of the internal market in its current definition. Rather, the EEA is a common economic space that comprises both the EU and the EEA EFTA States. This is affirmed by Article 2 EEA Agreement and Recital 5 of its preamble which list the free movement of goods, persons, services and capital, rules on competition law and 'strengthened

---

[107] G De Búrca and J Scott (n 27) 2; B De Witte, A Ott and E Vos (eds.), *Between Flexibility and Disintegration: The Trajectory of Differentiation in EU Law* (Edward Elgar Publishing 2017); M Cremona, 'Internal Differentiation and External Unity' in F Amtenbrink and others (eds.), *The Internal Market and the Future of European Integration* (Cambridge University Press 2019) 605;

[108] See N Walker (n 22) 356.

[109] A Lazowski, 'Box of Chocolates Integration: The European Economic Area and the Swiss Models Revisited' in S Blockmans and S Prechal (eds.), *Reconciling the Deepening and Widening of the European Union* (T.M.C. Asser Press 2007) 87, 89.

and broadened cooperation in flanking and horizontal policies' such as research and development, the environment, education and social policy as the specific objectives of the EEA. An explicit reference to a borderless area, which is a defining feature of the 'internal market' is, nevertheless, excluded.

The EEA Agreement specifies that the legal area thus created is to be 'homogeneous'. Homogeneity is one of the 'fundamental principles' of the EEA Agreement.[110] The main question is whether 'homogeneity' in this context should be understood as uniformity of law within the EEA, uniformity between EEA law and EU law, or rather the chosen and accepted path in European integration – unity constructed around a common hard core allowing for permissible differentiation. Another question is whether the internal market as extended to third countries retains the same component of unity as inherent to the EU's internal market.

When considering the uniformity/unity/homogeneity of legal orders that incorporate parts of EU law, the notion of unity assumes two dimensions.[111] The first is unity within the legal order that is created by 'exporting' the internal market rules. From an empirical point of view, it calls for comparing the adoption, implementation and application of the rules in all states parties to the respective multilateral agreement. From a functional perspective, it requires the proper functioning of the legal order in accordance with its stated aims. This dimension of unity is, subsequently, called the uniformity/unity/homogeneity of the EEA, the Energy Community, the ECAA or the Transport Community.[112] For those parts of the multilateral agreements that do not reproduce EU law, homogeneity can only appear in this dimension. The second dimension of unity, or homogeneity, pertains to the 'EU – non-EU Member States' axis. This situation is roughly similar to the relationship between the EU and its Member States but refrains from looking at the differences in the internal application of rules in the countries parties to the multilateral agreement. The two dimensions are to some extent intertwined.

---

[110] Case E-3/97 *Opel Norge* [1998] EFTA Ct Rep 1, para. 30.
[111] See H Haukeland Fredriksen, 'One Market, Two Courts: Legal Pluralism vs. Homogeneity in the European Economic Area' (2010) 79 *Nordic Journal of International Law* 481, 483.
[112] For example, 'homogeneity in the interpretation and application of the law in the EEA' in S Norberg and others, *The European Economica Area: A Commentary on the EEA Agreement* (Fritzes 1993) 187.

Recital 4 of the preamble to the EEA Agreement attempts to clarify the objective of homogeneity in the EEA:

[. . .] [T]he objective of establishing a dynamic and homogeneous European Economic Area, based on common rules and equal conditions of competition and providing for the adequate means of enforcement including at the judicial level, and achieved on the basis of equality and reciprocity and of an overall balance of benefits, rights and obligations for the Contracting Parties.

This provision suggests that 'homogeneous' in the context of the EEA is to be understood as referring to the EEA as a whole, including the EU, its Member States and the EEA EFTA States. It does not create a direct link of uniformity with the EU legal order. For a common economic space to come into existence, no uniformity as between itself and the EU's internal market is necessary because it exists independently of the EU. In this respect, the EEA must not be regarded as a legal framework resting on two distinct pillars, the EU and its Member States, on the one side, and the EEA EFTA States, on the other, notwithstanding its two-pillar institutional structure.[113] The EEA Agreement is an international agreement that derives its legal context from the EU and has set up mechanisms, which allow for legislative updates in the EEA parallel to the occurrence of legislative developments in the EU, but the EU and the EEA are not identical twins. 'Homogeneity' in the EEA Agreement should, thus, be considered as referring to the harmony between the different components of the EEA legal order.

On the uniformity–unity scale, the homogeneity of the EEA resembles the unity rather than uniformity of the EU legal order. Both strive towards integration through the creation of a single market in which total commonality is not a decisive factor. In Recital 4, the qualities of 'dynamic and homogeneous', which describe the EEA, are presented not as means of achieving a higher level of integration but rather as a characterisation of the economic area. This is similar to the idea of unity constituting an inherent part of the internal market. How the homogeneous EEA is to be achieved is explained in the same provision: the EEA is grounded on 'equality and reciprocity' and an 'overall balance of benefits, rights and obligations'.[114]

---

[113] C Baudenbacher, 'If Not EEA State Liability, Then What: Reflections Ten Years after the EFTA Court's Sveinbjornsdottir Ruling' (2009) 10 *Chicago Journal of International Law* 333, 338. The Court, too, understands the 'twin-pillar' system of the EEA as institutional rather than substantive: see Opinion 1/00 *ECAA* EU:C:2002:231, para. 7. A complete analysis is provided in Chapters 7 and 8.

[114] Recital 4, preamble to the EEA Agreement.

Recital 15 of the preamble to the EEA Agreement further elaborates on the aspect of equality, which was first introduced in Recital 4 through the idea of a balance of benefits, rights and obligations: '[the objective] is to arrive at equal treatment of individuals and economic operators as regards the four freedoms and the conditions of competition'. This provision reflects the functional character of the concept of homogeneity. The driving force behind integration in the EEA is the common objective of equality rather than the application of identical legislation that may or may not lead to equal outcomes. Further support for the functional aspect of homogeneity in the EEA can be found in Article 1 EEA Agreement:

The aim of this Agreement of association is to promote a continuous and balanced strengthening of trade and economic relations between the Contracting Parties with equal conditions of competition, and the respect of the same rules, with a view to creating a homogeneous European Economic Area [...]

Recital 15 proceeds to link EEA law with EU law by stating the objective of the contracting parties to 'arrive at, and maintain, a uniform interpretation and application of this Agreement and those provisions of Community legislation which are substantially reproduced in this Agreement [...]'. The link reflects the choice to use EU law as a framework of reference on which to base the legal framework of the EEA, but it does not create a functional link of uniformity between the two legal orders. Complete uniformity of interpretation would require both the Court of Justice and the EFTA Court to interpret the 'exported' rules in an identical manner and to follow in so doing the former's interpretation of 'original' EU law. This possibility was, however, deemed incompatible with the autonomy of the EU legal order.[115]

The above provisions strongly emphasise the EEA-internal dimension of homogeneity. The EEA legal order is homogeneous as to its own constituent elements and their application in the states parties to the EEA Agreement rather than in relation to the EU legal order. Equal conditions and the respect for the same rules, for example, do not require that the legal framework of the EEA be based exclusively on EU rules, but EU law was chosen as the substantive regulatory basis for the newly established EEA. This choice connects the EEA-internal and the EU-EEA level dimensions of homogeneity.

---

[115] See further in Chapters 6 and 8.

The normative framework of the EEA, which originates from the EU, is dynamically updated and developed along the three foundations of homogeneity, pertaining to the legislative, enforcement and judicial review procedures. On the one hand, Article 6 of the EEA Agreement provides a mechanism for the dynamic evolution of EEA acquis in line with developments in the EU internal market legislation. On the other hand, the EEA rules must be applied and interpreted in conformity with EU law following the procedures of surveillance and judicial review established under the EEA Agreement.[116] Contrary to Haukeland Fredriksen, this interpretation of Article 6 EEA Agreement does not imply the 'legal homogeneity between the EEA rules and the interpretation of the Court of Justice on underlying EU law' as an objective of the EEA Agreement.[117] Article 6 paves the ground for judicial homogeneity in terms of uniform interpretation of identically worded EU and EEA rules, but uniform interpretation shall be ensured on part of the EU by the national courts of the EU Member States and the Court of Justice, and on part of the EEA EFTA States, their respective national courts and the EFTA Court.

Hartley has suggested that homogeneity in the EEA means identical quality to EU law.[118] In a more nuanced contribution, Magnússon has substantiated the concept of homogeneity with comparable rights and obligations between the EU and the EEA EFTA States leading to comparable rights and obligations of individuals regardless of the 'side' of the EEA Agreement on which they find themselves.[119] Magnússon's interpretation constitutes another example of the distinction made between the EU and the EFTA pillars within the EEA. Yet not only the EEA EFTA States but also the EU Member States are bound by EEA rules as parties to a mixed agreement. Under the EEA Agreement, the Member States are subject to the same rights and obligations, as those conferred upon the EEA EFTA States. Differences may only occur on the institutional level owing specifically to the fact that the Court of Justice interprets the acquis in the EU pillar and the EFTA Court in the EFTA pillar of the EEA.[120]

---

[116] The EFTA Court recognises these as two foundations; see Case E-9/97 *Sveinbjörnsdóttir* [1998] EFTA Ct Rep 95, paras. 52–54.

[117] H Haukeland Fredriksen, 'The EFTA Court 15 Years On' (2010) 59 *International and Comparative Law Quarterly* 731, 733.

[118] TC Hartley, 'The European Court and the EEA' (1992) 41 *International and Comparative Law Quarterly* 841, 845.

[119] S Magnusson (n 75) 9.

[120] See further in Chapter 8.

The EEA was created as a separate legal order. It has its own objectives and methods for achieving them, and neither replicates those of the EU. According to the EFTA Court, the EEA Agreement is an 'international treaty *sui generis* which contains a distinct legal order of its own'.[121] The EFTA Court has further clarified that the EEA Agreement differs from the EU Treaties by the 'less far-reaching' depth of integration whereas both the scope and the objective of the EEA Agreement are more extensive than those of regular agreements concluded under public international law.[122]

Contesting the interpretation of the EFTA Court, Haukeland Fredriksen has contended that if anything, the EEA represents an extension of the EU legal order.[123] Displaying a high degree of integration, the EEA, indeed, represents an enhanced free trade area, the objectives of which go beyond a mere free trade area.[124] However, the level of integration envisaged in the EEA Agreement is less profound than in the EU Treaties.[125] The EFTA Court has interpreted the objectives of the EEA Agreement to be the setting up of a 'fundamentally improved free trade area but no customs union with a uniform foreign trade policy'.[126] Moreover, the EEA EFTA Member States did not, upon concluding the EEA Agreement, adhere to the EU policies on a borderless area,[127] agriculture and fisheries, taxation, economic and monetary union, and the common foreign and security policy.[128] Because of these restrictions – several of which form if not the core then at least crucial elements of the EU legal order – one cannot consider the EEA to be a true extension of the EU legal order in the broadest sense of the term.

Homogeneity in the EEA Agreement is not an objective by itself but rather a notion describing the common economic space as envisaged by the treaty makers. When assessing the level of homogeneity in the EEA, account must be taken of the same considerations as with regard to the EU legal order and the internal market. The establishment and

---

[121] Case E-9/97 *Sveinbjörnsdóttir* (n 116) para. 59.
[122] Ibid.
[123] H Haukeland Fredriksen. 'Bridging the Widening Gap between the EU Treaties and the Agreement on the European Economic Area' (2012) 18 *European Law Journal* 868, 881.
[124] Case T-115/94 *Opel Austria v. Council* EU:T:1997:3, para. 107; Case E-9/97 *Sveinbjörnsdóttir* (n 116) para. 59.
[125] Case E-9/97 *Sveinbjörnsdóttir* (n 116) para. 59.
[126] Case E-2/97 *Maglite* [1997] EFTA Ct Rep 127, para. 27.
[127] All four EFTA countries participate in the Schengen area but the Schengen Agreement is not part of the EEA Agreement.
[128] W van Gerven, 'The Genesis of EEA Law and the Principles of Primacy and Direct Effect' (1992) 16 *Fordham International Law Journal* 955, 960.

functioning of a single market require not a set of identical norms but rather a core set of elements representing the defining features of the market and/or the legal order in question. There are three possible ways of looking at the defining features of the single market created by exporting the EU internal market acquis: (1) the defining features of a single market; (2) the defining features of a single market that includes the fundamental freedoms and competition policy as in the EEA, the Energy Community, the ECAA and the Transport Community; and (3) the core of the EU internal market. The three may coincide but may also differ significantly.

The benchmark for determining the existence of unity in the internal dimension of the EEA legal order is a similar 'core' of the main elements of the agreement as in the case of the EU legal order. In the EU-EEA dimension, the yardstick should comprise the defining elements commonly shared by both the EU Treaties and the EEA Agreement. Comparing the definitions of the internal market and the common economic space of the EEA, it becomes apparent that the concept of homogeneity in the EEA pertains to the fundamental freedoms of the internal market. Since the aims of the EU are more extensive in terms of integration in Europe, it is possible that the core of the EEA single market, insofar as the EEA EFTA States do not partake in the achievement of European unity but 'merely' cooperate in trade and certain flanking areas, encompasses a more limited set of essential elements than the EU internal market.

From an empirical point of view, participation in the EEA amounts for the EEA EFTA States to a 'quasi- or semi-membership' in the EU.[129] On the one hand, the policy areas featured in the EEA Agreement are often harmonised in the EEA EFTA States on a level comparable to the EU Member States or even higher.[130] Due to the homogeneity requirement, the interpreters of EEA law in the EEA EFTA States may, at times, also take account of pre-transposition EEA legislation.[131]

The objectives of the EEA Agreement, however, rather point towards a functional interpretation of 'homogeneity' in the EU-EEA dimension. In its written observations to Opinion 1/91, the Commission claimed that the EEA was established as ' ... a homogeneous economic area in

---

[129] M Egeberg and J Trondal, 'Differentiated Integration in Europe: The Case of EEA Country, Norway' (1999) 37 *Journal of Common Market Studies* 133, 134.

[130] Ibid.

[131] See Joined Cases E-5/04, E-6/04 and E-7/04 *Fesil and Finnfjord* [2005] EFTA Ct Rep 117, para. 110.

which law, substantially identical to that which is in force within the EEC, is to be applied as uniformly *as possible*'.[132] Hence, along the EU-EEA axis absolute uniformity has not been a separate goal. In the emphasised part of the observation, leeway is left for a functional interpretation. Opting for unity rather than uniformity in the EU-EEA dimension enables the interpreters of the EEA Agreement to take into account the specific aims of the EEA vis-à-vis the EU. The benchmark for assessing the level of homogeneity in the EEA along the EU-EEA axis should, therefore, not differ from the EEA-internal dimension, and amount to unity rather than uniformity. The 'core' of the internal market expanded to the EEA EFTA States must, subsequently, be considered to include the same vertical elements as the core of the EU internal market with the possibility of excluding certain horizontal policy areas. The horizontal-vertical division of the core elements of the internal market will be the focus of the following subsections on the homogeneity requirements in the Energy Community, the ECAA and the Transport Community agreements.

4.3.2 Energy Community

The EnCT is much less elaborate in scope than the EEA Agreement. Of sectoral remit only, the Treaty aims to establish a 'single regulatory space for trade in gas and electricity'.[133] This objective is to be achieved by implementing the *acquis communautaire* on energy,[134] and creating for the contracting parties a market in Network Energy without internal frontiers.[135] In broad terms, the EnCT employs the same type of methods for expanding the EU internal market in energy as does the EEA Agreement in respect of the internal market in a more comprehensive manner. However, the EnCT features much less explicit aims concerning the link of homogeneity between the EU acquis and the Energy Community acquis, and the level of integration envisaged between the EU and the Energy Community treaties, which essentially feature identical sets of rules. Differently from the EEA Agreement, the EnCT is silent on any references to 'uniformity', 'unity' or 'homogeneity' of the Energy Community legal order vis-à-vis the EU legal order.

---

[132] General observations submitted by the Institutions and the Governments, Opinion 1/91 *EEA I* EU:C:1991:490, para. 9 (emphasis added).

[133] Recitals 10, 13 and 16, preamble to the EnCT; Article 2(1)(b) EnCT.

[134] Article 3(a) EnCT.

[135] Article 3(c) EnCT.

Closest to a reference to homogeneity is the ambitious heading of Title IV of the EnCT that reads 'The Creation of a Single Energy Market'. The Single Energy Market comprises the prohibition of quantitative restrictions and measures having equivalent effect as well as justifications for deviations equivalent to those provided in Article 36 TFEU.[136] Also, the EnCT lays out that the parties may agree upon creating a 'single market without internal frontiers' for Network Energy – hence an internal market – and take the necessary measures to that effect.[137] Yet the creation of an internal market in Network Energy that would constitute a direct extension of the EU internal energy market is not the proclaimed objective of the EnCT. Very limited in scope, this sectoral market in energy is not to cover either fiscal measures, the free movement of persons or provisions on the rights of workers.[138] Freedom of establishment may be gradually granted to Network Energy companies upon separate agreement among the parties to the Treaty,[139] but no provision on the free movement of services or capital is included.

Being closest to a true extension of the internal market by the first part of the definition, the limited substantive scope of the envisaged internal market in Network Energy, nevertheless, renders it questionable whether this particular sectoral market would, indeed, correspond to an extension of the EU internal market. Since it excludes several of the core elements of the internal market – the free movement of persons, services, capital and, unless the contracting parties decide otherwise, the freedom of establishment – it is difficult if not impossible to regard the internal market in Network Energy as a true extension of the EU internal market. The conclusion would be different if the specific nature of both the sectoral market in Network Energy and the EU internal market in energy excluded entirely elements such as the free movement of persons or services. In that hypothetical scenario, it would be impossible to regard these fundamental freedoms as essential elements of the core of the energy sector of the EU internal market and the internal market in Network Energy could, subsequently, be considered equivalent thereto.

Article 5 EnCT provides that the Energy Community is to follow the development of EU acquis in the relevant areas – energy, environment,

---

[136] Article 41 EnCT.
[137] Article 42(1) EnCT.
[138] Article 42(2) EnCT.
[139] Article 34 EnCT.

competition and renewables. Throughout the Treaty, the term 'extension of the *acquis communautaire*' is used but references to the EU acquis
do not establish any level of envisaged uniformity comparable to the
EEA Agreement. The EEA Agreement generally provides for a degree of
uniformity in its application, subject to adaptations in accordance with
Article 119 EEA Agreement.[140] Adaptations of the relevant EU acquis are
also enabled by the EnCT to suit both the institutional framework of the
EnCT and the specific situations of the contracting parties, for the sake
of investment security and optimal investments,[141] as well as by the
ECAA Agreement,[142] and the TCT.[143]

The Single Energy Market set up by the EnCT functions separately
from the EU legal order. Of sectoral scope and custom-designed for the
participants of the Energy Community, the EnCT does not present the
Single Energy Market as a literal extension of the energy sector of the EU
internal market. This approach is in principle similar to the EEA that
forms a separate legal order albeit drawing heavily on the regulatory
framework of the EU.

The EnCT does not expressly aim at ensuring uniformity either within
the Energy Community or between the acquis of the EU internal market
and the law of the Energy Community. First, the method used by the
Energy Community to update its legal framework to changes in EU law
is articulated in a less imperative manner than its equivalent in the EEA
Agreement.[144] Second, although both Article 98 EEA Agreement[145] and
Articles 25 and 42(1) EnCT[146] state that the respective legal areas *may*
amend their legal frameworks to follow changes in the EU acquis, the
EEA Agreement provides for an extensive procedural framework for
simultaneously updating EEA law to reflect relevant changes in EU
law.[147]

---

[140] On the nature of adaptation clauses, see EFTA Secretariat, 'Adaptation texts to EU acts
upon incorporation into the EEA Agreement' (2019) EFTA Bulletin 37.

[141] Articles 5 and 24 EnCT.

[142] Article 3 and Annex II ECAA Agreement.

[143] Annex II TCT.

[144] For details see Chapter 7, Section 7.1.2.2.

[145] 'The Annexes to this Agreement and Protocols [...] may be amended by a decision of
the EEA Joint Committee [...].'

[146] Article 25 EnCT reads: 'The Energy Community may take Measures to implement
amendments to the *acquis communautaire* described in [Title II], in line with the evolution of European Community law'; Article 42(1) EnCT reads: 'The Energy Community
may take Measures with the aim of creating a single market without internal frontiers
for Network Energy'.

[147] See Article 102 EEA Agreement.

The adaptation clauses of Article 24 EnCT and Article 119 EEA Agreement are comparable to Article 27 TFEU, which accommodates the possibility of temporary exceptions from internal market harmonisation measures for developing economies. Considering that the TFEU exceptions clause does not conflict with the idea of the unity of the internal market, especially given the temporary nature of the permitted derogations, if the adaptations made under Article 24 EnCT, too, are only temporary in nature, there is little reason to regard them as contrary to the idea of a uniform[148] Energy Community. The adaptation provisions do not, however, impose a temporal limitation on the adaptation of the acquis, which may lead to harmful effects on homogeneity if differing from similar adaptations applicable to the EU Member States. As concerns the single market in Network Energy, the EnCT refrains from specifying any grounds for deviation from the measures that the Energy Community may adopt in order to create the single market. Any other differentiation between the EU and the Energy Community acquis are to be introduced via the usual decision-making procedure.

For the Single Energy Market to be regarded as an extension of the EU's internal market in energy, full uniformity is not required. Unity in case of a true extension of the internal market in energy presupposes adherence to the basic set of core principles that apply to the overall concept of the single market. In the case of the EnCT, the objectives regarding uniformity with EU acquis are worded in an ambiguous manner. This imprecision is, in turn, greatly reflected in the limited scope of application of the fundamental freedoms in the Energy Community as well as in its institutional framework.[149]

4.3.3 European Common Aviation Area

Compared to the EnCT, the aims of the ECAA Agreement are significantly more ambitious and, indeed, similar to those of the EEA Agreement. The aim of the ECAA Agreement is to create a highly integrated[150] ECAA based on mutual/free access to the air transport markets of the contracting parties along with the freedom of establishment, equal conditions of competition and respect of the same rules.[151] In Opinion 1/00, the Court had the opportunity to directly compare the

---

[148] In the meaning of unity, not uniformity.
[149] Elaborated in Chapters 7 and 8.
[150] Opinion 1/00 *ECAA* (n 113) para. 2.
[151] Recital 1, preamble to the ECAA Agreement; Article 1(1) ECAA Agreement.

objectives of the ECAA and the EEA agreements. The similarity of the aims of the respective agreements was confirmed to the extent of 'extend[ing] the *acquis communautaire* to new States, by implementing in a larger geographical area rules, which are essentially those of Community law', notwithstanding the narrower, sectoral scope of the ECAA Agreement.[152] The text of the ECAA Agreement contains no explicit references to 'homogeneity'. In Opinion 1/00, however, the Court refers to the uniformity objectives of the ECAA in terms of both 'uniform interpretation' and 'homogeneous interpretation'.[153]

The basic idea of homogeneity in the ECAA, too, lies in equal conditions of access to the aviation markets of all contracting parties, both inside and outside the EU.[154] For this, Article 1 ECAA Agreement envisages free market access, freedom of establishment, equal conditions of competition and common rules in certain key areas – all based on EU acquis. Equal access to the common aviation market requires that the uniform rules as well as the permissible derogations therefrom, which are considered compatible with the idea of unity of the market, must extend to the non-EU contracting parties. Cases in point are the transitional arrangements provided in Article 27 ECAA Agreement that also occur in the EU Treaties and are generally considered an example of permissible differentiation. Homogeneity in the ECAA does not, therefore, amount to complete uniformity of rules and interpretation as the objective of the agreement – equal market access – can be fulfilled under the conditions of unity, just like in the EU internal market. The ECAA, too, is constructed upon a core of internal market principles and permissible derogations surrounded by peripheral provisions, which do not require uniform adherence in order to ensure the proper functioning of the Agreement. As in the case of the Energy Community, however, unless the specificities of the EU aviation market allow for the absence of certain fundamental freedoms, the lack of these elements in the ECAA is detrimental to the unity of the ECAA vis-à-vis the EU internal market in aviation.

4.3.4 Transport Community

The TCT does not mention as its objective the creation of a single regulatory space but instead 'the progressive integration of transport

---

[152] Opinion 1/00 *ECAA* (n 113) paras. 3 and 7.
[153] Ibid., paras. 11 and 40.
[154] Ibid., para. 9.

markets of the South East European [(SEE)] parties into the EU transport market on the basis of the relevant acquis'.[155] The TCT covers legislative integration in the areas of technical standards, interoperability, safety, security, traffic management, social policy, public procurement and the environment. Rules on non-discrimination and competition law, too, are included.[156] The acquis shall apply to all sectors of transport not already covered by the ECAA Agreement. The similarity of the ECAA and the TCT agreements points at their perceived complementary effects, providing for broad cooperation with the SEE neighbourhood across the entire transport sector.

Similar to the ECAA Agreement, the treaty makers concede that the transport markets can only be integrated gradually.[157] The specific transitional arrangements have limited duration,[158] and the transition is subject to assessments carried out by the Commission in cooperation with the SEE contracting parties concerned.[159] Despite the strong temporal conditionality, the TCT features an implicit homogeneity aim. The integration of third country markets into the single EU transport market is to be achieved by the application of the EU acquis, which shall be given 'homogeneous interpretation' throughout the Transport Community.[160] The TCT's objectives and means to achieve them do not, therefore, differ much from those featured in the other multilateral agreements under scrutiny, and the unity in the EU-TCT axis is similarly limited by the lack of application of all four fundamental freedoms.

4.3.5 The Legal Nature of Homogeneity Clauses

It was concluded, on the one hand, that the EU internal market enjoys a degree of inherent unity that forms part of its definition. The unity of a legal order, on the other hand, is necessary for upholding the balance of rights and obligations among the parties to a common undertaking. The unity in both a legal order and the internal market is determined by the presence of a distinct set of central elements – the core. In the EU-related dimension of homogeneity of the multilateral agreements, the unity of the extended internal market or a sector thereof is determined

---

[155] Article 1(1) TCT.
[156] Articles 16 and 17 TCT.
[157] Recital 6, preamble to the TCT. Compare with the almost identically worded Recital 5, preamble to the ECAA Agreement.
[158] Laid out in detail in Protocols I to VI annexed to the TCT.
[159] Article 40(2) TCT.
[160] Article 24(7) TCT.

by the core, which is characteristic to the internal market or the particular sector, be it all four fundamental freedoms and competition policy including the relevant non-economic elements or only those aspects that are relevant for the sector of the internal market in question.

In general terms, it is not justified to regard the homogeneity claim presented in the multilateral agreements any differently from unity in the EU legal order. The internal dimension of homogeneity in the multilateral agreements should, thus, be equalised with unity rather than uniformity. Concerning the link between the EU, on the one hand, and the EEA, the Energy Community, the ECAA or the Transport Community, on the other, there is neither any reason to impose on the third country counterparts a stronger obligation of adherence to EU rules than on the EU Member States. Unity should, thus, be the norm even in this dimension of homogeneity, requiring that all core elements of the internal market or a sector thereof be in place as well as the inherent unity of those elements within the limits of permissible differentiation.

The provisions of international agreements generally lay out obligations as well as the means for achieving them. A proper performance of the provisions of the multilateral agreements by employing the substantive, institutional and procedural means stipulated therein should lead to a homogeneous EEA, Energy Community, ECAA and Transport Community. The obligation of achieving a homogeneous result rests with the treaty makers and the decision-making bodies envisaged by the agreements whereas the duty to maintain homogeneity is equally the responsibility of the states parties to the agreement.

The homogeneity clauses can be considered either an obligation of result or best endeavour.[161] Obligations of result set explicit goals to be achieved, whereas obligations of best efforts require that all necessary means be employed without an imperative of reaching the goal, notwithstanding the legal character of the obligation. The latter type of obligations is particularly characteristic of public international law.[162] The distinction between a legal or normative and a non-legal, political

---

[161] French law knows *obligations de résultat* directed at achieving a result and *obligations des moyens* concerning the use of appropriate means, see EA Farnsworth, 'On Trying to Keep One's Promises: The Duty of Best Efforts in Contract Law' (1984) 46 *University of Pittsburgh Law Review* 1, 3.

[162] See P Weil, 'Towards Relative Normativity in International Law' (1983) 77 *American Journal of International Law* 413.

or pre-normative obligation lies in the enforceability of the obligation in a court or tribunal, and the possibility of incurring responsibility for non-performance.[163] The performance of the substantive provisions of an international agreement is in EU law, with regard to the EU Treaties, further strengthened by the principle of sincere cooperation,[164] and in public international law by the general principle of good faith.[165] An example of an obligation of result in EU law includes the rule of equal treatment, which 'by its nature' is enforceable in a court.[166] An example of an obligation of best endeavour is contained in Article 2 of Annex III to the ECAA Agreement providing that the ECAA contracting parties shall seek to gradually approximate their laws on state aid and competition to the EU acquis.

The homogeneity clauses of the multilateral agreements are not as explicit as the latter example and are, moreover, mostly found in the preambles to the agreements. They resemble more closely the general political objectives of the EU provided in, for example, Article 3(3) TEU than the concrete legal obligations regarding the means of establishing the internal market in the TFEU. The programmatic nature of the homogeneity clauses makes them legally unenforceable. They, therefore, serve primarily as guidance to lawmakers. As such, it is unnecessary to regard the question of homogeneity in the multilateral agreements vis-à-vis the EU legal order as a question of compliance but rather as a common objective justifying the means for its achievement.

4.4 Conclusion

Both the EU legal order in general and the internal market in particular are to some extent flexible notions. Strict uniformity is neither required nor always desirable in order to accommodate various differences between the EU Member States. Neither, however, are the EU and the internal market a collection of separate national legal orders. A certain, and important, notion of unity is inherent especially to the concept of the internal market but also to the EU legal order as a whole. The perception of unity as part of the definition of the EU and the central part of its legal order – the internal market – is closely related to the

---

[163] Ibid., 415.
[164] Article 4(3) TEU.
[165] *Nuclear Tests (Australia v. France)*, Judgment, 1974 ICJ Reports 253, 268.
[166] Case C-171/01 *Wählergruppe Gemeinsam* EU:C:2003:260, para. 58.

functional understanding of the tasks of the Union. In order for the EU to be able to successfully deliver the outcomes expected from it by the contracting parties, it is necessary that the legal order and the internal market feature a certain degree of unity. To comply with the understanding of unity, all derogations must be accepted by the other Member States either in the form of generally agreed derogations provided in the Treaties or individual opt-outs separately negotiated by the individual Member States. The limits of permissible differentiation are found in the core of the EU legal order and the internal market and amount in the latter to the four fundamental freedoms, equal conditions of competition and the relevant non-economic elements that affect the scope of the core economic principles.

As well as EU acquis, the international agreements that extend the internal market to third countries also extend the concepts of EU law and the EU's internal market as comprising a uniform set of rules. The legal orders of the EEA, the Energy Community and the ECAA feature inherent unity or homogeneity, as well as a degree of unity vis-à-vis the EU internal market. To constitute a real extension of the EU internal market or a sector thereof, the EEA, the Energy Community, the ECAA and the Transport Community legal orders must also feature the same core set of indispensable elements that are characteristic of the internal market as a whole or the corresponding sector of the EU's internal market in the case of sectoral agreements. Without a sufficient link between the international agreements exporting the acquis and the EU internal market to the extent of the core elements of the internal market, these extensions cannot, however, neither empirically nor functionally, be equalised with the conditions offered to market participants in the internal market of the EU.

5 Internal Market
The Constitutional Context

Before the famous assertion of the Court of Justice in *Van Gend en Loos* that the EEC constitutes a 'new legal order of international law',[1] the European Communities as established by the European Coal and Steel (ECSC) Treaty and the Rome Treaties were yet another example of international organisations established and functioning under public international law. Not before long, however, the Court confirmed that the legal character of the Communities, and especially of the rules created by it, went far beyond the traditional concept of an international organisation. Subsequently, the traditional conception of the effect of internationally adopted rules in the national legal orders underwent a significant change.

The following analysis is dedicated to the question of how the changing nature of the Union, which is created by a 'constitutional charter',[2] from an international organisation to a 'new legal order' affects the internal market. Focusing on four of the constitutional principles – direct effect, primacy, state liability and consistent interpretation – comparisons are made between the potential operation of internal market rules in legal settings governed by public international law, EU law and, finally, the multilateral legal orders of the EEA, the Energy Community, the ECAA and the Transport Community, which operate in a grey area between the former two.

5.1 The Effect of Internal Market Provisions in the National Legal Orders

1.1 Public International Law

The EU's founding Treaties were concluded as ordinary multilateral international agreements between the six original members of the

---

[1] Case 26/62 *Van Gend en Loos* EU:C:1963:1, para. 3.
[2] Opinion 1/91 *EEA I* EU:C:1991:490, para. 21.

European Communities – sovereign states exercising their sovereign powers. The operation of the agreements was governed by the international law of treaties and their domestic effects initially determined by the national legal systems. Pursuant to one of the most fundamental provisions of the international law of treaties, states, when concluding international agreements, only bind themselves with respect to one another. This is an expression of the concept of international legal personality and the idea that the subjects of international law can only assume rights and obligations vis-à-vis other subjects of international law. Consequently, the responsibility for a breach of an international obligation under the law of treaties rests primarily with states as the bearers of the obligation rather than the citizens of that state.

The concept of state sovereignty is the primary factor shaping the relationship between international law and domestic law and determining the effect of rules of international law origin in the domestic legal orders. In order to fulfil the obligations arising from a treaty vis-à-vis the other contracting parties, a state must in most cases first give effect to the provisions of international law by transferring them into the domestic legal system. This can be done either by a general constitutional provisions giving effect to all international agreements on the basis of a set of pre-determined criteria or by introducing each treaty into the domestic legal order separately. International law does not, however, prescribe the methods by which it should be made part of the domestic legal orders. On the international plane, states are bound by the principle of *pacta sunt servanda* provided in Article 26 of the Vienna Convention on the Law of Treaties (VCLT),[3] to perform every treaty which is binding on them in good faith.[4]

The two well-known positions on the relationship between international law and national law – monism and dualism – and their many variations have been widely discussed in literature.[5] In monist states, international obligations become part of domestic law from the moment a treaty enters into force for that state. Strict adherence to the constitutional law of the state in question is required at the moment the

---

[3] 23 May 1969, 1155 UNTS 331, 8 ILM 679.
[4] Recital 3, preamble to the VCLT.
[5] See, for example, A Aust, *Modern Treaty Law and Practice* (Cambridge University Press 2013); J Crawford, *Brownlie's Principles of Public International Law* (Oxford University Press 2012); MD Evans, *International Law* (Oxford University Press 2014); MN Shaw, *International Law* (Cambridge University Press 2014).

international obligations are assumed. No further domestic legislation is usually necessary to render the rules binding for the state and its citizens.

The fact that an international agreement has become 'the law of the land'[6] does not, however, provide definite guidance about whether citizens can extract concrete rights and obligations from its provisions. 'Self-executing' and 'non-self-executing' are terms frequently used to describe the judicial enforceability of international norms.[7] Self-executing treaties, originating in the United States (US) legal system,[8] grant rights and obligations to individuals directly from the moment the treaty has been ratified by the state. Non-self-executing treaties require implementing legislation to have an effect on individuals; their direct applicability in the domestic legal systems is contested.[9]

In dualist systems, the state assumes the rights and obligations conferred by an international agreement upon expressing its consent to be bound by the agreement and its entry into force. For the treaty to assume effect in the domestic legal order, further legislative action in accordance with domestic constitutional law is needed. The rights and obligations, which can be invoked by citizens, are provided in domestic law and not in the international agreement itself. The pure dualist model does not recognise the effect of unincorporated treaties in the domestic legal order. In practice, there exist hybrid states such as the dualist United Kingdom where unincorporated treaties can be used for interpreting domestic statutes.[10]

The self-executing character of a provision of an international agreement is generally determined by a court, either domestic or international, with the exception of treaties that explicitly require implementation by domestic legislation.[11] In monist legal systems, the judiciary usually

---

[6] Article VI of the US Constitution reads as follows: '[. . .] all Treaties made, or which shall be made, under the authority of the United States, shall be the Supreme Law of the Land'.

[7] In fact, what should be considered self-executing or not are the separate provisions of an international agreement rather than the agreement in its entirety.

[8] See Y Iwasawa, 'The Doctrine of Self-Executing Treaties in the United States: A Critical Analysis' (1985) 26 *Virginia Journal of International Law* 627, 627–628.

[9] D Sloss, 'Domestic Application of Treaties' in DB Hollis (ed.), *The Oxford Guide to Treaties* (Oxford University Press 2012) 367, 386–388.

[10] Examples of UK case law: *James Buchanan & Co. Ltd.* v. *Babco Forwarding and Shipping (UK) Ltd.* [1978] AC 141; *Fothergill* v. *Monarch Airlines Ltd.* [1981] AC 251; TC Hartley, *The Foundations of European Union Law* (Oxford University Press 2014) 204.

[11] A distinctive example subject to great controversy are the 'non-self-executing declarations' issued by the US Senate. See LF Damrosch, 'Role of the United States Senate Concerning Self-Executing and Non-Self-Executing Treaties' (1991) 67 *Chicago-Kent Law Review* 515.

decides on the direct applicability of a treaty provision, whereas in dualist legal systems the analysis is rather carried out by the legislature upon adopting the necessary implementing legislation.[12] The provisions of some treaties are commonly regarded as self-executing, also in the meaning of creating private rights that can be invoked directly by individuals. Cases in point are, increasingly, environmental and human rights treaties, such as the ECHR.[13] The task of creating appropriate remedies in the domestic legal system rests with the national legislature by virtue of Article 13 ECHR, which states that the contracting parties must ensure that 'effective remedies before a national authority' are in place. Depriving individuals of such effective recourse will constitute a direct breach of the international law obligation. Another example of international agreements containing specific provisions allowing individuals – in this case companies – to bring claims against states for breaches of their treaty obligations are international investment treaties establishing special dispute settlement tribunals.[14]

The monist-dualist dichotomy, albeit widely rehearsed, is increasingly being deemed both unnecessary and uninformative.[15] An alternative to the formalistic construction is provided by a functional method asking for the domestic courts' actual practices with international agreements granting rights to individuals.[16] The functional approach asserts that judges in dualist systems often find ways to incorporate international agreements concluded by the state whether incorporated in the domestic legal order or not, whereas judges in monist legal systems seek possibilities to avoid applying ratified treaties by relying on their non-self-executing character.[17] The growing inclination of domestic courts to give effect to unincorporated international norms has been called 'creeping monism'.[18]

---

[12] A Aust (n 5) 174.

[13] EB Weiss, 'Invoking State Responsibility in the Twenty-first Century' (2002) 96 *American Journal of International Law* 798, 809ff.

[14] G Van Harten and M Loughlin, 'Investment Treaty Arbitration as a Species of Global Administrative Law' (2006) 17 *European Journal of International Law* 121, 129.

[15] See E Denza, 'The Relationship between International and National Law' in MD Evans (ed.), *International Law* (Oxford University Press 2006) 423, 429; A von Bogdandy, 'Pluralism, Direct Effect, and the Ultimate Say: On the Relationship between International and Domestic Constitutional Law' (2008) 6 *International Journal of Constitutional Law* 397, 400.

[16] D Sloss (n 9) 368.

[17] Ibid., 376.

[18] For a definition, see MA Waters, 'Creeping Monism: The Judicial Trend toward Interpretive Incorporation of Human Rights Treaties' (2007) 107 *Columbia Law Review* 628, 633.

Courts are most likely to opt for the functional approach in cases where an international agreement creates rights either between individuals within the state or between individuals in different countries – vertical and transnational provisions, respectively.[19]

International courts, too, deal with the domestic effect of international rules, albeit more implicitly. The first international court to recognise the direct effect of treaty provisions was the Permanent Court of International Justice (PCIJ) in *Jurisdiction of the Courts of Danzig*. The PCIJ had to consider whether the '*Beamtenabkommen*' concluded between Poland and the Free City of Danzig provided the Danzig railway officials who had passed to the Polish railway service with the right to bring claims against the Polish Railways Administration.[20] The question concerned the direct effect of those provisions in the meaning of whether or not they conferred rights on individuals. The PCIJ had to establish whether the domestic effect of the provisions of an international agreement should be determined by each contracting party on the domestic plane or whether the effect of the provisions could be ascertained internationally and, thus, be extracted from the intention of the parties and the wording of the treaty.[21] The latter was affirmed.

In its reasoning, the PCIJ restated the general principle of international law according to which international agreements only bind the contracting parties, yet recognised that, if the contents of the agreement demonstrated that the essence of the international obligation was to grant rights and obligations to individuals, which can be enforced in domestic courts, then this must be considered to be the very substance of the obligation.[22] The direct effect of the *Beamtenabkommen* was established with the help of, firstly and implicitly, the sufficiently clear and unconditional wording of the provision conferring rights on individuals; and, secondly, the fact that the contracting parties through the execution of the agreement had given effect to its provisions even in the absence of implementing legislation.[23]

5.1.2 EU Law

The introduction of the principle of direct effect of international law in the domestic legal orders is not attributable to the

---

[19] D Sloss (n 9) 377–378.
[20] *Jurisdiction of the Courts of Danzig*, Advisory Opinion, 1928 PCIJ Series B No 15, 17.
[21] Ibid., 17.
[22] Ibid., 17–18.
[23] Ibid., 18.

EU.[24] However, by setting up a Court of Justice to interpret the Treaties and adjudicate on disputes arising therefrom, the European Communities were set on a path fundamentally different from other existing international organisations. From the very beginning, the EU Treaties were intended to go beyond the prevailing ad hoc recognition of the direct effect of international law by international courts and tribunals. The new type of an international organisation thereby created would not only comprise cooperation between Member States, but also penetrate the sovereignty of the Member States to a degree unprecedented in international law.

The aim of the Communities was to join together not only the Member States but also their citizens. The 'ever closer union between the peoples of Europe' as articulated in the preamble to the EEC Treaty has proven crucial for the development of EU law. Since the founding of the Communities, the 'peoples of Europe' have progressively become the European individuals. The distinction between the actors – the states and the peoples – is barely noticeable at first sight yet has assumed immense importance in the narrative of the EU and may constitute one of the main reasons for why rules of EU origin, such as the internal market acquis, function differently inside and outside the EU.

From the perspective of international treaty law, the EU Treaties are not completely revolutionary. They are concluded under international law by states as subjects of international law and are subject to the conventional rules of international treaty law comprising customary international law as well as the VCLT, which largely codifies the former. As a result, the Member States determine the international validity of the provisions of the Treaties, and their constitutional law the validity of the provisions in the national legal orders. For the monist Member States, the introduction of EU law into the national legal order was uncomplicated whereas the dualist states had to resort to implementing legislation or even constitutional amendment. The provisions of the EU Treaties are binding on all Member States and their applicability – direct or indirect – is not subject to discussion. Questions as to the direct effect of their provisions, on the contrary, continue to be subject to debate. The effect which provisions that are identical to the EU internal market

---

[24] See, for example, O Spiermann, 'The Other Side of the Story: An Unpopular Essay on the Making of the European Community Legal Order' (1999) 10 *European Journal of International Law* 763, 766.

acquis assume in the legal orders of non-EU Member States is also crucial for evaluating their effectiveness.

The distinction between the 'direct application' and 'direct effect' of EU law is, in the first place, a linguistic one. Since only the former appears in the Treaties but both are featured in the Court's case law, a need arose to substantiate them differently.[25] 'Direct applicability' denotes the immediate legal force that a legal act or a provision thereof assumes in the legal orders of the Member States, not requiring or even allowing further legislative action[26] to become 'the law of the land'. The direct applicability of EU law serves to give the same binding force to EU law provisions in all Member States leading, ideally, to their uniform application. The Treaties are directly applicable because all Member States have fulfilled the requirements under their national constitutional law to give force to them domestically. The direct applicability of regulations is not disputed owing to Article 288 TFEU, and decisions, too, can be directly applicable.[27] The enforceability of recommendations, on the other hand, is unproblematic due to their lack of binding force.

The notions of direct applicability and direct effect assume greatest relevance with respect to directives. Initially not envisaged to be directly applicable, directives were intended to reflect the more general policy objectives whereas the Member States retained 'a choice of form and methods' to achieve the planned results.[28] This idea, also expressed by the subsidiarity principle provided in Article 5(3) TEU is, however, without prejudice to the fact that the Member States are not entirely free to choose between any available implementation methods.[29] Until the passing of the implementation deadline, a directive is neither directly applicable nor directly effective.

Differently from direct applicability, direct effect concerns the objective 'nature' of the legal provisions subject to definite criteria, and not the effect attributed thereto by the constitutional law of the Member

---

[25] TC Hartley (n 10) 215; A Dashwood, 'The Principle of Direct Effect in European Community Law' (1977) 16 *Journal of Common Market Studies* 229, 230.

[26] Case 39/72 *Commission* v. *Italy* EU:C:1973:13, para. 17.

[27] Case 93/71 *Leonensio* v. *Minstero dell' Agricoltura e Foreste* EU:C:1972:39, para. 22; Case 9/70 *Grad* v. *Finanzamt Traunstein* EU:C:1970:78, para. 5.

[28] Article 288 TFEU.

[29] For restrictions in the form of 'guidelines', effectiveness and appropriateness, see case law indicated in D Curtin, 'Directives: The Effectiveness of Judicial Protection of Individual Rights' (1990) 27 *Common Market Law Review* 709, 715–716.

States.[30] Not all directly applicable regulations have direct effect,[31] whereas some decisions that are not directly applicable may still have direct effect.[32] Direct effect itself can be divided into two categories. The one called 'objective direct effect' refers to the obligations that bind the authorities of the Member States.[33] The other, 'subjective' direct effect of EU law, pertains to the possibility for individuals to derive rights from the directive that can be invoked before a court.[34] Yet, the direct effect of a provision does not depend on whether it is intended to confer rights on individuals.[35] Individuals may rely on a provision conferring individual rights because the obligation has become binding on the Member States from the date of the implementation deadline.[36] It is, moreover, not only individuals who must take action in order to ascertain the direct effect of EU law. 'Administrative direct effect'[37] requires national administrations as well as national courts to enforce the directly effective provisions.[38]

The creation of the doctrine of direct effect in EU law is not an immediate consequence of the EU constituting a 'new legal order'. Instead, the latter proclamation followed from the fact that the existence of direct effect could be determined by the Court rather than the constitutional law of the Member States. The Court's recognition of the direct effect of EU law was triggered by the idea of the EU being founded for the benefit of the peoples of Europe. The Court found that the spirit and nature of the Treaties, which reflect the will of the contracting parties, require that EU law in certain cases be enforceable directly by

---

[30] For example, Case 26/62 *Van Gend en Loos* (n 1) para. 11: 'The very nature of this prohibition makes it ideally adapted to produce direct effects in the legal relationship between member states and their subjects.'

[31] JA Winter, 'Direct Applicability and Direct Effect: Two Distinct and Different Concepts in Community Law' (1972) 9 *Common Market Law Review* 425, 435.

[32] LJ Brinkhorst, 'S.A.C.E. v. Ministry of Finance of the Italian Republic. Case 33/70. Decision of December 17, 1970. Preliminary Ruling on Request of the District Court of Brescia, Italy' (1971) 8 *Common Market Law Review* 384, 390.

[33] W van Gerven, 'Of Rights, Remedies and Procedures' (2000) 37 *Common Market Law Review* 501, 506.

[34] M Ruffert, 'Rights and Remedies in European Community Law: A Comparative View' (1997) 34 *Common Market Law Review* 307, 320.

[35] Ibid., 321.

[36] Case 103/88 *Fratelli Costanzo* EU:C:1989:256, para. 30.

[37] M Verhoeven, 'The 'Costanzo Obligation' of National Administrative Authorities in the Light of the Principle of Legality: Prodigy or Problem Child?' (2009) 5 *Croatian Yearbook of European Law and Policy* 65.

[38] Case 103/88 *Fratelli Costanzo* (n 36) paras. 31–32; Case C-224/97 *Ciola* v. *Land Vorarlberg* EU:C:1999:212, para. 33.

the EU individuals without prior action by the Member States. The Court thus interpreted the Treaties not by 'what the drafters of the Treaty had in mind but what they ought to have had in mind'.[39] The Court's teleological approach to interpreting the Treaty provisions has equipped the EU with a set of concepts and principles characteristic of a federal system and has, thereby, removed the EU legal order from a pure international law setting.[40]

In a broad sense, direct effect serves to ensure Member States' compliance with EU law. The obligation of the Member States to observe EU law includes the duty to grant rights to individuals, which the latter derive directly from EU law.[41] The fact that individuals have the possibility to hold the Member States liable for breaches of EU law before national courts is a central feature of ensuring adherence to EU law and thereby enhancing integration in the Union.[42]

At the time of the conclusion of the founding Treaties, the scope of the provisions granting rights to individuals was unique in international law. The Court stated in *Van Gend en Loos* that individuals enjoy rights 'not only where they are expressly granted by the Treaty, but also by reason of obligations which the Treaty imposes in a clearly defined way upon individuals as well as upon the Member States and upon the institutions of the Community'.[43] The position of the individuals in the EU is, moreover, reinforced by their participation in the governance of the Union via, for example, the European Parliament and the Economic and Social Committee.[44]

The reognition that EU law confers rights on individuals directly without requiring further implementation by the Member States meant that an appropriate system of enforcement had to be devised. In fact, the setting up of a judicial system composed of national courts to ensure the uniform interpretation of EU law via the preliminary ruling procedure enshrined in Article 267 TFEU was an expression of the Member States' will to grant their nationals the possibility to invoke EU law

---

[39] JA Winter (n 31) 433.

[40] A Dashwood (n 25) 245.

[41] Case C-213/89 *Factortame* EU:C:1990:257, para. 19; Joined Cases C-430/93 and C-431/93 *Van Schijndel and Van Veen* v. *SPF* EU:C:1995:441, para. 14; Case C-72/95 *Kraaijeveld* EU: C:1996:404, para. 58.

[42] See D Curtin (n 29) 712; A Dashwood (n 25) 232.

[43] Case 26/62 *Van Gend en Loos* (n 1) para. 9. The three traditional criteria for determining the existence of direct effect require the provision to be clear, unconditional and not in need of further legislative action: Case 26/62 *Van Gend en Loos* (n 1) paras. 11–12.

[44] Ibid., para. 8.

directly.[45] This leads to the other, connected doctrines of primacy of EU law, indirect effect/consistent interpretation and state liability.

The functional purpose of direct effect in EU law and the fact that the existence of direct effect is determined by the Court is to ensure the uniform application of EU law throughout the Union and to maintain unity in the EU legal order. Direct effect contributes to the 'operability' of EU law, which, through the principle of effectiveness,[46] is 'the very soul of legal rules'.[47] Since the EU aims for a level of integration unprecedented among other international organisations, it is paramount that the rules adopted by the organisation are applied uniformly across the Union. For the internal market, the uniform application of rules is central for the task of abolishing barriers to trade between Member States, especially non-tariff barriers. The three fundamental functions of the internal market that direct effect has had significant impact on include liberalisation, harmonisation and equal competitive conditions.[48] Yet lacking from full effect of EU law in the national legal systems is the horizontal direct effect of directives – the possibility for individuals to enforce the directly effective provisions of directives in disputes between themselves and other individuals rather than the state.[49]

The possible direct effect of international agreements concluded by the EU including those exporting the EU acquis is a matter slightly different from the direct effect of EU law. The Court determines the existence of direct effect of international agreements in the EU legal order[50] whereas the Member States in the instance of mixed agreements,[51] and third country contracting parties make their own determination in the light of their respective constitutional laws. Uniformity in the EU legal order is guaranteed by the fact that the provisions of international agreements that fall within the scope of EU law enjoy the same effect across the Union regardless of who – the EU or the Member States – give effect to its provisions.[52]

The EU may, together with the other contracting parties, determine the effect of the provisions of an international agreement during the

---

[45] Ibid., para. 9.
[46] Case C-213/89 *Factortame* (n 41) paras. 20–22.
[47] P Pescatore, 'The Doctrine of "Direct Effect": An Infant Disease of Community Law' (1983) 8 *European Law Review* 155, 177.
[48] A Dashwood (n 25) 232.
[49] D Curtin (n 29) 738.
[50] Case C-240/09 *Lesoochranárske zoskupenie VLK* EU:C:2011:125, para. 33.
[51] Joined Cases C-300/98 and C-392/98 *Dior* EU:C:2000:688, para. 48.
[52] Case 104/81 *Kupferberg* EU:C:1982:362, para. 14.

negotiations. If the agreement is silent on the matter, the effect of its provisions in the EU legal order will be determined by the Court.[53] The Court is, however, not bound to recognise direct effect regardless of whether the other contracting parties do so.[54] Since the effect of treaty provisions is a matter of national constitutional law and serves to protect a state's sovereign rights, granting automatic direct effect to all provisions of international agreements that satisfy the criteria for direct effect in EU law may place the EU in a less favourable position in comparison to the other contracting parties.

The court uses a two-stage test to determine the existence of direct effect of the provisions of international agreements. In the first stage, 'the spirit, the general scheme and the terms of the general agreement' are considered.[55] Reciprocity, the possibility of consultations and the existence of safeguard clauses do not, in themselves, preclude the existence of direct effect of the respective provisions,[56] but the existence of direct effect needs to be established in the context of the agreement, taking into account its object and purpose.[57] Once it has been confirmed that the purpose and nature of the agreement allow for direct effect, the *Van Gend en Loos* criteria of clarity and unconditional nature of the provision and the absence of a need to adopt further implementing measures apply.[58]

Generally, the Court has been accommodating towards the direct effect of the provisions of AAs.[59] First, in *Haegeman*, the Court considered the AA concluded between the EEC and Greece to form an integral part of Community law.[60] In *Kziber*, the Court recognised the direct effect of the national treatment provisions of the EEC-Morocco Cooperation Agreement.[61] For the purposes of establishing direct effect, the objectives of the agreement do not, however, have to amount to setting up an association with the EU or refer to future membership in the Union.[62] In

---

[53] Case 270/80 *Polydor v. Harlequin Records* EU:C:1982:43, para. 17.

[54] Case 104/81 *Kupferberg* (n 52) para. 18.

[55] Joined Cases 21–24/72 *International Fruit Company* EU:C:1972:115, para. 20.

[56] Case 104/81 *Kupferberg* (n 52) paras. 18 and 20–21.

[57] Ibid., para. 23.

[58] Ibid.; Case 12/86 *Demirel* EU:C:1987:400, para. 14.

[59] See PJ Kuijper, 'Customary International Law, Decisions of International Organisations and Other Techniques for Ensuring Respect for International Legal Rules in European Community Law' in J Wouters, A Nollkaemper and E de Wet (eds.), *The Europeanisation of International Law* (T.M.C. Asser Press 2008) 87, 98.

[60] Case 181/73 *Haegeman* EU:C:1974:41, paras. 4–5.

[61] Case C-18/90 *Kziber* EU:C:1991:36, paras. 15–22.

[62] See, for example, ibid., paras. 21–22.

Simutenkov, the Court found that the narrower scope of PCAs as compared to AAs and the EU Treaties does not necessarily limit the effect of its provisions in the EU legal order. *Simutenkov* concerned the possible direct effect of an equal treatment provision in the EC-Russia PCA. AG Stix-Hackl found that the PCA 'lags behind' the EAs with respect to its substantive content by not establishing an FTA and providing only for limited freedom of movement; the institutional set-up including the dispute resolution mechanism; as well as the fact that the PCA does not aim at an association with the EU let alone accession to the Union.[63] The Court confirmed the findings of the AG and, recalling the narrower purpose of PCAs as compared to AAs, concluded that the PCA was designed to set up a more limited partnership.[64] When considering the legal effect of the provisions of the PCA within the EU legal order, however, the Court disregarded the disparities and accorded the same direct effect to the PCA's provision on non-discrimination on the basis of nationality as to the corresponding provisions in AAs or in the EC Treaty.[65]

One of the fundamental aspects of the Court's case law on the recognition of direct effect of the provisions of international agreements concluded by the EU has been determining whether the system of reciprocal rights and obligations set up by the agreement would preclude the recognition of direct effect on behalf of the EU if it might deprive the EU of a certain advantage. This is specific to the General Agreement on Tariffs and Trade (GATT) and the succeeding WTO agreements, which are characterised by 'reciprocal and mutually advantageous arrangements' allowing for considerable flexibility of its provisions.[66] Negotiations between the contracting parties and countervailing measures form a crucial part of these agreements, and the EU would place itself in a less advantageous position by granting direct effect to their provisions in the EU legal order. This flexibility was the reason for the Court denying

---

[63] Case C-265/03 *Simutenkov* EU:C:2005:6, Opinion of AG Stix-Hackl, paras. 33–34.
[64] Case C-265/03 *Simutenkov* EU:C:2005:213, paras. 27–28 and 35. See Chapter 2, Section 2.1 at n 8.
[65] The possible grounds for derogations from the general non-discrimination clause differ, suggesting different functions of the non-discrimination clauses in the EC Treaty and the PCA, respectively, and in turn referring to the distinct objectives of the two agreements: C Hillion, 'Case C-265/03, *Igor Simutenkov* v. *Ministerio de Educación y Cultura, Real Federación Española de Fútbol*' (2008) 45 *Common Market Law Review* 815, 830. This reasoning is in line with the Court's ruling in Case 270/80 *Polydor* v. *Harlequin Records* (n 53) paras. 14–21. For detailed discussion see Section 5.3.1.3.
[66] Joined Cases 21–24/72 *International Fruit Company* (n 55) para. 21.

the direct effect of the provisions of the 1947 GATT.[67] In *Portugal* v. *Council*, the Court held that the provisions of the WTO agreements cannot be given direct effect as this would not enable the EU to adequately respond to the actions of the other contracting parties and, thus, upset the balance of reciprocal relations within the WTO.[68]

Not always, though, is the question of reciprocity decisive in recognising direct effect. The nature of development cooperation agreements, especially, predetermines that the one party is at the giving and the other at the receiving end. The provisions of the Yaoundé and Lomé Conventions, for example, have been deemed by the Court to have direct effect although being development cooperation agreements the relationship between the contracting parties is unbalanced.[69]

5.1.3 Multilateral Agreements Exporting EU Internal Market Acquis

Determining the direct effect of international agreements by authorities other than the national judiciaries is a growing trend in light of the ever-increasing regulatory cooperation between states. This holds most clearly true for the EU but direct effect may also be granted to the provisions of multilateral agreements that export the internal market acquis to non-EU Member States by institutions other than the third country national courts. Here, two dimensions of direct effect assume relevance: the possible direct effect of the provisions of these agreements in the EU legal order, and in the legal orders of the third country contracting parties.

Reciprocity is a crucial element of the EEA Agreement. With regard to the FTAs concluded between the EEC and the former EFTA countries, the Commission considered the 'balance of advantages and disadvantages' to be especially disturbed as the EFTA states assumed all of the advantages but rejected all of the disadvantages associated with Community membership.[70] The preamble to the EEA Agreement speaks of grounding the EEA on 'equality and reciprocity and [...] an overall balance of benefits, rights and obligations for the Contracting Parties'. The overall balance is significant from the point of view of establishing the direct effect of the provisions of the EEA Agreement, at least within the EU. The

---

[67] Ibid., para. 27.

[68] Case C-149/96 *Portugal* v. *Council* EU:C:1999:574, paras. 45–47.

[69] Case 87/75 *Bresciani* EU:C:1976:18, paras. 22–23; Case C-469/93 *Chiquita Italia* EU: C:1995:435, para. 35.

[70] Submissions of the Commission during the oral procedure, Case 270/80 *Polydor* v. *Harlequin Records* (n 53) 343.

EEA Agreement does not contain a reference to the peoples of the EU and the EFTA as did the original EEC Treaty, yet the preamble recognises in Recital 8 'the important role that individuals will play in the European Economic Area through the exercise of the rights conferred on them by this Agreement and through the judicial defence of these rights'.

Similar to the EU Treaties, the EEA agreement does not determine the direct applicability or direct effect of its provisions in the national legal orders. The direct applicability – but not necessarily the direct effect – of the EEA Agreement in the legal orders of the contracting parties is uncontroversial because the national procedures for making the provisions of the agreement valid in the national legal orders have been complied with upon conclusion. Regarding direct effect, the preamble to the EEA Agreement expresses the explicit will of the contracting parties to confer rights on individuals as well as to provide 'judicial defence of these rights'. The direct effect of the provisions of the EEA Agreement could be recognised with relative ease for the purposes of protecting individual rights and, possibly, beyond to achieve the effectiveness of the EEA Agreement conditional upon the fulfilment of the *Van Gend en Loos* criteria.

The EFTA Court acknowledged in *Sveinbjörnsdóttir* that the depth of integration envisaged by the EEA Agreement is less far reaching than what is provided by the EC Treaty.[71] The degree of integration in the EEA is, however, higher than in a customs union or a regular free trade area,[72] even though the EEA itself is not a customs union.[73] The Court of Justice, too, contended in Opinion 1/91 that a parallel cannot be drawn between the objectives of the EU Treaties and the EEA Agreement, which has a more limited scope.[74] The latter is, however, not conclusive in establishing the potential direct effect of the provisions of the agreement. Article 6 EEA Agreement, in fact, precludes consideration being given to the different scopes of the two agreements. The rationale is well articulated by van Gerven according to whom the direct effect of EU law, including when extended to third countries, which concerns the fundamental freedoms should not be affected by the broader scope of legislative activity of the EU in areas outside the internal market.[75]

---

[71] Case E-9/97 *Sveinbjörnsdóttir* [1998] EFTA Ct Rep 95, para. 59.
[72] Ibid., para. 59; Case T-115/94 *Opel Austria* v. *Council* EU:T:1997:3, para. 107.
[73] Case E-2/97 *Maglite* [1997] EFTA Ct Rep 127, para. 27.
[74] Opinion 1/91 *EEA I* (n 2) paras. 15–16.
[75] W van Gerven, 'The Genesis of EEA Law and the Principles of Primacy and Direct Effect' (1992) 16 *Fordham International Law Journal* 955, 977.

The Sole Article of Protocol 35 to the EEA Agreement on the implementation of EEA rules provides that the EEA EFTA States are to introduce in their national legal orders 'a statutory provision to the effect that EEA rules prevail' in cases of conflict between the EEA and national law. In Opinion 1/91, the Court found that by virtue of that provision, the homogeneity requirement in Article 6 EEA Agreement does not convey to the EEA legal order the 'essential elements' of the Court's case law, such as the principles of direct effect and primacy, 'which are irreconcilable with the characteristics of the agreement'.[76] A question still remaining is whether the principles of direct effect and primacy really are irreconcilable with the characteristics of the EEA Agreement. van Gerven, for example, finds that a broad interpretation of Article 6 EEA can also accommodate the foundational principles of EU law such as primacy and direct effect insofar as permitted by Protocol 35.[77] He asserts that the principles of direct effect and primacy form the core of the EU legal order in the absence of which in the EEA one can hardly speak of a legal order 'homogeneous' with the EU.[78] This interpretation is supported by Baudenbacher who has offered an alternative classification of the types of homogeneity in the EEA, adding to the substantive and procedural dimensions of homogeneity 'homogeneity with regard to effect'. The latter pertains to the implicit application in the EEA legal order of the foundational principles of the EU – primacy, direct effect and state liability.[79]

Noteworthy is the Court's statement in Opinion 1/91 that the EEA is established by an international agreement that 'essentially, merely creates rights and obligations as between the contracting parties and provides for no transfer of sovereign rights to the inter-governmental institutions which it sets up'.[80] Through the Court's argumentation in *Van Gend en Loos*, the aims of the EEA Agreement regarding individuals in its legal order and the homogeneity claim, strong support is presented for the recognition of the equivalence of the 'essential characteristics' in the EU Treaties and the EEA Agreement,[81] as well as the direct effect

---

[76] Opinion 1/91 *EEA I* (n 2) paras. 27–28. See also S Magnússon and ÓÍ Hannesson, 'State Liability in EEA Law: Towards Parallelism or Homogeneity?' (2013) 38 *European Law Review* 167, 168.

[77] W van Gerven, 'The Genesis of EEA Law' (n 75) 971.

[78] Ibid., 973.

[79] C Baudenbacher, 'The EFTA Court and Court of Justice of the European Union: Coming in Parts but Winning Together' in *The Court of Justice and the Construction of Europe: Analyses and Perspectives on Sixty Years of Case-law* (T.M.C. Asser Press 2013) 183.

[80] Opinion 1/91 *EEA I* (n 2) para. 20.

[81] W van Gerven, 'The Genesis of EEA Law' (n 75) 979.

of the provisions of the EEA Agreement under the *Van Gend en Loos* criteria.

The case law of the Court demonstrates clearly its willingness to extend the interpretation of EU law, including direct effect, to the identical provisions found in the EEA Agreement. First, in *Opel Austria*, the Court of First Instance (CFI, now General Court) accorded direct effect in the EU legal order to Article 10 EEA Agreement drawing directly on the case law setting out the conditions for direct effect in the EU.[82] *Opel Austria* has since been followed by a number of other cases,[83] proving that the recognition of identical interpretation as well as the direct effect of exported acquis vis-à-vis EU law is not considered as problematic.

The monopoly of determining the effect of the provisions of the EEA Agreement in the national legal orders of the EEA EFTA States does not, however, rest with the Court of Justice but with the national courts of the EEA EFTA States and, eventually, the EFTA Court. In *Restamark*, the EFTA Court established for the first time that a provision of EEA law fulfils the conditions for being unconditional and sufficiently precise to have direct effect.[84] The EFTA Court, in turn, referred to the *Manghera* decision of the Court of Justice[85] in which the Court established the direct effect of 37(1) EC Treaty, which is the equivalent of Article 16 EEA Agreement considered in the *Restamark* case.[86] With the *Restamark* ruling, the EFTA Court filled the gap in the EFTA pillar of the EEA Agreement as concerns the direct effect of the provisions of the latter, yet with respect to rules that had already been implemented in the national legal order, hence the notion 'quasi-direct effect'.[87] The relationship between non-implemented EEA law and national law, including the possible direct effect of the former, is subject to a decision by the EEA EFTA States and their wish to, thereby, avoid a violation of EEA law without escaping the obligation to duly transpose directives into domestic law.[88]

---

[82] Case T-115/94 *Opel Austria* v. *Council* (n 72) paras. 100–102.
[83] Case C-355/96 *Silhouette* EU:C:1998:374, para. 36; Case C-465/01 *Commission* v. *Austria* EU:C:2004:530; Case C-85/12 *LBI* v. *Kepler Capital Markets* EU:C:2013:697.
[84] Case E-1/94 *Restamark* [1994–1995] EFTA Ct Rep 15.
[85] Case 59/75 *Manghera* EU:C:1976:14.
[86] Case E-1/94 *Restamark* (n 84) para. 79.
[87] C Baudenbacher, 'If Not EEA State Liability, Then What: Reflections Ten Years after the EFTA Court's Sveinbjornsdottir Ruling' (2009) 10 *Chicago Journal of International Law* 333, 358.
[88] Case E-1/07 *Criminal proceedings against A* [2007] EFTA Ct Rep 246, para. 41.

The possible direct effect of the provisions of the multilateral sectoral agreements has not been clarified to the same extent as with regard to the EEA. The preamble to the EnCT makes no reference to the role of individuals. Recital 7 of the preamble states that the 'Parties', that is, the Union and the non-EU contracting parties have resolved to 'establish an integrated market in natural gas and electricity, based on common interest and solidarity'. It may, nevertheless, be possible to extract the creation of individual rights from Recital 12 of the preamble, which expresses the aim of furthering 'high levels of gas and electricity provision to all citizens based on public service obligations' whereas the overall aim of the agreement is to create 'a single regulatory space'.[89] Article 94 EnCT provides for consistent interpretation of the terms and concepts of the treaty with the interpretation provided by the Court, yet the limited reference renders it doubtful whether the Treaty is able to convey a similar degree of homogeneity between EU law and the exported acquis as the EEA Agreement.

The ECAA Agreement and the TCT differ in this regard slightly from the EnCT. Recital 2 of the preamble to the ECAA Agreement and Recital 3 of the preamble to the TCT provide that 'the rules concerning the [ECAA/Transport Community] are to apply on a multilateral basis within the [ECAA/Transport Community]'. The preamble to the ECAA Agreement mentions that the agreement is concluded in order to provide 'mutual market access to the air transport markets of the Contracting Parties and freedom of establishment, with equal conditions of competition, and respect of the same rules'.[90] Insofar as the agreement is envisaged to regulate market relations among the specific group of air transport companies the latter can be considered as the economic operators who could, possibly, claim the direct effect of the provisions of the ECAA Agreement. Recital 7 of the preamble to the TCT makes an explicit reference to transport operators who must not be treated in a discriminatory manner regarding their access to transport infrastructures, hence affirming a personal dimension of the Treaty. Furthermore, Articles 16 ECAA Agreement and Article 19 TCT replicate, in essence, Article 6 EEA Agreement as concerns the conform interpretation of identical provisions. Differently from the EEA Agreement, however, the sources of authoritative interpretation in the ECAA and the Transport Community include the European Commission.

---

[89] Recital 13, preamble to the EnCT.
[90] Recital 1, preamble to the ECAA Agreement.

The object and purpose of a treaty cannot, nevertheless, be derived from its stated objectives only. The nature of the provisions, too, reflects the intention of the contracting parties. In the cases of the EnCT, the ECAA Agreement and the TCT, the intention of the contracting parties must also be deduced from the fact that the identical acquis can have direct effect in the EU legal order as the agreements strive after a certain level of homogeneity with the original EU acquis. It can thus be concluded that the provisions of the multilateral sectoral agreements can, in the light of the objectives of the agreements, have direct effect under conditions comparable to those invoked in the EU and the EEA. The fundamental difference between the EU and the EEA, on the one hand, and the Energy Community, the ECAA and the Transport Community, on the other, lies in the institutional framework set up by the agreements, especially the absence of a court endowed with jurisdiction to determine the effect of the rules of the agreements in the national legal orders. In the non-EU contracting states, therefore, direct effect is largely to be determined by the national courts.[91]

5.2 The Hierarchy of Norms and Rules of Conflict between Internal Market Rules and National Legislation

5.2.1 Public International Law

Differently from the effect of international law in the domestic legal orders, the hierarchy of norms cannot be determined by the international rules themselves or by international courts but falls exclusively within the realm of domestic constitutional law. For example, some monist countries such as the Netherlands grant international treaties a rank higher than ordinary domestic laws, whereas others such as the United States do not. In dualist countries, where international agreements are incorporated into the domestic legal system by domestic laws, the rank assumed by the international law provisions is usually equal to that of the act giving force to it domestically. In consequence, a later statute can override an earlier one according to the principle of *lex posterior derogat prior* unless the international law instrument itself establishes its rank. The fact that international law

---

[91] Unless the third countries have agreed to a possibility to obtain binding preliminary rulings from the Court of Justice: see Chapter 8, Sections 8.2.2.4 and 8.2.2.5.

obligations can thereby be infringed assumes relevance primarily on the international plane and not in the domestic legal order.

The responsibility of states is to give effect to their obligations incurred under international law. States are, thus, bound to ensure that treaties which have been incorporated in the domestic legal systems are given proper effect domestically. A failure to correctly implement a treaty by duly amending or repealing domestic law cannot justify a breach of an international law obligation under Article 27 VCLT. Depending on the treaty's provisions on dispute settlement, the breach can be enforced by other states or international organisations or, in some cases such as the ECHR, the EU Treaties and international investment agreements, also by individuals. The state can also incur liability for damages.[92] The actual rank of international law in the domestic legal order assumes significance only in cases where the international law instrument provides concrete implementation methods.[93]

5.2.2 EU Law

In the EU, the hierarchical relationship between EU law and national law was, to a certain extent, left for the national legal orders to determine. In *Costa* v. *ENEL*, the Court ruled that EU law takes precedence over conflicting national law.[94] Together with direct effect, the primacy of EU law is a key principle of the Union's constitutional set-up, even suggested to be the foundation of the EU's constitutional order.[95] The principle appears in Declaration No 17 annexed to the Treaties and is substantiated with references to the case law of the Court. The fact that the Court opted for proclaiming precedence rather than establishing a general rule and deeming invalid the conflicting national rules means that the primacy of EU law does not constitute an absolute rule of hierarchy.[96] The reasoning of the Court drew, once again, on the 'terms and the spirit of the Treaty' and established that the reciprocal system of the EU cannot allow national measures to prevail over the EU

---

[92] A Aust (n 5) 161.

[93] TC Hartley (n 10) 206.

[94] Case 6/64 *Costa* v. *ENEL* EU:C:1964:66, 594.

[95] B De Witte, 'International Agreement or European Constitution?' in JA Winter and others (eds.), *Reforming the Treaty on European Union: The Legal Debate* (Kluwer Law International 1996) 3, 12–13.

[96] 'Primacy of application' as compared to 'primacy of validity': see FC Mayer, 'Supremacy – Lost? Comment on Roman Kwiecien' in P Dann and M Rynkowski (eds.), *The Unity of the European Constitution* (Springer 2006) 87, 88.

legal system. In the meantime, the Court avoided fully separating the EU from the Member States, which are 'intimately and even organically tied'.[97] The Court's reasoning rested on the need to attain the objectives of the Treaties and to avoid the discriminatory behaviour which they prohibit.

The primacy principle was established with reference to Article 189 EEC Treaty (now Article 288 TFEU), which grants direct applicability to regulations.[98] The conclusion of the Court is explainable in the light of the general rationale by which the provisions that determine the means to be employed in order to introduce an international law measure into the EU legal order should not be overridden by national legislation. Adopting additional national measures would, possibly, defeat the objective of the measure, which includes uniform application.

The principle of primacy emerged from the Court's teleological inter-pretation of the Treaties with the purpose of ensuring the uniformity and effectiveness of EU law.[99] The teleological and effectiveness-driven approach is generally characteristic of international organisations and multilateral cooperation schemes.[100] The primacy of EU law requires that the validity of EU rules be determined only with relation to EU law rather than national law, including even the fundamental principles of national constitutional law.[101] The primacy of EU law vis-à-vis provi-sions of national constitutions has been established in a number of cases.[102] The most significant concern of the Member States – the protection of fundamental rights by their constitutions – is partly resolved by Article 6(3) TEU, which provides that the EU legal order protects fundamental rights originating both from the ECHR and from the constitutional traditions common to the Member States. EU law accommodates fundamental rights as general principles of EU law[103] as well as via the Charter.

The principle of primacy does not constitute complete supremacy over national laws. The national legal systems are protected, first, by

---

[97] Case 6/64 *Costa* v. *ENEL* EU:C:1964:51, Opinion of AG Lagrange, 605.
[98] Case 6/64 *Costa* v. *ENEL* (n 94).
[99] Case 106/77 *Simmenthal* EU:C:1978:49, para. 18; Case 11/70 *Internationale Handelsgesellschaft* EU:C:1970:114, para. 3.
[100] O Spiermann (n 24) 788.
[101] Case 106/77 *Simmenthal* (n 99).
[102] For example, Case C-285/98 *Kreil* EU:C:2000:2; Case C-462/99 *Connect Austria* v. *Telekom-Control-Kommission* EU:C:2003:297; Case C-213/07 *Michaniki* EU:C:2008:731.
[103] Case 11/70 *Internationale Handelsgesellschaft* (n 99) para. 4.

the initial adoption or transposition of the EU Treaties, which has taken place pursuant to the national constitutions and by which they have accepted the EU legal order; second, by the principle of conferral that limits the Union's powers to those conferred upon it by the Member States; third, by the fact that EU law which has been adopted *ultra vires* is invalid; and, fourth, by the impossibility for the Court to declare national law invalid. Yet, while national courts may be faced with questions regarding the validity of EU legal acts, the exclusive jurisdiction to declare EU acts invalid is vested with the Court under Article 263 TFEU.[104]

The fact that the principle of primacy, too, was enforced by the Court distinguished the EU legal order and judicial structure from other international organisations established to the date of the founding of the European Communities. Similar to direct effect, the actual effect of the principle of primacy is, however, subject to its acceptance by national courts.[105] Whereas direct effect is to some extent determined by the nature of the international rule, the hierarchy of the sources of law is established solely by the legal order. Moreover, while the principle of direct effect does not infringe upon national legislation to the extent that it does not affect the application of national law, the principle of primacy renders conflicting national law inapplicable. It is not surprising, therefore, that the primacy of EU law has been challenged in national courts and that the latter have been called upon to condition their acceptance of EU law in the light of the national constitutions.[106]

5.2.3 Multilateral Agreements Exporting EU Internal Market Acquis

Whether the EU internal market acquis takes precedence over conflicting national norms in the third states parties to the multilateral agreements exporting the acquis depends primarily on their domestic legal orders owing to the limits of the jurisdiction of the Court as concerns these agreements.

---

[104] Case 314/85 *Foto-Frost v. Hauptzollamt Lübeck-Ost* EU:C:1987:452, para. 20; Joined Cases C-143/88 and C-92/89 *Zuckerfabrik Süderdithmarschen and Zuckerfabrik Soest* EU:C:1991:65, para. 17.

[105] See also F Morgenstern, 'Judicial Practice and the Supremacy of International Law' (1950) 27 *British Yearbook of International Law* 42, 91.

[106] For example, 2 BvR 197/83 *Solange II* [1986] BVerfG 73, 339; 2 BvR 2134, 2159/92 *Maastricht* [1993] BVerfG, 89, 155; 2 BvE 2/08 et al *Lissabon* [2009] BVerfG 123, 267; see also J Baquero Cruz, 'The Legacy of the Maastricht-Urteil and the Pluralist Movement' (2008) 14 *European Law Journal* 389.

In Opinion 1/91, the Court found that the principles of primacy and direct effect did not necessarily form part of the EEA legal order. Contrary to the EU where the Member States have surrendered part of their sovereignty and the Treaties bind not only the states but also their nationals, the EEA was, according to the Court, founded by an international agreement that only affects the contracting parties and not their nationals.[107] As demonstrated, though, this is not exactly the case with the EEA.[108]

Protocol 35 to the EEA Agreement provides that the EEA Agreement does not entail a transfer of legislative powers to any institutions of the EEA. The effectiveness of EEA law is to be ensured by the obligation of the contracting parties to introduce in their national legal orders a statutory provision giving precedence to EEA rules in cases of conflict. The direct effect of EEA law is, however, only fully realised when the EEA rules also enjoy primacy in the EEA.[109] The EFTA Court has, therefore, established a 'quasi-primacy'[110] of the EFTA pillar of the EEA Agreement.[111] Naturally, this only affects provisions that have been implemented in the national legal orders of the EEA EFTA States and create rights for individuals.[112] Differently from the Court of Justice, however, the EFTA Court did not need to analyse the nature of the EEA to acknowledge the principle of primacy. Instead, the EFTA Court based its argumentation on Protocol 35 and its own prior recognition of the 'quasi-direct effect' of the provisions of the EEA Agreement that have been implemented by the EEA EFTA States.

The EnCT, the ECAA Agreement and the TCT are silent on the question of primacy. The non-EU and non-EEA EFTA contracting parties to these agreements are, thereby, bound to implement the agreements in good faith,[113] while the relationship between the agreements and the national legal orders is governed by the rules of public international law and national constitutional law. One significant limitation to extending the principle of primacy to the non-EU EEA contracting parties to these agreements is the fact that there is no court to establish the principle in

---

[107] Opinion 1/91 *EEA I* (n 2) para. 21; Case 26/62 *Van Gend en Loos* (n 1).
[108] See Section 5.1.3.
[109] V Kronenberger, 'Does the EFTA Court Interpret the EEA Agreement as If It Were the EC Treaty? Some Questions Raised by the Restamark Judgment' (1996) 45 *International and Comparative Law Quarterly* 198, 210.
[110] C Baudenbacher, 'If Not EEA State Liability, Then What' (n 87) 358.
[111] Case E-1/01 *Einarsson* [2002] EFTA Ct Rep 1, paras. 51–55.
[112] Ibid., paras. 52–53.
[113] Article 6 EnCT; Article 4 ECAA Agreement; Article 4 TCT.

an authoritative manner except for the Court of Justice with respect to the application of the agreements in the EU legal order and the domestic legal orders of the EU Member States, where applicable.[114] International law that is binding on the EU forms part of the EU legal order without any implementing legislation.[115] The jurisdiction of the Court with respect to the application of the EnCT, the ECAA Agreement and the TCT in the non-EU contracting states is, however, very limited.

Another question about the primacy of the exported acquis pertains to the possibility of inserting the principle into the framework of those agreements at all. When establishing the primacy of EU law, the Court relied on the nature of EU law that necessitated the primacy of application of EU law vis-à-vis national law, as well as the principles of effectiveness and uniformity of EU law. The effectiveness and uniformity of the multilateral agreements could, possibly, also justify the principle of primacy in those agreements. It would also be conceivable to insert a primacy rule similar to the one found in the EEA Agreement directly into the treaties. However, the narrower scope and simpler institutional structure of the sectoral agreements witness of a lower degree of integration thereby envisaged as well as the difficulty of motivating the ensuing loss of sovereignty on behalf of the third countries.

A primacy principle might also conflict with the constitutional law of the non-EU treaty partners. On the one hand, since the EU Treaties do not apply to the third countries, the latter are not protected by the Union's fundamental rights guarantees under Article 6 TEU. Also, their constitutional traditions fall outside the range of principles, which affect the application of the internal market acquis in the EU legal order.[116] On the other hand, the protection of fundamental rights in the EU legal order as reflected in the exported acquis could be considered adequate by the third countries. In the EEA, it might be possible to ensure the application of fundamental rights via the homogeneity clauses of Articles 1 and 6 EEA Agreement in spite of neither the Charter nor the ECHR[117] forming part of the EEA Agreement; also, from the fact that the EEA Agreement creates individual rights an interpretation can be derived of the identical acquis that is homogeneous with

---

[114] Institutional aspects are discussed, in detail, in Chapter 8.
[115] Case 181/73 *Haegeman* (n 60) paras. 3–6.
[116] H Haukeland Fredriksen, 'One Market, Two Courts: Legal Pluralism vs. Homogeneity in the European Economic Area' (2010) 79 *Nordic Journal of International Law* 481, 491.
[117] All EEA EFTA States as well as the non-EU and the non-EEA contracting parties to the multilateral sectoral agreements except for Kosovo are parties to the ECHR.

the interpretation provided by the Court, which takes account of the protection of fundamental rights.[118] Furthermore, in the Oporto Protocol which guides the interpretation of the EEA Agreement, it was agreed that insofar as and until the EEA Agreement does not provide for the fulfilment of the existing treaty obligations of the contracting parties including those providing for individual rights, the latter agreements continue to be applied.[119] This concerns most directly human rights treaties and the protection of fundamental rights.

5.3 The Effective Application and Enforcement of the Internal Market Rules

5.3.1 Consistent Interpretation

5.3.1.1 Public International Law

One further possibility of increasing the effectiveness of a legal system is through the choice of interpretative methods. The rules for interpreting international agreements are laid down in Articles 31–33 VCLT, resulting from comprehensive analysis conducted by the International Law Commission (ILC), which reflects customary international law.[120] The general rules provided in Article 31(1) VCLT read as follows:

A treaty shall be interpreted in good faith in accordance with the ordinary meaning to be given to the terms of the treaty in their context and in the light of its object and purpose.

Should the result of the interpretation carried out on the basis of Article 31 VCLT prove inadequate or when the situation requires that the preliminary interpretation be confirmed, a secondary means of recourse is provided by Article 32 VCLT, which lists the 'preparatory work of the treaty and the circumstances of its conclusion' as additional sources of interpretation.

---

[118] W Kälin, 'The EEA Agreement and the European Convention for the Protection of Human Rights' (1992) 3 *European Journal of International Law* 341, 341–342 and 347–348. On the EFTA Court's practice, see E-U Petersmann, 'Human Rights, International Economic Law and "Constitutional Justice"' (2008) 19 *European Journal of International Law* 769, 785.

[119] Joint Declaration on the relation between the EEA Agreement and existing agreements, annexed to the EEA Agreement.

[120] *Kasikili/Sedudu Island (Botswana/Namibia)*, Judgment, 1999 ICJ Reports 1045, 1059; *Territorial Dispute (Libyan Arab Jarnahiriya/Chad)*, Judgment, 1994 ICJ Reports 6, 21.

Lauterpacht has divided the principles guiding the interpretation of treaties into two categories – a restrictive literal interpretation, and a teleological interpretation promoting the principle of effectiveness.[121] Literal interpretation is strongly connected to the idea of state sovereignty. It helps ensure that no encroachment upon state sovereignty to which the contracting parties have voluntarily consented will go beyond a literal analysis of what was established at the stage of conclusion. Teleological interpretation seeks to go beyond the textual construction and draws on the object and purpose of the treaty, which may have to be inferred implicitly from the wording of the treaty provisions.[122]

If the provisions of a treaty are worded in a clear manner, there is no need to go beyond a textual interpretation for reasons other than to confirm its correctness.[123] There is no strict hierarchy between the two methods.[124] Pursuant to Article 31(1) VCLT, the ordinary meaning of the terms of the treaty is to be construed in the light of the object and purpose and the context of the agreement, thus accommodating both methods,[125] with a certain priority given to textual interpretation.[126]

Article 27(1) VCLT codifies the maxim *ut res magis valeat quam pereat*, which reflects the principle of effectiveness. The principle requires that whenever a choice can be made between two possible interpretations of a treaty of which one gives effect to the provision and the other does not, the former should be given preference due to the principles of good faith and the object and purpose of the treaty.[127] The interpretation should not, however, lead to a result that does not correspond to the

---

[121] H Lauterpacht, 'Restrictive Interpretation and the Principle of Effectiveness in the Interpretation of Treaties' (1949) 26 *British Yearbook of International Law* 48.

[122] E Gordon, 'The World Court and the Interpretation of Constitutive Treaties: Some Observations on the Development of an International Constitutional Law' (1965) 59 *American Journal of International Law* 794, 796.

[123] *Acquisition of Polish Nationality*, Advisory Opinion, 1923 PCIJ Series B No 7, 20; *Aegean Sea Continental Shelf*, Judgment, 1978 ICJ Reports 3, 22; ILC Draft Articles on the Law of Treaties with commentaries, (1966) II *Yearbook of the International Law Commission*, 220, para. 11.

[124] DP O'Connell, *International Law* (Stevens & Sons 1970) 254.

[125] RY Jennings, 'Treaties' in M Bedjaoui (ed.), *International Law: Achievements and Prospects* (Martinus Nijhoff Publishers 1991) 135, 145.

[126] A Aust (n 5) 209.

[127] ILC Draft Articles on the Law of Treaties with commentaries (n 123) 219, para. 6; *Free Zones of Upper Savoy and the District of Gex*, Order, 1929 PCIJ Series A No 22, 13; *Legal Consequences for States of the Continued Presence of South Africa in Namibia (South West Africa) notwithstanding Security Council Resolution 276 (1970)*, Advisory Opinion, 1971 ICJ Reports 16, 35.

intention of the parties as expressed in the 'letter and spirit' of the treaty, or amount to treaty revision.[128]

Both international and domestic courts employ different procedures and seek guidance in different principles of treaty interpretation.[129] Notably, in dualist legal systems when international agreements are transposed into the domestic legal order, the domestic courts must combine the domestic procedures and principles of interpretation with the requirement to ensure compliance with the state's international law obligations.[130] As long as the former can accommodate the latter and the real intent of the parties will not become obscured, no problems will arise on the international plane. In most cases, the choice between interpretative methods is not about those that have some effect and those that have none but instead about the different levels of effectiveness.[131] Treaties establishing international organisations – constitutive treaties – are particular because they create evolving legal regimes; moreover are more contracting parties usually involved than the original signatories whose intent should be looked for.[132]

The interpretation of constitutive treaties falls within the realm of 'international constitutional law'.[133] The intent of the parties to such treaties tends to be the decisive factor in the development of the legal order thereby created,[134] as well as when resolving uncertainties about the interpretation of comprehensive agreements, which cover a plethora of legal relationships. An ambiguous provision should therefore be construed in a manner allowing for the achievement of the purpose of the agreement by, first, seeking a way to extend the application of the agreement over the specific legal question and, second, by considering

---

[128] *Interpretation of Peace Treaties (second phase)*, Advisory Opinion, 1950 ICJ Reports 221, 229; ILC Draft Articles on the Law of Treaties with commentaries (n 123) 219, para. 6.

[129] MA Rogoff, 'Interpretation of International Agreements by Domestic Courts and the Politics of International Treaty Relations: Reflections on Some Recent Decisions of the United States Supreme Court' (1996) 11 *American University Journal of International Law and Policy* 559, 609–610.

[130] MF Sturley, 'International Uniform Laws in National Courts: The Influence of Domestic Laws in Conflicts of Interpretation' (1986) 27 *Virginia Journal of International Law* 729; AM Donner, 'National Law and the Case Law of the Court of Justice of the European Communities' (1963) 1 *Common Market Law Review* 8, 9.

[131] H Lauterpacht (n 121) 70.

[132] E Gordon (n 122) 797.

[133] T Opsahl, 'An International Constitutional Law?' (1961) 10 *International and Comparative Law Quarterly* 760, 768.

[134] E Gordon (n 122) 798.

the agreement as an authoritative source for dealing with the issue in question.[135]

When interpreting constitutive treaties, special attention is given to the competences attributed to the international organisation or regime, leading to a frequent use of teleological interpretation by courts, especially in instances where the competences have to be asserted by implication.[136] This observation is coherent with the modern regime theory, which focuses on international regimes as opposed to international organisations. International regimes can be defined as 'governing arrangements constructed by states to coordinate their expectations and organize aspects of international behaviour in various issue-areas',[137] comprising principles and norms, specific rules, procedures and programs.[138] Regime theory influences the interpretative methods of international agreements by leading the interpreters towards a broader perspective of maintaining and developing the regime.[139] This approach is clearly reflected in the case law of the Court of Justice. In turn, the national courts of the EU Member States must, when interpreting EU law, depart from the national canons of interpretation of national legislation and observe the EU's broader integration objectives. In international law, it is unusual for treaties themselves to create an interpreting mechanism, although treaty bodies may be tasked with questions of interpretation.[140] The ECHR, the EU Treaties and the EEA Agreement are among the limited number of treaties that set up a court with an express mandate to interpret the constitutive instrument.

5.3.1.2 EU Law

In order to avoid fragmentation in the interpretation of EU law and to preserve the autonomy of the EU legal order, the Treaties provide a stable framework for treaty interpretation. EU law is interpreted by the EU institutions and the Court of Justice as well as by the national authorities and courts. Article 19 TEU confers the Court with the task of ensuring that the law is observed in the interpretation and application

---

[135] MA Rogoff (n 129) 570.

[136] E Gordon (n 122) 816.

[137] F Kratochwil and JG Ruggie, 'International Organization: A State of the Art on an Art of the State' (1986) 40 *International Organization* 753, 759.

[138] MA Levy, OR Young and M Zürn, 'The Study of International Regimes' (1995) 1 *European Journal of International Relations* 267.

[139] OR Young, 'Regime Dynamics: The Rise and Fall of International Regimes' in SD Krasner (ed.), *International Regimes* (Cornell University Press 1983) 93.

[140] A Aust (n 5) 207.

of the Treaties. Article 267 TFEU, moreover, provides for a preliminary reference procedure in which the national courts may, and highest courts must, when doubtful about the correct interpretation of EU law, have recourse to the Court for an authoritative interpretation. Under Article 267(b) TFEU, the Court is the only judicial body that may rule on the validity of secondary EU law.[141] Moreover, the Court holds the monopoly of interpretation of the Treaties by virtue of Article 344 TFEU, which precludes the Member States from submitting a dispute arising from the Treaties to a dispute settlement mechanism other than those provided for in the Treaties. All of the above applies equally to international agreements concluded by the EU.

One of the specific methods of ensuring the effectiveness of EU law and coherence in the EU legal order is consistent interpretation. Originating from the principle of sincere cooperation enshrined in Article 4(3) TEU and 'inherent in the system of the Treaty',[142] it allows for a rule to be construed in the light of another, hierarchically higher-standing rule, thus avoiding a conflict between the two and refraining from challenging the validity of either. Consistent interpretation can be employed in the dimensions of national law–EU law, secondary–primary EU law, as well as EU law–public international law.[143]

Directive-conform interpretation, or 'indirect effect', is the most prominent area of application of consistent interpretation. The doctrine entails an obligation on behalf of the national courts to interpret all national law,[144] whether or not intended to implement a directive at hand, 'in the light of the wording and the purpose of the directive' in order to achieve the objectives of the latter.[145] The *effet utile* of unimplemented directives lacking direct effect needs to be achieved by 'any appropriate measure, general or particular'.[146] Whereas the doctrine of direct effect emerged out of a need to ensure adequate protection of the rights of individuals where Member States had failed to give effect to directly applicable provisions,[147] consistent interpretation assumes relevance in instances of a directive lacking direct effect, that is, when

---

[141] Case 314/85 *Foto-Frost* v. *Hauptzollamt Lübeck-Ost* (n 104).
[142] Joined Cases C-397/01 to C-403/01 *Pfeiffer* EU:C:2004:584, para. 114.
[143] G Betlem, 'The Doctrine of Consistent Interpretation – Managing Legal Uncertainty' (2002) 22 *Oxford Journal of Legal Studies* 397, 398.
[144] Case C-106/89 *Marleasing* EU:C:1990:395, para. 8.
[145] Case 14/83 *von Colson* EU:C:1984:153, para. 26. This includes the case law of the national courts: Case C-456/98 *Centrosteel* v. *Adipol* EU:C:2000:402, para. 17.
[146] Article 4(3) TEU.
[147] See Section 5.1.2.

the *Van Gend en Loos* criteria do not apply,[148] or in horizontal relations between individuals.[149] Both the doctrines of direct effect and consistent interpretation concern the effective judicial protection granted to individuals, which can be considered a general principle of EU law.[150]

The duty of consistent interpretation also applies to national legislation that has duly implemented a directive because the mere fact of transposition does not rule out the possibility of a national court 'de-implementing' a directive by deficient interpretation.[151] Consistent interpretation for the purpose of providing accurate interpretation for a piece of national legislation that has correctly implemented a directive should, thus, be distinguished from consistent interpretation which, in a temporary fashion, seeks to compensate for faulty or lacking implementation.[152]

Via the duty of consistent interpretation, the Court imposes upon national courts an obligation to apply teleological interpretation that is considerate of the objectives sought by the directive. A national court's possibilities to interpret national law in conformity with EU law are limited by the national legislation. National law must both exist and allow for directive-conform interpretation.[153] Furthermore, national legal traditions play a role, notably in the form of the methods of interpretation recognised by the national legal system[154] and within the confines of discretion provided in national law.[155] A method of interpretation cannot replace legislative action. As a next step in giving effect to a directive, which has no direct effect and for the effective implementation of which national law cannot be interpreted in a consistent manner, recourse must be had to state liability.[156]

Further limitations to implementing the duty of consistent interpretation are of a substantive nature, arising from the general principles of

---

[148] Case 14/83 *von Colson* (n 145) paras. 27–28.

[149] Joined Cases C-397/01 to C-403/01 *Pfeiffer* (n 142) para. 119.

[150] W van Gerven, 'Non-Contractual Liability of Member States, Community Institutions and Individuals for Breaches of Community Law with a View to a Common Law for Europe' (1994) 1 *Maastricht Journal of European and Comparative Law* 6, 11–12.

[151] JDN Bates, 'The Impact of Directives on Statutory Interpretation: Using the Euro-Meaning?' (1986) 7 *Statute Law Review* 174, 185.

[152] 'Judicial implementation' and 'remedial interpretation', respectively: S Prechal, *Directives in EC law* (Oxford University Press 2006) 190–191.

[153] T Tridimas, 'Horizontal Effect of Directives: A Missed Opportunity?' (1994) 19 *European Law Review* 621, 624.

[154] Joined Cases C-397/01 to C-403/01 *Pfeiffer* (n 142) para. 116.

[155] Case 14/83 *von Colson* (n 145) para. 28.

[156] Case C-91/92 *Faccini Dori* v. *Recreb* EU:C:1994:292, para. 27.

law and serving to protect individuals.[157] Relevant general principles include, for example, legal certainty and non-retroactivity,[158] which require an individual not to be placed in an unfavourable situation as a result of giving effect to a directive, which is otherwise not intended to have effects on individuals.[159]

5.3.1.3 Multilateral Agreements Exporting EU Internal Market Acquis

The interpretation of international agreements, including the multilateral agreements exporting EU acquis to third countries by national courts is subject to the choice of interpretation methods and procedures of each contracting party. Both the multilateral agreements exporting the EU acquis as well as the EU Treaties being 'regimes' under the regime theory, their contracting parties can be expected to be more inclined towards teleological interpretation. There is, however, no guarantee to that effect. For example, the development of the doctrine of consistent interpretation demonstrates that the Court has perceived it necessary to enhance the effectiveness of EU law by placing upon the Member States an explicit obligation to adopt conforming interpretation rather than relying on the interpretative practices of the national courts. In this vein, it is perhaps unreasonable to expect a level of market integration similar to the EU to be achieved in an expanded internal market without the multilateral agreements featuring similar duties of consistent interpretation and corresponding enforcement mechanisms as provided in the EU legal order.

There are two dimensions to the interpretation of the multilateral agreements exporting the internal market acquis. The first concerns the consistent interpretation of national legislation in the light of the multilateral agreements, and the second the uniform interpretation and application of the agreements and the corresponding EU acquis. The EEA Agreement, the EnCT, the ECAA Agreement and the TCT all provide rules on interpretation for the purpose of preserving the homogeneous interpretation of the agreements.[160] In the absence of interpretative guidelines,

---

[157] The same rationale is used by the Court to reject the horizontal direct effect of directives: Case 152/84 *Marshall* EU:C:1986:84, para. 48.

[158] Case 80/86 *Kolpinghuis Nijmegen* EU:C:1987:431, para. 13.

[159] G Betlem (n 143) 407.

[160] Recital 15, preamble to the EEA Agreement and Articles 6, 58, 105, 106, 111 EEA Agreement; Article 94 EnCT; Articles 16, 18, 20 ECAA Agreement and a number of references in the Annexes to the ECAA Agreement; Articles 19, 24 and 37 TCT.

however, it falls upon the national courts to choose the appropriate interpretative methods in the national legal orders.

In the EFTA pillar of the EEA, the EFTA Court has adopted a similar effectiveness-driven approach to interpreting EEA law as the Court of Justice. The EFTA Court has ruled in *Karlsson* that although EEA law does not prescribe the direct effect of unimplemented EEA rules before national courts because the EEA lacks legislative powers, the domestic courts of the EEA EFTA States must, nevertheless, take into consideration 'any relevant element of EEA law, whether implemented or not when interpreting national law'.[161] The direct effect of unimplemented EEA law is, therefore, replaced by a duty of consistent interpretation. The duty derives from the 'general objective of the EEA Agreement of establishing a dynamic and homogeneous market, [...] the ensuing emphasis on the judicial defence and enforcement of the rights of individuals, as well as [...] the public international law principle of effectiveness',[162] following closely the case law of the Court of Justice. The methods of interpretation recognised by national law must, furthermore, be employed to the greatest extent possible to ensure the effectiveness of the EEA Agreement.[163] The EFTA Court has, however, restricted the possibility of relying on the provisions of EU law that have not been made part of EEA law.[164]

Neither the EnCT, the ECAA Agreement nor the TCT establish supranational judiciaries endowed with the powers to enforce the principle of consistent interpretation of national laws with EU acquis.[165] The non-performance of the obligations assumed under the agreements will, nevertheless, entail the responsibility of the state vis-à-vis the other contracting parties.

The consistent interpretation of EU law and the identical acquis exported by the multilateral agreements is best exemplified by the *Polydor* doctrine and the subsequent case law. The *Polydor* case concerned the interpretation of a provision of the 1972 EEC-Portugal FTA. Two British companies were selling in the United Kingdom records

---

[161] Case E-4/01 *Karlsson* [2002] EFTA Ct Rep 240, para. 28.
[162] Ibid.
[163] Case E-1/07 *Criminal proceedings against A* (n 88) para. 39.
[164] Joined Cases E-5/04, E-6/04, and E-7/04 *Fesil and Finnfjord* [2005] EFTA Ct Rep 117, para. 110.
[165] With the exception of the possibility of the Court to give preliminary rulings on the interpretation of the ECAA Agreement and the TCT: see Chapter 8, Sections 8.2.2.4 and 8.2.2.5.

imported from a Portuguese producer. Since the records did not comply with the UK copyright laws, a copyright infringement action was subsequently brought against the companies. The defendants relied on a provision in the FTA on the abolition of restrictions to trade in goods that have been lawfully placed on the market in Portugal that replicated provisions of the EEC Treaty. The Court of Justice, however, refused to interpret the provision of the FTA in a manner identical to the corresponding provisions of the EEC Treaty. The identical wording of provisions contained in the EU Treaties and in international agreements does not, therefore, entail an automatic uniformity of interpretation.

The Court maintained that the interpretation of the EEC Treaty follows from its 'objectives and activities',[166] whereas the provisions of the FTA must, in line with Article 31 VCLT, be given an interpretation in the light of its own specific objectives. A comparison between the objectives of the EEC Treaty and the FTA revealed the narrower scope of the latter.[167] A mere similarity between the provisions of the two agreements did not, therefore, justify an extension of the interpretation given in the context of the EEC Treaty to the provisions of the FTA.[168]

The *Polydor* doctrine has had a crucial impact on all attempts to extend the actual effect of EU law beyond the Union by means of exporting internal market acquis. In order for third country nationals to enjoy the same rights as conferred by the Treaties on EU citizens, international agreements exporting the acquis must contain similarly worded provisions as well as demonstrate a similarity of objectives as concerns the internal market. A mere FTA neither entails such similarity of objectives nor provides a guarantee for identical interpretation.

In subsequent case law, the Court has elaborated on the *Polydor* doctrine by assessing the aims pursued by the provisions of international agreements in their particular context and comparing the objectives and context of the agreements with the EU Treaties. In some instances, the provisions of FTAs and AAs have thereafter been interpreted in a manner consistent with the interpretation of a Treaty provision,[169] in others

---

[166]   Case 270/80 *Polydor* v. *Harlequin Records* (n 53) para. 16.
[167]   Ibid., paras. 16–18.
[168]   Ibid., paras. 15 and 18.
[169]   For example, Case 17/81 *Pabst & Richarz* EU:C:1982:129 concerning the EEC-Greece AA; Case C-207/91 *Eurim-Pharm* EU:C:1993:278 concerning the EEC-Austria FTA; Case C-162/00 *Pokrzeptowicz-Meyer* EU:C:2002:57 concerning the EC-Poland EA; Case C-438/00 *Deutscher Handballbund* EU:C:2003:255 concerning the EC-Slovakia EA; Case C-171/01

not.[170] The determination is always made with reference to a concrete provision and is not extended to an international agreement in its entirety.

The institutional context of an international agreement may also affect the possibility of establishing the equivalence of the legal contexts of the EU Treaties and the agreement. In A, the Court claimed that the same interpretation of the provisions on the free movement of capital within the Community cannot be extended to capital movements between the Community and third countries insofar as the mutual assistance between competent authorities does not extend to the third countries in question.[171] The Court maintained this requirement even with respect to the EEA Agreement.[172]

There is abundant case law of the Court on the interpretation of provisions of international agreements including those that replicate EU acquis. The Court's interpretation of three (sets of) agreements – the EEC-Turkey AA, the EU-Switzerland bilateral agreements and the EEA Agreement – are particularly relevant. Having different scopes, each of these (groups of) agreements also aims at different levels of integration.

Regarding the EEC-Turkey AA, the Court has repeatedly ruled that the free movement of Turkish workers in the EU is limited and does not comprise the general freedom of movement that applies to EU citizens.[173] Third country nationals may enjoy the same freedom from discrimination on grounds of nationality provided that they belong to the privileged categories of long-term residents or family members or that the principle extends to them by virtue of an international agreement.[174]

Wählergruppe Gemeinsam EU:C:2003:260 concerning the EEC-Turkey AA; Case C-265/03 *Simutenkov* (n 64) concerning the EC-Russia PCA.

[170] For example, Case C-312/91 *Metalsa* EU:C:1993:279 concerning the EEC-Austria FTA; Case C-63/99 *Gloszczuk* EU:C:2001:488 concerning the EC-Poland EA; Case C-235/99 *Kondova* EU:C:2001:489 and Case C-101/10 *Pavlov and Famira* EU:C:2011:462 concerning the EC-Bulgaria EA; Case C-257/99 *Barkoci and Malík* EU:C:2001:491 concerning the EC-Czech EA.

[171] Case C-101/05 *A* EU:C:2007:804, paras. 60–63.

[172] Case C-72/09 *Établissements Rimbaud* EU:C:2010:645, para. 40; Case C-48/11 *Veronsaajien oikeudenvalvontayksikkö* v. *A* EU:C:2012:485, para. 34. In the former, the conditions for administrative assistance were not satisfied whereas in the latter, they were.

[173] For example, Case C-171/95 *Tetik* EU:C:1997:31, para. 29; Case C-325/05 *Derin* EU:C:2007:442, para. 66.

[174] See S Boelaert-Suominen, 'Non-EU Nationals and Council Directive 2003/109/EC on the Status of Third-Country Nationals who are Long-term Residents: Five Paces Forward and Possibly Three Paces Back' (2005) 42 *Common Market Law Review* 1011.

Demirkan provides another good example of how the Court delimits the scope of the free movement provisions in the EEC-Turkey AA.[175] Previously, the Court had interpreted the 'freedom to provide services' in EU law as entailing a passive dimension – the freedom of movement for the purpose of receiving services.[176] In *Demirkan*, the Court decided not to extend this interpretation to the EEC-Turkey AA. Resorting to the *Polydor* doctrine, the Court found that the 'purely economic purpose' of the EEC-Turkey AA fell short of the purpose of the EU Treaties to 'bring [. . .] about freedom of movement for persons of a general nature'.[177] Pursuant to the Court, the protection of the passive freedom to provide services is part of the specific internal market objective, which distinguishes the EU Treaties from the EEC-Turkey AA.[178] *Demirkan* thereby clearly demonstrates that a fundamental freedom cannot be guaranteed to retain the same scope as within the EU when exported to third countries and extended to non-EU nationals.

The EU-Switzerland bilateral agreements are, on the one hand, separate from one another and pursue their own objectives. On the other hand, each bilateral agreement contributes to the comprehensive management of the EU-Switzerland relations and can, thus, be placed in the collective context of the agreements.[179] When interpreting the agreements, the Court has adopted the latter, comprehensive perspective.[180] It has, for example, found that regarding the internal market, the objectives of the EU-Swiss agreements are not comparable to those of the EEA Agreement. By rejecting the EEA Agreement and refraining from implementing the free movement of services and establishment, Switzerland did not 'join the internal market of the Community', which is an 'area of total freedom of movement analogous to that provided by a national market'.[181] Therefore, the provisions of the EU-Switzerland bilateral agreements cannot automatically be interpreted in line with the corresponding provisions of the EU Treaties unless the agreement provides so explicitly.[182]

---

[175] Case C-221/11 *Demirkan* EU:C:2013:583.
[176] Joined Cases 286/82 and 26/83 *Luisi and Carbone* EU:C:1984:35, para. 16. See also Chapter 3, Section 3.3.1.
[177] Case C-221/11 *Demirkan* (n 175) paras. 44, 51 and 53.
[178] Ibid., para. 56.
[179] This applies in particular to the 'Bilateral I' set of seven agreements, which are bound together by a so-called guillotine clause. All of the agreements entered into force together and none of them can be terminated individually, see Chapter 2, Section 2.4.1.
[180] Case C-351/08 *Grimme* EU:C:2009:697.
[181] Ibid., para. 27.
[182] Ibid., para. 29; Case C-541/08 *Fokus Invest* EU:C:2010:74, para. 28; Case C-70/09 *Hengartner and Gasser* EU:C:2010:430, para. 42.

This does not, however, preclude the possibility of identical interpretation provided that in the relevant fields the objectives of the bilateral agreements are comparable to those of the EU Treaties. In *Ettwein*, the Court interpreted the relevant provisions of the EC-Switzerland agreement on the free movement of persons in the light of the agreement itself without comparing its objectives to the EU Treaties nor to the EEA Agreement.[183] In spite of the lack of automaticity, the Court deemed the objectives of the agreement and the EU Treaties to be equivalent and interpreted the provisions of the agreement in question in light of the interpretation previously given to the corresponding provisions of EU law.

Among all international agreements concluded by the EU, the EEA Agreement comes closest to the level of integration in the EU internal market. Homogeneous interpretation of the EEA acquis with the EU acquis is, moreover, pursued by Article 6 EEA Agreement, which provides that provisions of the EEA Agreement that are identical in substance to EU acquis must be interpreted in conformity with the pre-1992 case law of the Court.[184] Even before the conclusion of the EEA Agreement, its objectives were subject to scrutiny by the Court. In Opinion 1/91, the Court, implicitly referring to the *Polydor* doctrine, found that the identical wording of the provisions of the EC Treaty and the EEA Agreement neither necessarily leads to their identical interpretation nor guarantees homogeneity between the treaties, unless their respective objectives justify such analogous interpretation.[185] Although the internal market objectives of the EU and the EEA are roughly identical, the Court claimed that the free trade and competition rules in the EEC Treaty 'far from being an end in themselves' serve the purpose within the Community of 'making concrete progress towards European unity' which is lacking in the EEA.[186]

Some nuance was provided by *Opel Austria*, in which the CFI rejected the Council's argument on the existence of major differences between the EU Treaties and the EEA Agreement that would preclude an identical interpretation of Article 10 EEA Agreement and the corresponding provision in the EC Treaty.[187] The CFI recognised the difference between the aims and context of the EEA Agreement and Community law without, however, perceiving them as a hindrance to

---

[183] Case C-425/11 *Ettwein* EU:C:2013:121.
[184] See Chapter 8, Section 8.1.2.2.
[185] Opinion 1/91 *EEA I* (n 2) paras. 14 and 22.
[186] Ibid., paras. 15–18.
[187] Case T-115/94 *Opel Austria* v. *Council* (n 72) paras. 105–106.

a homogeneous EEA. Instead, the CFI deemed the integration objectives of the EEA Agreement to 'exceed those of a mere free-trade agreement', thus justifying the inapplicability of the *Polydor* doctrine.[188] The CFI argued that the conclusions in Opinion 1/91 referred to the envisaged judicial system of the EEA and its effect on the autonomy of the EU legal order rather than the identical interpretation of similar provisions.[189] The EEA Agreement contains certain safeguard clauses that allow the Joint Committee to refuse the entry into the EEA legal order of post-1992 acquis, leading to derogations from substantive uniformity between the EU and the EEA legal orders. The CFI, however, regarded the possibility of certain substantive divergences in the composition of the acquis not to be of importance for the purpose of interpreting Article 10 EEA Agreement,[190] and did not, therefore, deem the objectives of the EEA Agreement to be incomparable to the EU Treaties.

The CFI's arguments in *Opel Austria* were in turn refuted by AG Cosmas in *Andersson*.[191] The case concerned the interpretation of Article 6 EEA Agreement with a view to determining whether secondary EU law and the principles established in the Court's case law – in this case, the *Francovich* doctrine – could be applied to the EEA legal order. Noting the 'fundamental differences' between the EU and the EEA legal systems, the AG contended that the contexts are too different to transfer to the EEA the fundamental principles of primacy, direct effect and state liability.[192] The analysis of AG Cosmas must be viewed within the specific context of the applicability of the fundamental principles of the EU in the EEA Agreement that pertain to the effect of the acquis outside the Union rather than the identical set of rights and obligations, which the EU and the EEA EFTA citizens receive from the EU Treaties and the EEA Agreement, respectively. As concerns the comparability of the objectives of the EEA Agreement and the EU Treaties for the purpose of interpreting Article 10 EEA Agreement, AG Cosmas fully endorsed the conclusions of the CFI in *Opel Austria*.[193]

The 'notorious' differences in character between the EU and the EEA treaties once noted by AG Fennelly[194] have not been upheld in

---

[188] Ibid., paras. 106–107.
[189] Ibid., para. 109.
[190] Ibid., paras. 110–111.
[191] Case C-321/97 *Andersson and Wakeras-Andersson* EU:C:1999:9, Opinion of AG Cosmas.
[192] Ibid., para. 49.
[193] Ibid., n 44.
[194] Case C-110/95 *Yamanouchi* EU:C:1996:34, Opinion of AG Fennelly, para. 30.

subsequent case law. In *Ospelt*, both AG Geelhoed and subsequently the Court contended that the objective of 'the fullest possible realisation of the free movement of goods, persons, services and capital within the whole European Economic Area' amounts to an extension of the EU internal market to the EEA EFTA States.[195] Exceptions occur only in situations where all rules relevant to the identical interpretation and application of the provisions of EEA law and the underlying EU law have not been made part of the EEA legal order.[196]

Several authors have shared the view that the internal market has, indeed, been 'extended' to the EEA EFTA States,[197] and that the *Polydor* doctrine does not apply to the EEA Agreement to the extent of precluding an identical interpretation of provisions which are identical in substance.[198] On the one hand, compared to the EEC-Portugal FTA, the EEA Agreement envisages much closer cooperation. On the other hand, Article 6 EEA Agreement precludes conflicting interpretations, at least vis-à-vis pre-signature case law. Moreover, although the EEA Agreement does not include a reference to the peoples of the EU and the EEA EFTA States as did the original EEC Treaty, the preamble to the EEA Agreement mentions the crucial role of individuals in the EEA, exercising and protecting the individual rights, which they derive from the Agreement.[199] Importantly, Recital 8 was only added to the preamble to the draft EEA Agreement after the Court had given its Opinion 1/91.[200] Compared to both the EEC-Turkey AA and the EU-Switzerland bilateral agreements, the objectives of the EEA Agreement do, indeed, to the extent of the internal market constitute a pre-determined guarantee for the identical interpretation of identically worded acquis. The

---

[195] Case C-452/01 *Ospelt* EU:C:2003:232, Opinion of AG Geelhoed, para. 69; Case C-452/01 *Ospelt* EU:C:2003:493, para. 29. The Court's ruling has been confirmed in a number of subsequent judgments. See, for example, Case C-286/02 *Bellio F.lli* EU:C:2004:212, para. 34; Case C-48/11 *Veronsaajien oikeudenvalvontayksikkö v. A* (n 172) para. 15.

[196] Case C-540/07 *Commission v. Italy* EU:C:2009:717, paras. 68–75.

[197] C Baudenbacher, 'If Not EEA State Liability, Then What' (n 87) 333; H Haukeland Fredriksen, 'Bridging the Widening Gap between the EU Treaties and the Agreement on the European Economic Area' (2012) 18 *European Law Journal* 868, 883.

[198] S Norberg, 'The European Economic Area' in PJ Oliver (ed.), *Oliver on Free Movement of Goods in the European Union* (Hart Publishing 2010) 487, 493; C Baudenbacher, 'The EFTA Court and Court of Justice of the European Union' (n 79) 191.

[199] Recital 8, preamble to the EEA Agreement. See also Section 5.1.3.

[200] H Haukeland Fredriksen, 'The EFTA Court 15 Years On' (2010) 59 *International and Comparative Law Quarterly* 731, 750.

type of the agreement plays no particular role here as all of the agreements discussed have been concluded as AAs.[201]

The three judgments of *United Kingdom* v. *Council* have provided a unique occasion to compare the objectives of the EEA Agreement,[202] the EC-Switzerland agreement on the free movement of persons[203] and the EEC-Turkey AA.[204] Although the judgments do not concern the interpretation of identical provisions, they illustrate the considerations of the objective and context of the international agreements, which is likely to be taken into account should a question of identical interpretation arise at a later point in time. Each of the cases concerned an annulment action brought by the United Kingdom against a Council decision on the EU's position to be taken in accordance with Article 218(9) TFEU in the respective treaty bodies. The amendments in question concerned the adoption into the EEA Agreement, the EC-Switzerland agreement and the EEC-Turkey AA of Regulation (EC) No 883/2004 on the coordination of social security systems replacing Regulation (EEC) No 1408/71. Instead of the internal market legal basis of Article 48 TFEU, the United Kingdom argued that the contested Council decisions should have been adopted on the basis of Article 79(2) TFEU regulating EU immigration policy.

In all three cases, the Court firmly overruled the United Kingdom's arguments. In the first judgment delivered, the Court cited its earlier judgment in *Ospelt* on the objectives of the EEA Agreement to extend the internal market to EEA EFTA States and found that the contested regulation served precisely the purpose of providing to EEA citizens the same social conditions for the exercise of their free movement rights as those enjoyed by EU citizens.[205] In the case concerning the EC-Switzerland agreement, the Court did not use the language of extending the internal market to Switzerland, probably due to the Swiss refusal to become party to the EEA Agreement. Instead, the Court referred to the objective of the agreement to 'bring about between [the EC and Switzerland] the free movement of persons on the basis of the rules applying in the

---

[201] Among the bilateral agreements concluded with Switzerland, agreements belonging to 'Bilateral I' are AAs but not those of the 'Bilateral II' package. The Agreement on the Free Movement of Persons is part of 'Bilateral I'. See Chapter 2, Section 2.4.1.
[202] Case C-431/11 *United Kingdom* v. *Council* EU:C:2013:589.
[203] Case C-656/11 *United Kingdom* v. *Council* EU:C:2014:97.
[204] Case C-81/13 *United Kingdom* v. *Council* EU:C:2014:2449.
[205] Case C-431/11 *United Kingdom* v. *Council* (n 202) paras. 50 and 58.

Community'.[206] Both the EEA and the EC-Switzerland agreements already contained EU acquis on the approximation of social security systems with a view of ensuring the effectiveness of the free movement provisions. An update to the EU acquis was necessary to incorporate the changes introduced by the Lisbon Treaty and to ensure a balance of rights between EU citizens and the citizens of Iceland, Liechtenstein, Norway and Switzerland regarding the social conditions connected to the free movement.[207] The scope of the amendment itself was insignificant.

However, the same does not hold true for the EEC-Turkey AA. The objective of the EEC-Turkey AA is narrower than the fullest possible realisation of the free movement of persons, stating merely the wish of the contracting parties to secure between them the freedom of movement for workers in progressive stages, one of which is the incorporation of the contested regulation into the AA.[208] As set out in *Demirkan* and other case law on the AA, there is neither general freedom of movement between the EU and Turkey nor have the contracting parties completed the progressive introduction of the free movement of workers provided in Article 12 of the EEC-Turkey AA. In the judgment, the Court compared the three agreements and concluded that as concerns the free movement of persons the objective of the EEC-Turkey Agreement is not comparable to the aims of either the EEA Agreement or the EC-Switzerland agreement. The EEA EFTA States and Switzerland can be 'equated with a Member State for the purposes of the application of those regulations' whereas Turkey cannot.[209] Even though Regulation (EEC) No 1408/71 had been incorporated into the EEC-Turkey AA and the Additional Protocol similar to the EEA and the EC-Switzerland agreements, it did not have the effect of extending to Turkey the rules on the coordination of social security systems.[210] As a result, Turkey was not covered by the extension of the internal market in a manner similar to the EEA EFTA States and Switzerland. In the case at hand, this meant that the Council decision could not be adopted solely on the basis of Article 48 TFEU but in conjunction with Article 217 TFEU, the legal basis for AAs.[211] The use of the additional legal basis was intended to emphasise the distinction between the EEC-Turkey AA and the EEA and EC-Switzerland agreements

---

[206] Case C-656/11 *United Kingdom* v. *Council* (n 203) para. 55.
[207] Ibid., para. 58.
[208] Case C-81/13 *United Kingdom* v. *Council* (n 204) paras. 43 and 45.
[209] Ibid., para. 57.
[210] Ibid., para. 58.
[211] Ibid., paras. 59–66.

yet is somewhat puzzling as all of the agreements are AAs. The Court highlighted that the legal basis of Article 48 TFEU may be used on its own only for adopting internal market measures within the EU or in external action vis-à-vis non-EU Member States that 'can be placed on the same footing' as EU Member States.[212] The difference between the decisions does not, therefore, lie in the actual divergences in the application of Regulation (EC) 883/2004 in the third countries concerned but rather in the perceived differences in the level of integration of the third countries in the internal market.

In addition, the Court made it explicit that an extension of the internal market to non-EU Member States comprises not only the extension of the EU free movement rights to third country nationals but also the free movement of EU nationals in the third states.[213] Nationals of the EFTA countries, furthermore, enjoy internal market freedoms even vis-à-vis one another. In this case, the individuals of Iceland, Liechtenstein, Norway and Switzerland have, indeed, been placed on an equal footing with EU citizens whereas the generalisation cannot automatically be carried on to all of the EU-Switzerland bilateral agreements owing to the lack uniformity in the application of the other fundamental freedoms, in particular the free movement of capital and services.

In Opinion 1/91, the Court held that the fundamental freedoms were only one of several possible means to achieve the internal market and an economic and monetary union and, eventually, greater European unity.[214] A reading of Opinion 1/91 in combination with the judgments in the three cases *United Kingdom* v. *Council*, however, reveals that the Court is not likely to restrict the application of EU acquis in countries with which the EU has concluded agreements featuring deep regulatory integration. By 2014, the Court's careful approach towards the EEA Agreement had been replaced by a recognition of the possibility of truly extending the internal market beyond the EU also in the light of the *Polydor* doctrine. The Court's affirmation of an extended internal market suggests that the Court is unlikely to impede the functioning thereof by refusing to interpret the EEA or even the EU-Switzerland acquis which is identical in substance to the underlying EU acquis differently from the latter.

---

[212] Ibid., para. 59.
[213] Case C-431/11 *United Kingdom* v. *Council* (n 202) para. 55.
[214] Opinion 1/91 *EEA I* (n 2) para. 19.

The EFTA Court is generally very accommodating towards the identical interpretation of identical provisions of EU and EEA law. This derives, on the one hand, from Article 6 EEA Agreement and Article 3 of the EFTA Surveillance and Court Agreement (SCA),[215] the latter providing that the EFTA Court must also pay due account to post-signature case law of the Court of Justice. On the other hand, the uniform interpretation of EU and EEA law stems from the 'main objective of the EEA Agreement [. . .] to create a homogeneous EEA' as provided by the EEA Agreement.[216] The reasoning of the EFTA Court is effectiveness-driven, thus corresponding to the teleological approach of the Court of Justice.[217] According to the EFTA Court, the homogeneity principle sets forth a presumption that identical provisions of the EU and the EEA treaties are to be interpreted in a similar manner.[218] Diverging interpretations are justified only in cases where the differences in the scope and purpose of the respective treaties so demand.[219] The threshold for the EEA EFTA States to prove the compelling circumstances that would justify diverging interpretation of EEA law from EU law is very high rendering the homogeneity guarantee on behalf of the EFTA Court equally strong.[220] Justification cannot, however, be granted on the basis of any unilateral expression of understanding made by the contracting parties.[221] Neither can the dynamic interpretation of the EEA Agreement lead to an expansion of the substantive scope of the EEA legal order, such as to cover agricultural products, which are excluded from the application of the Agreement.[222] Albeit not legally bound to, the EFTA Court has extended the principle of uniform interpretation also to procedural rules including, for example, the rules on costs recoverable from the party ordered to pay the costs, which are worded identically in the Rules of Procedure of the EFTA Court, the Court of Justice and the General Court.[223] The

---

[215] Agreement between the EFTA States on the Establishment of a Surveillance Authority and a Court of Justice [1994] OJ L344/3.

[216] Joined Cases E-9/07 and E-10/07 L'Oréal [2008] EFTA Ct Rep 259, para. 27.

[217] 'Homogeneous interpretation and application of common rules is essential for the effective functioning of the internal market within the EEA': ibid.

[218] Case E-2/06 EFTA Surveillance Authority v. Norway [2007] EFTA Ct Rep 164, para. 59.

[219] Case E-3/98 Rainford-Towning [1998] EFTA Ct Rep 205, para. 21, referring to the Maglite case in which such different circumstances did, indeed, occur: Case E-2/97 Maglite (n 73) para. 27.

[220] H Haukeland Fredriksen, 'The EFTA Court 15 Years On' (n 200) 743.

[221] Case E-2/06 EFTA Surveillance Authority v. Norway (n 218) para. 59.

[222] Case E-4/04 Pedicel [2005] EFTA Ct Rep 1, para. 28.

[223] Order in Case E-9/04 European Banking Federations [2007] EFTA Ct Rep 74, para. 16.

voluntarily homogeneous interpretation has been justified by a need for equal treatment and foreseeability for the parties appearing before the courts.[224]

The provisions of the ECAA Agreement and the TCT, too, are to be given an interpretation uniform with the underlying EU acquis. Both agreements generally fail to distinguish between the ECAA/TCT-level homogeneity and homogeneity along the ECAA/TCT-EU axis. Article 16(1) ECAA Agreement and Article 19 TCT provide the standard clauses of conforming interpretation of identical acquis. In Opinion 1/00 on the compatibility of the ECAA Agreement with the EU Treaties, the Court was firm to make a distinction between the EU and the ECAA legal orders and reassured that identical rules are to be given autonomous interpretation.[225] Autonomous interpretation, which the Court refers to for the purposes of safeguarding the autonomy of the EU legal order, does not exclude identical interpretation but enables the Court to take due account of the differences in the objectives and context of the separate legal orders that may affect the interpretation of individual provisions, just as in the case of the EEA Agreement.

It is likely that the rules which the Court considers 'identical as to substance but distinct as to form'[226] will receive exactly the same kind of uniform interpretation as EEA law provided that the identically worded provisions pursue the same objectives in the EU, the ECAA and the TCT legal orders. Article 94 EnCT furthermore provides in the absence of a judiciary set up by the treaty that the institutions of the Energy Community must ensure conforming interpretation of its acquis with the case law of the Court of Justice. There is no case law of the Court that would shed light on the interpretation of the objectives and purpose of the EnCT vis-à-vis the EU Treaties. Nevertheless, the Court's rulings on international agreements that 'extend' the internal market to third countries clearly indicate that in general terms the broad objectives of both the ECAA Agreement, the EnCT and the TCT could be considered equivalent to the EU Treaties for the purposes of granting identical interpretation to identical acquis.

---

[224] Ibid.
[225] Opinion 1/00 *ECAA* EU:C:2002:231, para. 41.
[226] Ibid.

5.3.2 Responsibility of the State for Violation of EU Acquis

5.3.2.1 Public International Law

In public international law, the responsibility for a failure to properly fulfil international law obligations is vested with the subjects of international law – states, international organisations, and, to a very limited degree, individuals. In the case of a breach of an international agreement, the treaty's own rules will be invoked first. In a second step, a breach of a treaty triggers responsibility under the international law of treaties and, in particular, the rule of *pacta sunt servanda*. The violation of a primary obligation, that is, of the treaty provisions, entails in the case of states responsibility under the VCLT. Third, following the breach of a primary obligation, the breach can, as a secondary obligation, entail state responsibility. Article 1 of the Articles on Responsibility of States for Internationally Wrongful Acts (ARSIWA)[227] provides that every internationally wrongful act of a State entails the international responsibility of that state, with no distinction being made between responsibility arising from a breach of a contract or tort.[228]

The main reaction to a treaty breach under the law of treaties is non-performance in the form of a suspension or termination of the treaty,[229] either on the basis of the provisions of the treaty itself or the general law of treaties under Articles 65–68 and Annex to the VCLT. It is also possible to invalidate the consent to be bound under Articles 49–52 VCLT. If these remedies have not been exhausted, the aggrieved party may instead invoke state responsibility under Articles 23 and 25 ARSIWA, whereas the procedures provided in the VCLT and the ARSIWA differ in terms of complexity.[230]

The possibilities for individuals to enforce international law against a violating state are extremely limited. Even though many treaties create rights for individuals that can be invoked in domestic courts, individuals themselves do not, for example, have standing in the

---

[227] Annex, General Assembly Resolution 56/83 of 12 December 2001, A/RES/56/83.

[228] *Rainbow Warrior Affair (New Zealand v. France)* (1990) 20 RIAA 217; J Verhoeven, 'The Law of Responsibility and the Law of Treaties' in J Crawford, A Pellet and S Olleson (eds.), *The Law of International Responsibility* (Oxford University Press 2010) 105, 106.

[229] B Simma and CJ Tams, 'Reacting against Treaty Breaches' in DB Hollis (ed.), *The Oxford Guide to Treaties* (Oxford University Press 2012) 576, 580.

[230] C Binder, 'Does the Difference Make a Difference? A Comparison between the Mechanisms of the Law of Treaties and of State Responsibility as Means to Derogate from Treaty Obligations in Cases of Subsequent Changes of Circumstances' in M Szabó (ed.), *State Responsibility and the Law of Treaties* (Eleven International Publishing 2010) 1, 17 and 22–23.

International Court of Justice (ICJ).[231] In the case of agreements between states, a breach of an international law obligation can, thus, mainly be invoked by the contracting parties. The situation is different in cases where the international law instrument itself creates remedies that can be invoked by individuals, such as access to judicial mechanisms under the ECHR, the EU Treaties and international investment agreements. In these cases, individuals can directly rely on the provisions of international law, provided that the treaty has become part of the domestic legal order and that its provisions confer rights on the individual. Regardless, the possible recourse to international courts and other dispute settlement mechanisms is complementary to the legal remedies provided by domestic law, to the extent that the rules on state immunity so permit.[232] In certain circumstances, individuals can also invoke international law in national disputes if a rule of international law that is binding on the state covers an aspect of the situation of the individual.[233] In the same vein, should individuals incur damages as a result of a state breaching an international law obligation, they can pursue remedial action in domestic courts or, for example, before the European Court of Human Rights (ECtHR), the Court of Justice of the EU or international investment tribunals.

5.3.2.2 EU Law

In the case of the EU and the treaties concluded by the EU, the matter of responsibility and liability of international organisations comes into play. The EU has not yet acceded to the Vienna Convention on the Law of Treaties between States and International Organizations or between International Organizations nor has the Convention entered into force, but the EU is, nevertheless, bound by those provisions of the Convention that have been recognised as international customary law. The responsibility of the EU as an international organisation is, moreover, regulated by the ILC Draft Articles on the Responsibility of International Organizations.[234] The latter impose conditions identical in essence to the ARSIWA for invoking the responsibility of international

---

[231] Articles 34(1) and 65 of the Statute of the International Court of Justice, San Francisco, 1945, UKTS 67 (1946) UKTS 67 (1946) Cmd 7015 (ICJ Statute).

[232] J Crawford, 'The System of International Responsibility' in J Crawford, A Pellet and S Olleson (eds.), *The Law of International Responsibility* (Oxford University Press 2010) 17, 21.

[233] See I Brownlie, *Principles of Public International Law* (Oxford University Press 2008) 35.

[234] (2011) II Yearbook of the International Law Commission Part II.

organisations for internationally wrongful conduct. Account, though, must in the case of the EU also be taken of the special characteristics of the EU as a supranational 'regional economic integration organisation'.[235] Article 340(2) TFEU provides that in the case of non-contractual liability, the Union shall make good the damage caused 'in accordance with the general principles common to the laws of the Member States' regardless of whether the damage is caused by the legislative, administrative or judicial activities of the Union's institutions,[236] or regardless of whether the act was discretionary or not.[237] As concerns the liability of the Member States for infringements of international agreements concluded by the EU, including mixed agreements, the Court has found that by not complying with its obligations under the EEA Agreement in an area that falls within the scope of EU law, a Member State failed to fulfil its obligations under EU law.[238]

The EU Treaties being governed by international law, the Member States of the EU, too, owe to each other obligations under international law. Under the VCLT, the Member States must perform their obligations assumed under the Treaties in good faith and may not invoke national law as a justification for a failure of performance.[239] The EU Treaties envisage sanctions for the non-performance of Treaty obligations. A Member State may take a case of non-performance by another Member State to the Court under Article 259 TFEU after first having brought the matter to the attention of the Commission. If an infringement is established by the Court, the infringing Member State must remedy the breach by paying a financial penalty under Article 260 TFEU. A special provision provided in Article 7 TEU establishes a procedure for dealing with 'serious and persistent breaches' by a Member State of the values enlisted in Article 2 TEU on which the EU is founded. Under the provision, the infringing Member State may temporarily lose certain rights under the Treaties, including voting rights in the Council. The Member States are, however, restricted from adopting countermeasures 'on [their] own authority, corrective or

---

[235] See E Paasivirta and PJ Kuijper, 'Does One Size Fit all?: The European Community and the Responsibility of International Organizations' (2005) 36 *Netherlands Yearbook of International Law* 169.

[236] Case C-352/98 P *Bergaderm and Goupil* EU:C:2000:361, para. 46.

[237] PP Craig, 'Once More unto the Breach: The Community, the State and Damages Liability' (1997) 113 *Law Quarterly Review* 67, 72–73.

[238] Case C-13/00 *Commission v. Ireland* EU:C:2002:184.

[239] Articles 26 and 27 VCLT.

protective measures' in reaction to a breach of EU law by another Member State.[240]

The responsibility of Member States for breaches of EU Treaties vis-à-vis one another is triggered much less frequently than the 'domestication' of responsibility, that is, the responsibility of the Member States for breaches of EU law towards individuals.[241] Under EU law, individuals enjoy direct access to courts to defend their rights against a breaching Member State. They can also bring complaints to the Commission in order to encourage the latter to initiate infringement proceedings against a Member State in a procedure of non-compliance under Article 258 TFEU, and seek reparation for damages incurred as a result of the breach.

The principle of state liability in EU law is a direct consequence of the doctrine of direct effect that was established by the Court to ensure the protection of individual rights and the effective application of EU law. In *Francovich*, the Court established state liability for breaches of EU law as 'a matter of principle', much like the ascertainment of direct effect and primacy. A piece missing from the effectiveness puzzle was the possibility for individuals to obtain redress for an infringement of their rights under EU law.[242] The subsequent *Brasserie du Pêcheur* consolidated the three conditions for establishing state liability: (1) the infringed provision must confer individual rights; (2) the breach of those rights must be sufficiently serious; and (3) a causal link must exist between the breach of EU law by the Member State and the damage sustained by the injured party.[243]

State liability in EU law requires extensive interface between the EU and the national legal systems. While the Treaties and secondary law create rights for individuals, the legal remedies in the event of a breach of those rights must, in the absence of relevant EU rules, be established by national law.[244] The Member States, therefore, enjoy certain procedural autonomy[245] to set up a system of national courts or tribunals for the protection of the rights of individuals in cases where the Member

---

[240] Case C-5/94 *Hedley Lomas* EU:C:1996:205, para. 20.
[241] J Crawford, 'The System of International Responsibility' (n 232) 21.
[242] Joined Cases C-6/90 and C-9/90 *Francovich and Bonifaci* EU:C:1991:428, paras. 33–34.
[243] Joined Cases C-46/93 and C-48/93 *Brasserie du Pêcheur and Factortame* EU:C:1996:79, para. 51.
[244] Case 45/76 *Comet* EU:C:1976:191, para. 13; Case 33/76 *Rewe* EU:C:1976:188, para. 5.
[245] Also called 'remedial autonomy': C Kilpatrick, 'The Future of Remedies in Europe' in C Kilpatrick, T Novitz and P Skidmore (eds.), *The Future of Remedies in Europe* (Hart Publishing 2000) 1, 4.

State or any other actor has failed to fulfil its obligations under EU law.[246]

Effectiveness is the principal argument underpinning the principle of state liability, and the latter is the most important factor in ensuring the effectiveness of EU law.[247] State liability is also crucial for substantiating the principle of primacy.[248] An extension of the internal market to third countries should, therefore, necessarily also include the principle of state liability to ensure comparable effectiveness of the internal market acquis in the third countries' legal orders.

5.3.2.3 Multilateral Agreements Exporting EU Internal Market Acquis

Similarly to the international law regime, the grounds for state liability for breaches of EU acquis contained in multilateral agreements must either be established by the agreements themselves or remain to be determined by the rules of international and domestic law.

The responsibility of the EEA contracting parties is governed by Articles 108–110 EEA Agreement. As in EU law, a breach of an obligation under the EEA Agreement entails a pecuniary penalty. Regarding remedies available for individuals, the EFTA Court has recognised the doctrine of state liability in the EEA alongside those of (quasi-)direct effect and (quasi-)primacy. In *Sveinbjörnsdóttir*, the Commission as well as the three EEA EFTA States argued that as a matter of principle, state liability cannot be recognised in the EEA on equal grounds to the EU legal order owing to the fact that the EEA legal order lacks 'important principles of Community law such as transfer of legislative powers, direct effect and primacy of Community legislation'.[249] The EFTA Court, nevertheless, introduced the principle of state liability into the EEA legal order through the back door. Drawing upon the example of *Francovich*, the EFTA Court found that the homogeneity objective and the establishment of individual rights by the EEA Agreement justify a similar doctrine of state liability for injuries suffered by individuals as a consequence of a Member State's breach of EEA rules as in the case

---

[246] The national measures must be equivalent and effective: see Case C-312/93 *Peterbroeck* EU:C:1995:437, para. 12; Joined Cases C-430/93 and C-431/93 *Van Schijndel and Van Veen v. SPF* (n 41) para. 17.

[247] T Tridimas, *The General Principles of EU Law* (Oxford University Press 2006) 498.

[248] Ibid., 500.

[249] Case E-9/97 *Sveinbjörnsdóttir* (n 71) para. 44.

of the EU.[250] Moreover, the EFTA Court held that the principle of state liability constituted nothing less than an 'integral part of the EEA Agreement as such'[251] and was justified by the obligation of the EEA contracting parties under Article 3 EEA Agreement to take all appropriate measures to ensure the fulfilment of their obligations under the Agreement, including remedies for loss or damages incurred as a result of a failure to implement a directive.[252] The Court of Justice later confirmed the existence of the principle of state liability in the EEA in *Rechberger*, referring to the objective of uniform interpretation and application of the EEA Agreement and EU law.[253] The three conditions that the EFTA Court defined for establishing state liability are identical to those in *Brasserie du Pêcheur*.[254]

The value of the principle of state liability in the EEA legal order has been contested. Some consider it to surpass in relevance the principles of primacy and direct effect.[255] Others argue that the absence of a sovereign rights transfer from the EEA EFTA States to the EEA cannot lead to the recognition of direct effect and primacy in the EEA.[256] It must be recalled, however, that the Court's doctrines of direct effect, primacy and, subsequently, state liability are embedded in the fact that the EU Treaties create rights for individuals, which must be protected by the Member States for the sake of effective and uniform implementation of EU law. The intent of the EEA founding fathers by which the EU internal market was extended to the EEA EFTA States necessarily entailed a conferral of rights to individuals. As a result, the development of principles such as those discussed in the current chapter is central to maintaining homogeneity between the identical acquis in the EU and the EEA. In the absence of supranational institutions, the foundational principles might not have been established. The national courts would, instead, have had to resort to public international law and, in the absence of rules in the latter as concerns the possibility of individuals to invoke the law, to national tort law. Insofar as the EFTA Court and the Court of Justice have, however, recognised the principles of direct effect and primacy in EEA and EU law, respectively, there is little

---

[250] Ibid., para. 60.
[251] Ibid., para. 63.
[252] Ibid., para. 61. See also Case E-7/97 *EFTA Surveillance Authority* v. *Norway* [1998] EFTA Ct Rep 62, para. 16.
[253] Case C-140/97 *Rechberger* EU:C:1999:306, para. 39.
[254] Case E-9/97 *Sveinbjörnsdóttir* (n 71) para. 66.
[255] C Baudenbacher, 'If Not EEA State Liability, Then What' (n 87) 357–358.
[256] S Magnússon and ÓÍ Hannesson (n 76) 170.

reason to question their existence. Beyond the role granted to the EFTA Court by the EEA Agreement and the status of the EFTA Court's judgments in the legal orders of the EEA EFTA States, the acceptance by the EEA Member States' courts of the foundational principles and their implementation is a separate matter and falls within the realm of enforcement rather than the recognition of the principles. When applying the principle of state liability, the national courts of the EEA EFTA States have relied both on the rulings of the EFTA Court and on national provisions on the non-contractual liability of the state.[257]

In *Karlsson*, the EFTA Court extended the principle of state liability to all breaches of primary and secondary EEA law.[258] Regarding parallels between the foundational principles in the EU and the EEA, the EFTA Court added that contrary to the connection between the principles of direct effect and state liability in EU law no such connection necessarily exists in the EEA legal order.[259] The principle of state liability exists in the EEA legal order regardless of the narrower scope of direct effect in the EEA as compared to the EU legal order.[260] When it comes to ensuring the effectiveness of EEA law, the principle of state liability, therefore, also fulfils the tasks of primacy and direct effect that are not given full application in the EEA legal order.[261]

In the Energy Community, the ECAA and the Transport Community, the responsibility of the contracting parties for breaches of the agreements is not regulated by a principle of state liability, owing greatly to the absence of separate judicial bodies created by the agreements. Certain procedural rules for non-performance are provided in Articles 90–93 EnCT, Article 20 ECAA Agreement and Article 37 TCT, respectively.[262] The protection of individual rights arising from the agreements must be guaranteed by national courts on the basis of remedies available in the respective legal orders to the detriment of homogeneity in the expanded sectoral markets.

---

[257] See C Baudenbacher, 'If Not EEA State Liability, Then What' (n 87) 347–354.
[258] Case E-4/01 *Karlsson* (n 161) para. 32.
[259] Ibid., para. 27.
[260] Ibid., para. 29.
[261] C Baudenbacher, 'If Not EEA State Liability, Then What' (n 87) 358.
[262] Discussed in detail in Chapter 8.

5.4 Conclusion

The principle of effectiveness, emerging from the principle of sincere cooperation enshrined in Article 4(3) TEU, is a guarantor of unity and coherence in the EU legal order.[263] As the subjects of the rights and obligations arising from the EU Treaties are not only the Member States but also their nationals, the principle of effectiveness is transformed into a question of empowering individuals. The Member States must grant individuals access to rights derived from the Treaties by taking all appropriate measures to ensure the fulfilment of the obligations under EU law, facilitating the achievement of the objectives of the Union and refraining from jeopardising their attainment.

The effectiveness of EU law is to be secured by a set of principles of a constitutional nature – direct effect, primacy, consistent interpretation and state liability. Effectiveness is a principle that also applies to public international law. In the light of the growing trend of international regimes, effectiveness is gaining ever more relevance just as the teleological interpretation of the rules of international law and organisations. Teleological, effect-giving interpretation has been of key importance in the creation of the foundational principles in EU law. Extending substantive elements of the EU legal order such as the internal market acquis to third countries amounts, in essence, to the act of creating new international regimes or expanding existing ones, which, too, strive towards effectiveness.

The Court of Justice's initial 'objective and context'-based construal of the transfer of constitutional principles to the EEA legal order in Opinion 1/91 was soon replaced by a more accommodating approach towards the principle of direct effect. Operating in the EFTA pillar of the EEA, the EFTA Court has been far more result-oriented in terms of creating a 'homogeneous legal order' on both substantive and procedural levels. The practice of the EFTA Court reflects a sincere devotion to an effectiveness-based interpretation of the EEA Agreement in the light of the EU Treaties and the foundational principles developed by the Court of Justice. Despite some empirical differences in the application of the acquis in the EU and the EFTA pillars of the EEA, the possibilities for achieving uniform interpretation of identical acquis in the EEA are not dangerously hampered by the fact that the EFTA states are not

---

[263] Case 33/76 *Rewe* (n 244) para. 5; Case C-213/89 *Factortame* (n 41) paras. 19–21; Case C-312/93 *Peterbroeck* (n 246) para. 12.

directly bound by the constitutional doctrines developed by the Court of Justice.

The 'European substantive supremacy'[264] relies on the interpretation adopted by the national courts and the remedies provided by the national legal systems. On the one hand, the expansion of the EU internal market is strengthened and sustained by the autonomous adoption of EU acquis by non-Member States.[265] On the other hand, unity in the extended market is jeopardised, just as in the EU, by national legislatures, administrations and judiciaries. These actors both uphold and challenge the effective application of EU rules through possible inconsistent implementation of the acquis and deficient procedural homogeneity.

In the EU, the Court of Justice enjoys the position of the authoritative interpreter of EU law and an engine for the development of legal doctrines. The EFTA Court serves essentially the same purpose in the EEA. When it comes to the other multilateral arrangements, such as the Energy Community, the ECAA and the Transport Community, it becomes apparent that in the absence of a strong judicial authority comparable to the Court of Justice or the EFTA Court, the burden of ensuring the effectiveness of the regime outside the EU and the EEA falls primarily on the national courts. The questions of the applicability of international law in municipal law, the rank provided to the acquis in the national legal orders and the legal remedies available to individuals to enforce their rights under EU acquis are left to be determined by the national constitutional systems. Likewise is the recognition of the direct effect of a provision of EU origin, unless the legal instrument itself specifies its effect, and the methods for interpreting treaties to be established by the national legal orders and national courts. Although there is nothing in international law to prevent a state from independently adopting an accommodating approach to EU acquis as international rules, in the absence of institutional guarantees one can neither ensure the protection of the individual rights embedded in the exported acquis nor the effectiveness of the expanded internal market. Upholding homogeneity in the multilateral sectoral agreements is, thus, considerably more challenging than in the EEA.

---

[264] JS Delicostopoulos, 'Towards European Procedural Primacy in National Legal Systems' (2003) 9 *European Law Journal* 599, 609.
[265] S Kux and U Sverdrup, 'Fuzzy borders and adaptive outsiders: Norway, Switzerland and the EU' (2000) 22 *Journal of European Integration* 237, 253.

Part II

Expanding the Internal Market:
Institutional Implications

.

6   Autonomy of the EU Legal Order

Achieving and preserving homogeneity in the expanded internal market inevitably calls for an appropriate institutional and procedural framework. Suitable mechanisms must be in place for creating and maintaining an identical body of rules across the territory of the expanded market space, as well as for implementing and interpreting identical acquis in a uniform manner. The claim of homogeneity in the project of extending the EU internal market to non-EU Member States pertains merely to the substantive dimension of the rules transfer; it does not prescribe any particular institutional design by which the desired level of uniformity is to be reached and maintained.

This chapter analyses the meaning and rationale of autonomy in the Union's legal order from the internal and external perspectives. The motivations for the creation, specification and continued application of the concept of autonomy – the unity and effectiveness of the EU legal order – help explain the limitations that the concept imposes on the feasibility of expanding the internal market. The relevant constraints, albeit neither static nor even fully developed, are illustrated by the case law of the Court of Justice whereby the principle of autonomy obstructs the creation of certain institutional structures that could best support the Union's norms export.

6.1 Autonomy of the EU Legal Order: The Concept

Manifestly undefined in scholarly debates,[1] the concept of autonomy of a legal order is not EU-specific but has developed with reference to its

---

[1] See M Klamert, 'The Autonomy of the EU (and of EU Law): Through the Kaleidoscope' (2017) 42 *European Law Review* 815, 815–816.

relationship with the Member States' national legal systems and international law. The principle of autonomy, while maintaining its relevance in the EU's internal context, is increasingly causing complications for the Union's external action, in particular the effective export of the Union's acquis to third countries. The following analysis explains the emergence of the concept of autonomy in the Court's jurisprudence and the role it has subsequently assumed in the EU's legal edifice, as well as illuminates its application in the specific context of international agreements concluded by the EU, including those exporting the internal market acquis.

6.1.1 Autonomy in Relation to the National Legal Orders

Originating from the idea of sovereignty, the concept of an autonomous legal order primarily refers to its self-referential character. An autonomous legal order is able to create, validate, apply and interpret legal rules on the basis of the tools found within the legal order itself without constant validation by another legal order.[2]

The allocation of competences and, thereby, powers between the EU and the Member States is ultimately a question of dividing sovereign powers.[3] The founding Treaties of the EU are concluded under public international law and in accordance with national constitutional requirements regarding their negotiation, signature, conclusion and application. By virtue of the Treaties, the Member States have set up a number of institutions tasked with decision-making, administrative and judicial duties. Although based on an original recognition by the Member States, the institutions of the EU enjoy the powers conferred on them to the extent specified by the Treaties.[4] Once established, the institutional framework thus operates independently of the Member States.

There exist several doctrinal approaches to the concept of autonomy of the EU legal order, illustrated by the renowned debate between Schilling, Weiler and Haltern. Proceeding from Schilling's classification, autonomy can refer to either the absolute, original constituent power ('original autonomy'); independent power that is, however, accorded by another, original constituent power ('derivative autonomy'); or the power to interpret the highest rules in a legal order

---

[2] R Barents, *The Autonomy of Community Law* (Kluwer Law International 2004) 172.
[3] P Pescatore, *The Law of Integration* (Sijthoff 1974) 30.
[4] Article 5(2) TEU.

('interpretive autonomy').[5] The latter, according to Schilling, belongs to the concept of original autonomy but not necessarily to the legal orders that enjoy derivative autonomy. By virtue of the Member States, the EU Treaties possess derivative autonomy.[6]

In contrast to Schilling, Weiler and Haltern have argued that the Member States do not possess the right of 'auto-decision' over the meaning of the Treaties; this is notwithstanding the practice of the Member States' judiciaries to delimit the competences between the EU and the Member States.[7] The Court is, indeed, the 'ultimate umpire' in the EU legal system. This position of the Court is enshrined in the Treaty articles that require Member State compliance with the Court's judgments under Article 260(1) TFEU; the jurisdiction of the Court to review the validity and legality of EU measures under Article 263 TFEU, among others on grounds of a lack of competence; and the obligation of the Member States' courts of last instance under Article 267 TFEU to refer for preliminary ruling to the Court any matter on the interpretation of the Treaties or the validity or interpretation of an EU legal act.

Another key assumption in the discussion is that the Court enjoys judicial *Kompetenz-Kompetenz* – the power to determine the limits of the EU's competences.[8] Article 267 TFEU allocates judicial *Kompetenz-Kompetenz* to the Court to provide authoritative interpretations of EU law and rule on its validity. The ultimate authority to rule on the limits of the powers conferred on the Union is exercised by the Court of Justice rather than the courts of the Member States.[9]

Several judgments of the Court of Justice as well as national courts indeed confirm that the Member States have transferred part of their

---

[5] T Schilling, 'The Autonomy of the Community Legal Order: An Analysis of Possible Foundations' (1996) 37 *Harvard International Law Journal* 389, 389–390.

[6] Ibid., 404.

[7] JHH Weiler and UR Haltern, 'The Autonomy of the Community Legal Order – Through the Looking Glass' (1996) 37 *Harvard International Law Journal* 411, 424–425.

[8] Ibid., 436–437.

[9] As concerns EU law or the Court's rulings adopted *ultra vires*, in violation of fundamental rights and infringing national constitutional identity, the German Constitutional Court and the Czech Constitutional Court beg to differ: see M Payandeh, 'Constitutional Review of EU Law after *Honeywell*: Contextualizing the Relationship between the German Constitutional Court and the EU Court of Justice' (2011) 48 *Common Market Law Review* 9; J Komárek, 'Czech Constitutional Court Playing with Matches: The Czech Constitutional Court Declares a Judgment of the Court of Justice of the EU *Ultra Vires*; Judgment of 31 January 2012, Pl. ÚS 5/12, *Slovak Pensions XVII*' (2012) 8 *European Constitutional Law Review* 323.

sovereignty to the EU.[10] This, in turn, is a crucial element in making the determination that the EU legal order is one of autonomous character,[11] recognised both by the supranational legal order itself and by the national legal orders from which the autonomy derives. For the EU Member States, the duty to fully apply the Treaties entails a partial loss of sovereignty insofar as the Union has been set up for 'unlimited duration, having its own institutions, its own personality, its own legal capacity and capacity of representation on the international plane and, more particularly, real powers stemming from a limitation of sovereignty or a transfer of powers from the States to the Community'.[12] It were incompatible with the terms and spirit of the Treaty as well as the obligation of the Member States to give effect to the Treaties in their national legal orders if the Member States could overrule the authority of the EU legal system by giving precedence to their own unilateral acts,[13] and, thereby, exercise 'auto-decision'.

Similarly to the foundational principles,[14] the fundamental rationale behind the claim for autonomy of the EU legal order is the desire to uphold the unity of the legal order and, consequently, to ensure its proper functioning.[15] Unity and effectiveness are also closely related to the principle of primacy. Were one legal order to penetrate the interpretation or application of the rules of another legal order, the latter could not justify its independent existence nor could the objectives of the Union be reached. This inevitably demands the creation of a supranational and autonomous legal order, which serves the common aims of the Member States.[16]

The concept of autonomy requires, in addition to the EU Treaties determining the legal remedies available under EU law, also that the content of those rights and obligations be found in the Treaties. For the sake of ensuring the uniformity and efficacy of EU law, the validity of the measures adopted by the EU institutions may only be judged in the light of EU law itself and not on the basis of national laws and legal

---

[10] Case 26/62 *Van Gend en Loos* EU:C:1963:1; Case 6/64 *Costa* v. *ENEL* EU:C:1964:66; the German Constitutional Court's ruling 1 BvR 248/63, 216/67 *EWG-Verordnungen* [1967] BVerfGE 22, 293, para. 15;

[11] FC Mayer, '*Van Gend en Loos*: The Foundation of a Community of Law' in M Poiares Maduro and L Azoulai (eds.), *The Past and Future of EU Law* (Hart Publishing 2010) 16, 20.

[12] Case 6/64 *Costa* v. *ENEL* (n 10) (emphasis added).

[13] Ibid.

[14] See Chapter 5.

[15] R Barents (n 2) 171–172.

[16] P Pescatore (n 3) 50–51.

concepts.[17] Moreover, recourse to national interpretation of EU law is impossible due to the Treaties constituting an 'independent source of law' thereby autonomous from the national legal orders.[18] As such, the validity of the Treaties cannot be questioned by national courts without questioning the very foundations of the EU legal order as a whole, not even on grounds of an alleged violation of fundamental rights as recognised by national constitutional law.[19]

The self-referential character of the EU legal order is inextricably linked to the EU's institutional framework. The latter upholds the independence of the legal order from external claims of authority and ensures that the rules of the legal order are interpreted and applied consistently with the principles inherent to the legal order.[20] The Court has repeatedly overruled the attempts of the Member States' governments to challenge the refusal of the EU institutions to take account of national laws and, thus, the autonomy of those institutions.[21] The autonomy of the institutions does not, however, mean that only they are endowed with the task of giving effect to EU law. National institutions and judiciaries form part of the general institutional framework of the EU whereas the ultimate authority to give binding interpretations of EU law and to declare the latter invalid rests with the Court pursuant to Article 267 TFEU.[22]

Reverting back to Schilling's classification, the Court of Justice and the national courts proceed to consider the EU legal order as one possessing 'derivative autonomy',[23] yet having reached 'interpretive autonomy' to the extent that it is the Court that interprets EU law and determines the validity of EU secondary legal acts, including draft international agreements, in the light of the Treaties. It is, therefore, also the Court that decides what is necessary to uphold the

---

[17] Case 11/70 *Internationale Handelsgesellschaft* EU:C:1970:114, para. 3.
[18] Ibid.
[19] Ibid.
[20] R Barents (n 2) 262–263.
[21] Case 1/58 *Stork v. High Authority* EU:C:1959:4, 26; Joined Cases 7/56 and 3–7/57 *Alegra v. Common Assembly* EU:C:1957:7, 57; Case 30/59 *Gezamenlijke Steenkolenmijnen* EU: C:1961:2, 22. This is notwithstanding the mutual application of the autonomy of the EU legal order – neither does the EU possess the power to annul national rules that conflict with the obligations of the Member States under EU law: Case 6/60 *Humblet* EU: C:1960:48, 568.
[22] Case 314/85 *Foto-Frost v. Hauptzollamt Lübeck-Ost* EU:C:1987:452, para. 17; G Bebr, 'The Relation of the European Coal and Steel Community Law to the Law of the Member States: A Peculiar Legal Symbiosis' (1958) 58 *Columbia Law Review* 767, 769–770.
[23] See, for example, 2 BvE 2/08 *Lissabon* et al. [2009] BVerfG 123, 231.

autonomous, self-validating character of the EU legal order for the purpose of attaining the Treaty objectives.

The effectiveness of the norms export from the Union to third countries is vitally dependent on institutions that support a timely and efficient transfer of new or amended rules from the Union's legal order to the third countries' legal orders. The role of efficient institutions is ever more relevant bearing in mind that norms transfer in this case takes place by means of 'regular' international agreements and not via the supranational EU Treaties, whereas the desired outcome of the norms exporting exercise is homogeneity of the acquis inside and outside the EU. Maintaining the autonomy of the Union's legal order, however, demands that even in this specifically external context, the Union shall retain 'auto-decision' over the content and scope of the acquis and that interpretations given by third country courts do not encroach upon the judicial *Kompetenz-Kompetenz* or the interpretative autonomy of the Court of Justice. Setting up institutions that are able to uphold homogeneity of the acquis in the EU and third countries while preserving the prerogatives of the Court is not an easy task.

6.1.2 Autonomy in Relation to International Law

From an external perspective, the autonomy of the EU legal order is a means of controlling the normative influence of legal norms and principles that emanate from outside the EU.[24] The EU legal order exists within the international community but its autonomous character precludes the authoritative influence of international norms that have not become part thereof. The EU is thus independent to determine the applicability and the legal effect of international law on its territory. The Court has generally taken an accommodating approach towards the influences of international law on EU law. It does not preclude an interpretation of EU law in the light of the general principles of international law or customary international law, the provisions of international agreements to which the EU is a party itself or by proxy of the Member States, or the decisions of international courts and tribunals the jurisdiction of which is binding on the Union.

When it has considered it necessary to protect the Union's legal order from excessive influence, however, the Court's stance has been firm. This is best illustrated by the landmark judgments *Kadi I* and *Kadi II*. The cases touched upon the fundamental issue of the interaction between

---

[24] R Barents (n 2) 261.

the EU Treaties and the Charter of the United Nations Organisation (UN). The EU not being a member of the UN, the obligations under its Charter do not bind the Union directly. A question, nevertheless, arose concerning the indirect influence of the UN Charter on the EU legal order. In *Kadi I*, the CFI ruled that the Member States' obligations under the UN Charter, including the resolutions of the Security Council, enjoy primacy over all domestic and international law obligations including the EU Treaties by virtue of international customary law and Articles 5, 27 and 30 VCLT as well as under Article 103 UN Charter and the case law of the ICJ.[25] Furthermore, since the Member States' obligations under the UN Charter predate the conclusion of the EU Treaties, the Member States must give precedence to the Charter and leave conflicting measures of EU law unapplied.[26]

In the appeal of *Kadi I*,[27] the Court of Justice ruled that in its legislative action, including when implementing UN anti-terrorist sanctions on the EU's territory, the Union is bound by the international requirements of fundamental rights protection. Also considering that the EU legal order is an autonomous one, the Court concluded in *Kadi II* that international obligations cannot prevail over the constitutional principles of the EU Treaties, including respect for fundamental rights, which is a precondition for the lawfulness of EU measures.[28] Neither can measures adopted by the Member States for the purpose of maintaining peace and international security nor international agreements concluded by the Member States prior to their accession to the EU be given precedence under Articles 347 and 351 TFEU at the expense of the protection of fundamental rights by the EU.[29] In *Kadi*, the main thrust of the Court's autonomy argument was to uphold the Union's standard of protection of fundamental rights rather than the jurisdiction of the Court.[30] The latter aspect has, however, been in the focus of a number of other cases.

Most frequently, the EU courts deal with the interaction between EU and international law in cases concerning the interpretation of EU or national rules, including EU law of international law origin, in the light of international law. The latter category includes international

---

[25] Case T-315/01 *Kadi* EU:T:2005:332, paras. 181–184; Case T-306/01 *Yusuf and Al Barakaat* EU:T:2005:331, paras. 231–234.

[26] Case T-315/01 *Kadi* (n 25) paras. 185–190; Case T-306/01 *Yusuf and Al Barakaat* (n 25) paras. 235–240.

[27] Joined Cases C-402/05 P and C-415/05 P *Kadi and Al Barakaat* EU:C:2008:461.

[28] Ibid., paras. 282 and 285; Case 5/88 *Wachauf* EU:C:1989:321, para. 19.

[29] Joined Cases C-402/05 P and C-415/05 P *Kadi and Al Barakaat* (n 27) paras. 302–304.

[30] M Klamert (n 1) 829.

agreements concluded by the EU, or by the Member States in instances where the EU as an international organisation cannot accede to an international instrument in its field of competence due to restrictions imposed by the international agreement. In *Cipra and Kvasnicka*, for example, the Court examined its own jurisdiction to interpret the European Agreement concerning the Work of Crews of Vehicles engaged in International Road Transport (the AETR Agreement).[31] The Agreement was concluded only by the EU Member States without the EEC, although it covers an area of shared competence. During the time when the initial negotiations took place, the EEC had not yet legislated in the field.[32] Following the adoption of Regulation (EEC) No 543/69 on the harmonisation of certain social legislation relating to road transport, the EU assumed exclusive competence over the subject matter of the Agreement.[33] In order not to undermine the ongoing negotiations, the Commission and the Council decided that the Member States could proceed to conclude the agreement.[34] In so doing, however, the Member States acted 'in the interest and on behalf of the [Union]'[35] and the provisions of the AETR Agreement, subsequently, formed part of EU law.[36] As a consequence, the Court of Justice claimed jurisdiction to interpret the agreement,[37] even though the Union was not formally party to the agreement. The sphere of EU law in which the Court enjoys judicial *Kompetenz-Kompetenz*, thus, exceeds measures officially adopted by the Union's institutions.

Close cooperation between the Member States and the EU is required in the stages of negotiation, conclusion as well as the fulfilment of the commitments entered into on the international plane,[38] including both AETR-type situations and mixed agreements. In fact, it is 'the inherent nature of the system'[39] of the EU to strive for unity in operation and representation through the cooperation between Union institutions and the Member States, including their judiciaries. The unity of standards protected in *Kadi II* and the unity of the EU's external action represent two sides of the same coin – safeguarding the effectiveness

[31] Case C-439/01 *Cipra and Kvasnicka* EU:C:2003:31.
[32] Case 22/70 *Commission* v. *Council (AETR)* EU:C:1971:32, paras. 82–83.
[33] Ibid., paras. 30–31.
[34] Ibid., paras. 86–87.
[35] Ibid., para. 90; Case C-439/01 *Cipra and Kvasnicka* (n 31) para. 23.
[36] Case C-439/01 *Cipra and Kvasnicka* (n 31) para. 24.
[37] Ibid.
[38] Opinion 1/94 *WTO* EU:C:1994:384, para. 108.
[39] Case C-53/96 *Hermès* v. *FHT* EU:C:1997:539, Opinion of AG Tesauro, para. 21.

of the Union's policies in addition to the good functioning of the Treaties and the attainment of the objectives set out therein.

Regarding mixed agreements, the Court has generally held that since agreements concluded by the Union are acts of EU institutions, it has jurisdiction to rule on their validity and interpretation at least regarding those parts of the agreement that fall within the scope of Union competence.[40] The Member States, in turn, have under Article 216(2) TFEU a duty vis-à-vis the EU to ensure the proper fulfilment of the obligations arising from international agreements concluded by the Union.[41] The question of the Court's jurisdiction to interpret those provisions of mixed agreements that deal with issues falling within a sphere of shared competences in which the EU has not yet legislated first arose in the context of the Agreement on Trade-Related Aspects of Intellectual Property Rights (TRIPs). In the cases Hèrmes[42] and Dior,[43] the Court found that the jurisdiction to interpret the provisions of the TRIPs Agreement, which was concluded jointly by the EU and the Member States, requires for the purpose of unity uniform interpretation by both the judiciaries of the Member States and of the EU.[44] In order to ensure this uniformity, the Court extended its jurisdiction in Dior to interpret Article 50 of TRIPs regarding intellectual property law beyond issues of trademark regulation, which fell within the scope of Community competence.[45] The Court thereby overstepped the competence boundaries between the EU and the Member States in a mixed agreement but refrained from clarifying the exact link between jurisdiction and competences.[46] Finally, in Merck Genéricos, the Court established that notwithstanding the jurisdiction of the Member States' courts to interpret those provisions of mixed agreements that fall within their sphere of competence, the assessment of the exact division of competences must for the purposes of ensuring uniformity on the EU level be made by the Court of Justice.[47] This includes determining whether a provision of a mixed agreement has direct effect; in areas

---

[40] See, for example, Case 181/73 Haegeman EU:C:1974:41, paras. 4–6; Case 12/86 Demirel EU:C:1987:400, para. 7.

[41] Case 104/81 Kupferberg EU:C:1982:362, para. 2.

[42] Case C-53/96 Hermès v. FHT EU:C:1998:292.

[43] Joined Cases C-300/98 and C-392/98 Dior EU:C:2000:688.

[44] Ibid., paras. 37–38; Case C-53/96 Hermès v. FHT (n 42) para. 32.

[45] Joined Cases C-300/98 and C-392/98 Dior (n 43) para. 39.

[46] Case C-240/09 Lesoochranárske zoskupenie VLK EU:C:2010:436, Opinion of AG Sharpston, para. 50.

[47] Case C-431/05 Merck Genéricos EU:C:2007:496, paras. 33–38.

that fall within Member States' competence, the determination shall be made by the national courts.[48] By protecting the division of competences laid out in the Treaties and its own role in the Union's institutional set-up, the Court shows deep determination to safeguard unity in the EU legal order, be it from the influence of its Member States or the third country counterparts to international agreements.

Other situations in which the interaction between international law and EU law can give rise to conflicts concern the interpretation of EU law by international actors. An example is provided by the *MOX Plant* case,[49] which concerned a non-EU judiciary – an international arbitral tribunal – being called upon by an EU Member State to rule on the application and interpretation of EU law. *MOX Plant* dealt with infringement proceedings initiated by the Commission against Ireland. The Irish government had submitted a case against the United Kingdom to an arbitral tribunal established under the 1992 Convention for the Protection of the Marine Environment of the North-East Atlantic, which the EU, too, has concluded. In addition, Ireland submitted a request for provisional measures to the International Tribunal for the Law of the Sea (ITLOS). The arbitral tribunal, recognising that it would have to rule on matters of EU law including the division of competences between the Union and the Member States and the exclusive jurisdiction of the Court of Justice, decided to suspend the proceedings and await the Court's decision as to its exclusive jurisdiction to adjudicate on the matter.[50]

The Court considered that the fact that the Tribunal was to interpret EU law constituted a threat to the autonomy of the EU legal order. This is a step further from *Hèrmes*, *Dior* and *Merck Genericos*, in which the Court made explicit links between its interpretative monopoly and with the unity but not the autonomy of the EU legal order. The legal rules that were the subject of Ireland's submission fell within the scope of EU competence, which triggered the Court's exclusive jurisdiction to rule on the matter.[51] The Court pointed out that the division of competences in the EU legal order between the Union and the Member States cannot be altered by an international agreement, as that would adversely affect the autonomy of the EU legal order.[52] The Court's judgment was based

---

[48] Joined Cases C-300/98 and C-392/98 *Dior* (n 43) para. 48; Ibid., para. 34.
[49] Case C-459/03 *Commission* v. *Ireland (MOX Plant)* EU:C:2006:345.
[50] Ibid., paras. 42–48.
[51] Ibid., paras. 120–121.
[52] Ibid., para. 123.

on Article 344 TFEU pursuant to which Member States undertake not to submit a dispute concerning the interpretation or application of the Treaties to any method of settlement other than those provided in the Treaties.[53] This rule is closely connected to the duty of sincere cooperation between Member States under Article 4(3) TEU.[54] In the case at hand, though, a solution to the question of conflicting jurisdictions was provided in the United Nations Convention on the Law of the Sea (UNCLOS) itself to which both the EU and its Member States are parties. Pursuant to Article 282 UNCLOS, if the parties to the Convention have agreed to submit disputes arising between them to a procedure that results in a binding decision, that procedure shall take precedence over the dispute settlement mechanisms provided by the UNCLOS. The Convention, therefore, pays full respect to the autonomy of the EU legal order in terms of not exercising jurisdiction over EU law, which, in *MOX Plant*, concerned both the provisions of an international agreement concluded by the EU and the Member States as well as EU directives. The matter under dispute fell within the competence of the EU by virtue of Ireland relying in its argumentation before the tribunal on EU directives.[55] Since the Convention is a mixed agreement and the EU enjoys exclusive competence in the relevant fields, the Court deemed the case to be decided on the basis of the EU Treaties, which included the exclusive jurisdiction of the Court.[56] Subsequently, Ireland was held to have breached its obligations under EU law.[57]

The above line of case law illustrates well the perception of the EU as an autonomous legal order – 'municipal' in the words of AG Poiares Maduro,[58] yet not as one completely isolated from the international legal regime. Respect for international law is deeply rooted in the EU legal order but does not lead to the Court abandoning its keenness to protect the many facets of unity and, thereby, also the autonomy of the legal order by controlling the influence of international law and alongside that its own jurisdiction to interpret and adjudicate EU law. The latter includes, especially, the parts of mixed agreements that fall within the scope of the EU's exclusive competence as well as

---

[53] Ibid.
[54] Ibid., para. 169.
[55] Ibid., paras. 119–121.
[56] Ibid., paras. 126–127.
[57] Ibid., para. 182.
[58] Joined Cases C-402/05 P and C-415/05 P *Kadi and Al Barakaat* EU:C:2008:11, Opinion of AG Poiares Maduro, para. 21.

agreements concluded by the Member States acting in the interests of the Union.

The multilateral agreements exporting the internal market acquis have been concluded as mixed or exclusively EU agreements and include, for the sake of guaranteeing unity, more or less elaborate institutional mechanisms. All of these aspects can, in the light of the case law discussed earlier, lead to conflicts between the Court of Justice safeguarding the effectiveness of the functioning of the Treaties, including its own prerogatives, and the effectiveness of norms transfer by means of international agreements.

6.2 The Implications of Autonomy for Expanding the Internal Market

The Court's broad view on its own jurisdiction and the requirements for maintaining the uniform interpretation and application of EU law have led to obstacles in the Union's effective pursuit of foreign policy. Many international agreements to be concluded by the Union may potentially encroach upon the autonomy of the legal order, leaving both the Union negotiators and their third country counterparts in limbo and in search for solutions that would pass the Court's rigorous scrutiny.

Whereas the key mechanism for maintaining the effectiveness of EU law is embedded in the EU's supranational principles such as primacy, direct effect and state liability,[59] the safeguards against threats to the autonomy of the EU legal order lie, primarily, in institutional arrangements and the legal rules that ensure its proper functioning.[60] By upholding the authority to determine its institutional structure, the EU is able to preserve its 'independence of action' or, in other words, 'autonomy'.[61] In a sequence of case law, the Court has examined the compatibility with the principle of autonomy of a number of institutional arrangements in international agreements. Many of the cases are opinions delivered under Article 218(11) TFEU and several concern agreements that export the EU's acquis to third countries. In order to

---

[59] D Leczykiewicz, 'Effectiveness of EU Law before National Courts: Direct Effect, Effective Judicial Protection, and State Liability' in A Arnull and D Chalmers (eds.), *Oxford Handbook of European Union Law* (Oxford University Press 2015) 212.

[60] See Opinion 2/13 *ECHR II* EU:C:2014:2454, para. 158.

[61] Opinion 1/76 *European laying-up fund for inland waterway vessels* EU:C:1977:63, para. 12. In the original French text the 'independence of action' is referred to as *'l'autonomie d'action'*.

achieve and maintain homogeneity with the internal market acquis,[62] the agreements must provide supporting institutional structures that enable swift and precise transferral of new acquis from the EU to the third country contracting parties. Suitable institutional arrangements, however, often give rise to conflicts with the principle of autonomy.

The conditions for deeming an institutional framework established by an international agreement compatible with the EU legal order can be divided into two distinct groups that have been summarised by the Court in Opinion 1/00.[63] The catalogue is broad but follows the essential aspects outlined by the Court in the case law discussed earlier. The first requirement of preserving the autonomy of the EU legal order demands that the essential character of the powers and the institutions of the EU remain unaffected so as not to necessitate an amendment of the Treaties. The second requirement stipulates that the EU and its institutions must maintain their independence in interpreting EU law – interpretive autonomy – in the exercise of their internal powers and may not be bound by an interpretation given to identical acquis in the context of an international agreement.

Maintaining the essential character of the EU's powers and institutions concerns a number of different issues: first, the relationship between the Member States in the context of the EU including the 'mutual trust' between them; second, the idea that the objectives of the EU must be obtained by 'common action' of the Member States; and, third, the understanding according to which the EU institutions may not transfer to 'non-EU organisms' powers of the Union. The fourth category of essential elements in safeguarding autonomy relates to the nature of the powers of the EU and of its institutions as conceived in the Treaties. On the one hand, the powers of the Commission may be extended to third countries provided that the nature of the powers remains intact; on the other, EU representatives cannot be replaced by those of the Member States in the organs of international organisations; and, moreover, the 'nature of the function of the Court' requires that its judgments be binding. The fifth and sixth aspect concern the role of national courts as 'ordinary' courts in the 'complete system of legal remedies and procedures', and remedies to individuals following an infringement of EU law by a Member State.

---

[62] Article 1(1) EEA Agreement; Article 2 EnCT; Article 1(1) ECAA Agreement; Article 1(1) TCT.

[63] Opinion 1/00 *ECAA* EU:C:2002:231, paras. 12–13.

Safeguarding the independence of the Union's institutions when interpreting EU law follows from the basic premise that the EU's institutions enjoy interpretive autonomy and the Court, in particular, possesses judicial *Kompetenz-Kompetenz*. Interpretive autonomy inevitably entails the exclusive jurisdiction of the EU judiciary to interpret and apply EU law, including the obligation of the Member States under Article 344 TFEU to refrain from submitting disputes concerning to the interpretation or application of EU law to other methods of adjudication than those provided in the Treaties. The judges of the Court must, moreover, maintain 'complete independence' when interpreting EU law. Judicial *Kompetenz-Kompetenz* necessitates the exclusive jurisdiction of the Court of Justice to delimit the competences between the EU and its Member States and to declare invalid an act of EU institutions under Article 263 TFEU. Each of these elements has been examined in the following case law.

6.2.1 Opinion 1/76 European Laying-Up Fund

The very first case to deal with an international agreement threatening to distort the institutional system of the EU was Opinion 1/76 on the Draft Agreement establishing a European laying-up fund for inland waterway vessels.[64] The Draft Agreement sought to set up an international organisation to regulate inland waterway navigation on the river Rhine. While the Court endorsed, generally, the establishment of such an international organisation, it contested certain solutions proposed for its institutional design. The Draft Agreement intended to privilege some Member States over others in terms of their participation in the organs of the organisation. This, according to the Court, was to 'alter in a manner inconsistent with the Treaty the relationships between Member States within the context of the Community'.[65] More precisely, pursuant to Recital 2 of the preamble to the EEC Treaty, the objectives of the Community must be obtained by 'common action'. The latter requires the participation of all Member States without even a voluntary exclusion of one or more Member States, as well as that the same participation rules of individual Member States as have been determined by the Treaties in the respective policy field apply to the decision-making procedures of an international agreement.[66]

---

[64] Opinion 1/76 *European laying-up fund for inland waterway vessels* (n 61).
[65] Ibid., para. 10.
[66] Ibid., para. 11(b).

Together these factors constituted, according to the Court, 'a surrender of the independence of action of the Community in its external relations' as well as an alteration in the 'internal constitution of the Community' by virtue of an alteration in the essential elements of the Community structure concerning the powers of the institutions as well as the relationship between the Member States.[67] In turn, these elements were deemed to conflict with the principles of unity and solidarity in the Community. Today, common action has in the light of the increased use of flexibility mechanisms, especially opt-outs, become accepted as compatible with both the unity and, subsequently, even the autonomy of the EU legal order. The absence of one or more Member States in any of those policies or decision-making procedures that are not subject to opt-outs would, on the other hand, still be likely to fail the test of compatibility with the Treaties.

Regarding decision-making procedures, the Court considered incompatible with the EEC Treaty provisions of the Draft Agreement that replaced the EEC's institutions with the Member States in the organs of the treaty that dealt with matters falling within the EEC's competence and, thereby, restricted the powers of the Commission.[68] Also, the Court analysed the compatibility with the EEC Treaty of a provision of the Draft Agreement by which direct applicability would be granted to all decisions of the Fund's organs in the territories of the contracting parties, including the Community. Here, a peculiar question of *Kompetenz-Kompetenz* arose. The question referred to the authority of the Community's institutions to transfer the Community's powers to 'non-Community organisms' and thereby subject the Member States to the direct applicability of rules created by an international body outside the decision-making framework of the EEC Treaty.[69] Indeed, a transfer of such powers to another international organisation would subject the Community's legal order to the authority of another legal order and, thus, deprive the former of its autonomous nature. The situation is different if the international agreement itself specifies the possible direct effect of its provisions.[70] The Court, however, refrained from answering the question because according to the provisions of the Draft Agreement, the powers to be transferred were of executive nature

---

[67] Ibid., para. 12.
[68] Ibid., paras. 10–11(a).
[69] Ibid., para. 15.
[70] Case 104/81 *Kupferberg* (n 41) para. 17.

only and thus not liable to bind the contracting parties, including the Community, to supranational rules.[71]

Regarding the judicial system envisaged by the Draft Agreement in Opinion 1/76, the Court considered that including a non-Member State in the legal system of the agreement would preclude the effective legal protection of the rights of individuals.[72] The participation of the judges of the Court of Justice in the fund tribunal would prejudice their impartiality in deciding cases brought before the Court after the same legal question had already been considered by the fund tribunal in the presence of the same judges and vice versa. Whereas homogeneity would be preserved, the uniformity of interpretation was not considered to outweigh the prospect of EU law developing lopin in a manner completely independent of external influences beyond those considered by the Court to be compatible with the Treaties.[73] The only acceptable solution from the perspective of the autonomy of the EU legal order would, therefore, be for the judges of the Court not to participate in judicial institutions established by international agreements concluded by the Union, at least in situations where the envisaged court or tribunal could potentially be called upon to interpret or apply EU law.

The Court of Justice recognised the value of the Draft Agreement as an example for future agreements concluded between the EU and/or its Member States and third countries. The latter must conform to the requirements pronounced by the Court in order to receive a green light in the opinion procedure under Article 218(11) TFEU.

6.2.2 Opinion 1/91 EEA I

Some of the issues that arose in Opinion 1/76 recurred in the landmark Opinion 1/91 concerning the compatibility with the Treaties of the draft EEA Agreement.[74] In the Opinion, the Court confined its analysis of the compatibility of the Draft Agreement with the autonomy of the EU legal order to the proposed judicial architecture only. Opinion 1/91 notably features explicit references to the notion of the autonomy of the EU legal order in the context of international agreements exporting EU acquis – a terminological affirmation, which the Court has upheld in subsequent case law.

---

[71] Opinion 1/76 *European laying-up fund for inland waterway vessels* (n 61) para. 16.
[72] Ibid., para. 21.
[73] Ibid., para. 22.
[74] Opinion 1/91 *EEA I* EU:C:1991:490.

The judicial autonomy of the EU legal order, as elaborated in Opinion 1/91, rests on two main premises: Articles 19(1) TEU and 344 TFEU. These provisions assert the exclusive jurisdiction of the EU judiciary to ensure that in the interpretation and application of the Treaties the law is observed, and the obligation of the Member States not to submit EU law disputes to external fora, respectively. The EEA Court envisaged by the draft EEA Agreement would have been conferred jurisdiction to hear disputes between the contracting parties. Subsequently, the EEA Court would have had to interpret the term 'Contracting Party' in the context of the EEA Agreement and thereby determine who – the EU, the Member States or the EU and the Member States together – were indeed contracting parties in the particular case brought before the EEA Court. The tasks of the EEA Court would, therefore, have entailed a delimitation of competences between the EU and its Member States that constitutes an interpretation of the Treaties by a judicial body other than the Court of Justice.[75] The Court maintained that the creation of an international court whose decisions are binding on EU institutions including the Court itself is not *per se* contrary to the Treaties.[76] Yet a distinction was made with respect to 'an essential part of the rules – including the rules of secondary legislation – which govern economic and trading relations within the Community and which constitute, for the most part, 'fundamental provisions of the Community legal order'.[77] A homogeneous interpretation of the exported acquis that is identical to EU provisions would, according to the Court, add up to an interpretation of EU law itself. In the absence of an obligation on behalf of the EEA Court to provide an interpretation of EEA law that is identical with the interpretations given by the Court of Justice after the signature of the EEA Agreement, the mechanism for maintaining homogeneity would have threatened the independence of the Court to determine the meaning and application of EU rules and thus the 'very foundations' of the EU and the autonomy of the EU legal order.[78]

The Court did not consider its freedom to deviate from the homogeneity objective in favour of preserving autonomy should a conflict arise between its own and the EEA Court's interpretation of the acquis. Instead, the Court endeavoured to ascertain whether the draft EEA Agreement complied fully with the requirements of the Treaties, and

[75] Ibid., paras. 31–35.
[76] Ibid., paras. 39–40.
[77] Ibid., para. 41.
[78] Ibid., paras. 44–46.

whether the autonomy of the EU legal order could be safeguarded without forcing the Court to breach its obligations under the EEA Agreement to maintain homogeneity within the EEA legal order. Homogeneity in the EEA was, thus, not sacrificed for the sake of autonomy.

In terms of the composition of the EEA Court, similarly to Opinion 1/76, the Court considered it incompatible with the concept of autonomy that judges of the Court of Justice sit on the EEA Court.[79] In such a setting, the judges of the Court of Justice would need to juggle between different methods of interpretation when applying and interpreting identical rules in two different treaty contexts that also feature different objectives regarding the depth of integration.[80] The Court was concerned that such a task would challenge the 'open minds' and 'complete independence' of its judges when interpreting EU law and thus jeopardise the idea of autonomy as independence from legal sources external to the EU.[81] While the Court has generally not been averse towards drawing inspiration from public international law or national legal systems for the purpose of interpreting EU law, here the problematic aspect was the Court's perception that the judges would, in a situation of multiple loyalties, not be fully independent to interpret EU law solely on the basis of the objectives and context of the EU Treaties.

Finally, the Court considered in Opinion 1/91 the compatibility with the Treaties of the system of preliminary rulings under the draft EEA Agreement. According to the draft Protocol 34 to the EEA Agreement, the courts of the EEA EFTA States would have been conferred a right to make references for a preliminary ruling to the Court of Justice. In the meantime, each of the contracting parties could determine the extent to which the protocol would apply to the courts and tribunals under their jurisdiction, whether there is an obligation for the highest courts to make a referral and whether the Court's rulings have binding effect.[82] It is not contrary to the Treaties to confer on the Court the task to provide preliminary rulings to third country courts on the basis of an international agreement or to allow third countries to decide whether to permit their courts and tribunals to make use of the preliminary ruling procedure; it was, however, considered incompatible with the Treaty

[79] Ibid., para. 47.
[80] Ibid., para. 51.
[81] Ibid., paras. 52–53.
[82] Ibid., paras. 56–58.

structure if in instances where the Court has given a preliminary ruling there are no guarantees to ensure its binding force.[83] Pursuant to the Court, the lack of binding force of its preliminary rulings would defeat 'the nature of the function of the Court of Justice [...] namely that of a court whose judgments are binding'.[84] It is remarkable that the Court considered only the binding effect of the preliminary rulings an issue and not the lack of a general obligation of the highest courts to request a preliminary ruling as if the latter did not belong to the 'nature of the function of the Court of Justice'. The first concerns the function of the Court as not being an advisory body and the other the function of the procedure that might not guarantee unity if requests for preliminary rulings are optional. As a clarification, the Court noted that all preliminary rulings, even those given in response to possible requests by the EEA EFTA countries, are binding on the Member States. Yet confusion could arise among the Member State courts as to the general effect of preliminary rulings when applying preliminary rulings that are not binding on their potentially direct addressees – the EEA EFTA States' courts.[85]

6.2.3 Opinion 1/92 EEA II

Having struck down the first version of the EEA Agreement, the Court had the opportunity to assess the compatibility with the Treaties of the second version of the Draft Agreement in Opinion 1/92.[86] The second version of the EEA Agreement no longer envisaged the creation of an EEA Court but instead an EFTA Court that would only adjudicate on disputes between the EEA EFTA States and in which only judges from the EEA EFTA countries would sit. The concerns raised by the Court in the previous Opinion 1/91 were, thus, met. Also, the Court was given the possibility to be involved in the dispute settlement procedure by giving rulings on the interpretation of those rules contained in the EEA Agreement that are identical to those of the Treaties. The EEA EFTA States were, furthermore, provided an opportunity to decide whether to allow its courts to request binding rulings from the Court of Justice on the interpretation of the provisions of the EEA Agreement. Finally, the requirement for the Court to take account of the decisions of other courts had been removed.[87] The Union's judicial

---

[83] Ibid., paras. 59–61.
[84] Ibid., para. 61.
[85] Ibid., paras. 62–63.
[86] Opinion 1/92 EEA II EU:C:1992:189.
[87] Ibid., paras. 13–16.

Kompetenz-Kompetenz, interpretive autonomy and the unity of the legal order were thereby safeguarded.

Instead of a common EEA Court, the updated EEA Agreement provides for the creation of a political body – the Joint Committee – to track the development of the case law of the Court. The Court deemed this solution to be compatible with the Treaties and the principle of autonomy insofar as it does not alter the binding force of the rulings of the Court within the EU.[88] Under Articles 105 and 111 EEA Agreement, which are linked together and 'must be interpreted systematically and consistently', the Joint Committee cannot issue decisions that would render the case law of the Court inapplicable in the contracting parties.[89]

The Court further stated that it could be conferred additional powers only upon a revision of the Treaties unless the new powers did not alter the 'nature of the function of the Court', such as altering the binding force of the Court's judgments.[90] The new procedures of the Court giving rulings on the interpretation of the EEA agreement and identical acquis envisaged in the updated EEA Agreement concern both the settlement of disputes under Article 111(3) EEA Agreement and the requests for rulings by the EEA EFTA States under Article 107 EEA Agreement and Protocol 34 to the EEA Agreement.[91] Since binding force is accorded to the interpretations provided by the Court it does not, therefore, affect the nature of the function of the Court in an adverse manner.[92] The arbitration procedure provided in Article 111(4) EEA Agreement and Protocol 33 to the EEA Agreement, on the other hand, cannot be used if the object of interpretation is the identical acquis. This means that EU acquis will not be given authoritative interpretation by non-EU judicial mechanisms, and that the autonomy of the EU legal order is thus upheld.[93]

In addition to the judicial mechanisms, the autonomy of the EU legal order also requires the preservation of other institutional arrangements established by the Treaties to the extent of maintaining the 'nature of [their] powers'.[94] The sharing of surveillance tasks in the field of competition between the Commission and the EFTA Surveillance Authority

---

[88] Ibid., paras. 22–24 and 29.
[89] Ibid., paras. 25 and 28.
[90] Ibid., paras. 32–33.
[91] The latter has not yet been made use of: see Chapter 8, Section 8.2.2.2 at n 157.
[92] Opinion 1/92 *EEA II* (n 86) paras. 35 and 37.
[93] Ibid., para. 36.
[94] Ibid., para. 41.

(ESA), in particular, was deemed compatible with the Treaties.[95] All in all, together with the governments of the EU Member States and the EEA EFTA States, the Commission finally succeeded in walking the tightrope between a homogeneity-preserving institutional and procedural mechanism upholding a close relationship between the EU and the EEA institutions and the autonomy of the EU legal order.

6.2.4 Opinion 1/00 ECAA

In the subsequent Opinion 1/00 on the draft Agreement establishing the ECAA, the Court consolidated its previous case law and recapitulated the main requirements on international agreements regarding compatibility with the autonomy claim. In the forefront of the compatibility test stands the essential character of the powers of the Community and its institutions and the canons of interpretation of EU law.[96] An alteration of the foundations of the EU would inevitably require an amendment of the Treaties, and international agreements cannot be used to circumvent the regular Treaty amendment procedures provided in Article 48 TEU.[97] This was also the reason for the Court in Opinion 2/94 to consider the planned accession by the Community to the ECHR incompatible with Community law on institutional as well as substantive grounds owing to the lack of competence of the EU under the now Article 352 TFEU.[98]

According to the Court, compatibility with the Treaties further requires that the institutional framework of an agreement aiming to export EU acquis either demonstrate a clearer separation between the EU and the non-EU pillars or feature one single organisation with distinct organs that function parallel to those of the EU, such as in the EEA.[99] In the field of air transport, there is no other international organisation comparable to the EFTA in the context of the EEA. The ECAA Agreement, therefore, provides for a 'single pillar' structure instead of the 'twin pillar' construction of the EEA Agreement.[100] The ECAA Agreement neither sets up a separate surveillance body nor

---

[95] Ibid., paras. 38–42.
[96] Opinion 1/00 ECAA (n 63) para. 5.
[97] Ibid.
[98] 'Fundamental institutional implications' of 'constitutional significance' would require an amendment of the Treaties: Opinion 2/94 ECHR I EU:C:1996:140, paras. 30 and 35.
[99] Opinion 1/00 ECAA (n 63) para. 6.
[100] Ibid., para. 7.

a separate court. Instead, a political organ – the ECAA Joint Committee – is tasked with the settlement of disputes and the contracting parties have a possibility to request preliminary rulings from the Court of Justice. Since the ECAA Agreement only extended the powers of the EU's institutions, including the Commission, in a geographical dimension, the nature or those powers remained intact and the agreement was found to be compatible with the Treaties.

A great advantage in terms of autonomy-conform institutional design is the conclusion of an agreement in a field of exclusive EU competence, such as the EnCT or the TCT. Where only the EU is party to the agreement without the Member States, there is consequently no need for the treaty organs to interpret the term 'Contracting Party' to the effect of ruling on the division of competences between the EU and its Member States.[101] Furthermore, a danger of the Member States violating Article 344 TFEU only occurs in the case of mixed agreements or agreements to which the EU is not a party despite their subject matter falling within EU competence.[102] The conclusion of the EnCT and the TCT, therefore, never necessitated an opinion of the Court under Article 218(11) TFEU.

In all of the opinions on agreements exporting the acquis the general tone of the Court has been protective towards the autonomy of the EU legal order. Differently from the reconciling tenor in Opinion 1/91, however, Opinion 1/00 demonstrates that the Court is undoubtedly willing to sacrifice the homogeneity objective of the acquis-exporting agreements for the need to preserve the autonomy of the EU legal order. In spite of being part of the EU legal order as a provision of an international agreement, the homogeneity objectives featured in, for example, the EEA and the ECAA Agreements do not belong to the core mechanisms preserving an effective functioning of the Treaties. The Court made clear that it is not bound to pursue a political agenda of expanding a homogeneous internal market beyond the EU but rather assesses the mechanisms put in place for that aim from the strict prism of maintaining the autonomy of the EU legal order.[103]

A common feature of the case law discussed in this section as well as *MOX Plant* is that they deal with the interpretation by a non-EU judiciary or body of either EU law or legal rules that mirror EU acquis. The Court has previously affirmed that it is not as such contrary to the concept of

---

[101] Ibid., para. 16.
[102] Ibid., para. 17.
[103] See, for example, ibid., paras. 41 and 45.

the autonomy of the EU legal order to accept the jurisdiction of an international court or tribunal for the purpose of interpreting rules of international law. A threat to autonomy, however, occurs in cases where an external judiciary is tasked with the interpretation of EU law and, thereby, potentially encroaches upon the Court's interpretive autonomy. While the latter can be accepted as a reasonable conclusion, it is nevertheless remarkable that the Court struck down the EEA Court for the reason that the participation of the judges of the Court would prevent them from remaining impartial when deciding on cases concerning identically worded provisions in either the EU Treaties or the EEA Agreement. The question of open minds is puzzling considering that the Court interprets both the provisions of the EU Treaties and the EEA Agreement and does, thereby, differentiate, where appropriate, between the different objectives of the agreements. The mere fact that the judges of the Court of Justice deal with the interpretation of identical internal market acquis in two or more different contexts does not *per se* jeopardise the autonomy of the EU legal order. The 'double-hatting' of the judges, however, is considered to do so by virtue of the fact that the individual judges, and not the Court, may encounter difficulties when switching identities between the Court of Justice and the EEA Court.

A slightly different situation involving the concept of autonomy occurred in *Reynolds* v. *Commission* where the Court was called upon to rule on the compatibility with the concept of a civil action brought by the Commission before a US court against certain American tobacco manufacturers.[104] The applicants submitted that if a US court were to determine the Commission's competence to commence proceedings in a non-Member State for recovery of allegedly unpaid customs duties and value-added tax, this would violate the autonomy of the EU legal order and breach Article 344 TFEU.[105] The Court swiftly overruled the arguments and stated that a third country court's decision as to the power of the Commission to bring before it legal proceedings does not bind the EU institutions to a particular interpretation of EU law when exercising their internal powers and, subsequently, does not affect the autonomy of the EU legal order.[106] The Court did, thus, not oscillate from the

---

[104] Case C-131/03 P *Reynolds* v. *Commission* EU:C:2006:541.
[105] Ibid., paras. 97–98.
[106] Ibid., para. 102.

previously developed criteria for assessing the preservation of the autonomy principle.

6.2.5 Opinion 1/09 Patents Court

The systematic application of the principle of autonomy continued in the next opinion on the compatibility of a draft international agreement with the Treaties. In Opinion 1/09, the Court was requested to assess the conformity with the Treaties and, in particular, the concept of autonomy of the envisaged agreement setting up a European and Community Patents Court.[107] The Court added to previous case law that it is not only compatible with but, in fact, part of the autonomy of the EU legal order to be able to voluntarily submit itself to the jurisdiction of an external judiciary.[108] However, the judicial mechanism created for the purpose of interpreting an international agreement may not violate the essential characteristics of the judicial power of the Court of Justice. The envisaged Patents Court was intended not only to interpret an international agreement but also future EU patent legislation and acquis in the fields of intellectual property, internal market and competition policy. In addition, the Patents Court would have been able to interpret the provisions of EU law in the light of fundamental rights, general principles of EU law, and even determine the validity of EU measures.[109]

The Court established, moreover, that the autonomy of the EU legal order reaches beyond EU law and EU institutions and includes the functions of the Member States' institutions in the general institutional framework of the Union that contribute to upholding the unity and effectiveness of the EU legal order. The task of the Patents Court was to unify patent litigation across the Union by assuming the respective responsibilities of the national courts to hear disputes between individuals. The fact that the Member States' courts would subsequently be dispossessed of their power to apply and interpret EU law and request preliminary rulings from the Court of Justice in the field of patent law was considered by the Court to deprive the national courts of their role as the 'ordinary' courts in the EU judicial system.[110] This, in turn, encroaches upon the 'very nature of EU law' by altering the complete system of legal remedies and procedures for reviewing the validity of EU

---

[107] Opinion 1/09 *Patents Court* EU:C:2011:123.
[108] Ibid., para. 74.
[109] Ibid., para. 78.
[110] Ibid., para. 80.

measures that includes both the Member States' courts and the EU judiciary without a due revision of the Treaties.[111]

A further shortcoming of the Patents Court system was the fact that in the EU legal system individual rights are protected by the obligation of the Member States to remedy damages incurred by individuals as a result of an infringement of EU law by the Member States including, under specific circumstances, the national judiciaries. Since the Patents Court could not be subjected to infringement proceedings under Articles 258–260 TFEU nor could its decisions give ground to financial liability on behalf of the Member States, the nature of EU law was considered to be altered to the extent incompatible with the provisions of the Treaties.[112] Overall, the Court did not accept either the proposed institutional format or the treatment of the foundational principles of EU law in the draft Patents Court agreement.

The Benelux Court under scrutiny in *Parfums Christian Dior* was, however, deemed by the Court to be compatible with the Treaties.[113] Differently from the Patents Court, the Benelux Court serves to provide a common interpretation to a set of rules common to the Benelux countries.[114] It is also embedded within the judicial system of the EU and, thereby, subject to the judicial review mechanisms provided by the Treaties.[115] Finally, since the proceedings before the Benelux Court form part of the proceedings before national courts, the latter maintain their powers to interact with the Court of Justice via the preliminary ruling procedure without adversely affecting the judicial system or the autonomy of the EU legal order.

6.2.6 *Opinion 2/13 ECHR II, Case C-284/16 Achmea and Opinion 1/17 CETA*

The most vividly contested of the Court's opinions given under Article 218(11) TFEU has been Opinion 2/13 on the EU's accession to the ECHR.[116] Following the first failed attempt in 1994 to design an agreement on the EU's accession to the ECHR,[117] a new Draft Agreement was

---

[111] Ibid., paras. 70 and 85; citing Case C-50/00 P *Unión de Pequeños Agricultores* EU: C:2002:462, para. 40.
[112] Ibid., paras. 86–89.
[113] Case C-337/95 *Parfums Christian Dior* EU:C:1997:517.
[114] Ibid., para. 22; Case C-196/09 *Miles and Others* EU:C:2011:388, para. 41.
[115] Opinion 1/09 *Patents Court* (n 107) para. 82.
[116] Opinion 2/13 *ECHR II* (n 60).
[117] Opinion 2/94 *ECHR I* (n 98).

drawn up in hope that the substantive shortcomings impeding the conclusion of the first agreement had been remedied by Article 6(2) TEU and that the new Draft Agreement would, therefore, be accepted by the Court of Justice. Both Article 6(2) TEU and Protocol No 8 to the Treaties as well as the Declaration on Article 6(2) annexed to the Treaties stipulate that the EU's accession to the ECHR must preserve the 'specific characteristics of the EU'[118] pertaining both to its 'constitutional structure' and 'institutional framework'.[119] The accession may, thus, neither affect the Union's competences, the powers of the institutions or the relationship between the Member States with respect to the ECHR, nor infringe Article 344 TFEU.[120] Unexpectedly to many,[121] the Court, however, refuted the compatibility of the Draft Agreement with the Treaties on a number of different grounds pertaining to the preservation of the specific characteristics and the autonomy of the EU legal order.

The Court first contended that Article 53 ECHR, which allows the Member States to lay down higher standards of fundamental rights protection must be coordinated with Article 53 of the EU Charter in order to restrict the Member States from introducing standards higher than necessary under the Charter and to maintain the primacy, unity and effectiveness of EU law.[122] Second, the Court found that in accordance with the principle of mutual trust, the Member States may not, especially in the field of the AFSJ, other than in exceptional circumstances, scrutinise the other Member States' performance of their obligations under EU law including fundamental rights.[123] The latter was considered by the Court to undermine both the 'underlying balance of the EU' and the autonomy of the EU legal order.[124] Both instances would threaten the effective and uniform application of EU law. In order to preserve the self-referential character of the EU legal order, any control over compliance with fundamental rights can only be undertaken by the Union itself in accordance with the EU-internal standards.

---

[118] Article 1, Protocol No 8 to the Treaties.
[119] Opinion 2/13 *ECHR II* (n 60) para. 165.
[120] Articles 2 and 3, Protocol No 8 to the Treaties.
[121] For a list of comments on Opinion 2/13 see, for example, D Halberstam, '"It's the Autonomy, Stupid!" A Modest Defense of *Opinion 2/13* on EU Accession to the ECHR, and the Way Forward' (2015) 16 *German Law Journal* 105, at n 3.
[122] Opinion 2/13 *ECHR II* (n 60) para. 189. See also Case C-399/11 *Melloni* EU:C:2013:107, paras. 56–60.
[123] Opinion 2/13 *ECHR II* (n 60) paras. 191–192.
[124] Ibid., para. 194.

As a third aspect, the Court pointed out the possibility of the Member States under Protocol No 16 to the ECHR to refer to the ECtHR requests for advisory opinions on the interpretation and application of the Convention. At the same time, upon the EU's accession to the ECHR, the Convention would become an inherent part of EU law and its interpretation would fall within the jurisdiction of the Court. Since the Draft Agreement did not regulate the relationship between the EU's preliminary ruling procedure and the advisory opinion procedure under Protocol No 16 to the ECHR, the latter might have jeopardised the autonomy and the effectiveness of the preliminary ruling procedure – 'a keystone of the judicial system' of the EU – insofar as the Member States would have been able to circumvent it via a procedure for the prior involvement of the Court.[125]

The connection between autonomy and the preliminary ruling procedure was again highlighted in *Achmea*, which concerned an arbitration clause in the bilateral investment treaty (BIT) in force between the Netherlands and Slovakia.[126] Pursuant to Article 8 of the BIT, the parties may submit disputes arising from the subject matter of the BIT to an arbitral tribunal. In the case at hand, Germany was chosen as the place of arbitration. The Court of Justice was called upon by the German Federal Court of Justice to provide a preliminary ruling on whether it is lawful under the EU Treaties to submit disputes arising from an 'intra-EU BIT' to arbitration. The Court's judgment was negative. Contrary to the Benelux Court, the BIT tribunal was not integrated in the Union's judicial system and fell, therefore, outside the preliminary ruling system.[127] The tribunal's interpretation and application of EU law could subsequently lead to a fragmentation of EU law and undermine its effectiveness by means of the Court losing its interpretive autonomy. On the one hand, the uniform interpretation of EU law, including the maintenance of the particular nature of EU law, which is ensured by the preliminary ruling procedure, is a manifestation of the mutual trust between Member States.[128] The principle of sincere cooperation, on the other hand, obliges the Member States to ensure that EU law is interpreted uniformly throughout the Union. A lack of mutual trust, therefore, leads to a breach of the principle of sincere cooperation and, hence, negatively affects the autonomy of the EU legal order.[129]

---

[125] Ibid., paras. 197–199.
[126] Case C-284/16 *Achmea* EU:C:2018:158.
[127] Ibid., para. 49.
[128] Opinion 2/13 *ECHR II* (n 60) para. 168; Case C-284/16 *Achmea* (n 126) paras. 34 and 58.
[129] Case C-284/16 *Achmea* (n 126) para. 59.

In the most recent example, Opinion 1/17 – the anticipated follow-up to *Achmea* – the Court was called upon to review the compatibility with the Treaties and, especially, the principle of autonomy, of the envisaged Comprehensive Economic and Trade Agreement between Canada, of the one part, and the EU and its Member States, of the other part (CETA).[130] The Court's scrutiny focused on whether it would be able to maintain its exclusive jurisdiction to give definitive interpretations of EU law in the light of the planned investor-state dispute settlement mechanism featuring a CETA Tribunal, an Appellate Tribunal and, eventually, a multilateral investment Tribunal. The Court was to answer questions on, first, whether the envisaged tribunals would be conferred any powers to interpret or apply EU law other than with regard to the rules and principles of international law; and, second, whether the tribunals might have the power to issue awards which, falling short of interpreting or applying EU rules, could curtail the possibilities of the EU's institutions to act within the Union's 'unique' constitutional framework.[131]

The Court pointed out the reciprocal nature of the CETA and the Union's need to maintain an international presence as grounds for accepting the Union's submission to the jurisdiction of dispute settlement bodies, which neither, however, directly interpret or apply EU law nor restrict the EU's institutions' operation in the EU's constitutional framework.[132] On the other hand, any interpretation of the CETA will be undertaken in accordance with the rules of public international law rather than EU law.[133] In the course of 'examining' (but not 'interpreting') the compatibility of EU or host State measures with the CETA, the latter must be treated 'as a matter of fact' and the CETA Tribunal must follow the Court's interpretation of relevant EU law as the 'prevailing interpretation' without binding either the Court, the other EU institutions or the Member States to a particular interpretation of EU law.[134]

It was also examined whether the CETA tribunals might be able to call into question the level of protection of a public interest in EU law in the course of reviewing possible restrictions to an investor's right to conduct business under the CETA.[135] The tribunals would thereby execute

---

[130] [2017] OJ L11/23.
[131] Opinion 1/17 *CETA* EU:C:2019:341, paras. 110 and 119.
[132] Ibid., paras. 117–118.
[133] Ibid., para. 122.
[134] Ibid., paras. 130–131.
[135] Such as public order or public safety, the protection of public morals, the protection of health and life of humans and animals, the preservation of food safety, the protection

a task, which under Article 19 TEU is conferred upon the Court to be carried out in accordance with the Treaties, the Charter and the general principles of EU law.[136] The autonomous operation of the EU's institutions would be impaired if the Union or the Member States would be bound to amend or repeal legislation following a decision of a judicial body outside the EU's judicial system.[137] However, the Court considered that no such authority had been granted to the CETA tribunals, thus rendering the agreement compatible with the principle of autonomy and, specifically, its regulatory dimension.[138]

Reverting to Opinion 2/13, the Court, fourth, found that its exclusive jurisdiction under Article 344 TFEU – and thereby its interpretive autonomy – was not protected by the Draft Agreement. The latter did not give explicit precedence to the EU's dispute settlement procedure over the corresponding procedure under the ECHR in disputes concerning EU law.[139] This is different from the situation in *MOX Plant* where the UNCLOS provided a clear rule on the priority of the EU dispute settlement procedures over those specified in the Convention.[140] According to the Court, Article 344 TFEU 'precludes any prior or subsequent external control'[141] and even a mere possibility to refer a case to a non-EU judiciary.[142]

Fifth, the Court scrutinised the co-respondent mechanism under the Draft Agreement and found that it infringed EU law in several ways. Pursuant to the Draft Agreement, the ECtHR would have the possibility to decide on the 'plausibility' of a request from either the Member States or the EU to become a co-respondent in a case before the ECtHR. This would enable the latter court to rule on matters concerning EU law such as the division of competences between the EU and the Member States.[143] The ECtHR would also be able to investigate the co-respondents' potential joint responsibility for a violation of the Convention, including an assessment of the allocation of powers between the EU and its Member States

---

of plants and the environment, welfare at work, product safety, consumer protection and fundamental rights.

[136] Opinion 1/17 *CETA* (n 131) para. 151.

[137] Ibid., para. 150.

[138] See P Koutrakos, 'More on Autonomy – Opinion 1/17 (CETA)' (2019) 44 *European Law Review* 293.

[139] Opinion 2/13 *ECHR II* (n 60) paras. 205–208.

[140] Ibid., para. 205.

[141] Ibid., para. 210.

[142] Ibid., para. 212.

[143] Ibid., paras. 220–225.

and the corresponding attribution of responsibility.[144] The Court was firm to establish that the latter assessment falls within its sole jurisdiction,[145] and is essential to uphold the Court's autonomous interpretation of EU law.

Sixth, the Draft Agreement provided for a procedure for the prior involvement of the EU, which the Court considered, indeed, necessary to preserve the competences of the Union and the powers of its institutions including the Court of Justice.[146] The ascertainment of who would determine whether a case before the ECtHR has already been decided by the Court of Justice, however, proved problematic. The Court did not regard the safeguards provided by the Draft Agreement as sufficient to ensure that the ECtHR would not be granted the jurisdiction to interpret the case law of the Court and were, thus, deemed inadequate from the perspective of preserving the specific characteristics of the EU legal order.[147] The Draft Agreement also provided that in the course of the procedure of prior involvement, the Court could only assess the validity of secondary law and interpret primary law in the light of the ECHR whereas the impossibility to interpret EU secondary law would defeat the Court's exclusive jurisdiction to give definitive interpretations of EU law.[148]

Finally, the Court considered it problematic that the Draft Agreement would grant the ECtHR the possibility to review the legality of certain CFSP acts under the ECHR. Article 275 TFEU limits the Court's jurisdiction in the area of CFSP monitoring compliance with Article 40 TEU that delimits the CFSP and other EU policies, and reviewing the legality of Council decisions that impose restrictive measures against natural or legal persons pursuant to Article 263 TFEU. The ECtHR would, thus, be granted more extensive jurisdiction than the Court of Justice to review the compatibility with the fundamental rights of at least some CFSP acts.[149] With reference to Opinion 1/09, the Court deemed this to conflict with the idea that the jurisdiction of the Court in the field of EU law may not be transferred on an exclusive basis to an international court that does not belong to the EU's institutional and judicial framework,[150]

---

[144] Ibid., paras. 229–231.
[145] Ibid., para. 234.
[146] Ibid., para. 237.
[147] Ibid., paras. 239–240 and 248.
[148] Ibid., paras. 242–246.
[149] Ibid., para. 254.
[150] Ibid., para. 256.

regardless of whether jurisdiction in the field of the CFSP ever belonged to the Court. Rather, the object of protection was the character of the CFSP as a policy area that remains outside supranational judicial control. Whereas the previous arguments of the Court can be found justified in the light of its previous case law, the final statement reflects a somewhat more egoistic attitude of the Court towards its role in the international community of courts and tribunals. From the perspective of the CFSP belonging to the same EU legal order as the other policies and the ECtHR becoming an EU constitutional court by gaining jurisdiction over CFSP matters, however, the Court's approach may receive more sympathisers.[151] The question that remains is whether the Court's stance towards the CFSP concerns the autonomy of the EU legal order at all, or simply one of its 'special characteristics'.

The Court's strong position on the protection of the autonomy of the EU legal order in Opinion 2/13, especially in comparison with Opinion 1/17, owes to the fact that in the heart of the Union's accession to the ECHR lies cooperation between two large judicial edifices.[152] The judgments of the ECtHR have much larger resonance than those of the EFTA Court or the decisions of the ECAA Joint Committee, which implies a more significant perceived threat to the Treaties arising from the Draft Agreement than from the agreements discussed earlier. A careful review of the case law has, however, demonstrated that the Court's meticulous approach to autonomy when issuing opinions under Article 218(11) TFEU has been consistent and that the (over)protection of the EU legal order from outside influence is a regular feature of its approach to interpreting the Treaties. Furthermore, Opinion 2/13 was not given solely on the basis of the concept of autonomy but also following the explicit requirement in Protocol No 8 to the Treaties to safeguard the 'specific characteristics' of the EU and EU law. Without getting entangled in the terminological variety employed by the Court throughout the autonomy jurisprudence, the safeguarding of the 'specific characteristics' of the EU legal order is a beast created by the Lisbon Treaty makers and used extensively in Opinion 2/13 owing to the formulation in Protocol No 8.

The Court's definition of autonomy, or the way in which the concept has been substantiated overtime, has not been systematised to detail. In

---

[151] D Halberstam (n 121) 141–142.
[152] On judicial dialogue between the two courts, see further P Eeckhout, 'Opinion 2/13 on EU Accession to the ECHR and Judicial Dialogue: Autonomy or Autarky?' (2015) 38 *Fordham International Law Journal* 955.

case law, a number of features have been identified in international agreements as conflicting with the concept of autonomy with the purpose of securing the unity and effectiveness of the Union's legal order, especially as concerns the Court's interpretive autonomy. Yet it is doubtful whether the interpretation of the concept of autonomy has been broadened to subsume all of the 'specific' and 'essential' characteristics of the EU legal order.[153] The Court has refrained from explicitly categorising all of the autonomy-threatening features of international agreements as the 'essential elements' of the EU legal order. A clear thread is visible in the autonomy case law along the lines of unity and effectiveness without, however, a concrete definition of autonomy to resort to when assessing the reasonableness of the Court's application of the concept, and none that the Court would consider itself bound to follow in future case law.

Furthermore, in Opinion 2/13, the Court does not conclude that the 'specific characteristics' of the EU and its legal order, which are numerous, are the same as the autonomy of the legal order.[154] Instead, the Court's treatment of the different shortcomings of the Draft Agreement is re-ordered in the concluding paragraph: only the coordination between Article 53 of the ECHR and Article 53 of the Charter, the principle of Member States' mutual trust under EU law and the relationship between the mechanism established by Protocol No 16 to the ECHR and the preliminary ruling procedure are considered to explicitly fall within the category of provisions likely to adversely affect the 'specific characteristics and the autonomy of EU law'.[155] While in the analysis of the other elements the Court has also occasionally referred to autonomy, its effort not to refer to the term in excess is notable. 'Autonomy' is not employed synonymously with the 'specific characteristics' of the EU and EU law; rather, the latter concept subsumes the former. Overall, albeit broad, vague and debatable as a concept, the autonomy of the EU legal order is not the cause for all questionable choices made by the Court in Opinion 2/13.

Opinion 2/13 provides further instruction on how the Court interprets the concept of autonomy and must be taken account of by the EU

---

[153] See to the contrary C Contartese, 'The Autonomy of the EU Legal Order in the ECJ's External Relations Case Law: From the "Essential" to the "Specific Characteristics" of the Union and Back Again' (2017) 54 *Common Market Law Review* 1627, 1628.

[154] 'In order to ensure that the specific characteristics and the autonomy of that legal order are preserved, [. . .]': Opinion 2/13 *ECHR II* (n 60) para. 174.

[155] Ibid., para. 258.

when concluding international agreements,[156] but its implications for exporting Union acquis to third countries should not be overstated. Existing frameworks provide plenty of examples of 'approved' institutional structures to support the Union's norms export and serve as benchmarks for similar arrangements in the future. The establishment and judicialisation of the post-Brexit relationship, which will be another likely example of the Union setting up close trade relations with a third country based on EU acquis to at least some extent, will more probably deviate from existing examples. It is, however, unlikely to ever reach the profundity of the judicial dialogue that would accompany the EU's accession to the ECHR and to, thus, become the second act in the drama of Opinion 2/13.

6.3 Conclusion

In terms of flexibility in EU integration, the multiplicity of the types of membership in the Union could be justified as a means to safeguard the 'integrity and autonomy' of the EU legal order.[157] Flexible integration does, nonetheless, demand that the unconventional form of membership be identified as such and that the multiplication of membership patterns enable the 'core' of the EU legal order to be preserved. In the interaction between the EU and third countries or international organisations, the integrity and autonomy claim is ever so strong.

The case law of the Court of Justice demonstrates that safeguarding the autonomy of the EU legal order is one of its key tasks. The Court's vigorous protection[158] of the autonomy of the EU legal order perforce places strong limitations on the Union's possibilities to enter into international agreements. Nevertheless, while the Court is more prone to preserve the autonomy of the EU legal order than to further the homogeneity objectives of the international agreements exporting the internal market acquis, this does not render the aims of exporting the acquis beyond the Union's borders and thereby expanding the internal market a mission impossible. By and large, conflicts with autonomy can

---

[156] See also P Eeckhout (n 152) 963.

[157] M Cremona, 'The "Dynamic and Homogeneous" EEA: Byzantine Structures and Variable Geometry' (1994) 19 *European Law Review* 508, 525.

[158] Or even 'selfishness': see B de Witte, 'A Selfish Court? The Court of Justice and the Design of International Dispute Settlement Beyond the European Union' in M Cremona and A Thies (eds.), *The European Court of Justice and External Relations Law: Constitutional Challenges* (Hart Publishing 2014) 33.

be obviated if the institutional structures of the agreements clearly separate the EU pillar from the non-EU pillar, such as in the multilateral sectoral agreements; or where a set of treaty organs are created to function in parallel to those of the EU, such as in the EEA.

The Court has repeatedly established that certain institutional designs in international agreements are incompatible with the current Treaty framework and that the Treaty amendment provisions cannot be replaced by concluding an international agreement. Virtually any institutional framework set up by an international agreement exporting the acquis could be reconciled with the Treaties and, subsequently, the requirement of autonomy of the EU legal order. In the fear of opening Pandora's box treaty amendment is, however, an unlikely option to be resorted to.[159]

All of the institutional aspects of the autonomy of the EU legal order considered have been accorded rigorous protection on behalf of the Court in the name of the essential characteristics of the Union. These features of the EU legal order can, indeed, be regarded as parts of the fundamental acquis[160] of the Union the protection of which is paramount – the 'untouchable hard core'[161] conditioning the EU's relations with its neighbourhood.

---

[159] T Lock, 'Walking on a Tightrope: The Draft ECHR Accession Agreement and the Autonomy of the EU Legal Order' (2011) 48 *Common Market Law Review* 1025, 1049.

[160] P Pescatore, 'Aspects judiciaires de l'«acquis communautaire»' (1981) 20 Revue trimestrielle de droit européen 617, 618. See Chapter 3, Section 3.2.1 at n 55.

[161] C Curti Gialdino, 'Some Reflections on the *Acquis Communautaire*' (1995) 32 *Common Market Law Review* 1089, 1108.

7 Institutional Framework
Defining the Core of the Internal Market

The project of expanding the EU internal market beyond the borders of the Union inevitably requires a solid institutional and procedural framework to ensure that the same fundamental characteristics of the internal market and the necessary degree of unity of the market are incorporated in the 'extended' internal market as in the EU. As discussed in Chapter 4, a homogeneous EEA, Energy Community, ECAA or Transport Community necessitate, ideally, that the same core body of rules and procedures be given the same effect across the entire territory of the respective legal orders at any point of time. In order to be considered homogeneous with the EU internal market, the acquis must thus feature unity in substance, time and territory. These aspects must be present at all stages – the adoption, implementation, application and enforcement of the acquis. Furthermore, homogeneity in the external dimension demands that there exists a sufficient institutional link between the EU legal order and the legal orders created by the multilateral agreements.

This chapter focuses on two essential aspects of the institutional frameworks that are set up to guarantee homogeneity in the expanded internal market – the exporting of the acquis and the defining of its key elements necessary for achieving homogeneity. The first part of the chapter deals with legal mechanisms that enable the acquis adopted in the EU to be exported to the EEA, the Energy Community, the ECAA and the Transport Community legal orders, scrutinising both institutional and procedural arrangements. The second part of the chapter explores the possible effects of third country participation in the stages of determining the substantive content of the core acquis on homogeneity in the expanded internal market and the possibilities of various non-EU actors to influence the making of the EU acquis.

7.1 Exporting Internal Market Acquis to Third Countries

In order to ensure homogeneity and a true extension of the internal market, the core of the internal market acquis – either comprehensive or characteristic of a particular sector – must be transposed into the legal orders of third countries in a timely and precise manner. Suitable institutional and procedural mechanisms need to be set up both by the international instruments and by the third countries' national legal orders.

Uniformity at the stage of adoption means, first, that the same set of rules come into force. Second, when new legislation or amendments to existing legislation in the sphere of the internal market or a sector thereof enter into force in the EU, the same acquis must also enter into force vis-à-vis the third countries. This is important both regarding the content of the legal rules – within the limits of what can be classified as 'permissible differentiation' – and the temporal dimension. Third, homogeneity demands that the same set of rules apply at the same point of time across the entire territory of the expanded internal market, thus excluding the possibility of adopting new legislation at different times and, thereby, proceeding at different speeds.[1]

Within the EU, general rules on the entry into force of new legislation apply equally to all Member States notwithstanding negotiated exceptions that are usually limited in number and scope. The entry into force following the adoption of new EU legislation is automatic across the entire Union. EU legislation becomes binding on the Member States to the extent that the measures adopted enjoy general application and have legally binding force at the moment of adoption or at a later date as may be specified by the instrument. Should the particular instrument have direct effect, it will also become enforceable by individuals.

In the case of exporting the acquis outside the Union, the automaticity no longer applies. The international agreements serve as a filter between the EU Treaties and the constitutional orders of the third countries. In all of the multilateral agreements under scrutiny, uniformity of the acquis is guaranteed only at the moment of their conclusion. Updating the acquis that forms part of the international agreement,

[1] See Chapter 4, Section 4.2.1.

either as inserted into the main text of the agreement or into an annex attached thereto, amounts to amending the agreement. Any amendments for the purpose of reflecting legislative changes in the EU must be carried out in accordance with the provisions of the agreement and international treaty law. Simplified treaty amendment procedures are often used to introduce new acquis into the multilateral agreements.

7.1.1 Institutions Exporting the Acquis

7.1.1.1 European Economic Area

The EEA is constructed upon two distinct pillars. The first, EU pillar, comprises the EU and its Member States and the institutions of the EU, whereas the second, EFTA pillar, includes the EEA EFTA States and the institutions of the EFTA, respectively. The EEA's parallel structure also features four joint institutions representing both the EU and the EFTA sides of the EEA Agreement.[2] These include the EEA Council, the EEA Joint Committee, the EEA Joint Parliamentary Committee and the EEA Consultative Committee. In addition, the institutions of the EFTA pillar comprise the EFTA Standing Committee, the ESA and the EFTA Court.

Similar to the European Council, the EEA Council is the main political body of the EEA. It comprises representatives of the contracting parties, including the Council of the EU, the Commission and the EEA EFTA States. The main task of the EEA Council is to give political impetus to the EEA and to lay down general guidelines for the EEA Joint Committee.[3] It also deals with difficult questions on which the Joint Committee has failed to reach a decision as well as urgent issues.[4] The EEA is characterised by consensual decision-making. The EEA Council adopts decisions 'by agreement between the [Union], on the one hand, and the EEA EFTA States, on the other'.[5] The requirement of consensus places the two pillars of the EEA on the opposing sides of the meeting table yet compels the parties to cooperate closely in order to reach an agreement. Furthermore, both the EU and its Member States as represented by the Commission and the Council as well as the EEA EFTA States must agree on a common message and communicate this with one voice. The EFTA Standing Committee serves as a forum for the EEA

---

[2] For an illustrative organigram, see 'Joint Committee' (EEA website) www.efta.int/eea/e ea-institutions accessed 10 February 2020.
[3] Article 89(1) EEA Agreement.
[4] Article 89(2) EEA Agreement.
[5] Article 90(2) EEA Agreement.

EFTA States to meet at and to adopt common positions to be presented in the EEA Joint Committee. The EEA Council is led by a President, alternating twice a year between a member of the Council of the EU and a representative of an EEA EFTA State,[6] with the aim of maintaining a balance between the EU and the EFTA pillars.

A rough equivalent of the Council of the EU, the EEA Joint Committee is involved in the day-to-day management of the EEA and adopts amendments to the EEA Agreement.[7] The division between the EU and the EFTA pillars is also reflected in the Joint Committee, which adopts decisions by agreement between the two blocks.[8] The Presidency of the EEA Joint Committee alternates twice a year between the Union, represented by the Commission, and a representative of one of the EEA EFTA States.[9]

The EEA Joint Parliamentary Committee is an advisory body and a venue for parliamentary cooperation between the European Parliament and the national parliaments of the EEA EFTA States, being composed of an equal number of parliamentarians from each pillar.[10] The task of the Parliamentary Committee is to raise awareness about the issues covered by the EEA Agreement through dialogue and debate without, however, any formal role in the EEA decision-making procedures.[11] The Committee's powers are limited to the adoption of resolutions, scrutinising the annual report of the Joint Committee and hearing the President of the EEA Council.[12]

The EEA Consultative Committee provides a venue for cooperation between the social partners of the EU and the EFTA States. The cooperation serves to 'enhance the awareness of the economic and social aspects of the growing interdependence of the economies of the Contracting Parties and of their interests within the context of the EEA'.[13] The Consultative Committee is composed of an equal number of members from the European Economic and Social Committee (EESC) and its EFTA equivalent, the EFTA Consultative Committee, and may adopt reports and non-binding resolutions to put forward its views.[14] It

---

[6] Article 91(2) EEA Agreement.
[7] Article 92 EEA Agreement.
[8] Article 93(2) EEA Agreement.
[9] Article 94(1) EEA Agreement.
[10] Article 95(1) EEA Agreement.
[11] Article 95(3) EEA Agreement.
[12] Article 95(4) EEA Agreement.
[13] Article 96(1) EEA Agreement.
[14] Article 96(2) EEA Agreement.

thereby enables the EEA social partners to participate in the EEA despite lacking a role in the decision-making process.

The EEA Agreement has been concluded as a mixed agreement. Similar to the EEA EFTA States and the EU Member States represented by the Council of the EU, the Union, too, has to decide on its positions to be put forward at the Joint Committee meetings or taken on possible amendments to the EEA Agreement, its annexes or protocols. Regulation(EC) No 2894/94 establishes the procedures to be followed by the EU when implementing the EEA Agreement.[15] Article 1 of the Regulation provides that at the stage of submitting a legislative proposal to the Council for adoption, the Commission must indicate whether the act falls within the ambit of the EEA Agreement. Should a Member State object to the EEA relevance of the proposed act, the Council will vote on the matter, whereas the same voting majority applies as during the adoption of the corresponding EU legal act. In the Joint Committee meetings where the extension of an EU legal act to the EEA is decided, the position of the EU is adopted by the Commission.[16] All other EU positions in the EEA Joint Committee must be endorsed by the Council on a proposal from the Commission. The EU's positions in the EEA Council require unanimous adoption in the Council unless the EEA Council deals with an EU legal act. In the latter case, the voting majority is determined by the legal basis of the legal act in question.[17] Analogous rules apply to the European Parliament who will, in parallel to adopting positions on EU legislation, also adopt positions on the 'EEA relevance' of those acts.[18]

7.1.1.2 Energy Community Treaty

The institutional mechanisms for achieving and maintaining homogeneity in the Energy Community are significantly less elaborate than their equivalents in the EAA Agreement. The institutional structure of the Energy Community is, in turn, more sophisticated than that created by the ECAA Agreement, although the sophistication does not necessarily translate into the effectiveness of the structure when safeguarding homogeneity in the Energy Community legal order.

The Energy Community comprises five institutions: the Ministerial Council, the Permanent High Level Group (PHLG), the Regulatory Board,

---

[15] Council Regulation (EC) No 2894/94 of 28 November 1994 concerning arrangements for implementing the Agreement on the European Economic Area [1994] OJ L305/6.
[16] Ibid., Article 1(2).
[17] Ibid., Article 2.
[18] Ibid., Article 3.

two Fora and the Secretariat. The Ministerial Council provides general policy guidelines to the Energy Community and ensures the attainment of the Treaty objectives. It adopts Measures and Procedural Acts and may also delegate legislative tasks to the other institutions.[19] The Ministerial Council is composed of one representative from each contracting party except for the EU that is represented by two persons.[20] Each contracting party holds the Presidency of the Energy Community in turn for a term of six months. Importantly, since the EnCT is not a mixed agreement, its institutions do not balance between two blocks of participants like the EEA.

One of the tasks of the Ministerial Council is to compose an annual report, which is forwarded to the European Parliament and to the parliaments of the Adhering Parties and of the Participants.[21] The EnCT's Adhering Parties are its non-EU contracting parties with the exception of Kosovo. Participants comprise the EU Member States that wish to be involved in the Energy Community's activities. They represent and participate in the discussions at the Energy Community's institutions without voting rights,[22] enjoying a status higher than the third country observers.[23]

The PHLG prepares the work of the Ministerial Council and reports to it on progress made towards the achievement of the objectives of the Treaty.[24] The PHLG may take Measures upon due delegation from the Ministerial Council. It also discusses the development of the acquis on the basis of reports submitted on a regular basis by the European Commission. The PHLG includes a representative from each contracting party and two from the EU.[25]

The Regulatory Board possesses the necessary technical expertise for the proper functioning of the Energy Community. The Board advises the Ministerial Council and the PHLG on the details of statutory, technical and regulatory rules and issues recommendations on cross-border disputes involving two or more regulators upon request by any of them.[26] The Regulatory Board is composed of representatives of each contracting party's energy regulators. The EU is represented by the Commission,

---

[19] Article 47 EnCT.
[20] Article 48 EnCT.
[21] Article 52 EnCT.
[22] Article 95 EnCT.
[23] Article 96(2) EnCT.
[24] Article 53 EnCT.
[25] Article 54 EnCT.
[26] Article 58 EnCT.

assisted by one regulator of each Participant, and one representative of the Agency for the Cooperation of Energy Regulators (ACER).[27]

The two Fora on electricity and gas, respectively, represent stakeholder groups. The Fora are composed of the representatives of all interested stakeholders including industry, regulators, industry representative groups and consumers, and play an advisory role in the Energy Community.[28] The conclusions of the Fora are forwarded to the PHLG.[29]

Finally, the Secretariat of the Energy Community provides administrative assistance to all of the other institutions and reviews the proper implementation of the EnCT by the contracting parties.[30] The Secretariat is impartial, thus also independent of the EU, and acts only in the interests of the Energy Community.[31]

7.1.1.3 European Common Aviation Area

Despite following the model of the EEA, the sectoral ECAA Agreement features much less elaborate institutional framework and decision-making procedures than the comprehensive EEA Agreement or even the equally sectoral EnCT.

The ECAA Agreement sets up one institution only, the ECAA Joint Committee, which is responsible for the administration and proper implementation of the Agreement.[32] The Joint Committee is composed of representatives of the contracting parties including the EU and its Member States as well as the third country participants. Differently from its EEA counterpart, though, the ECAA Joint Committee does not strive for consensus. Decisions are adopted by unanimous vote unless the Joint Committee itself lays down majority voting rules for certain specific issues.[33] The ECAA Joint Committee is presided over in turn by an ECAA Partner[34] or the EU and its Member States and, like in the EEA, this arrangement mirrors the two blocks representing the EU and its Member States, and the non-EU ECAA contracting parties, respectively.[35]

---

[27] Article 59 EnCT.
[28] Article 63 EnCT.
[29] Article 65 EnCT.
[30] Article 67 EnCT.
[31] Article 70 EnCT.
[32] Article 18(1) ECAA Agreement.
[33] Article 18(3) ECAA Agreement.
[34] ECAA Partners include the third country contracting parties to the ECAA Agreement: Article 2 ECAA Agreement.
[35] Article 18(6) ECAA Agreement.

7.1.1.4 Transport Community

The TCT comprises four institutions: the Ministerial Council, the Regional Steering Committee (RSC), the Social Forum and the Permanent Secretariat. The Ministerial Council shall ensure the attainment of the objectives of the Treaty and is composed of one representative per contracting party.[36] The RSC, an equivalent to the ECAA Joint Committee, comprises representatives of the contracting parties and is responsible for the administration and proper implementation of the Treaty. The RSC can make recommendations and adopt decisions,[37] and acts by unanimity.[38] In addition, the RSC is mandated to establish technical committees as ad hoc working groups consisting of participants from all of the contracting parties, which may submit proposals for decisions to be adopted by the RSC.[39] The EU Member States may participate as observers in all of the institutions and bodies of the TCT, including the technical committees.[40] The contracting parties shall also establish a Social Forum including representatives from the contracting parties' governments, workers' and employers' organisations and any other relevant bodies. Representatives of the European social dialogue committees related to the transport sector and of the EESC shall participate in the meetings. Finally, the Permanent Secretariat, acting independently and in the interest of the Transport Community,[41] is to assist all of the institutions and bodies of the TCT.[42]

7.1.2 Procedures for Ensuring Homogeneity

7.1.2.1 European Economic Area

Newly adopted, amended or repealed EU acquis becomes part of or is excluded from the EEA legal order only upon due amendment of the EEA Agreement. The amendment procedure involves the institutions of both the EEA and the EEA EFTA States. The former amend the annexes or protocols to the EEA Agreement, whereas the latter implement the acquis in the national legal orders. The sophisticated institutional framework of the EEA allows for a 'quasi-automatic' procedure for amending the annexes to the EEA Agreement that contain the

---

[36] Articles 21 and 22 TCT.
[37] Article 24(1),(2) TCT.
[38] Article 24(3) TCT.
[39] Article 26(1) TCT.
[40] Articles 22, 24(2) and 26(1) TCT.
[41] Article 31 TCT.
[42] Article 28 TCT.

relevant acquis,[43] which is indispensable considering the vast scope of the agreement.

A first evaluation of the EEA relevance of EU acquis is made by the EU.[44] After the legal act has been adopted, the EEA EFTA States' experts review it to establish its EEA relevance and provide an opinion as to whether the annexes to the EEA Agreement should be amended.[45] Occasionally, EU legislation must be adapted before incorporation into the EEA such as by removing the non-EEA relevant parts of the legal acts.[46] This procedure is coordinated by the EFTA Secretariat. The EFTA Secretariat also drafts the decision of the Joint Committee. Following approval by the EFTA States and the subcommittees dealing with the matter in question, the draft decision is passed on to the Commission via the European External Action Service (EEAS). After endorsement by the Commission, the draft decision is forwarded to either the Commission or the Council, depending on whether the proposed revisions are minor or substantive. The aim of the procedure is to ensure the simultaneous entry into force of new or amended legislation in the entire EEA and to thereby maintain homogeneity and legal certainty.[47] A certain delay is nevertheless embedded in the procedure as the Joint Committee incorporates into the EEA Agreement acquis that has already been adopted in the EU, including acts that enter into force immediately or with minor delay vis-à-vis the EU Member States.[48]

Since no voting takes place in the Joint Committee, great emphasis is placed on finding consensus.[49] Consensus is also striven for in the equally elaborate 'decision-shaping' procedure in which the EEA EFTA States participate.[50] Should the contracting parties not succeed in

---

[43] S Lavenex, D Lehmkuhl and N Wichmann, 'Modes of External Governance: A Cross-National and Cross-Sectoral Comparison' (2009) 16 *Journal of European Public Policy* 813, 818.

[44] See, for example, Directive 2013/36/EU of the European Parliament and of the Council of 26 June 2013 on access to the activity of credit institutions and the prudential supervision of credit institutions and investment firms [2013] OJ L176/338, which proclaims that the text has EEA relevance.

[45] Not always, though, is acquis that has been declared EEA relevant actually relevant for the EEA Agreement and vice versa, see H Haukeland Fredriksen and CNK Franklin, 'Of Pragmatism and Principles: The EEA Agreement 20 Years On' (2015) 52 *Common Market Law Review* 629, 652–653.

[46] Norwegian Government, 'Parliament White Paper – The EEA Agreement and Norway's other agreements with the EU' No 5 (2012–2013), 12 and 16.

[47] Article 102(1) EEA Agreement.

[48] H Haukeland Fredriksen and CNK Franklin (n 45) 657.

[49] Article 102(3) EEA Agreement.

[50] The influence of the EEA EFTA States in the procedure of developing new EEA relevant acquis in the EU is discussed in detail in Section 7.2.2.1.

reaching an agreement about the incorporation of an amendment of EU acquis into the EEA Agreement, the Joint Committee will continue working towards a commonly acceptable solution. One solution, albeit imperfect, is to recognise an equivalence of legislation in the EU and the EFTA pillars of the EEA.[51] A decision on taking notice of the equivalence of legislation must be made at least six months after the matter has been referred to the Joint Committee or, at the latest, on the day of the entry into force of the corresponding EU legislation.

If the EEA Joint Committee fails to reach agreement by the above deadlines, the relevant part of an annex to the EEA Agreement is suspended unless the Joint Committee decides differently.[52] The Joint Committee will continue to work on the matter until the parties agree to a solution. The time span between the adoption of an EEA relevant EU act and the possible suspension of a part of an annex attached to the EEA Agreement will be one year in total.[53] The practical effect of a suspension will be discussed in and decided by the Joint Committee.[54] The suspension does not, however, affect the rights and obligations that individuals and undertakings have already acquired under the EEA Agreement.[55] In practice, although the EEA Agreement allows for a time lag of a maximum of twelve months, the incorporation of EEA relevant acquis into the EEA Agreement has in some instances taken up to six years.[56] A suspension of the EEA Agreement has never been resorted to.

A suspension will affect an entire part of an annex to the EEA Agreement.[57] A failure by any EEA EFTA State to agree to update the EEA Agreement will, therefore, have consequences for all. The aim of the suspension mechanism is to avoid a patchwork situation whereby different acquis applies in different parts of the EEA defeating the homogeneity of the EEA legal order. In the case of a suspension, homogeneity vis-à-vis the EU pillar of the EEA will certainly be interrupted.

Joint Committee decisions are binding on the EEA contracting parties but their implementation is subject to national constitutional requirements. The parties must ensure that the decisions of the Joint Committee

---

[51] Article 102(4) EEA Agreement.
[52] Article 102(5) EEA Agreement.
[53] The sum of the two six-month periods provided in Article 102(4) and (5) EEA Agreement.
[54] Article 102(5) EEA Agreement.
[55] See, for example, J Pelkmans and P Böhler, 'The EEA Review and Liechtenstein's Integration Strategy' (2013) *Centre for European Policy Studies*, 53.
[56] See, for example, H Haukeland Fredriksen and CNK Franklin (n 45) 657–658.
[57] C Reymond, 'Institutions, Decision-Making Procedure and Settlement of Disputes in the European Economic Area' (1993) 30 *Common Market Law Review* 449, 466.

are duly applied and implemented.[58] Failure by a contracting party in that regard will incur international responsibility towards the others. Subject to the applicable constitutional provisions, amendments to the EEA Agreement, its annexes or protocols may have to be approved separately by the legislatures of one or more contracting parties. Seeking parliamentary approval may, however, delay the procedure and pose a threat to the temporal dimension of homogeneity in the EEA legal order.

The contracting parties must notify each other upon fulfilling the national constitutional requirements to give effect to decisions made by Joint Committee.[59] A contracting party's failure to do so within six months will result in a provisional application of the Joint Committee's decision until the notification is provided.[60] During that period there is, thus, a time lag between the acquis becoming applicable in the EU and the time it enters into force with vis-à-vis one or several of the EEA EFTA States. The provisional application of a piece of acquis that has not received parliamentary approval in an EEA EFTA State may be refused provisional application by another contracting party. Such refusal will, as well as a notification by a contracting party that the amendment has not been ratified by their parliament, lead to a suspension of the relevant part of an annex to the EEA Agreement. The suspension will take place within a month of those circumstances arising but not before the entry into force of the corresponding EU legal act.[61]

Article 97 of the EEA Agreement is one of the key provisions for ensuring homogeneity. It provides that subsequent amendments to the contracting parties' domestic legislation are only compatible with the Agreement if they comply with the principle of non-discrimination, and if other EEA members are duly informed of the amendments. Following a notification in this regard, the domestic legislative amendment may be given green light by the EEA Joint Committee if the latter does not consider it to affect the good functioning of the EEA Agreement, hence not be EEA relevant. The amendment may, however, also be deemed to necessitate a revision of the annexes or protocols to the EEA Agreement in accordance with Article 98. The good functioning of the EEA Agreement, therefore, requires legal homogeneity both within the EU and between the EU and the EEA legal orders.

---

[58] Article 104 EEA Agreement.
[59] Article 103(1) EEA Agreement.
[60] Article 103(2) EEA Agreement.
[61] Ibid.

In conclusion, the institutional and procedural framework of the EEA supports the objective of dynamic homogeneity to almost the greatest extent possible for an international agreement lacking supranational character. The substantive dimension of homogeneity is safeguarded by the continuous monitoring of the 'EEA relevance' of EU acquis by both the EU and the EEA EFTA contracting parties, and subsequent action taken by the EEA Joint Committee to update the annexes to the Agreement. The two distinct – EU and EFTA – pillars of the EEA influence the territorial dimension of homogeneity insofar as a part of the Agreement can be suspended upon a failure of the Joint Committee to update the annexes in accordance with the developments in the EU acquis, or if one or several EEA EFTA States' legislatures fail to duly implement the amendments. In such instances, legislative uniformity between the EU and the EFTA pillars will be lost and homogeneity within the EEA will be distorted. However, the fact that no EEA EFTA States are allowed to surpass others in keeping up with the changes in the EU acquis, unless on a voluntary basis and without corresponding rights vis-à-vis the EU pillar, places extra pressure on the defaulting party.

A certain time gap is inevitable owing to the quasi-automatic system of updating the EEA Agreement and the need to await parliamentary approval in order for the amendments of the EEA Agreement to enter into force vis-à-vis the EEA EFTA countries. One of the reasons for the time gap is the increasingly cross-sectoral nature of the EU's legislative activity that makes it difficult to determine the EEA relevance of EU acquis, including whether a legal act affects the internal market.[62] The impossibility of always arriving at a homogeneous result is, moreover, recognised by the EFTA Court.[63] In practice, achieving homogeneity may be more vulnerable than what the regulatory framework sets out to be, although the current backlog of legal acts awaiting incorporation into the EEA Agreement[64] and implementation in the EEA EFTA States[65] is small.

---

[62] Norwegian Government, 'Parliament White Paper' (n 46) 15.

[63] Case E-3/97 *Opel Norge* [1998] EFTA Ct Rep 1, para. 30.

[64] More than 600 legislative acts in 2014: see G Baur, 'From EU Law to EEA Law: The Decision-Making Process' (2015) EFTA Bulletin 18, 29.

[65] For example, as of July 2019, Iceland had a transposition deficit of 0.7 per cent (6 directives), Liechtenstein 0.9 per cent (7 directives) and Norway 0.4 per cent (3 directives). In Iceland and Norway, regulations, too, must be incorporated in the respective legal orders. Iceland had 38 overdue regulations (1.2 per cent) and Norway 17 (0.5 per cent): EFTA Surveillance Authority, 'Internal Market Scoreboard – EEA EFTA States' No 44 July 2019, 1.

7.1.2.2 Energy Community

The decision-making procedures for adopting Energy Community Measures differ according to whether they are adopted under Title II EnCT on the extension of the *acquis communautaire*, under Title III on the Mechanism for operation of Network Energy Markets or under Title IV on the creation of a Single Energy Market. The Measures, which are either decisions or recommendations, can be adopted by the Ministerial Council or, upon a delegation from the latter, another institution of the Energy Community.[66]

The EU Commission holds a central position in the Energy Community and maintains a strong link between the EU and the Energy Community. It coordinates all activities of the Energy Community[67] as well as makes proposals for the adoption of Measures.[68] Measures can be adopted either by the Ministerial Council, the PHLG or the Regulatory Board. Each EnCT contracting party has one vote and a Measure is adopted by a majority of votes cast,[69] yet for a decision to be taken two-thirds of the contracting parties must be present.[70] Measures under Title III are adopted by the Ministerial Council, the PHLG or the Regulatory Board on a proposal from a contracting party or the Secretariat,[71] the necessary voting majority being two-thirds of the votes cast including a positive vote by the EU.[72] The EU is, thereby, granted a right of veto. Measures under Title IV are adopted by a unanimous vote in the Ministerial Council, the PHLG or the Regulatory Board on a proposal from a contracting party.[73]

The decisions adopted under the EnCT are binding on the contracting parties and must be implemented in the domestic legal orders.[74] A failure of a contracting party to implement the EnCT or a Measure may be brought to the attention of the Ministerial Council by a reasoned request of any party, the Secretariat or the Regulatory Board, whereas private bodies may issue complaints to the Secretariat.[75] A serious and persistent breach of the obligations under the EnCT may lead to a

---

[66] Article 76 EnCT.
[67] Article 4 EnCT.
[68] Article 79 EnCT.
[69] Articles 80–81 EnCT.
[70] Article 78 EnCT.
[71] Article 82 EnCT.
[72] Article 83 EnCT.
[73] Articles 84 and 85 EnCT.
[74] Article 89 EnCT.
[75] Article 90 EnCT.

suspension of certain rights under the Treaty, including voting rights and exclusion from meetings or other mechanisms.[76]

Pursuant to Article 25 EnCT, the Energy Community 'may take Measures' to implement amendments to the *acquis communautaire* provided in Title I of the Treaty to reflect the evolution of EU acquis. The limited degree of automatism provided by this provision reflects the somewhat lower ambitions of the EnCT concerning homogeneity as compared to the EEA. The acquis provided in Title II of the Treaty is, moreover, applied flexibly vis-à-vis the non-EU contracting parties. The acquis shall be adapted to both the institutional framework of the EnCT and to the specific situations of the contracting parties.[77]

The EnCT makes no distinction between measures adopted for the purpose of updating the acquis and other measures. Subsequently, no special procedure has been established to tackle specifically the failure of an Energy Community institution or a contracting party to implement changes in relevant EU acquis in the EnCT. The inability of an Energy Community institution to adopt a decision to update the acquis provided in the Treaty has no consequences for its functioning. Although a situation in which a contracting party does not comply with the Treaty is considered a breach thereof, the EnCT does not provide mechanisms to safeguard the homogeneity of its legal order or the homogeneity between the EU acquis and the Energy Community acquis other than a suspension of the rights deriving from the EnCT in the case of a serious and persistent breach.

7.1.2.3 European Common Aviation Area

Similar to the EEA Agreement, the ECAA Agreement does not restrain the contracting parties from unilaterally adopting new or amending existing legislation in the field of air transport or other associated areas covered by the Agreement as long as they do not conflict with its provisions.[78] A contracting party including the EU must, upon amending ECAA relevant national legislation, notify the other contracting parties via the Joint Committee within a month of the legislative change.[79] At the request of a contracting party, the Joint Committee will discuss the amended acquis within a two-month timeframe.[80] The

---

[76] Article 92 EnCT.
[77] Articles 5 and 24 EnCT. See further in Chapter 4, Section 4.3.2.
[78] Article 17(1) ECAA Agreement.
[79] Article 17(2) ECAA Agreement.
[80] Ibid.

Joint Committee may either adopt a decision to revise Annex I of the ECAA Agreement and incorporate the amendment of the acquis into the Agreement, approve the amendment as being in accordance with the Agreement or 'decide on any other measures to safeguard the proper functioning of the agreement' without further specification.[81]

The ECAA Joint Committee decisions have the same effect as the decisions of the EEA Joint Committee. Both are binding on the contracting parties under international law and must, therefore, be implemented in accordance with national constitutional requirements,[82] following which the Joint Committee must be informed.

The significantly simpler decision-making procedure envisaged by the ECAA Agreement as compared to the EEA reflects the more limited opportunities to safeguard homogeneity in the ECAA legal order. While the ECAA Agreement can be updated by a simplified treaty amendment procedure, there are no safeguards comparable to the EEA Agreement in place against a failure to reach agreement in the Joint Committee, or the non-implementation of a Joint Committee decision by a contracting party. Neither does the ECAA Agreement provide for a possibility to suspend a part of the Agreement when homogeneity is jeopardised. As a result, it is more challenging in the ECAA to maintain the intended homogeneous character of its legal order vis-à-vis the EU aviation market.

7.1.2.4 Transport Community

The procedures foreseen by the TCT to safeguard legislative homogeneity in the TCT legal order are virtually identical to the ECAA Agreement. The TCT contracting parties exchange information on new legislation or decisions relevant for the TCT and may hold consultations within the RSC, including on social issues, at the request by any contracting party.[83] The SEE Parties may adopt new or amend existing legislation in the fields of transport and associated areas covered by the Treaty on condition that the amendments neither breach the Treaty nor conflict with the principle of non-discrimination.[84] The other contracting parties shall be notified of the legislative changes via the RSC within a month.[85] Upon request by a contracting party, the respective technical committee shall hold an exchange of views within two months to discuss the implications

---

[81] Article 17(3)(c) ECAA Agreement.
[82] Article 19(1) ECAA Agreement.
[83] Article 24(4) TCT.
[84] Article 20(1) TCT.
[85] Article 20(2) TCT.

of the new or amended legislation for the 'proper functioning' of the TCT.[86] In case of new relevant EU acquis, the RSC may either adopt a decision revising Annex I to the Treaty to incorporate the new legal act or recognising the equivalence between the new piece of acquis and the TCT, or decide on any other measure to ensure the proper functioning of the TCT, without specifying the latter.

In sum, the EnCT, the ECAA Agreement and the TCT feature institutional and procedural possibilities to update the agreements in accordance with developments in the relevant EU acquis. Similar to the EEA Agreement, however, there are no absolute guarantees to the effect of maintaining homogeneity. Homogeneity in the Energy Community, the ECAA and the Transport Community depends largely on the willingness of the contracting parties to duly update the agreements and to, thereafter, implement the amendments to the agreements in their domestic legal orders.

7.2 Actors Defining the Core of the Internal Market

An important aspect of maintaining homogeneity is ensuring that the exported acquis is incorporated into the agreements and into the third countries' national legal orders in a dynamic and speedy fashion. This presupposes that sufficient information and consultation possibilities are provided to the non-EU contracting parties before the acquis is adopted on the EU level. Each of the three main stages in the EU policy-making – the pre-proposal agenda setting, the decision-making and the policy implementation stages[87] – is relevant for exporting EU acquis to third countries and identifying the essential characteristics of an optimal institutional framework for achieving and maintaining homogeneity.

This section considers the importance of the first, exploratory stage of decision-shaping on the homogeneity of the expanded internal market. In the pre-proposal stage, the acquis, including the 'core' acquis, which provides a benchmark for evaluating the level of homogeneity in the expanded internal market, is defined. Yet, the legislative preparatory stage serves not only as a venue for elaborating the content of a

---

[86] Ibid.
[87] T Christiansen and T Larsson, 'Introduction: The Role of Committees in the Policy-Process of the European Union' in T Christiansen and T Larsson (eds.), *The Role of Committees in the Policy-Process of the European Union* (Edward Elgar Publishing 2007) 1, 3.

legislative act.[88] It also provides a possibility to consult with different actors and thereby guarantee support for the proposed act at the decision-making stage, in addition to ensuring the effective implementation of the acquis by the EU Member States as well as by the third countries.[89] The decision-makers notably include the EU legislator, the decision-making bodies of the international agreements exporting the acquis and the national parliaments.

7.2.1 EU Actors Defining the Core of the Internal Market

The substance of EU internal market acquis is determined during the legislative procedure. Post-Lisbon Treaty, Article 289 TFEU provides for two types of legislative procedures: the ordinary and the special legislative procedures. Internal market legislation based on Article 114 TFEU is usually adopted following the ordinary legislative procedure, save fiscal provisions and rules on the free movement of persons and labour law.[90]

In the ordinary legislative procedure,[91] the main actors preparing and adopting a legislative act are the European Commission, the Council of the EU and the European Parliament. The Commission submits a proposal to the European Parliament followed by a deliberation in the Council that will either approve or reject the proposal. The Commission provides an opinion on the proposed amendments. In order to bypass a negative opinion of the Commission, the Council may adopt the act by unanimous vote. Yet, legislative initiative in the EU does not rest solely with the Commission. Pursuant to Article 289(4) TFEU, in special cases defined by the Treaties, legislative initiative may also be taken by a group of Member States or the European Parliament, or on a recommendation from the European Central Bank, or at the request of the Court of Justice or the European Investment Bank.

On certain conditions, a legislative act may delegate a power to adopt non-legislative acts to the Commission for the purpose of supplementing or amending some of its non-essential elements.[92] The Commission may also adopt measures to implement legislative acts in cases where uniformity in implementation is deemed necessary.[93] This implementation is carried out by the so-called comitology committees.

---

[88] Ibid., 4.
[89] Ibid., 5.
[90] Article 114(2) TFEU.
[91] See Article 294 TFEU.
[92] Article 290(1),(2) TFEU.
[93] Article 291 TFEU.

A further group of institutions only recently included in the EU's legislative process are the Member States' national parliaments. The role of the latter has been laid out in Article 12 TEU and Protocols No 1 and No 2 to the Treaties. In the context of the internal market, national parliaments are kept informed about the EU's legislative activity including draft legislation, and they are guarding the application of the principle of subsidiarity by the EU.[94] In addition to their individual roles in reviewing draft EU legislation, there is a framework in place for cooperation between national parliaments and the EU Parliament. The national parliaments are, thus, involved in the EU's legislative procedures beyond the ratification of the EU Treaties and amendments thereto. In the process of preparing legislative proposals, local conditions are also considered during consultations held with a wide range of interested parties, allowing the Commission to gain an insight into whether a proposed legislative act should be best adopted on the EU or the national level.[95] Among third countries, similar consultations take place only with the EEA EFTA States.

Participation is one of the defining features of EU governance. In an attempt to increase legitimacy, transparency and effectiveness in the EU policy-making, a number of stakeholders and other interested parties partake in the stages of policy initiative, development and implementation. These actors represent and reflect the political, social, economic and regional realities across the EU and channel those elements into the internal market legislation, thus providing the EU internal market with a unique character beyond its substantive content.

The most institutionalised forms of stakeholder participation in the EU's legislative procedure are represented by the EESC and the Committee of the Regions.[96] The former is composed of the representatives of the civil society – social partners and other interest groups from the Member States; the latter comprises representatives of regional and local bodies of the Member States. Both exercise an advisory role vis-à-vis the European Parliament, the Council and the Commission. Although the Committees are composed of representatives of the

---

[94] Via the 'yellow card procedure': see Protocol No 1 on the Role of National Parliaments in the European Union and Protocol No 2 on the Application of the Principles of Subsidiarity and Proportionality annexed to the Treaties.
[95] Article 2, Protocol No 2 to the Treaties..
[96] Article 300 TFEU.

Member States, the members must be completely independent in their activities and act only in the general interest of the EU.

The EESC must be consulted by the decision-making institutions where the Treaties so provide including both under Articles 114 and 115 TFEU. In all other cases, the EU institutions are free to consult the Committee. The EESC may also submit opinions on issues that it itself considers necessary to address.[97] The same rules apply to the Committee of the Regions, except for compulsory consultation in the procedures of adopting legislation on the internal market legal bases.[98]

In addition to these formalised channels of consultation, the Commission also launches public consultations at the stage of developing proposals for envisaged legislative acts. The Commission calls for input from interested individuals as well as industry and civil society stakeholders. In the absence of national limitations to participation, third country citizens and entities, too, may submit opinions, observations and suggestions to the Commission.

The Commission, furthermore, seeks for external expertise itself, both via formal expert groups set up by a Commission decision or by a Commission department; single consultations in the form of meetings, conferences, and so on; comitology committees; independent experts in the fields of research and technological development; social dialogue committees; and joint entities that monitor the implementation of international agreements.[99] Advisory groups that participate in the stages of preparing and implementing EU legislation include 'expert committees' composed of national officials and experts, and consultative committees, also called expert groups, involving stakeholder representatives.[100] All of these external expert configurations fulfil a consultative function. They provide unbinding expertise to the Commission, which remains independent in shaping the content of its proposals.[101]

Additional local expertise in the preparatory stage is provided to the Commission by seconded national experts (SNEs). Working on temporary secondment from their home countries, SNEs contribute to an

---

[97] Article 304 TFEU.
[98] Article 307 TFEU.
[99] Commission, 'Framework for Commission Expert Groups: Horizontal Rules and Public Register' (Communication from the President to the Commission) C (2010) 7649 final, 5–6.
[100] N Nugent, *The European Commission* (Palgrave Macmillan 2001) 244–245; T Larsson and J Murk, 'The Commission's Relations with Expert Advisory Groups' in T Christiansen and T Larsson (eds.), *The Role of Committees in the Policy-Process of the European Union* (Edward Elgar Publishing 2007) 64, 67.
[101] Commission, 'Framework for Commission Expert Groups' (n 99) 3.

exchange of experience and expertise between the EU and its Member States and beyond. Importantly, SNEs are not limited to EU citizens but include experts seconded from the EFTA, EU candidate countries and public inter-governmental organisations (IGOs).[102] Although SNEs' possibilities to act independently in the Commission are limited[103] and they are, during their period in the Commission bound to be loyal to the Commission and not to external parties,[104] the SNEs can make Commission staff aware of national circumstances that may affect the contents of a proposed legislative act.[105]

EU citizens can directly participate in the Union's policy-making via the European Citizens' Initiative. Introduced by the Treaty of Lisbon, Articles 11(4) TEU and 24(1) TFEU provide that at least one million citizens who are nationals of a 'significant number' of Member States may submit an initiative to the European Commission for the latter to initiate, within its powers, a legislative procedure for the adoption of a legal act, which the group of citizens consider essential for the purpose of implementing the Treaties. The Citizens' Initiative falls within the broader scheme of bringing EU institutions closer to the people by providing opportunities to the latter to express their views on EU policies and actions.[106] It enables a group of nationals from at least seven Member States to submit an invitation to the Commission to propose new legislation.[107] Differently from the public consultations, the European Citizens' Initiative is exclusively reserved for EU citizens. Despite a theoretical possibility to influence the outcome of EU legislation, non-EU resident third country nationals cannot, therefore, take legislative initiative to impact the direction of internal market legislation in a broader sense.

Finally, EU citizens may also submit petitions to the European Parliament under Article 227 TFEU on matters falling within the remit of the EU that are of direct concern to the petitioner. The opportunity is available to all EU citizens as well as to the members of associations,

---

[102] Article 1(1) and (3) of Commission Decision of 12 November 2008 laying down rules on the secondment to the Commission of national experts and national experts in professional training, C (2008) 6866 final.

[103] Ibid., Article 6.

[104] Ibid., Article 7(1)(a).

[105] The SNEs should not, however, be regarded as national 'Trojan Horses', see J Trondal, Z Murdoch and B Geys, 'On Trojan Horses and Revolving Doors: Assessing the Autonomy of National Officials in the European Commission' (2015) 54 *European Journal of Political Research* 249, 250.

[106] Article 11(1) TEU.

[107] See Regulation (EU) No 211/2011 of the European Parliament and of the Council of 16 February 2011 on the citizens' initiative [2011] OJ L65/1.

companies and organisations whose headquarters are located in any of the Member States. Petitions that are declared admissible are discussed by the relevant parliamentary committee, which may take further action on the basis of the petition.[108] Petitions submitted by non-nationals and non-residents who cannot claim an EU-based right to petition will be filed separately and made available to the parliamentary committee upon request.[109]

7.2.1.1 EU Social Governance

Participatory governance modes in the EU have become most institutionalised in the area of social policy, which as a horizontal and flanking policy has significant relevance also for the multilateral agreements exporting the internal market acquis. The novel and experimental approach to law making in social policy owes to the great variation in social, labour, legal and industrial relations' cultures across the EU.[110] On the one hand, the diversity is reflected in the choice of legislative acts: in the field of social policy, soft law measures are often preferred to hard law, minimum standards and partial harmonisation to total harmonisation, and directives to regulations.[111] On the other hand, the making of social policy is characterised by the inclusion of social partners. Both of these aspects reflect the rise of new governance methods to complement the classic Community method.

The classic Community method, partly incorporated in the ordinary legislative procedure,[112] comprises the European Commission solely responsible for legislative proposals, the Council and the European Parliament adopting legislation, the Commission and the Member States in charge of implementing EU policies and the Court of Justice guaranteeing respect for the rule of law.[113] As opposed to the classic Community method, new governance is generally characterised by participation and power-sharing, multi-level integration, diversity and decentralisation, deliberation, flexibility and revisability, and experimentation and knowledge creation.[114]

---

[108] Rule 227, Rules of Procedure of the European Parliament, 9th Parliamentary Term – December 2019.

[109] Ibid., Rule 226(15).

[110] C Barnard, *EU Employment Law* (Oxford University Press 2013) 47.

[111] Ibid., 61 and 63.

[112] Article 294 TFEU.

[113] Commission, 'European Governance – A White Paper' (Communication) COM (2001) 428 final (European Governance White Paper), 8.

[114] J Scott and DM Trubek, 'Mind the Gap: Law and New Approaches to Governance in the European Union' (2002) 8 *European Law Journal* 1, 5–6.

New governance pertains both to the adoption and implementation stages, often blurring the boundary between the two.[115] With regard to the former, new governance addresses the range of actors involved – promoting the engagement of the civil society and stakeholders – as well as the instruments adopted; as concerns the latter, new governance departs from the idea of uniformity through harmonisation and prefers an enhanced role for the Member States to determine the legislative outcome through consultations and coordination of national policies.[116] The distinction between the stages of policymaking and implementation as well as the importance in some situations accorded to procedure rather than the uniformity of outcome is reflected in the case law of the Court of Justice. In *Standley and Metson*, in particular, the Court ruled that the different ways in which the Member States may apply a directive does not conflict with the nature of the directive if the latter does not create harmonised rules and leaves wide discretion for the Member States.[117]

In response to an image of the EU as complex and intrusive, the Commission proposed reforming EU governance with the aim of increasing openness, involvement, flexibility and coherence, better policies and regulation and enhancing the Union's contribution to global governance.[118] The European Parliament reacted with a Resolution stating that the Community approach should not be replaced completely.[119] According to the Parliament, stakeholder consultations for the purpose of improving the quality of draft legislation 'can only ever supplement and can never replace the procedures and decisions of legislative bodies which possess democratic legitimacy', including the Council and the Parliament as co-legislators, and opinions provided by other actors specified in the Treaties, such as the EESC and the Committee of the Regions.[120]

An example of a new inter-governmental method in EU social policy is the Open Method of Co-ordination (OMC), first emerging in the framework of the European Employment Strategy in the 1990s. The aim of the OMC was to create a de-centralised decision-making process

---

[115] Ibid., 8.
[116] Ibid., 6.
[117] Case C-293/97 *Standley and Metson* EU:C:1999:215, para. 39.
[118] European Governance White Paper (n 113) 8.
[119] European Parliament, 'Resolution on the Commission White Paper on European governance COM(2001) 428' A5-0399/2001, 29 November 2001.
[120] Ibid., Recital 11(c).

in which the Member States play the main role.[121] Under the OMC, the Member States jointly identify non-binding objectives and guidelines, measuring instruments and benchmarking in a given field not falling within the EU's exclusive competence. The EU institutions are involved in the first and the third stage – the Council adopting the objectives and the Commission monitoring the benchmarking procedures. Since the 1990s, the OMC has been employed in a number of areas of social policy. Its use is encouraged both by the challenges of a common market and monetary policy and the interdependence between the Member States.[122] Although the OMC does not produce any hard legal obligations, its instruments form part of the Union's acquis.

Innovative governance does not, however, only appear in the realm of soft law. Maastricht Treaty introduced a new procedure for law making – the European Social Dialogue. The social dialogue originates from the Protocol on Social Policy and its Agreement attached to the Maastricht EC Treaty. The Amsterdam Treaty integrated the Social Protocol and the Agreement into the EC Treaty.

Social dialogue originates from the principle of subsidiarity and the assumption that the social partners are 'as a rule closer to the reality and to social problems',[123] although the major differences between the Member States in terms of the density of unionisation greatly undermine this supposition.[124] The European Social Dialogue includes discussions, consultations, negotiations and joint actions between the management and the labour sides of industry. Comprising both legislative and collective action, it introduces into EU law making collective agreements between the Social Partners that can be of both cross-industry and sectoral scope. In essence, the legislative procedure in which the social partners participate constitutes a European level collective agreement.

---

[121] S Smismans, 'EU Employment Policy: Decentralisation or Centralisation through the Open Method of Coordination?' (2004) EUI Working Paper LAW 2004/1, 4, https://cadmus.eui.eu/bitstream/handle/1814/1881/law04-1.pdf?sequence=1&isAllowed=y accessed 10 February 2020.

[122] DM Trubek and LG Trubek, 'Hard and Soft Law in the Construction of Social Europe: the Role of the Open Method of Co-ordination' (2005) 11 European Law Journal 343, 345 and 348.

[123] Council Resolution 94/C 368/03 of 6 December 1994 on certain aspects for a European Union social policy: a contribution to economic and social convergence in the Union [1994] OJ C368/6.

[124] OECD, 'Trade Union density' www.oecd-ilibrary.org/employment/data/trade-unions/trade-union-density_data-00371-en?isPartOf=/content/datacollection/lfs-tu-data-en accessed 10 February 2020.

Collective bargaining can be used for implementing EU law instead of legislation but not without complications. Under Article 153(3) TFEU, a Member State may entrust management and labour, at their joint request, with the implementation of a directive or a Council decision adopted in accordance with Article 155 TFEU. The Member State must ensure that by the implementation deadline the management and labour have, indeed, adopted a collective agreement that effectively implements the legislative act in question. On the EU level, the Member State remains responsible for the proper implementation of the directive or decision.[125] National legislation must be enforced with regard to all workers, not only those covered by the collective agreement.[126]

Social dialogue rests on the process of negotiations between the social partners – labour and management. It does not replace social legislation; rather together they form the two pillars of the EU 'Social Dimension'.[127] Social dialogue is, furthermore, encouraged on the EU level as the Union is required to promote the role of social partners as well as facilitate cooperation between them.[128] In the meantime, the Union must also respect national diversity in the field of social policy and the autonomy of the social partners.[129] If the social partners are involved in social dialogue, the institutions cannot subject them to the EU's policy agenda.

Specific tasks are placed on the Commission in this regard. The Commission must promote the consultation of the social partners on EU level and facilitate their dialogue by supporting both parties.[130] This means taking any relevant measures. To this end, the Commission organises meetings, supports joint studies and working groups and provides technical assistance.[131] Article 156 TFEU provides that the Commission will encourage cooperation between the Member States. The Commission provides coordinating assistance, conducts studies,

---

[125] Article 153(3) TFEU.

[126] See Case 143/83 *Commission* v. *Denmark* EU:C:1985:34, para. 8; Case C-187/98 *Commission* v. *Greece* EU:C:1999:535, para. 47.

[127] M Rhodes, 'A Regulatory Conundrum: Industrial Relations and the Social Dimension' in S Leibfried and P Pierson (eds.), *European Social Policy: Between Fragmentation and Integration* (The Brookings Institution 1995) 78.

[128] Article 152 TFEU.

[129] Ibid.

[130] Article 154(1) TFEU.

[131] Commission, 'The application of the Agreement on social policy' (Communication) COM (93) 600 final, para. 12.

delivers opinions after consulting the EESC and sets up consultations. The particular aim of such assistance is to encourage the sharing of best practices, benchmarking and other forms of new governance in the field of social policy.

During the legislative procedure, the Commission first consults management and labour before submitting legislative proposals on the general direction of future EU action.[132] As the next step, should the Commission wish to pursue legislation, it must also consult the social partners on the content of the draft proposal, the latter having the opportunity to provide either opinions or recommendations.[133] During both stages of consultation, the social partners may decide to leave the legislative pillar and continue with collective bargaining in the social dialogue pillar,[134] called 'bargaining in the shadow of law'.[135] The duration of the social dialogue procedure is at the most nine months, unless the Commission, the management and the labour jointly decide to extend the length of the this phase.[136]

Social dialogue between the management and labour may result in an agreement, but only upon the wish of the parties.[137] The resulting Europe-level collective agreements may be implemented by the Member States in accordance with their national procedures.[138] In matters falling within the scope of Union competence and outlined in Article 153 TFEU, should both sides so desire, they may jointly request a Council 'decision' to implement their agreement on a proposal from the Commission,[139] the term referring to any of the binding legal instruments provided in Article 288 TFEU – a regulation, directive or decision – as proposed by the Commission.[140] The involvement of the European Parliament, however, is limited to being informed.

Without the Council adopting the text of the agreement reached by the social partners as legislation, the EU-level agreements have no binding legal force on the Member States. The Commission both evaluates the representativity of the participants in the social dialogue as well

---

[132] Article 154(2) TFEU.
[133] Article 154(3) TFEU.
[134] Article 154(4) TFEU.
[135] B Bercusson, *European Labour Law* (Cambridge University Press 2009) 146.
[136] Article 154(4) TFEU.
[137] Article 155(1) TFEU.
[138] Article 155(2) TFEU.
[139] Ibid.
[140] See Commission, 'Proposal for a Council Directive on the framework agreement on parental leave concluded by UNICE, CEEP and the ETUC' COM (1996) 26 final, 7.

as assesses the content of the agreement with a view to possibly complementing it with legislation on its own proposal whereby all necessary consultation procedures will have to be followed. In practice, the Union legislation in the social field usually avoids harmonisation and rather allows the Member States or the social partners to arrive at a solution that best fits within the national circumstances.[141]

The Social Partners are autonomous to decide upon their structures and procedures for negotiating, conforming to certain criteria.[142] First, the participating social partners must either be of cross-industry scope or relate to a specific sector or category, and be organised on the European level. Second, they must form an 'integral and recognized part' of the Member States' social partner structures and, to the extent possible, represent all Member States. Third, the social partners must have 'adequate structures' to enable them to participate in the consultations.

The recognition of some social partners with regard to fulfilling the above-mentioned criteria has previously proved problematic. The most challenging issue has been representativity. In the landmark case *UEAPME*, in which a trade organisation representing craft and small and medium sized enterprises challenged the Parental Leave Directive,[143] the CFI asserted that because in social dialogue the European Parliament is excluded from the legislative procedure, the principle of democratic legitimacy requires that parties to the social dialogue be 'sufficiently representative'.[144] This criterion must be fulfilled separately in relation to each new agreement between the social partners.[145] Representativity contains two elements: sufficiency and collective representativity. Whereas sufficient representativity does not equal absolute participation, collective representativity demands that a wide range of Member States be represented.[146] Moreover, rather than the number of members it is important that an adequate number of interests are represented.[147]

---

[141] C Barnard (n 110) 66.

[142] Commission, 'Adapting and promoting the social dialogue at Community level' (Communication) COM (1998) 322 final, 5–6.

[143] Council Directive 96/34/EC of 3 June 1996 on the framework agreement on parental leave concluded by the Union des Confédérations de l'Industrie et des Employeurs d'Europe (UNICE), the Centre Européen de l'Entreprise Publique (CEEP) and the Confédération Européenne des Syndicats (ETUC) [1996] OJ L145/4.

[144] Case T-135/96 *UEAPME* EU:T:1998:128, paras. 89–90.

[145] Ibid., para. 90.

[146] B Bercusson, 'Democratic Legitimacy and European Labour Law' (1999) 28 *Industrial Law Journal* 153, 157–158.

[147] Ibid., 159.

So far, the Commission has recognised as cross-industry Social Partners the Confederation of European Business (BUSINESSEUROPE, formerly UNICE) and the European Centre of Employers and Enterprises providing Public Services (CEEP) representing private and public sector management, respectively; and the European Trade Union Confederation (ETUC) representing workers. These three organisations were participating in the original Val Duchesse talks with the Commission that came to be known as the social dialogue and paved way for the Social Policy Agreement attached to the Maastricht Treaty.[148] More recently, recognition has been granted to the European Association of Craft, Small and Medium-Sized Enterprises (SMEunited, formerly UEAPME), the Council of European Professional and Managerial Staff (Eurocadres) and European Confederation of Executives and Managerial Staff (CEC), the latter two participating in negotiations as part of the ETUC delegation. However, the question of representativity mainly plays a role if the social dialogue participants wish for the Council to implement their agreement by a decision; in other cases, the agreement can be implemented in accordance with the procedures and practices of the Member States.[149] Beyond the social dialogue pillar that results in an EU legislative act, the question of participation is generally a matter of mutual recognition of the social partners, rather than a prescription by the Commission.[150] The success of the social dialogue depends also on the internal rules of the representative organisations and the leeway given to them by their constituent national organisations, as reflected in the necessary voting majorities.[151] In practice, the cross-industry social partners have seldom managed to reach agreement.[152] In 2015, therefore, President Juncker of the European Commission launched a new start for social dialogue to enhance the involvement of the social partners in the EU's policy and law making.[153]

Social dialogue notably includes social partners from non-EU Member States. BUSINESSEUROPE, for example, engages representatives from

---

[148] E Franssen and ATJM Jacobs, 'The Question of Representativity in the European Social Dialogue' (1998) 35 *Common Market Law Review* 1295, 1298.

[149] Ibid., 1311.

[150] Commission, 'The Development of the Social Dialogue at Community level' (Communication) COM (96) 448 final, 4.

[151] B Keller and B Sörries, 'The New European Social Dialogue: Old Wine in New Bottles?' (1999) 9 *Journal of European Social Policy* 111, 114.

[152] See Commission, *A new start for Social Dialogue* (Publications Office of the European Union 2016) 8.

[153] Ibid.

Iceland, Montenegro, Norway, Serbia, San Marino, Switzerland and Turkey; CEEP representatives from Norway and Turkey; and ETUC from Andorra, Iceland, Liechtenstein, Montenegro, North Macedonia, Norway, San Marino, Serbia, Switzerland and Turkey. The new governance regime provides opportunities for third countries to participate in the making of EU acquis yet, paradoxically, by replacing the European Commission in the legislative procedure which includes consultations with expert groups, other third country stakeholders are effectively eliminated from the shaping of the acquis.[154]

7.2.1.2 EU Environmental Governance

Environmental protection provides another example of the application of new governance methods by the EU. The evolution of environmental governance is exemplified by four regimes: (1) the technocratic environment regime, (2) the internal market regime of harmonisation, (3) the integration regime of effectiveness and efficiency and (4) the strategy-based sustainable development regime.[155] Whereas the former two represent the classic Community method, the emergence of the integration regime in the 1990s shifted focus to effectiveness and efficiency.

The new orientation signalled by the integration regime demanded that the factors that influence the efficiency and effectiveness of environmental policies be targeted already in the stage of decision-making.[156] As a result, the decision-making processes increasingly include stakeholders and experts as well as locally tailored solutions, incorporated through consultations, negotiations and public information.[157] The sustainable development regime further demands that environmental policy be integrated into all EU policies.[158] An example of this is the environmental integration principle enshrined in Article 11 TFEU,[159] which has been considered a distant equivalent to the OMC in the sphere of environmental policy.[160] Since it is, however, not the only horizontal provision in the TFEU, it may be

---

[154] The different possibilities for third-countries to participate in the EU policy-making are discussed in Section 7.2.2.
[155] I von Homeyer, 'The Evolution of EU Environmental Governance' in J Scott (ed.), *Environmental Protection* (Oxford University Press 2009) 1.
[156] Ibid., 15.
[157] Ibid., 15 and 18.
[158] Ibid., 19.
[159] Discussed in detail in Chapter 3 Section 3.4.2.
[160] J Scott and DM Trubek (n 114) 5.

argued that other horizontal provisions too, could be regarded as examples of new governance.

New governance calls for cooperation between public and private undertakings on various levels and discretion and flexibility in the decision-making process. In addition, new governance departs significantly from the specific objectives of the classic Community method. The defined objectives are broad and consist primarily of procedural guidelines rather than objectives of result.

The new environmental policy instruments (NEPIs)[161] fall into three sub-categories: (1) suasive instruments, such as informational measures and voluntary agreements; (2) market-based instruments including taxes and tradable permits; and (3) regulatory instruments.[162] These measures can be used by the EU as well as the Member States. Despite their unconventional form, the NEPIs can nevertheless be considered part of the internal market acquis to the extent that they affect the functioning thereof, and are thereby relevant also for the purposes of expanding the internal market or a sector thereof to third countries.

Attention on new types of norms instead of the procedure for their adoption is the main feature distinguishing between the application of new governance in EU environmental policy and social policy. This is notwithstanding the fact that a significant element of the new governance norms themselves is participation.[163] Participation includes access to information, which is generally regulated in the Aarhus Convention.[164] Article 1 of the Convention stipulates the right of EU citizens to receive environmental information from the EU's institutions, agencies, bodies and offices; public participation in decision-making; and access to justice in environmental matters. A corresponding obligation is conferred on the EU to make information regarding the environment available to the public.[165]

Article 8 of the Aarhus Convention endorses effective public participation in the drafting of legislative proposals that may have a significant

---

[161] A Jordan and others, 'European Governance and the Transfer of 'New' Environmental Policy Instruments (NEPIs) in the European Union' (2003) 81 *Public Administration* 555.

[162] RKW Wurzel, AR Zito and AJ Jordan, *Environmental Governance in Europe* (Edward Elgar Publishing 2013) 30–34.

[163] J Scott and DM Trubek (n 114) 3.

[164] Convention on Access to Information, Public Participation in Decision-Making and Access to Justice in Environmental Matters done at Aarhus, Denmark, on 25 June 1998, approved by Council Decision 2005/370/EC of 17 February 2005 [2005] OJ L124/1 (Aarhus Convention).

[165] Ibid., Article 5.

effect on the environment. This rule is widely applied on the EU level and not only with respect to the environment. All Commission initiatives including legislative proposals, non-legislative initiatives and implementing measures are subject to impact assessment as to their economic, social and environmental effects. Impact assessment is conducted in the form of consultations between the Commission, on the one hand, and stakeholders and interested parties, on the other. Impact assessment may take the form of Green and White papers, Commission Communications, expert groups, ad hoc consultations and so on.[166] In addition, the European Parliament and the Member States, too, gather public and expert opinions on EU legislative proposals.[167] Yet the sphere of environmental protection features no alternative decision-making procedure comparable to the social dialogue in the field of social policy. Nor might such a governance method be suitable in this context. A compulsory system including a legislative role for environmental policy stakeholders parallel to that of the Commission might instead hamper the current possibilities for taking swift legislative action.[168] For actors outside the EU institutions, the decision-making procedures in the environmental sphere do not provide increased participation opportunities, but further opportunities may avail themselves to third country stakeholders in the initial phases of agenda setting.

7.2.2 Third Country Actors Defining the Core of the Internal Market

7.2.2.1 European Economic Area

The most prominent example of third country influence on EU legislation in the absence of a right to participate in the formal law-making procedures is the inclusion of the EEA EFTA countries in the EU decision-shaping process.

During the negotiations of the EEA Agreement, it was considered whether to grant the EEA EFTA States a formal stake in the decision-making procedures. This would have required an amendment of the Treaties, as well as a significant alteration of the EU's legal and institutional order. The Commission's firm position was that the EU would not make concessions for the benefit of the EEA EFTA States insofar as the

---

[166] European Governance White Paper (n 113) 15.
[167] Ibid., 16.
[168] JH Jans, 'EU Environmental Policy and the Civil Society' in JH Jans (ed.), *The European Convention and the Future of European Environmental Law* (Europa Law Publishing 2003) 53, 59.

Union itself is facing a challenge to complete the internal market by the 1992 deadline.[169] In a speech given at the 1987 EC-EFTA Ministerial Meeting, Commissioner De Clercq established three principles for the cooperation between the Community and the EEA EFTA States: (1) priority for integration within the Community; (2) safeguarding the autonomy of the Community's decision-making; and (3) ensuring 'a fair balance between benefits and obligations' between the parties to the EEA Agreement.[170] The reference to Community integration comes from an assumption that the participation of countries who are not bound by the supranational principles of the EU and must, therefore, follow their national legislative procedures in order to implement EU legislation would cause undue delays in the law-making process and, thereby, render the Union less efficient. The three principles have greatly influenced the decision-making frameworks in the multilateral agreements exporting the acquis and the possibilities of arriving at and maintaining homogeneity in the extended internal market. A compromise solution provided for an inclusion of the EEA EFTA States in the informal stages preceding the initiation of the formal EU legislative procedure. Involvement in the decision-shaping stage allows both the EU and the EEA EFTA States to preserve their decision-making autonomy, whereas it is exercised at different stages and at different venues – the EU in the Council and the EEA EFTA States in the EEA Joint Committee.

Decision-shaping allows the EEA EFTA States to participate in various committees and submit opinions. When preparing legislative proposals, the Commission seeks national expertise both from the Member States and from the EEA EFTA countries.[171] Similar to the Member States' national experts, their EEA EFTA counterparts serve as independent experts and do not represent their respective states. Article 100 EEA Agreement requires that the Commission grant the EEA EFTA States 'as wide as possible' participation in the procedure of preparing draft measures before these are passed on to the committees assisting the Commission. Experts from the Member States and from the EEA EFTA countries must be included on an equal basis. The EEA EFTA States may submit comments to the EU institutions on various policy issues. The so-called EEA EFTA comments are approved by the

---

[169] W De Clercq, speech held at the EC-EFTA ministerial meeting, Interlaken, 20 May 1987, SPEECH/87/32, 5.
[170] Ibid., 5–6.
[171] Article 99(1) EEA Agreement.

EFTA Standing Committee and are forwarded to the relevant EU institutions as well as presented to the EEA Joint Committee.

When a proposal is submitted to the Council, the Commission must ensure that the Council is informed about the views of the EEA EFTA States. At the same time, the Commission must submit a copy of the proposal to the EEA EFTA States.[172] This is without prejudice to the fact that the latter do not participate in the EU legislative procedures. The EEA EFTA States may be invited to attend informal Council meetings upon decision by the Council Presidency.[173] A special arrangement, albeit not part of the EEA Agreement, has been established under Schengen cooperation. All EFTA States are parties to the Schengen Agreement and participate in the Schengen Mixed Committee where proposals for new Schengen acquis are discussed without a right to vote in the Council that adopts the legislative act.[174]

The two keywords that best characterise the participation of the EEA EFTA States in the preparatory stages of the Union's decision-making are information and consultation. All parties to the EEA Agreement must act in good faith as regards the flow of information and consultation.[175] Despite a lack of voting rights, the EEA EFTA States must be kept well informed throughout the legislative process. At the point when the legislative proposal is submitted to the Council any EEA Contracting Party may request that the proposal be discussed at a Joint Committee meeting for a 'preliminary exchange of views'.[176] Information sharing and consultation continue in the Joint Committee before a decision on the draft legislation is taken by the Council.

The scope of the EEA Agreement is not strictly limited to the four fundamental freedoms and competition policy. The Agreement also includes provisions on cooperation between the EU and the EEA EFTA States in relevant EU programmes. The Union's programmes and agencies are increasingly open towards external participation.[177] Cooperation

---

[172] Article 99(2) EEA Agreement.

[173] S Lavenex, 'Concentric circles of flexible "EUropean" Integration: A Typology of EU External Governance Relations' (2011) 9 *Comparative European Politics* 372, 377.

[174] For example, Articles 3 and 8(1) of the Agreement concluded by the Council of the European Union and the Republic of Iceland and the Kingdom of Norway concerning the latters' association with the implementation, application and development of the Schengen acquis [1999] OJ L176/36.

[175] Article 99(4) EEA Agreement.

[176] Article 99(2) EEA Agreement.

[177] See further M-L Öberg, 'Third Countries in EU Agencies: Participation and Influence' in HCH Hofmann, E Vos and M Chamon (eds.), *The External Dimension of EU Agencies and Bodies* (Edward Elgar 2019) 204.

in EU programmes extends to fields such as information services, the environment, education, social policy, consumer protection, and so on.[178] Pursuant to Article 80 EEA Agreement, the EFTA States may participate in the EU's framework programmes, specific programmes, projects and similar undertakings as well as, for example, joint activities, information exchange and parallel legislation. In cases where the EEA EFTA States take part in a programme, project or other action mentioned above and specified in Protocol 31 to the EEA Agreement, the EEA EFTA States enjoy full participation rights,[179] including in programme committees that assist the Commission in the management of the particular activity. In addition, the EEA EFTA States participate in the work of thirteen EU agencies including, for example, the European Union Aviation Safety Agency (EASA), the European Chemicals Agency, the European Food Safety Authority and the European Network and Information Security Agency.[180] The participation of the EEA EFTA States in EU agencies is subject to a decision by the EEA Joint Committee.[181]

The EEA EFTA experts are, furthermore, granted a right to participate in committees in specific areas falling outside the scope of Articles 81 and 100 EEA Agreement. This includes committees listed in Protocol 37 to the EEA Agreement. The committees currently listed in Protocol 37 include, for example, the Administrative Commission for the coordination of social security systems, the Advisory Committee on Restrictive Practices and Dominant Positions and a number of committees on pharmaceutical and medicinal products. The Protocol 37 list is subject to amendments by the Joint Committee,[182] when the 'good functioning' of the EEA Agreement demands the association of EEA EFTA States with additional committees.[183]

The role of the EEA EFTA States in shaping the EU's policies extends to the implementation of EU law by the comitology committees.[184]

---

[178] Article 78 EEA Agreement.
[179] Article 81 EEA Agreement.
[180] For full list, see 'EU Agencies' (EEA website) www.efta.int/eea/eu-agencies accessed 10 February 2020.
[181] For example, Decision of the EEA Joint Committee No 160/2009 of 4 December 2009 amending Protocol 31 to the EEA Agreement, on cooperation in specific fields outside the four freedoms [2010] OJ L62/67, which extended the cooperation between the parties to the EEA Agreement to Council Regulation (EC) No 2062/94 of 18 July 1994 establishing a European Agency for Safety and Health at Work [1994] OJ L216/1 as amended by Council Regulations (EC) No 1643/95, 1654/2003 and 1112/2005.
[182] Article 101(2) EEA Agreement.
[183] Article 101(1) EEA Agreement.
[184] Article 100 EEA Agreement.

Comitology committees have been established to assist the Commission in its task to implement EU law in accordance with Article 291 TFEU. Comitology committees comprise representatives of the Member States as well as, where relevant to the EEA Agreement, representatives of the EEA EFTA countries.[185]

In the comitology procedure, the Member States' and the EEA EFTA States' representatives exercise control over the Commission's activities.[186] Two procedures are available: the examination and the advisory procedure. Examination committees scrutinise the Commission's implementation activities. They are composed of representatives of the Member States and, where appropriate, the EEA EFTA States and are chaired by the Commission. The examination procedure is used in the case of general or potentially important measures. In the event of a negative opinion expressed by a qualified majority of the component members, the Commission may either amend the text or forward the matter to an appeal committee for further discussion.[187] Should the examination committee fail to give an opinion, the Commission may, on certain conditions, adopt the draft.[188] The second advisory procedure is used for the adoption of implementing acts in all other cases. The opinions of the advisory committee are adopted by simple majority and the Commission must take 'utmost account' thereof.[189] The EEA EFTA States do not enjoy voting rights but are able to influence the outcome through informal means.[190] Furthermore, information gathered in the committees facilitates the later implementation of the acts adopted in the comitology procedure in the EEA EFTA States.[191]

The EEA EFTA States' participation in the various stages of EU decision-shaping procedures serves a dual objective. The first is increasing democratic legitimacy and autonomy.[192] Notwithstanding the possibility of the EEA EFTA States to refuse the incorporation of a new or

---

[185] Regulation (EU) No 182/2011 of the European Parliament and of the Council of 16 February 2011 laying down the rules and general principles concerning mechanisms for control by Member States of the Commission's exercise of implementing powers [2011] OJ L55/13.

[186] See T Christiansen and T Larsson (n 87) 5.

[187] Article 5 of Regulation No 182/2011 (n 185).

[188] To trade policy different rules apply.

[189] Article 4 of Regulation No 182/2011 (n 185).

[190] EEA Joint Parliamentary Committee, 'EC comitology and the EEA' (Report and Resolution) M/20/R/029, 21 June 2011, 8.

[191] Ibid.

[192] Commission, 'Future Relations between the Community and EFTA' (Press Release) P/89/72, 22 November 1989.

amended EU legal act into the EEA Agreement and the international law character of the arrangement, the ability to influence the content of the legislation means, on the one hand, that EU legislation is not completely 'foreign' to the EEA EFTA States. On the other hand, both the EEA EFTA States and the EU maintain their autonomy of decision-making in their respective pillars of the EEA and, thus, the overall balance of benefits and obligations. The second, more pragmatic reason for the EEA EFTA States' participation is to facilitate consensus in the Joint Committee both when classifying a new piece of acquis as EEA relevant and when amending the EEA Agreement.[193] Continuous information sharing and consultation during the legislative procedure will also contribute to a swift parliamentary procedure where required by the EEA EFTA States' constitutions which is crucial for timely implementation of the acquis. Participation in decision-shaping, therefore, aims to reinforce both the substantive and temporal dimensions of homogeneity.

Although described as 'semi-colonial',[194] the importance of the 'mere' participation of the EEA EFTA States in the preparatory stages of the EU's legislative procedure should not be underestimated. Especially in the light of the increasing importance of various new governance modes, participation in the norm-shaping may prove almost as relevant as participation in the formal decision-making procedures.[195] This holds especially true for the comitology committees, which exercise quasi-legislative functions and in which the EEA EFTA States, with the exception of voting, possess participation rights equal to the EU Member States.[196] What may curb the effectiveness of the EEA EFTA States' participation are, however, the limits of their own administrative capacity that require prioritising among different policy concerns.[197]

Finally, due to the ensuing need for parliamentary approval for many of the updates to the EEA Agreement as compared to the EU Treaties, the

---

[193] Article 99(4) EEA Agreement.
[194] A Tovias, 'Exploring the "Pros" and "Cons" of Swiss and Norwegian Models of Relations with the European Union – What Can Israel Learn from the Experiences of These Two Countries?' (2006) 41 *Cooperation and Conflict* 203, 219.
[195] S Lavenex (n 173) 377.
[196] GF Schaefer and A Türk, 'The Role of Implementing Committees' in T Christiansen and T Larsson (eds.), *The Role of Committees in the Policy-Process of the European Union* (Edward Elgar Publishing 2007) 182, 184.
[197] S Kristjánsson and R Kristjánsson, 'Delegation and Accountability in an Ambiguous System: Iceland and the European Economic Area (EEA)' (2000) 6 *The Journal of Legislative Studies* 105, 118.

national parliaments of the EEA EFTA States are involved in the EEA decision-making to a much higher degree than their counterparts in the EU Member States. Theoretically, this role of the national parliaments poses a significant risk to the homogeneity of the EEA legal order. In practice, however, the EEA EFTA States' parliaments have to this date not vetoed any amendments to the EEA Agreement.[198]

7.2.2.2 Energy Community

The EnCT, the ECAA Agreement and the TCT feature simpler structures than the well-elaborated framework of the EEA Agreement but all three agreements share a similar set of basic characteristics. Like the EEA Agreement, the EnCT, too, contains provisions on stakeholder consultations. In the two Fora established under Article 63 EnCT, interested stakeholders from industry, regulators, industry representative groups and consumers are represented. The Fora have an advisory function in the Energy Community, dealing with electricity and gas matters, respectively,[199] and play a highly institutionalised role in stakeholder consultations. Among third countries and international organisations, Switzerland, Liechtenstein and the ESA have been represented in the Gas Regulatory Forum, and Norway and the ESA in the Electricity Regulatory Forum.[200] The EnCT does not provide information about the participation of non-EU third country experts in the Commission's committees or working groups but neither is the possibility explicitly excluded.

The Energy Community itself does not contribute to the making of the EU acquis nor are the non-EU contracting parties to the EnCT currently involved in the work of the ACER. Contrary to the EEA EFTA States, the possibilities available to the third country contracting parties

---

[198] See, for example, Foreign Affairs Committee, *The future of the European Union: UK Government policy* (HC 2013–14 1-II) 53.

[199] In addition, an Oil Forum was established by Ministerial Council Decision 2008/03/MC-EnC implementing certain provisions of the Treaty and creating Energy Community Oil Forum. The more recently established Law Forum, Sustainability Forum and Dispute Resolution Forum convene on the initiative of the Secretariat.

[200] See, for example, Attendance List, 27th meeting of the European Gas Regulatory Forum, Madrid, 20–21 April 2015, https://ec.europa.eu/energy/en/topics/markets-and-consumers/wholesale-market/gas-network-codes/madrid-forum-meetings#33rd-meeting-of-the-madrid-forum accessed 10 February 2020; List of participants, 27th meeting of the European Electricity Regulatory Forum, Florence, 27–28 November 2014, https://ec.europa.eu/energy/sites/ener/files/documents/meeting_027_participants.pdf accessed 10 February 2020.

to affect the making of the relevant EU acquis via participation in the Energy Community are, therefore, very modest.[201]

7.2.2.3 European Common Aviation Area

Information and consultation are prominent features of the ECAA Agreement. The ECAA contracting parties exchange information on legislative changes relevant for the ECAA Agreement and, upon request, engage in consultations with the Joint Committee on any pertinent issue, notably including social matters.[202]

Annex II to the ECAA Agreement lays out the procedure for consultations with the associated parties within the relevant committees of the EU. The general clause on exchange of information applies.[203] According to Point 4 of Annex II, the Commission consults with experts of the non-EU ECAA states. Like the EU Member State experts, the ECAA experts may submit their advice and opinions whenever ECAA relevant acts are discussed in the EU committees. The consultation procedure consists of a meeting in the ECAA Joint Committee, which is convened and chaired by the Commission. It takes place prior to the meeting of the EU Committee in question. The ECAA associated parties do not, therefore, participate in the exchange of views that takes place within the Commission between the EU Member States and the EEA EFTA States on proposed legislative acts of EEA relevance. The Commission 'shall take due account' of the views of the ECAA parties and consider them together with all other opinions gathered at the stage of expert consultations. A special consultation procedure provided in Annex III to the ECAA Agreement applies to competition rules.

The ECAA associated parties can, furthermore, directly participate in the activities of the EU committees such as the Single Sky Committee (SSC) that exercises comitology functions by examining draft implementing rules before adoption by the Commission. The 73rd meeting of the SSC, for example, was attended by the Commission, the EU Member States, the EFTA States as Members without voting rights, the EASA, the European Defence Agency and the ESA as observers.[204]

---

[201] See also B Hofmann, T Jevnaker and P Thaler, 'Following, Challenging, or Shaping: Can Third Countries Influence EU Energy Policy?' (2019) 7 *Politics and Governance* 152, 156.
[202] Article 18(4) ECAA Agreement.
[203] Point 5, Annex II to the ECAA Agreement.
[204] See, for example, the list of participants: Summary Report of the 73rd meeting of the Single Sky Committee (SSC) Held in Brussels, 27 November 2019, https://ec.europa.eu/transparency/regcomitology/index.cfm?do=search.documentdetail&Dos_ID=18467&ds_id=65246&version=1&page=1 accessed 10 February 2020.

Importantly, Regulation (EC) No 549/2004 on the Single European Sky[205] envisages in addition to the establishment of the SSC also an industry consultation body that comprises air navigation service providers, associations of airspace users, airport operators, the manufacturing industry and professional staff representative bodies.[206] The industry consultation body advises the Commission on the implementation of the SES. Insofar as this Regulation applies to the ECAA Agreement it can be assumed that non-EU ECAA stakeholders, too, may participate in its activities. In the context of the SES, particular attention is paid to information and consultations with the social partners on measures with substantial social implications, for example by means of consulting the Sectoral Dialogue committee established under Commission Decision 1998/500/EC.[207]

Norway and Iceland being parties to the ECAA Agreement, the provisions of the latter are without prejudice to the respective rules in the EEA Agreement.[208] Article 5 ECAA Agreement is intended to eliminate potential conflicts between the different scopes of the EEA and the ECAA Agreements with respect to the same legislation. Should the ECAA Joint Committee reject an amendment to the ECAA Agreement to adapt its content to changes in the EU acquis, Iceland and Norway would remain bound by the obligations assumed under the EEA Agreement. Vice versa, this would also apply in the hypothetical situation where the EEA Joint Committee rejects an amendment concerning EU legislation that forms part of the ECAA Agreement. In the process of interpretation and application, the different scopes of the ECAA and the EEA Agreements and their respective objectives and context may result in the different scope of identical rules. Council Directive 93/13/EEC on unfair terms in consumer contracts,[209] for example, is incorporated into both the EEA and the ECAA agreements. The sectoral scope of the ECAA Agreement may require a narrower interpretation of the

---

[205] Regulation (EC) No 549/2004 of the European Parliament and of the Council of 10 March 2004 laying down the framework for the creation of the single European sky [2004] OJ L96/1.

[206] Ibid., Article 6.

[207] Ibid., Recital 17 of the preamble; Commission Decision of 20 May 1998 on the establishment of Sectoral Dialogue Committees promoting the Dialogue between the social partners at European level (98/500/EC) [1998] OJ L225/27.

[208] Recital 11, preamble to the ECAA Agreement; Article 5 ECAA Agreement.

[209] Council Directive 93/13/EEC of 5 April 1993 on unfair terms in consumer contracts [1993] OJ L95/29.

provisions of the Directive than in the EEA or the EU but will, by virtue of Article 5 EEA Agreement, primarily concern the legal relations between an EEA EFTA State and a non-EEA and non-EU party to the ECAA Agreement. The Court recognised in Opinion 1/00 the problem of two sets of identical rules – those of the ECAA and of the EU – being applicable on the same territory but not subject to identical implementation and enforcement mechanisms.[210] The same holds true for the EEA-ECAA axis in which the adoption of identical rules will not necessarily result in their homogeneous interpretation and application across the entire expanded aviation market.

7.2.2.4 Transport Community

Annex II paragraph 4 to the TCT provides a procedure for consulting the SEE Parties' experts by the Commission in parallel to the consultation procedure taking place with the EU committees. The procedure, which is identical to the one provided by the ECAA Agreement with the exception of the RSC being the venue for the consultations, allows third country experts to submit their advice or opinion to the Commission which shall take due account thereof. In both agreements, therefore, third countries adopting EU acquis have been granted an important opportunity to influence the making of the acquis in a preliminary phase. Furthermore, the SEE Parties to the TCT do not participate in the meetings of the Management Board of the European Union Agency for Railways but are included in the activities of the European environment information and observation network (Eionet) as 'cooperating countries'. The Eionet is involved in assisting the European Environment Agency with environmental information, data and assessment. The SEE Parties have a possibility to, thereby, exert indirect and limited influence on the making of the EU acquis by contributing essential data in the information-dependent field of environmental policy.[211]

Environmental and social issues are firmly embedded in the Transport Community's institutional and procedural set-up. With the aim of increasing input from non-traditional decision-makers, civil society organisations, especially those dealing with environmental issues, may be invited to participate in the meetings of the technical

---

[210] Opinion 1/00 *ECAA* EU:C:2002:231, para. 10.
[211] See G Majone, 'The New European Agencies: Regulation by Information' (1997) 4 *Journal of European Public Policy* 262, 264.

committees as ad hoc observers,[212] hence without voting rights but possibly with a right to speak. The views of the observers can be considered in the preparation of proposals to be submitted to the RSC for decision, such as on matters concerning the implementation of the agreement. Additionally, a variety of social issues including workers' fundamental rights, labour laws, health and safety at work, and equal opportunities[213] are addressed by the Social Forum. The Social Forum involves a multitude of actors and is specifically tasked with promoting social dialogue in the monitoring of the implementation of the TCT and its effects.[214] The stakeholders do not, however, participate in the stage of integrating EU acquis into the Treaty nor exert influence on the making of the acquis in the EU.

7.3 Conclusion

The level of sophistication of the institutional and procedural arrangements for ensuring homogeneity in the expanded internal market mirrors the scope of the international agreement in question. The EEA Agreement envisages strong guarantees not only in terms of the substantive aspects of homogeneity – the transferral of a large part of relevant acquis from the EU to the EEA – but also in terms of the temporal and territorial aspects thereof. By imposing strict deadlines for the incorporation of new acquis and establishing consequences for all EEA EFTA States in the event of non-compliance by a contracting party, significant effort has, on the one hand, been made to ensure that the EFTA pillar of the EEA remains homogeneous. On the other hand, conceiving the EFTA pillar as one whole and subjecting all three EEA EFTA States to a potential suspension of a part of the agreement is a further guarantee for maintaining homogeneity in the EU-EEA dimension. Less elaborate mechanisms and, thus, weaker guarantees for homogeneity are in place in the sectoral agreements, regarding both the substantive, temporal and territorial aspects of homogeneity.

Different categories of third countries can exert different degrees of influence on the making of the EU acquis. Limited by the 'balance of benefits and obligations' and the autonomy of the EU legal order, the participation of third countries in the defining of the acquis cannot

---

[212] Article 26(1) TCT.
[213] Article 27 TCT.
[214] Article 27(1) TCT.

extend to formal decision-making. In the EEA, well-structured procedures are in place for engaging the EEA EFTA States in the preparatory
stages of the formal law-making procedure. Although efforts have
been made to include input from the non-EU parties to the EnCT, the
ECAA Agreement and the TCT into the making of the acquis in the
Union, the respective procedures are significantly narrower in scope
than those available to the EEA EFTA States, reflecting the less ambitious integration objectives of the sectoral agreements. Early information and consultation procedures are, however, crucial from a
democratic perspective as well as for encouraging the acceptance
and implementation of EU acquis in third countries. This applies to
the incorporation of new or amended acquis into the multilateral
agreements as well as into the national legal orders. Prior exchanges
of views are even more relevant in the case of the EEA where the Joint
Committee's decisions on updating the acquis are taken by consensus
rather than by formal voting.

Although the classic Community method remains prevalent in the
making of EU law,[215] the strongly emerging use of new governance
methods has influenced the range of actors involved in the Union's
decision-shaping and decision-making and provided a particular, inclusive character to EU acquis. The essence of new governance is embodied
in the use of soft law measures as well as in increased information
sharing and consultations, which apply mainly to horizontal and flanking policies such as the social and environmental policies that are relevant for the core of the internal market. For third countries, on the one
hand, the increased dissemination of information about new legislative
proposals and inclusion in early stage discussions may generate more
participatory opportunities. Rule-making procedures that depart from
the classic Community method are generally not regulated by the EU
Treaties and are, therefore, more flexible towards non-traditional participation, which may in turn entail stronger acceptance of and increased
compliance with EU acquis by the third countries. On the other hand,
where new governance translates into alternative procedures for EU law
making, such as in the case of social dialogue, third country representatives may become more excluded from the policy-making processes than
under the classic Community method. Importantly, the agreements
exporting the acquis display an intention to include stakeholders in the

---

[215] K Holzinger, C Knill and A Schäfer, 'Rhetoric or Reality? "New Governance" in EU
Environmental Policy' (2006) 12 *European Law Journal* 403.

implementation stage, thus echoing the inclusive character of EU acquis in the acquis of the respective multilateral agreements. Meanwhile, the initial range of stakeholders that have been consulted prior to the adoption of the acquis in the EU is broadened with third country representatives at the implementation stage, and further dialogue is promoted between the EU and the non-EU stakeholders.

Both quasi-sanctions such as the suspension of a part of the agreement, and the participation of third countries in the preliminary stages of the EU law-making procedures such as via expert consultations, participation in the comitology committees and the EU agencies are important factors in supporting the general acceptance, timely adoption and implementation of the acquis necessary for achieving and maintaining homogeneity. The main responsibility for homogeneity, however, rests on the third country lawmakers and authorities to duly incorporate and implement the exported acquis in the national legal orders.

8 Institutional Framework
Safeguarding the Core of the Internal Market

In a homogeneous expanded internal market, the uniformity of rules goes hand in hand with uniform application and effective enforcement. Individuals and economic operators shall enjoy the same rights regardless of whether they find themselves on the EU or non-EU side of the market. The following analysis proceeds from the assumption that the EU internal market features an adequate level of protection of individual rights through procedural means. In order to be deemed equally effective, the institutions, procedures and remedies provided by the international agreements exporting the acquis must reproduce as a minimum the core of the surveillance, enforcement and judicial protection elements found in the EU Treaties.

This chapter explores the different models of surveillance and enforcement set up by Treaties and the multilateral agreements exporting the internal market acquis, respectively. The analysis is structured along to the modes of centralisation and decentralisation. It looks both at the centralised institutions and procedures for surveillance and enforcement in the EEA, the Energy Community, the ECAA and the Transport Community, and the cooperation between these institutions and those of the Union; as well as the procedural links between the international or supranational institutions, on the one hand, and national authorities and individuals, on the other.

8.1 Safeguarding Homogeneity: Centralising Dynamics

8.1.1 Surveillance and Enforcement

The main institutional guardian of the functioning of the EU Treaties, including the internal market, is the European Commission. Within the

EU legal order, the Commission is specifically tasked to investigate the Member States' compliance with their duties under the Treaties.

First, the Commission may take initiatives under Article 258 TFEU. Suspecting that a Member State has infringed the Treaties, the Commission may issue a reasoned opinion and allow the Member State to submit observations.[1] If the Member State in question fails to comply with the reasoned opinion, the Commission may initiate infringement proceedings before the Court of Justice.[2]

Second, the Commission may follow the initiative taken by a Member State under Article 259 TFEU. Here, the Commission acts as a link between the Member State alleging infringement by another Member State and the Court of Justice. The Commission receives complaints from the Member States, hears each State concerned and submits a reasoned opinion after which the matter may be brought to the Court.[3] Member States cannot take infringement actions directly to the Court without first informing the Commission and allowing the latter to issue a reasoned opinion. Should the Commission fail to deliver an opinion within three months, the Member State may refer the matter to the Court. A decision of the Court establishing a breach of the Treaty obligations is binding on the Member State concerned.[4] The Commission must further monitor the Member State's compliance with the judgment. In case of a failure to rectify the breach, the Commission may bring a new case to the Court specifying a lump sum or penalty payment due by the Member State.[5]

The Commission plays a central role also where breaches of EU law by individual market participants are concerned, especially in the field of competition law. The Commission conducts investigations of suspected competition law infringements and proposes measures to bring them to an end.[6] Similar to infringement proceedings against the Member States, the Commission may act either on its own initiative or upon application by a Member State. If the proposed measures prove ineffi-cient, the Commission may issue a reasoned decision and authorise the Member State in question to remedy the situation.[7]

---

[1] Article 258 TFEU.
[2] Ibid.
[3] Article 259 TFEU.
[4] Article 260(1) TFEU.
[5] Article 260(2) TFEU.
[6] Article 105(1) TFEU. A special surveillance and enforcement procedure in the field of state aid is provided in Article 108 TFEU.
[7] Article 105(2) TFEU.

In the field of competition law, the EEA Agreement meticulously replicates the surveillance system of the EU. The EEA Agreement establishes both 'an independent surveillance authority' – the ESA – and 'procedures similar to those existing in the [Union]' for the purposes of both monitoring compliance with the EEA Agreement and reviewing the legality of the acts of the ESA.[8] For the latter purpose, the EFTA Surveillance and Court Agreement was concluded between the EEA EFTA States.[9]

The ESA's set-up resembles that of the Commission. The ESA features three independently acting members, equivalent of EU Commissioners.[10] At least two EEA EFTA States must be represented among the members. The specific tasks of the ESA are to monitor the functioning of the EEA Agreement and the SCA.[11] Like the Commission, the ESA monitors the compliance of EEA EFTA States both with the EEA Agreement generally[12] and competition rules specifically.[13] If the ESA considers an EEA EFTA State to have breached its obligations under the EEA Agreement, it delivers a reasoned opinion upon which the state concerned has the possibility to submit observations.[14] If the state fails to comply with the opinion, the ESA may bring the matter to the EFTA Court.[15] Differently from the EU Member States, though, the EEA EFTA States cannot initiate infringement proceedings against one another.

Compliance with the EEA competition rules is monitored by both the European Commission and the ESA acting within their respective pillars of the EEA yet in close cooperation in order to guarantee uniformity in the surveillance of the EEA Agreement.[16] To this end, the Commission and the ESA exchange information and consult each other both on general surveillance policy issues and on individual cases.[17] Should a complaint on the application of the EEA Agreement be handed in to the wrong institution, it will be forwarded to the institution competent to handle the issue.[18] In case of disagreement

---

[8] Article 108 EEA Agreement.
[9] See Chapter 5, Section 5.3.1.3, at n 215.
[10] Articles 7 and 8 SCA.
[11] Article 22 SCA.
[12] Article 31 SCA.
[13] Articles 23–25 SCA.
[14] Article 31 SCA.
[15] Ibid.
[16] Articles 58 and 109(1) EEA Agreement; Protocols 23 and 24 to the EEA Agreement.
[17] Article 109(2) EEA Agreement.
[18] Article 109(3) and (4) EEA Agreement.

between the Commission and the ESA concerning action to be taken with regard to a complaint or the results of an examination, either body may refer the issue to the EEA Joint Committee.[19] However, no penalty system similar to the one provided in Article 260(2) TFEU exists under the EEA Agreement.

The Commission and the ESA investigate alleged competition law violations in the EEA on their own initiative, by request of an EEA EFTA State on its territory or by request of the other surveillance authority.[20]

Generally, the ESA deals with cases that only affect trade between the EEA EFTA States or where the turnover of the undertakings concerned in the territory of the EEA EFTA States equals 33 per cent or more of their turnover in the entire EEA.[21] The remaining cases, including where trade between the EU Member States is affected, are to be decided by the Commission – if the latter is not appreciable, the case is decided by the ESA.[22] The surveillance authority competent to decide the case may request copies of important documents from the other authority during all stages of the procedure as well as make observations.[23]

Should either surveillance authority deem that the implementation of state aid control by the other fails to uphold equal conditions of competition within the EEA, an exchange of views will be held.[24] If no common solution is found, the competent authority of the contracting party concerned may immediately adopt interim measures to remedy the distortion of competition. A commonly acceptable solution will thereafter be sought in the EEA Joint Committee. If the Joint Committee cannot find a solution within three months, the interim measures may be replaced by definitive measures. Priority will be given to measures that will least affect the functioning of the EEA Agreement. The fact that differences will be settled in the EEA Joint Committee rather than through judicial means – which may have granted exclusive jurisdiction to the Court of Justice – ensures the equal footing of the EU and the EFTA pillars in the field of the surveillance of the functioning of the EEA Agreement.

---

[19] Article 109(5) EEA Agreement.
[20] Article 55(1) EEA Agreement.
[21] Article 56(1),(2) EEA Agreement.
[22] Article 56(3) EEA Agreement.
[23] Article 7, Protocol 23 to the EEA Agreement.
[24] Article 64(1) EEA Agreement.

Uniform effect is granted to surveillance decisions by virtue of Articles 280 and 299 TFEU and Article 110 EEA Agreement pursuant to which the enforcement decisions of the Commission and the ESA that impose a pecuniary obligation on individuals are enforceable in the EU as well as in the EEA. The same applies to the judgments of the EEA and the EU judiciaries.[25]

Both the Commission and the ESA can be held liable for failures to act. The institutions may be subject to infringement proceedings under Article 265 TFEU and Article 37 SCA, respectively. An infringement action can be brought before the Court of Justice by an EU Member State and to the EFTA Court by an EEA EFTA State if the respective surveillance authorities have previously been called upon to act. Any natural or legal person may also complain to the Court of Justice or the EFTA Court, respectively, if an institution, body, office or agency of the Union or the ESA has failed to address to that person 'any act other than a recommendation or an opinion' in the case of the EU or a decision in the case of the EEA EFTA States. In the meantime, EEA EFTA nationals can bring to the national courts cases challenging the legality of national legal acts implementing ESA decisions whereas EU citizens can only challenge individual decisions in the Court of Justice.[26]

The grounds on which the enforcement and surveillance of the internal market acquis takes place in the Energy Community, the ECAA and the TCT differ significantly from those applicable to the EU and the EEA. Neither the EnCT, the ECAA Agreement nor the TCT establish a separate surveillance authority. The surveillance of their proper functioning is instead conducted by the Commission in the EU pillar of the agreements and the national authorities in the non-EU pillar. The EU institutions, primarily the Commission, exercise surveillance duties where the competition rules or secondary legislation of the respective treaties so provide.[27] For example, the Commission enjoys special powers granted to it under EU acquis in cases that may affect the authorisation of actual or potential air services,[28] and may monitor compliance with aviation security rules.[29] In the TCT, the Permanent

---

[25] Article 110 EEA Agreement.
[26] HP Graver, 'The Efta Court and the Court of Justice of the EC: Legal Homogeneity at Stake?' in P-C Müller-Graff and E Selvig (eds.), *EEA-EU Relations* (Berlin Verlag Arno Spitz 1999) 31, 40–42.
[27] Opinion 1/00 *ECAA* EU:C:2002:231, para. 7.
[28] Article 15(2) ECAA Agreement.
[29] Article 12(4) ECAA Agreement.

Secretariat is tasked with acting as a Transport Observatory for the specific task of monitoring the TEN-T extension of the networks to the Western Balkans.[30]

Whereas the EEA Agreement features substantial institutional safeguards for maintaining homogeneity in the EEA and between the EEA and the EU acquis, no elaborate guarantees are envisaged by the sectoral agreements. Yet this does not necessarily pose a threat to homogeneity. In situations where EU institutions including the Commission have power to act, homogeneity may be preserved more effectively than in the EEA where it is to be secured by two institutions. In cases where the EU institutions have no power to act, they equally lack such power in the EU Member States, leading to a rather equal outcome in terms of (a lack of) homogeneity. This is notwithstanding the practical difficulties that the Commission or other EU institutions may encounter when exercising their powers to investigate the implementation of the acquis in the non-EU Member States rather than within the Union.

8.1.2 Interpretation and Dispute Settlement

8.1.2.1 European Union

The Court of Justice provides authoritative interpretations of EU law and, thereby, the benchmark for uniformity in the interpretation and application of EU acquis in the expanded internal market. Pursuant to Article 19(1) TEU, the Court shall observe that in the interpretation and application of the Treaties the law is observed. The Court rules on direct actions brought by the Member States, EU institutions or natural and legal persons, and in other cases provided in the Treaties,[31] whereas the General Court decides on all other cases that are assigned neither to the Court nor to a specialised court under Article 257 TFEU.[32] Article 273 TFEU, furthermore, allows the Member States to grant the Court of Justice jurisdiction in any dispute between them that relates to the subject matter of the Treaties under a special agreement. In the meantime, Article 344 TFEU forbids the Member States to submit a dispute concerning the interpretation or application of EU law to any other forum than the courts of the EU. The rulings of the Court of Justice are binding and enforceable in the Member States.[33]

---

[30] Article 28(b) TCT.
[31] Article 19(3) TEU.
[32] Article 256(1) TFEU.
[33] Articles 280 and 299 TFEU.

8.1.2.2 European Economic Area

The EEA features a hybrid system of maintaining homogeneity in the interpretation and application of the acquis, including both judicial and political elements.[34] The EEA judicial system consists of the EFTA Court, the Court of Justice of the EU, the General Court and the courts of last instance of the EEA EFTA States.[35]

The EFTA Court is established under Article 108(2) EEA Agreement. Its tasks include conducting surveillance of the EEA Agreement in the EEA EFTA States, deciding on appeals on the decisions rendered by the ESA in the field of competition law, and settling disputes between the EEA EFTA States.[36] The EFTA Court comprises three judges all of whom must participate in the deliberations in order for a decision of the EFTA Court to be valid.[37] The jurisdiction of the EFTA Court includes disputes between two or more EEA EFTA States regarding the interpretation or application of the EEA Agreement,[38] penalties imposed by the ESA[39] and actions brought by an EFTA state against a decision of the latter.[40] Individuals, too, may institute proceedings against a decision of the ESA provided that the decision was addressed to the individual or if the decision is of direct and individual concern to the person initiating the proceedings.[41]

The EU and the EFTA courts do not exist and work in isolation. The EEA Agreement has set up a system of exchange of information regarding judgments of the Court of Justice, the General Court, the EFTA Court and the courts of last instance of the EEA EFTA States. To this end, the Registrar of the Court of Justice receives copies of the judgments of the above courts which concern the interpretation or application of either the EEA Agreement, the EU Treaties or EEA relevant acquis and transmits the relevant documents to the contracting parties.[42]

Maintaining homogeneity in the interpretation of the common rules across the EEA is primarily the task of the EEA Joint Committee.

---

[34] C Reymond, 'Institutions, Decision-Making Procedure and Settlement of Disputes in the European Economic Area' (1993) 30 *Common Market Law Review* 449, 475.
[35] Article 106 EEA Agreement.
[36] Article 108(2) EEA Agreement.
[37] Articles 28 and 29 SCA.
[38] Article 32 SCA.
[39] Article 35 SCA.
[40] Article 36 SCA.
[41] Ibid.
[42] Article 106 EEA Agreement.

Pursuant to Article 105(2) EEA Agreement, the Joint Committee constantly reviews the development of the case law of the Court of Justice and the EFTA Court, thereby comparing the interpretations given to identical rules by the two courts. If necessary, the Joint Committee acts 'so as to preserve the homogeneous interpretation of the Agreement', which in accordance with Article 105(1) EEA Agreement, applies to both the EEA and the EU-EEA dimensions. If the Joint Committee fails to find a solution within two months, the matter will be dealt with under the dispute settlement procedure provided in Article 111 EEA Agreement.[43] It has been questioned whether the EEA Joint Committee could in the process of preserving the homogeneous interpretation of the EEA Agreement also incorporate new case law of the Court into the EEA.[44] Albeit homogeneity-advancing, it is questionable whether the Joint Committee could in effect amend the EEA Agreement and the SCA, which in their respective Articles 6 and 3(2) stipulate that the post-1992 case law of the Court is not binding on the EEA EFTA States and the EEA institutions.[45]

The process under Article 105(2) EEA Agreement of establishing a divergence in case law as well as finding a homogeneity-preserving solution is strictly political, not judicial. Apart from Article 106 EEA Agreement, the means of action available to the Joint Committee are not further specified but may certainly not affect the case law of the Court of Justice as was agreed by the drafters of the EEA Agreement.[46] Since it is not clear whether the prohibition concerns only the Court's rulings on EU law or also EEA law one should assume that it concerns both.

The homogeneity provision laid down in Article 1(1) EEA Agreement is neutral as to the authoritative source of the interpretation and application of the internal market acquis that would serve as a benchmark for homogeneity. From several provisions of the EEA Agreement, it appears, however, that the upper hand in determining the effect of the homogeneous acquis in the EEA rests with the Court of Justice. This notwithstanding, in the procedure provided in Article 105(2) EEA

---

[43] Article 105(3) EEA Agreement.

[44] C Baudenbacher, 'Between Homogeneity and Independence: The Legal Position of the EFTA Court in the European Economic Area' (1997) 3 *Columbia Journal of European Law* 169, 220.

[45] Ibid.

[46] '*Procès-verbal agréé ad article 105*': see Opinion 1/92 *EEA II* EU:C:1992:189, para. 6; also Protocol 48 to the EEA Agreement concerning Articles 105 and 111, which reads as follows: 'Decisions taken by the EEA Joint Committee under Articles 105 and 111 may not affect the case-law of the Court of Justice of the European Communities.'

Agreement, what is homogeneous is ultimately to be determined by the contracting parties.[47]

Yet the Joint Committee may not adversely affect the binding nature of the rulings of the Court within the EU legal order.[48] If the Joint Committee were to bind the EEA Contracting Parties, which include the EU and its Member States, to an interpretation of EEA law, which diverges from the interpretation given by the Court to identical provisions under EU law, the Joint Committee would itself undermine homogeneity in the EEA. Whether the Joint Committee could challenge an interpretation provided by the EFTA Court is, however, questionable from the point of view of judicial independence.[49]

In the case of disputes arising from the application or interpretation of the EEA Agreement, either the EU or an EEA EFTA State, but not an EU Member State, may bring the matter before the EEA Joint Committee.[50] The task of the Joint Committee is to gather all relevant information and find an acceptable solution to the case at hand by examining 'all possibilities to maintain the good functioning of the EEA Agreement'.[51] The link between Articles 105(3) and 111 EEA Agreement 'necessarily implies' that the '*procès-verbal agréé ad article 105*' and Protocol 48 to the EEA Agreement also apply to the dispute settlement procedure meaning that the case law of the Court of Justice must not be affected.[52]

The Joint Committee must find a solution to divergent interpretations of EEA acquis that is identical to EU law within three months.[53] If a solution cannot be found, the parties to the dispute may decide to request a binding interpretation of the rules under dispute from the Court of Justice.[54] In practice, it is unlikely for the Court to be called upon to rule on whether its own interpretation or that provided by the EFTA Court will prevail.[55] If no solution is found by the Joint Committee within six months and the parties have not requested a ruling from the

---

[47] The same applies to the legislative means of achieving and maintaining homogeneity in the form of, for example, updating the EEA Agreement and the, in practice rather subjective, determination of the EEA relevance of a piece of EU acquis. See further in Chapter 7, Section 7.1.2.1.

[48] Opinion 1/92 *EEA II* (n 46) para. 22.

[49] C Baudenbacher, 'Between Homogeneity and Independence' (n 44) 222–223.

[50] Article 111(1) EEA Agreement.

[51] Article 111(2) EEA Agreement.

[52] Opinion 1/92 *EEA II* (n 46) para. 28.

[53] Article 111(3) EEA Agreement.

[54] Ibid.

[55] T van Stiphout, 'Homogeneity vs. Decision-Making Autonomy in the EEA Agreement' (2007) 9 *European Journal of Law Reform* 431, 442–443.

Court, the contracting parties may either take safeguard measures or apply the procedure of Article 102 EEA Agreement, which is used in cases of inability to duly incorporate changes in EU acquis into the EEA Agreement.[56] The latter includes an assessment of the situation in the Joint Committee,[57] taking all efforts to arrive at an agreement on matters relevant to the EEA Agreement,[58] and, as a last resort, the EEA Joint Committee examining 'all further possibilities to maintain the good functioning of [the] Agreement' and taking 'any decision necessary to [that] effect'.[59] The solution calls for political agreement, not necessarily strict judicial homogeneity. The ultimate solution is to suspend the affected part of the EEA Agreement under Article 102(5). Since the final remedy is the suspension of the Agreement rather than a possibility of appeal, the hybrid system of dispute resolution is, in general, not likely to benefit the weaker party, which is the EEA EFTA State.[60] Only in specific cases that do not involve an interpretation of the acquis may a dispute between the EEA contracting parties be referred to arbitration under Protocol 33 to the EEA Agreement.[61]

In the polycentric[62] EEA legal order, both the EU and the EEA EFTA courts, including national courts, interpret the internal market acquis. A homogeneous outcome requires that the different judicial bodies arrive at a common interpretation of the rights conferred on individuals by the EEA Agreement. The EEA Agreement and the SCA clarify how uniformity in interpretation should be maintained Article 6 EEA Agreement stipulates that the provisions of the EEA Agreement that mirror EU acquis, must be interpreted in conformity with the rulings of the Court of Justice of the EU, including the Court of Justice and the General Court,[63] given prior to the date of signature of the EEA Agreement. The Agreement was signed in Oporto on 2 May 1992. The EFTA Court and the national courts of the EEA EFTA States are not obliged to follow the post-1992 case law of the Court of Justice yet neither are they discouraged from doing so. Quite to the contrary, owing to the institutional shortcomings of the EEA Agreement as

---

[56] Article 111(3) EEA Agreement.
[57] Article 102(2) EEA Agreement.
[58] Article 102(3) EEA Agreement.
[59] Article 102(4) EEA Agreement.
[60] C Reymond (n 34) 475–476.
[61] Article 111(4) EEA Agreement.
[62] H Haukeland Fredriksen, 'One Market, Two Courts: Legal Pluralism vs. Homogeneity in the European Economic Area' (2010) 79 *Nordic Journal of International Law* 481, 482.
[63] Case E-2/94 *Scottish Salmon Growers* [1994–1995] EFTA Ct Rep 59, para. 13.

concerns the lack of obligation on behalf of the numerous judiciaries of the EEA to always follow one another's rulings, homogeneity of the EEA legal order can in practice only be upheld by the goodwill of the contracting parties. Furthermore, the case law of the Court of Justice has no *stare decisis* effect of precedent. Although such situations occur very seldom,[64] the Court of Justice may deviate from its previous interpretations of EU law. In this respect, homogeneity necessarily requires careful consideration of the evolution of the Court's case law in time instead of stagnating in the pre-1992 state of the internal market.

Article 6 EEA Agreement is, furthermore, without prejudice to Article 3 SCA which only binds the EEA EFTA States. Whereas Article 3(1) SCA replicates in essence Article 6 EEA Agreement, paragraph 2 of the same article stipulates that the ESA and the EFTA Court 'shall *pay due account* to the principles laid down by the relevant rulings by the Court of Justice of the European [Union]'[65] post-1992 when interpreting and applying EEA law which is identical to EU acquis. Taken by the wording, paying due account to the Court's case law does not equal being obliged to follow the Court's interpretation. The EFTA Court has held that it is 'an inherent consequence' of the institutional system of the EEA that consists of two judiciaries that, occasionally, the two may arrive at different interpretations of common rules.[66] In practice, the EFTA Court has been accommodating towards the rulings of the Court regardless of their time of delivery.[67] There are numerous examples of case law that illustrate the EFTA Court's homogeneity-prone attitude.[68] However, there exist also examples of the EFTA Court deviating from the case law of the Court of Justice, albeit not to the extent of triggering a dispute settlement procedure under Article 111 EEA Agreement.[69]

The responsibility for maintaining judicial homogeneity in the EEA leans strongly towards the EFTA Court. One of the reasons for this is the fact that the Court of Justice is not only tasked with upholding homogeneity in the EEA but also with securing the uniform interpretation of

---

[64] For example, Case 192/73 *Hag I* EU:C:1974:72; Case C-10/89 *Hag II* EU:C:1990:359.
[65] Emphasis added.
[66] Joined Cases E-9/07 and E-10/07 *L'Oréal* [2008] EFTA Ct Rep 259, para. 28.
[67] Ibid.
[68] EFTA Court's case law citing post-1992 Court of Justice case law includes, for example, Case E-1/94 *Restamark* [1994–1995] EFTA Ct Rep 15; Case E-3/98 *Rainford-Towning* [1998] EFTA Ct Rep 205; Case E-5/98 *Fagtún* [1999] EFTA Ct Rep 51.
[69] C Baudenbacher, 'The EFTA Court and the European Court' in P-C Müller-Graff and E Selvig (eds.), *EEA-EU Relations* (Berlin Verlag Arno Spitz 1999) 69, 80–81.

EU law. When interpreting EEA rules that replicate the EU acquis, it is to be expected that the Court, first and foremost, considers the proper functioning of the internal market. Normally, this would only prove problematic in cases where EEA law is not interpreted in a manner identical to EU law, that is, where the particular context of the EEA rule differs from that of the EU provision. The latter requires interpretation that takes into consideration the EU's deeper integration objectives. Not many such examples exist, though.[70] Whenever the Court has provided an interpretation of the internal market acquis, the EFTA Court is likely to follow that by virtue of both Article 6 EEA Agreement and Article 3 SCA. From the perspective of homogeneity, problems arise when the EFTA Court is the first of the two to be faced with the task of interpreting a provision of EEA legislation that the Court has not yet reviewed, neither in the context of the EU nor of the EEA. This situation is also known as the 'going first constellation'.[71] The EEA Agreement and the SCA are silent on whether the Court, too, has an obligation to maintain a homogeneous interpretation of EEA law by following the case law of the EFTA Court. In practice, the Court of Justice often follows the interpretations given by the EFTA Court.[72] Yet it is highly doubtable that the Court would consider itself bound by any obligation in this regard, including the objective of maintaining homogeneity in the EEA. There are examples of the Court both not referring to a judgment of the EFTA Court[73] and deviating from the latter's interpretation.[74]

The best-known cases dealing with deviations from and re-alignment with previous case law are those belonging to the *Maglite-Silhouette-L'Oréal* saga. The cases concern the interpretation of Article 7(1) of the

---

[70] For an example, see the discussion on *Maglite-Silhouette-L'Oréal* cases below.

[71] C Baudenbacher, 'The EFTA Court and the European Court' (n 69) 81.

[72] For example, Joined Cases E-8/94 and E-9/94 *Mattel and Lego* [1994–1995] EFTA Ct Rep 113 in Joined Cases C-34/95, C-35/95 and C-36/95 *De Agostini* EU:C:1997:344; Case E-3/00 *Kellogg's* [2000–2001] EFTA Ct Rep 73 in Case C-192/01 *Commission v. Denmark* EU: C:2003:492 and Case C-41/02 *Commission v. Netherlands* EU:C:2004:762; Case E-3/02 *Paranova* [2003] EFTA Ct Rep 101 in Case C-348/04 *Boehringer Ingelheim* EU:C:2007:249. Advocates General, too, refer to the EFTA Court's case law: see, for example, Joined Cases C-34/95, C-35/95 and C-36/95 *De Agostini* EU:C:1996:333, Opinion of AG Jacobs.

[73] For example, Case C-189/95 *Franzén* EU:C:1997:504 in which the Court of Justice did not refer to the EFTA Court's advisory opinion in Case E-6/96 *Wilhelmsen* [1997] EFTA Ct Rep 53. The Court of Justice reached the same conclusion as the EFTA Court but on a different justification.

[74] Cases in which the Court of Justice has deviated from the EFTA Court's case law include, for example, Joined Cases C-34/95, C-35/95 and C-36/95 *De Agostini* (n 72) deviating from Case E-5/96 *Nille* [1997] EFTA Ct Rep 30; Case C-379/05 *Amurta* EU: C:2007:655 deviating from Case E-1/04 *Fokus Bank* [2004] EFTA Ct Rep 11.

Trade Marks Directive[75] and the question of whether the Directive settled in addition to the EEA-wide exhaustion of trade mark rights also the question of international exhaustion or whether that determination was left for the national courts.[76] In *Maglite*, the EFTA Court found that the different objectives and contexts of the EU and the EEA – the one being a customs union and the other not – may justify different interpretations of the rule of international exhaustion of trade mark rules and that the Directive as it applies to the EEA, therefore, does not prohibit compulsory international exhaustion of trade mark rights.[77] In *Silhouette*, however, the Court of Justice found that the Directive did, indeed, preclude the Member States from applying the principle of international exhaustion of trade mark rights in addition to the EEA-wide exhaustion.[78] The divergences in the two interpretations arose from the fact that the EFTA Court approached the issue from the angle of free trade and competition whereas the Court of Justice emphasised the functioning of the internal market.[79] The differences in the interpretation of the acquis did not result in a procedure in the EEA Joint Committee. Instead, the next time the EFTA Court dealt with the matter, in the *L'Oréal* case,[80] it followed the Court's interpretation in *Silhouette* and, thus, restored homogeneity by using the judicial means available.[81] The differences between the EU Treaties and the EEA Agreement did not, in the end, call for divergent interpretations in the two legal orders.[82]

Cases where the EFTA Court goes first raise, moreover, valid concerns for legal certainty. In spite of the homogeneity claim, a specific legal issue at hand cannot be considered to have been settled authoritatively in the EEA for as long as the Court of Justice has not expressed itself on the same matter. Should the Court, moreover, depart from the interpretation previously given by the EFTA Court, no final solution is reached until the latter has had a new opportunity to pronounce itself on the

---

[75] Council Directive 89/104/EEC of 21 December 1988 to approximate the laws of the Member States relating to trade marks [1989] OJ L40/1.

[76] O-A Rognstad, 'The Conflict between Internal Market and Third Country Policy Considerations in the EEA. Maglite Vs. Silhouette' in P-C Müller-Graff and E Selvig (eds.), *EEA-EU Relations* (Berlin Verlag Arno Spitz 1999) 131, 132.

[77] Case E-2/97 *Maglite* [1997] EFTA Ct Rep 127, paras. 25–28.

[78] Case C-355/96 *Silhouette* EU:C:1998:374, para. 52.

[79] Joined Cases E-9/07 and E-10/07 *L'Oréal* (n 66) para. 30.

[80] Ibid.

[81] H Haukeland Fredriksen, 'One Market, Two Courts' (n 62) 497.

[82] Joined Cases E-9/07 and E-10/07 *L'Oréal* (n 66) para. 37.

matter and, possibly, align its case law with that of the Court of Justice. In the particular case of *Maglite*, the EFTA Court's change of mind was not unpredictable. In the judgment, the EFTA Court had made a reservation by establishing a minimum standard of exhaustion subject to future developments in case law.[83] Due to this proviso, the impact of the later change in direction cannot be considered significant for individuals in terms of legal certainty.[84]

With respect to the EFTA Court's reservation in *Maglite*, van Stiphout has deemed the EFTA Court to perceive itself as not having more than 'provisional authority',[85] whereas Magnússon claims that the same can be said about the Court of Justice.[86] Both opinions can be considered justified to a certain extent but the scales of provisional authority lean more strongly towards the EFTA Court.

One can distinguish between the binding and the persuasive authority of judicial decisions.[87] The former category comprises judgments that must be followed in later case law unless the judge can find good reasons for not doing so, or even if the judge could, in fact, give good reasons for not doing so.[88] The latter category refers to previous decisions that have informative rather than obligatory value.[89] The rulings of the Court of Justice given prior to 1992 have binding authority on the EFTA Court but no rulings of the EFTA Court have binding authority on the Court of Justice. It is apparent from *Maglite* and *Silhouette* that the Court of Justice does not set the homogeneity objective of the EEA Agreement above its own judicial authority. Contrary could be proven in cases in which the EFTA Court would depart from the case law of the Court of Justice and the Court would later follow the EFTA Court's precedent, which to this date has never happened.

The seeming difference between the two courts is that the Court of Justice changes path in its case law on its own determination whereas the EFTA Court in the *L'Oréal* case reversed its previous interpretation to

---

[83] Case E-2/97 *Maglite* (n 77) para. 22.
[84] S Magnússon, 'Judicial Homogeneity in the European Economic Area and the Authority of the EFTA Court. Some Remarks on an Article by Halvard Haukeland Fredriksen' (2011) 80 *Nordic Journal of International Law* 507, 532.
[85] T van Stiphout, 'The L'Oréal Cases – Some Thoughts on the Role of the EFTA Court in the EEA Legal Framework: Because it is worth it!' (2009) 1 *Jus & News* 7, 15.
[86] S Magnússon, 'Judicial Homogeneity in the European Economic Area' (n 84) 531.
[87] AG Toth, 'The Authority of Judgments of the European Court of Justice: Binding Force and Legal Effects' (1984) 4 *Yearbook of European Law* 1, 20.
[88] R Cross and JW Harris, *Precedent in English Law* (Oxford University Press 1991) 4.
[89] AG Toth (n 87) 20.

realign itself with the Court. When accepting the EFTA Court's interpretation, however, the Court of Justice does not perceive the EFTA Court as exercising judicial authority over its own judicial activity. Rather, the Court refers to the judgments of the EFTA Court because it finds no reason to deviate from the interpretation given by the latter in the given case and, possibly, because it regards such references relevant from the perspective of maintaining homogeneity in the EEA.

When the Court of Justice arrives at a similar interpretation as the EFTA Court, a reference to the ruling of the latter is informative of the EFTA Court having previously reached the same conclusion as the Court itself in its subsequent ruling. Whereas agreement with the approach of the EFTA Court in given cases may be coincidental, the references that the Court of Justice makes to the EFTA Court's case law are not. Instead, the fact that the Court does refer to the EFTA Court's rulings, regardless of who had first ruled on the issue in question, shows that the Court, too, perceives that the proper functioning of the EEA Agreement requires homogeneity in the interpretation of identical rules. This is accompanied with a need to signal the existence of homogeneity as long as it does not conflict with the Court's own judicial authority. Although the rulings of the EFTA Court do not formally bind the Court nor do the post-1992 rulings of the Court bind the EFTA Court beyond 'duly taking them into account', it cannot be denied that the persuasive authority of these rulings is still an authority, if not of a 'soft' nature.

Another example illustrating the generally weaker position of the EFTA Court in the EEA equation is the fact that the Court of Justice but not the EFTA Court has jurisdiction to rule on the validity of the internal market acquis. The Court enjoys exclusive jurisdiction to review the legality of legislative acts adopted by the EU institutions and, if necessary, to declare them void.[90] In the EU pillar of the EEA, the Court of Justice may, moreover, rule on the validity of the Council decision concluding the EEA Agreement as well as the Council decisions by which the Union's positions to be taken in the EEA Joint Committee are adopted.[91] Should the Court declare void the former, the international obligations of the EU vis-à-vis the other contracting parties would remain in place until the Agreement is denounced in accordance with international treaty law. The EFTA Court possesses no comparable powers. The EFTA Court can neither review the legality of EU law nor

---

[90] Articles 263–264 TFEU.
[91] See, for example, Case C-431/11 *United Kingdom* v. *Council* EU:C:2013:589.

the legality of the decisions of the EEA Joint Committee.[92] In the EFTA pillar of the EEA, only the EEA EFTA States' national courts can review the validity of the national legislation implementing EEA law.

The EEA also features a number of procedural arrangements adopted to promote homogeneity. First, the EU and the Commission may intervene in proceedings before the EFTA Court,[93] and the EEA EFTA States and the ESA may intervene in proceedings before the Court of Justice in cases that concern the application of EEA law or EU acquis replicated by the EEA Agreement.[94] The EEA EFTA States and the ESA may appear in proceedings between EU institutions and EU Member States as well as in preliminary ruling proceedings provided that the cases concern one of the fields of application of the EEA Agreement.[95] Natural or legal persons including the ESA may, however, only intervene in a case before the Court of Justice if they can establish an interest in the result of that case.[96] Article 36 of the Statute of the EFTA Court does not restrict the intervention rights of the EU and the Commission in a similar manner. In practice, the Court has seldom refused to allow the ESA to intervene in the proceedings of a case having relevance for the EEA Agreement, such as where the parties to the dispute have been an EU institution and a Member State.[97] In other similar cases, the EEA EFTA States have been granted leave to intervene in proceedings before the Court of Justice.[98]

The lack of reciprocity in the intervention rights under the Statutes of the Court of Justice and of the EFTA Court, respectively, has prompted criticism for a perceived lack of procedural homogeneity in the EEA.[99]

---

[92] The EFTA Court has, however, under Article 34 SCA the jurisdiction to assess the limits of the competences of the EEA Joint Committee. See, for example, Case E-6/01 CIBA [2002] EFTA Ct Rep 281, paras. 21–23.

[93] Article 36 of the Statute of the EFTA Court, Protocol 5 to the EEA Agreement.

[94] Articles 23 and 40 of the Statute of the Court of Justice of the European Union provided in Protocol No 3 annexed to the Treaties. See also Declaration by the European Community on the Rights for the EFTA States before the EC Court of Justice annexed to the EEA Agreement, para. 1.

[95] Article 1(4) of the Council Decision of 22 December 1994 amending the Protocol on the Statute of the Court of Justice of the European Community (94/993/EC) [1994] OJ L379/1.

[96] Order of 19 January 2012 in Joined Cases T-289/11, T-290/11 and T-521/11 Deutsche Bahn EU:T:2012:20, para. 7.

[97] Order of 15 July 2010 in Case C-493/09 Commission v. Portugal EU:C:2010:444, paras. 11–12.

[98] See, for example, Case C-377/98 Netherlands v. Parliament and Council EU:C:2001:523; Order of 10 July 2006 in Joined Cases C-14/06 and C-295/06 Parliament and Denmark v. Commission EU:C:2006:452.

[99] S Magnusson, 'Procedural Homogeneity v. Inconsistency of European Courts – Comments on Order of the EFTA Court President of 15 June 2012 in Case E-16/11 EFTA Surveillance Authority v. Iceland' (2012), http://papers.ssrn.com/sol3/papers.cfm?abstract_id=2140717

Albeit generally unknown as a concept within EU law, procedural homogeneity has been recognised by the EFTA Court.[100] It is not explicit in either the EEA Agreement, the EnCT, the ECAA Agreement or the TCT that the homogeneity principle would extend to the procedural realm. For the sake of homogeneity, however, the institutions set up for ensuring the proper functioning of these agreements should also be equipped with the tools necessary to safeguard the uniform interpretation and application of the internal market acquis contained therein. This necessarily includes interpreting the identical procedural and institutional rules of the EU and the multilateral agreements in a coherent and uniform manner.[101]

8.1.2.3 Energy Community

The EnCT does not establish any judicial institutions. Article 94 EnCT allocates the task of interpreting the aspects of the Treaty that mirror EU acquis to the Ministerial Council, which may, in turn, delegate the matter to the PHLG. Energy Community law that replicates EU acquis must be interpreted in conformity with the case law of the Court of Justice. Compared to the EEA Agreement, Article 94 EnCT contains no reservation for post-signature case law suggesting that the Energy Community acquis might be more dynamic than the EEA acquis. Considering the experience from the EEA, though, the practical consequences of the distinction are minor. If no interpretation has yet been given by the Court, 'guidance' on how to interpret the EnCT will be provided by the Ministerial Council or, upon delegation from the latter, the PHLG. The interpretation agreed on by the political institutions does not subsequently bind the Court to a certain interpretation of EU law, nor of the Energy Community acquis. Article 94 EnCT, furthermore, states that the 'institutions' of the Energy Community must interpret Energy Community law in conformity with the case law of the Court without reference to the national courts of the non-EU contracting parties to the EnCT. Neither Article 6 EEA Agreement, Article 16(1) ECAA Agreement nor Article 19(1) TCT restricts the requirement of conforming interpretation

accessed 10 February 2020; C Baudenbacher, 'The EFTA Court and Court of Justice of the European Union: Coming in Parts but Winning Together', in *The Court of Justice and the Construction of Europe: Analyses and Perspectives on Sixty Years of Case-law* (T.M.C. Asser Press 2013) 183.

[100] '[...] for the sake of procedural homogeneity [...]': Order of 25 March 2011 in Case E-14/10 *Konkurrenten.no* [2011] EFTA Ct Rep 266, para. 9.

[101] S Magnusson, 'Procedural Homogeneity' (n 99) 4–5. See also C Baudenbacher, 'The EFTA Court and Court of Justice of the European Union' (n 99) 194.

to the institutions only. On the contrary, they refer to the 'implementation and application' of identical provisions. Nevertheless, the instances in which the Energy Community institutions interpret the Energy Community acquis include the dispute settlement procedures in the Ministerial Council. A centralised means, albeit of a political nature, is thus available to ensure judicial homogeneity in the Energy Community.

In the Energy Community, furthermore, any party to the EnCT, the Secretariat or the Regulatory Board may notify the Ministerial Council of a failure by another contracting party to comply with a Treaty obligation or implement a decision addressed to it.[102] Private bodies may submit complaints to the Secretariat. In the case of a serious and persistent breach of the treaty obligations, certain rights incumbent upon the party concerned under the Treaty may be suspended.[103] Since the Energy Community lacks an independent surveillance authority and a court, the procedures for determining the existence of an infringement are entirely political. The link between the Commission and the institutions of the Energy Community is in the non-compliance procedure limited to the Commission's participation in the institutions and the voting procedures. This mechanism is based on inter-governmental cooperation and does not possess additional synchronising tools, such as close cooperation between the Energy Community institutions and the Commission.

8.1.2.4 European Common Aviation Area

Similar to the EEA Agreement, only the pre-signature judgments of the Court of Justice are subject to conforming interpretation in the ECAA.[104] Later decisions are communicated to the contracting parties who may request the ECAA Joint Committee to determine the implications of the post-signature rulings and decisions. The respective decisions of the ECAA Joint Committee must conform to the Court's case law.[105] The ECAA Joint Committee must keep under constant review the development of the Court's case law. To this end, the EU forwards relevant case law to the ECAA Partners. The ECAA Joint Committee shall act so as to preserve the homogeneous interpretation of the ECAA Agreement in a timeframe of three months.[106]

---

[102] Article 90(1) EnCT.
[103] Article 92(1) EnCT.
[104] Article 16(1) ECAA Agreement.
[105] Ibid.
[106] Article 18(7) ECAA Agreement.

Dispute settlement in the ECAA is carried out by the ECAA Joint Committee. Matters of dispute concerning the application or interpretation of the ECAA Agreement may be brought to the Joint Committee by the EU acting together with its Member States, or by an ECAA Partner.[107] The dispute settlement procedure starts with immediate consultations between the parties to the dispute. The EU is always involved in the procedure, if not as a party to the dispute then as an invited participant to the consultations. If the disputing parties manage to agree to a solution, a proposal is drafted and submitted to the ECAA Joint Committee which shall take a decision on the matter. In the absence of an ECAA court, the ECAA Joint Committee is more likely to become involved in the settlement of disputes between the parties than the EEA Joint Committee.[108]

Also in the case of the ECAA, the Court of Justice enjoys a special position as the authoritative interpreter of EU acquis. The ECAA Joint Committee must respect the case law of the Court of Justice in the dispute settlement procedure.[109] Furthermore, if the ECAA Joint Committee is unable to solve a dispute between the contracting parties within four months, the parties to the dispute may refer it to the Court whose decision shall be final and binding.[110] In such case, the disputing parties may, moreover, take appropriate safeguard measures for a maximum period of six months after which each contracting party may denounce the ECAA Agreement with immediate effect. Referring a dispute to the Court of Justice, however, precludes the adoption of safeguard measures except in cases of aviation safety or compliance with mechanisms provided for in individual acts.[111] Finally, similar to the EEA and implicitly also the Energy Community, the jurisdiction of the Court of Justice also extends to a legality review of the decisions taken by the EU institutions under the ECAA Agreement.[112]

8.1.2.5 Transport Community

The procedural framework for interpretation and dispute settlement in the TCT follows closely those provided by the EnCT and the ECAA Agreement. Identical acquis in the TCT must be interpreted in conformity with the pre-signature case law of the Court of Justice and the decisions of

---

[107] Article 20(1) ECAA Agreement.
[108] Opinion 1/00 *ECAA* (n 27) para. 8.
[109] Article 20(2) ECAA Agreement.
[110] Article 20(3) ECAA Agreement.
[111] Article 20(4) ECAA Agreement.
[112] Article 15(3) ECAA Agreement.

the European Commission.[113] To ensure homogeneity in the interpretation of the TCT acquis, the RSC shall keep the development of the Court's case law and the Commission's decisions under constant review upon due notification by the EU to the other contracting parties.[114] Any of the latter may request the RSC, assisted by the technical committees, to establish the implications of the later rulings and decisions in order to ensure the proper functioning of the Treaty.[115] Homogeneity in the post-signature acquis is, thus, subject to political agreement in the RSC whereas all questions concerning the legality of the EU acquis replicated in the TCT fall within the exclusive competence of the Court.[116] The RSC shall 'act so as to preserve the homogeneous interpretation' of the TCT within three months.[117]

The dispute resolution mechanism set up by the TCT is similar to its equivalent in the ECAA Agreement. Any contracting party may bring a dispute concerning the application or interpretation of the TCT before the RSC, except where the TCT provides specific procedures. In its decisions, the RSC is bound to conform with the case law of the Court of Justice. The Court of Justice will, moreover, provide final and binding decisions in disputes, which the RSC has failed to solve within four months.[118] Overall, whereas the homogeneity objectives of the TCT are modestly framed, the institutional design of the TCT demonstrates that homogeneity in the Treaty is envisaged not only within the Transport Community but also along the EU-Transport Community axis.

8.2 Safeguarding Homogeneity: Decentralising Dynamics

8.2.1 Surveillance and Enforcement

In the area of surveillance, the decentralising dynamics of the EU legal order is reflected in the role of the EU Member States' institutions in the EU's institutional architecture. Here, the concepts of unity of the internal market and of the EU legal order assume particular relevance. In order to preserve the 'Community character'[119] or the 'Community

---

[113] Article 19(1) TCT.
[114] Ibid. and Article 24(7) TCT.
[115] Article 19(1) TCT.
[116] Article 18(2) TCT.
[117] Article 24(7) TCT
[118] Article 37 TCT. The modalities for this procedure are provided in Annex IV to the TCT.
[119] Case 166/73 *Rheinmühlen I* EU:C:1974:3, para. 2.

nature'[120] of EU law, the Union relies on a set of common procedures and institutions, including those of the Member States. Direct administration of EU law on the Union level is limited to certain specific areas only; instead, the Member States are the primary implementers and enforcers of EU law.[121] For example, the Member States' customs authorities act as EU customs authorities,[122] and the Member States' competition authorities assist the Commission in its investigation procedures.[123] National authorities are also empowered to implement and apply the EU acquis, which is exported to non-Member States as well as to investigate breaches of those rules. When implementing EU law, the national authorities are, however, under general obligation to abide by the principles of unity and solidarity.[124] The Member States must ensure the 'effective defence of the common interests of the [Union]'[125] and may not act if concurrent action would compromise the 'unity of the [Internal] Market and the uniform application of [Union] law'.[126]

Decentralisation also finds expression in the possibilities for individuals and economic operators to indirectly trigger infringement proceedings for non-compliance with EU law. Individuals may, for example, submit complaints to notify the Commission of possible breaches of EU law by a Member State. However, there is no guarantee for an EU individual to have their rights upheld by the Commission. The Commission enjoys discretion about whether to initiate infringement proceedings against a Member State for failure to fulfil their obligations under EU law. Considering the vast volume of individual complaints received, the Commission only takes up a fraction of the cases.

In the EEA, individuals may lodge complaints either to the ESA about alleged infringements of EEA law by the EEA EFTA States, or to the European Commission about supposed breaches of the EEA Agreement by the EU or its Member States. In the Energy Community, the ECAA and the Transport Community, there exists no possibility to

---

[120] Case 104/81 *Kupferberg* EU:C:1982:362, para. 14.
[121] HCH Hofmann and AH Türk, 'Policy implementation' in HCH Hofmann and AH Türk (eds.), *EU Administrative Governance* (Edward Elgar Publishing 2006) 74, 74.
[122] See, for example, Report of the Panel, *European Communities – Customs Classification of Certain Computer Equipment (LAN case)*, WT/DS62/R, WT/DS67/R, WT/DS68/R, para. 4.14.
[123] Article 105(1) TFEU.
[124] Opinion 1/76 *European laying-up fund for inland waterway vessels* EU:C:1977:63, para. 12.
[125] Opinion 1/75 *Re Understanding on a Local Costs Standard* EU:C:1975:145, paras. 15–18.
[126] Case 22/70 *Commission v. Council (AETR)* EU:C:1971:32, para. 31.

submit such general complaints. Since anyone can lodge a complaint with the Commission regarding a breach of EU law by a Member State, theoretically, also nationals of the non-EU contracting parties to the multilateral sectoral agreements may do so, but only against the EU Member States. Finally, the complaints procedure is established for the purpose of informing the Commission of potential breaches. Individual remedies must, thus, in principle, be sought in national courts.

8.2.2 Interpretation and Dispute Settlement

8.2.2.1 European Union

Individual rights derived from internal market acquis in and outside the EU are protected by the judicial system. The protection of individual rights rests on the principle of effective legal protection. The principle is provided in Article 67(4) TFEU, which obliges the Union to facilitate access to justice and in Article 47 of the Charter establishing the right to an effective remedy and to a fair trial. Underlying the constitutional traditions of the EU Member States, effective legal protection is a general principle of EU law.[127] Moreover, by virtue of Articles 6 and 13 ECHR the principle is binding on all EU Member States as well as all non-EU parties to the EEA Agreement, the EnCT, the ECAA Agreement and the TCT, except for Kosovo.

The duty of cooperation enshrined in Article 4(3) TEU obliges the Member States to contribute to the protection of the rights that individuals derive from EU law.[128] The two-tier judicial system of the EU envisages the participation of both the Court and the Member States' courts in the protection of individual rights arising from the Treaties, the latter forming an indispensable part of the EU's judicial architecture.[129] Albeit separate, the EU and the Member States' judiciaries are 'closely interlinked, dependent on and related to each other'.[130] Where no jurisdiction has been conferred upon the Court, the national courts must apply EU law in a manner that guarantees its effectiveness through appropriate remedies in accordance with the requirements of

---

[127] Case 222/84 *Johnston* EU:C:1986:206, para. 18; Case C-432/05 *Unibet* EU:C:2007:163, para. 37.

[128] Case 33/76 *Rewe* EU:C:1976:188, para. 5; Case 106/77 *Simmenthal* EU:C:1978:49, para. 21; Case C-432/05 *Unibet* (n 127) para. 38;

[129] Case 26/62 *Van Gend en Loos* EU:C:1963:1; Case 166/73 *Rheinmühlen I* (n 119) para. 2; Opinion 1/09 *Patents Court* EU:C:2011:123, paras. 83–85.

[130] Case 106/77 *Simmenthal* (n 128) para. 16. See also I Pernice, 'Multilevel constitutionalism and the Treaty of Amsterdam: European Constitution-Making Revisited' (1999) 36 *Common Market Law Review* 703, 710.

unity and diversity in the Union.[131] The national courts must also make proper use of the preliminary ruling procedure provided in Article 267 TFEU, pursuant to which the Court has jurisdiction to rule on the interpretation of the Treaties and on the validity and interpretation of secondary EU legislation.

The proper use of the preliminary ruling procedure requires, first, an obligation on behalf of a national court of last instance to refer a question on EU law for preliminary ruling if necessary to enable it to give a judgment in the case, and a possibility in this regard for the other courts; and, second, that the preliminary ruling is binding on the national court.[132] The aim of the procedure is to ensure that all questions relating to the interpretation and application of EU law, which have not yet been considered by the Court,[133] or constitute an *acte clair*[134] are decided centrally by the Court. Whether or not to refer a request to the Court of Justice is strictly for the national court to determine and the Court is generally bound to give the ruling.[135]

The preliminary reference procedure is primarily considered a venue for judicial dialogue between the EU and the national judiciaries but judicial dialogue alone does not always lead to effectiveness in legal protection. The national judicial systems must also feature certain effectiveness-ensuring elements. The quest for effectiveness may, therefore, in some circumstances conflict with the notion of national procedural autonomy,[136] whereas the Court has asserted that it will not itself interfere with the specific procedures of the national legal systems provided that the Member States can guarantee the effective protection of individual rights.[137] National rules may not be 'less favourable than those governing similar domestic actions (principle of equivalence)' or 'render virtually impossible or excessively difficult the exercise of rights

---

[131] Article 19(1) TEU; Case 166/73 *Rheinmühlen I* (n 119) para. 2; K Lenaerts, 'The Rule of Law and the Coherence of the Judicial System of the European Union' (2007) 44 *Common Market Law Review* 1625, 1625.

[132] Article 267 TFEU; Opinion 1/91 *EEA I* EU:C:1991:490, para. 61.

[133] Case 283/81 *CILFIT* EU:C:1982:335, para. 13.

[134] 'Where the correct application of Community law [is] so obvious as to leave no scope for any reasonable doubt as to the manner in which the question is to be resolved': ibid., para. 16.

[135] Case C-36/02 *Omega* EU:C:2004:614, para. 19.

[136] The two are closely linked: see M Accetto and S Zleptnig, 'The Principle of Effectiveness: Rethinking Its Role in Community Law' (2005) 11 *European Public Law* 375, 394.

[137] Case C-224/01 *Köbler* EU:C:2003:513, para. 47.

conferred by [EU] law (principle of effectiveness)'.[138] The national legal orders must, consequently, guarantee that individuals can uphold their rights regardless of whether these have been acquired through directly effective EU law or national law, as long as EU law does not regulate the matter.[139] In the absence of national procedures ensuring the effectiveness of EU law, the Court has not shunned from ordering national courts to create such procedures.[140]

It is obvious that the EU's legal architecture cannot by itself support achieving a level of uniformity in EU law that were comparable to uniformity in the Member States' legal orders. The question is whether this apparent impossibility should be accepted as an inevitable feature of a supranational legal order that must preserve a certain degree of sovereignty of its constituent states, or whether the aim of uniformity should prevail at all costs for the purpose of effective legal protection. The principle of effectiveness meets its natural limits in the need to include national courts, which enjoy their own autonomy and can demonstrate certain reluctance towards external authority.

Because individuals generally lack direct access to the Court, their only possibility of directly enforcing their rights under the Treaties is through the national judiciaries. Under the duty of sincere cooperation, the Member States must take 'all appropriate measures' to ensure that all of their authorities including the courts fulfil the obligations under the Treaties.[141] Should a national court incorrectly refrain from referring a request for a preliminary ruling to the Court or fail to implement a subsequent ruling by the Court, the Member State will breach its treaty obligations. Similar to public international law in which a state including its judiciary is generally regarded as a single entity,[142] the liability of a Member State for a breach of EU law does not depend on the national authority whose act or omission gave ground to the breach.[143]

Holding a Member State liable for breaches of EU law committed by the courts of last instance is, moreover, central to the question of effectiveness of EU law, as the highest courts' incompliance with the

---

[138] Case C-129/00 *Commission* v. *Italy* EU:C:2003:656, para. 25, consolidating earlier cases 33/76 *Rewe* (n 128) para. 5, and Case C-255/00 *Grundig Italiana* EU:C:2002:525, para. 33.

[139] Case 45/76 *Comet* EU:C:1976:191, paras. 13 and 15–16.

[140] Case C-213/89 *Factortame* EU:C:1990:257, para. 21.

[141] Joined Cases C-397/01 to C-403/01 *Pfeiffer* EU:C:2004:584, para. 110.

[142] Case C-224/01 *Köbler* (n 137) para. 32.

[143] Joined Cases C-46/93 and C-48/93 *Brasserie du Pêcheur and Factortame* EU:C:1996:79, paras. 32 and 34; Case 77/69 *Commission* v. *Belgium* EU:C:1970:34, para. 15.

preliminary ruling procedure severely limits the remedies available to individuals for asserting their rights under EU law.[144] An individual cannot appeal against a decision of the highest court but can only seek reparation for the loss incurred.

The Court has been cautious to establish state liability in cases of a national court failing to make proper use of the preliminary ruling procedure. However, it has been established that the actions or omissions of the 'constitutionally independent' actors of the Member States, too, may constitute a breach of EU law by the latter.[145] Moreover, the protection of individual rights necessarily entails redress for damage caused to an individual by a breach of EU law by a national court adjudicating at last instance.[146] State liability can be invoked following such a breach when three conditions are fulfilled: (1) the infringed rule is intended to confer rights on individuals; (2) the breach is sufficiently serious; and (3) there is a direct causal link between the breach of an obligation and the loss or damage suffered by the injured party.[147] National law, however, provides the procedural framework for making reparation for the loss and damage.[148] Since the bearers of responsibility under the Treaties are the Member States rather than the national courts or judges, the independence of the judiciary is not contested.[149]

Concerns have been raised about the possible damage that the principle of state liability for actions and omissions of the national judiciaries causes to the judicial dialogue between the EU and the Member States' national courts.[150] There is, indeed, a delicate balance between

[144] Case C-224/01 *Köbler* (n 137) paras. 33–34.
[145] Case 77/69 *Commission* v. *Belgium* (n 143) para. 15. The Court has subsequently clarified the liability of Member States for breaches of EU law by the national judiciary and especially the highest courts: see Case C-453/00 *Kühne & Heitz* EU:C:2004:17; Case C-129/00 *Commission* v. *Italy* (n 138); Case C-173/03 *Traghetti del Meditteraneo* EU:C:2006:391; Case C-154/08 *Commission* v. *Spain* EU:C:2009:695.
[146] Case C-224/01 *Köbler* (n 137) paras. 36–37.
[147] Case C-424/97 *Haim* EU:C:2000:357, para. 36.
[148] Case C-224/01 *Köbler* (n 137) para. 58.
[149] Ibid., para. 42. AG Geelhoed, however, has interpreted the independence of the judiciary as independence from external influence when deciding on specific cases, not independence from a declaration that the case law of the national court has constituted an infringement of EU law by the Member State: Case C-129/00 *Commission* v. *Italy* EU:C:2003:319, Opinion of AG Geelhoed, para. 56.
[150] J Komárek, 'Federal Elements in the Community Judicial System: Building Coherence in the Community Legal Order' (2005) 42 *Common Market Law Review* 9, 23. See also PJ Wattel, '*Köbler, CILFIT* and *Welthgrove*: We can't go on meeting like this' (2004) 41 *Common Market Law Review* 177.

ensuring the effective protection of individual rights across the Union and, thereby, the unity of EU law, on the one hand, and national procedural autonomy and other procedural principles, on the other. Neither of these aspects can light heartedly be sacrificed for the benefit of the other. The dilemma proves that the EU's institutional framework is not flawless when it comes to the objective of setting up an internal market in which all market participants enjoy the same set of rights and obligations. Insofar as several layers of institutions are involved in the interpretation and application of identical rules without a clear hierarchy, discrepancies are likely to occur and some of them rather difficult if not impossible to remedy.

8.2.2.2 European Economic Area

The EEA Agreement, too, contains a principle on effective judicial protection,[151] confirmed by the EFTA Court in *Ásgeirsson*.[152] The EEA Agreement has established an advisory ruling procedure to contribute to the 'proper functioning of the EEA Agreement to the benefit of individuals and economic operators'.[153] In *Bellona*, the EFTA Court stated that access to justice constitutes an essential element of the EEA legal framework, subject to the conditions and limitations following from EEA law.[154] Furthermore, similar to the Court of Justice vis-à-vis the EU legal order, in the absence of EEA rules on the matter, it is for the national legal systems to create procedures for the protection of the rights that individuals derive from EEA law with the qualification that the national procedures may not discriminate against persons deriving their rights from EEA law or restrict their fundamental freedoms.[155]

The EEA and the ECAA Agreements as well as the TCT promote judicial dialogue as a means of ensuring the effectiveness of the acquis. Under Article 107 EEA Agreement, the EEA EFTA States may allow their courts or tribunals to request the Court of Justice to decide on the interpretation of a provision of the EEA Agreement. This procedure is explained in Protocol 34 to the EEA Agreement. The EEA EFTA States are at liberty to determine the scope and modalities of this possibility, and communicate their intentions in this regard to the Depositary of the

---

[151] Recital 8, preamble to the EEA Agreement.
[152] Case E-2/03 *Ásgeirsson* [2003] EFTA Ct Rep 185, para. 28.
[153] Ibid., para. 24.
[154] Case E-2/02 *Bellona* [2003] EFTA Ct Rep 52, para. 36.
[155] Case E-5/10 *Kottke* [2009–2010] EFTA Ct Rep 320, paras. 26–27.

Court of Justice,[156] but to this date, none of the EEA EFTA States has enabled their courts to engage in direct dialogue with the Court.[157]

The EEA also features other types of judicial dialogue. The Court of Justice and the EFTA Court operate as a 'system of parallel functions and competencies'.[158] The EEA Agreement being part of the EU legal order, the EU Member States are bound to apply it as EU law.[159] Failure to do so, including in the form of not requesting a preliminary ruling from the Court or not upholding the Court's interpretation of the EEA Agreement may result in infringement proceedings against the Member State and possible state liability for damage caused to individuals. In the EFTA pillar of the EEA, the EFTA Court provides advisory opinions on the interpretation of the EEA Agreement.[160] Any court or tribunal of the EEA EFTA States may request an advisory opinion from the EFTA Court on the interpretation of the EEA Agreement if necessary for delivering a ruling in a pending case. The SCA endows the right to request an advisory opinion upon all EEA EFTA States' national courts. States may limit the possibility to make requests to those courts and tribunals against whose decisions there are no judicial remedies under national law,[161] but this opportunity has neither been made use of.[162]

An advisory opinion given by the EFTA Court is 'a specially established means of judicial co-operation between the Court and national courts'.[163] National courts are 'entitled' rather than obliged to request an advisory opinion from the EFTA Court.[164] In the meantime, the EFTA Court has recognised the identical wording of Articles 267 TFEU and 34 SCA in the essential elements of the provisions,[165] as well as interpreted the prerogatives of the national courts to request an advisory opinion in the light of the case law of the Court of Justice.[166] Importantly, the EFTA Court has considered the procedures to be identical as to their essential elements notwithstanding the fact that the one is compulsory for the courts adjudicating at last instance whereas the other is not.

[156] Article 2, Protocol 34 to the EEA Agreement.
[157] H Haukeland Fredriksen, 'One Market, Two Courts' (n 62) 487.
[158] HP Graver (n 26) 49.
[159] Case 181/73 *Haegeman* EU:C:1974:41; Case 87/75 *Bresciani* EU:C:1976:18.
[160] Article 34 SCA.
[161] Ibid.
[162] See also S Magnusson, 'On the Authority of Advisory Opinions' (2010) 13 *Europarättslig Tidskrift* 528, n 61.
[163] Case E-1/95 *Samuelsson* [1994–1995] EFTA Ct Rep 145, para. 13.
[164] Ibid.
[165] Ibid.
[166] Case E-5/96 *Nille* (n 74) para. 12.

The title of a procedure is not always indicative of its binding nature. The advisory opinions of the ICJ given under Article 96 UN Charter and Article 65 of the ICJ Statute may be conferred binding force in disputes between parties.[167] The opinions of the Court of Justice provided under Article 218(11) TFEU are binding to the effect that the envisaged international agreement, which the Court deems incompatible with the Treaties, may not enter into force unless either the draft is amended or the Treaties revised.[168] Similarly, paragraphs 2 and 3 of Article 105 EEA Agreement do not distinguish between rulings in direct actions and preliminary rulings/advisory opinions. The treaty makers' choice for an 'advisory opinion' rather than a 'preliminary ruling' in the EEA Agreement, however, demonstrates the EEA EFTA contracting parties' intention not to vest the EFTA Court with the authority of a sole authoritative interpreter of EEA law in the EEA EFTA States.

The twofold objectives of the advisory opinion procedure in the EEA include homogeneity as well as the equal protection of individual rights arising, first, from the EEA Agreement and, second, from the EU internal market acquis. According to the EFTA Court, the principle of homogeneity creates a presumption that provisions worded identically in the EU Treaties and the EEA Agreement will be given the same interpretation,[169] notwithstanding the differences between the agreements that may eventually lead to diverging interpretations.[170]

The EFTA Court is generally keen on finding parallels between the procedures established by the EU Treaties and the EEA Agreement. The requirement in Article 3(1) SCA that the acquis which originates from the EU be interpreted in conformity with the case law of the Court of Justice does not extend to either the main part of the EEA Agreement nor to the SCA that lays down the procedural rules governing the operation of the EFTA Court and the ESA. The EFTA Court has nonetheless striven towards homogeneity also in the procedural realm aligning its case law on the identical concepts found in EU and EEA law with the relevant rulings of the Court of Justice.[171]

---

[167] R Ago, 'Binding Advisory Opinions of the International Court of Justice' (1991) 85 *American Journal of International Law* 439.

[168] Opinion 1/91 *EEA I* (n 132) para. 61.

[169] Case E-2/06 *EFTA Surveillance Authority* v. *Norway* [2007] EFTA Ct Rep 164, para. 59.

[170] Case E-3/98 *Rainford-Towning* (n 68) para. 21.

[171] See, for example, Case E-1/94 *Restamark* (n 68) paras. 23–24; Case E-2/94 *Scottish Salmon Growers* (n 63) paras. 11 and 15.

The explicit differences between the EU preliminary ruling procedure and the EEA advisory opinion procedure provoke questions about the role of the EEA EFTA national courts in the EEA legal order. The EFTA Court has not been minded by the different title of the procedure and has held that the objective of the advisory opinion procedure, too, is to ensure the uniform interpretation of the EEA Agreement.[172] The aim of the judicial dialogue with the EEA EFTA States' courts is, thus, to maintain homogeneity from which one can imply the need to give effect to the EEA acquis. Moreover, roughly the same conditions as to the preliminary rulings procedure, with the exception of the obligation to refer, apply to the advisory opinion procedure of the EFTA Court.[173] This is without prejudice to the fact that the lack of exclusive jurisdiction of the EFTA Court renders the hierarchical relationship between the EFTA Court and the EEA EFTA States' national courts weaker. The latter, therefore, maintain a more central role as the interpreters of EEA law. The EEA EFTA States' national courts are certainly 'EEA courts' but subject to a lesser degree of subordination. This notwithstanding, a failure by a national court to give due effect to EEA law will result in a breach of the EEA Agreement by the EEA EFTA State.

The question of a national judiciary's liability for breaches of EEA law has remotely been considered in *Kolbeinsson*.[174] Following an alleged failure by Icelandic courts including the Supreme Court to properly apply EEA law, a case was brought against the Icelandic state claiming compensation for damages incurred as a result of the initial wrongful judgment. On appeal, the Supreme Court refused to refer to the EFTA Court for an advisory opinion a question concerning the Supreme Court's own liability for a wrongful interpretation of national law. The EFTA Court could, therefore, only consider a possible breach by the legislature whereas Icelandic procedural law does not allow for a lower court to review the decisions of the Supreme Court. In previous rulings,[175] the EFTA Court had established that it is the task of the national court to assess the facts of a case and to determine whether the conditions for state liability for a breach of EEA law have been met, whereas the EFTA Court can provide guidance in that regard.[176] Since the EFTA Court has repeatedly referred to the Court of Justice's interpretation

---

[172] Case E-1/94 *Restamark* (n 68) para. 25.
[173] Case E-1/95 *Samuelsson* (n 163) para. 15.
[174] Case E-2/10 *Kolbeinsson* [2009–2010] EFTA Ct Rep 234.
[175] Case E-4/01 *Karlsson* [2002] EFTA Ct Rep 240; Case E-8/07 *Nguyen* [2008] EFTA Ct Rep 224.
[176] Case E-2/10 *Kolbeinsson* (n 174) para. 81.

on the procedural elements of the principle of state liability, and considering the EFTA Court's generally dynamic interpretation of the EEA Agreement[177] it is likely that the EFTA Court would have ruled for state liability of the judiciary of an EEA EFTA State had the opportunity presented itself.

The appeal system set up by the EEA EFTA States for submitting requests for advisory opinions to the EFTA Court differs from its EU equivalent. In the EU legal order, the preliminary ruling system is deemed by the Court to serve as 'direct cooperation between the Court of Justice and the national courts' not requiring the involvement or initiative by the parties to the original case and dependent only on the referring court's assessment of necessity.[178] In *Cartesio*, the Court further clarified the scope of the direct cooperation between itself and the national courts, stating that any appeal system against a Member State court's requests for a preliminary ruling to the Court would be contrary to the Treaties by jeopardising the 'autonomous jurisdiction' which Article 267 TFEU confers on the referring court.[179]

The EFTA Court finally discussed the appeals system in *Irish Bank*.[180] The facts of the case regarding the request for an advisory opinion were similar to *Kolbeinsson*: an Icelandic district court intended to refer a question to the EFTA Court, but the defendant appealed against the ruling on the request for an advisory opinion to the Supreme Court of Iceland. The latter upheld the request but amended the questions to be referred to the EFTA Court. The district court submitted to the EFTA Court both its own ruling and the ruling of the Supreme Court on the questions to be referred. During the proceedings at the EFTA Court, the plaintiff claimed that *Cartesio* constitutes a precedent in EEA law because of the similarity of the purposes of Article 267 TFEU and Article 34 SCA. Moreover, it was submitted that the objective of achieving a balance in rights for individuals and economic operators in the EEA demands equal access to courts and judicial remedies across the EEA including equivalent access to the respective referral procedures,[181] especially since Iceland had not reserved the right to request advisory opinions only to courts adjudicating at last instance.[182]

---

[177] Case E-4/04 *Pedicel* [2005] EFTA Ct Rep 1, para. 28.
[178] Case C-2/06 *Kempter* EU:C:2008:78, paras. 41–42.
[179] Case C-210/06 *Cartesio* EU:C:2008:723, para. 95.
[180] Case E-18/11 *Irish Bank* [2012] EFTA Ct Rep 592.
[181] Ibid., para. 44.
[182] Ibid., para. 45.

In earlier case law, the EFTA Court had found that only the national court before which a dispute has been brought is to decide both on whether to request an advisory opinion from the EFTA Court and on which questions to refer.[183] The EFTA Court noted the differences between the preliminary ruling and the advisory opinion procedures finding its relationship with the national supreme courts of the EEA EFTA States to be 'more partner-like', and recalled the duty of loyalty enshrined in Article 3 EEA Agreement.[184] Unable to make equally bold statements as the Court of Justice, the EFTA Court referred to the possibility that a refusal by a court of last instance to permit a request to the EFTA Court by a lower court may infringe the principle of access to justice laid out in Article 6(1) ECHR.[185] With reference to the case law of the ECtHR, the EFTA Court specified that the infringement is particularly apparent if the refusing court fails to provide adequate reasoning for its decision.[186] Moreover, in addition to a refusal to refer, a national court of last instance may also breach the ECHR if it upholds the decision to refer but amends the question to be put before the EFTA Court.[187]

The voluntary nature of the EFTA Court's advisory opinion procedure is in some respects comparable to the EU Member States' courts determining whether or not an interpretation of EU law in a case at hand constitutes an *acte clair* and whether, subsequently, a preliminary reference to the Court of Justice is due. Compared to the EFTA pillar of the EEA, though, an omission of an EU Member State court to make a request may, if it constitutes a manifest error of appraisal, give rise to the Member State's breach of its obligations under EU law. Establishing the potential liability of an EEA EFTA State in a similar case is much more complicated. The preamble to the EEA Agreement states that uniformity in the interpretation and application of the EEA Agreement must be maintained 'in full deference to the independence of the courts'.[188] At first glance, and considering that the EEA is not a supranational legal order, the sovereignty of the EEA EFTA States may rule out any obligation on behalf of the EEA EFTA States' national courts to follow the case law of the Court of Justice. The EFTA Court has, however, ruled that the

---

[183] Case E-13/11 *Granville* [2012] EFTA Ct Rep 400, para. 18.
[184] Case E-18/11 *Irish Bank* (n 180) paras. 57–58.
[185] Ibid., para. 64.
[186] Ibid.
[187] Ibid.
[188] Recital 15, preamble to the EEA Agreement.

objectives of the EEA Agreement as well as the homogeneity clause provided in its Article 3 oblige the national courts to interpret national law in conformity with EEA law, as well as to apply teleological interpretation in the limits set by the national legal order.[189]

It has been argued that Article 3 EEA Agreement can be interpreted as imposing a duty on the EEA EFTA States' national courts to request advisory opinions from the EFTA Court even in the absence of an express obligation in the EEA Agreement.[190] The view can be supported by the EFTA Court's ruling in *Pedicel*, in which the EFTA Court recognised the necessity of a dynamic interpretation of EEA law in order to achieve the objective of homogeneity.[191] Although the case concerned a substantive provision of the EEA Agreement, the interpretation could be extended also to the procedural provisions of the Agreement or the SCA. In *Fokus Bank*, the EFTA Court, moreover, drew a parallel between the homogeneity claim provided in Article 3 EEA Agreement and Article 4(3) TEU, stating that the national procedural autonomy of the EEA EFTA States must be exercised in a manner that does not impair the enjoyment of individual rights provided by the EEA Agreement.[192] Whether the dynamic interpretation of Article 34 SCA could be stretched to confirm an obligation on behalf of the EEA EFTA States to request advisory opinions without arriving at a *contra legem* interpretation of the provision is, however, highly unlikely. The homogeneity obligation enshrined in Article 3 EEA Agreement applies to the contracting parties rather than national courts, and does not contain an obligation of result but rather of best efforts, providing a framework for the concrete legal obligations contained in the Agreement that serve the purpose of achieving and maintaining homogeneity.

Article 33 SCA further provides that the EEA EFTA States must take the measures necessary to comply with the judgments of the EFTA Court but omits a reference to advisory opinions, whereas the preliminary rulings of the Court of Justice are binding on the national court.[193] Although the obligation to follow the Court's rulings does not explicitly extend to either the same court when ruling in other cases or to other courts, it follows implicitly. A decision by a Member State court to divert from the Court's interpretation of EU law would collide with the

---

[189] Case E-1/07 *Criminal Proceedings against A* [2007] EFTA Ct Rep 246, para. 39.
[190] S Magnusson, 'On the Authority of Advisory Opinions' (n 162) 539–540.
[191] Case E-4/04 *Pedicel* (n 177) para. 28.
[192] Case E-1/04 *Fokus Bank* (n 74) para. 41.
[193] Order of 5 March 1986 in Case 69/85 *Wünsche* EU:C:1986:104, para. 13.

obligation incumbent upon the national court, if adjudicating at last instance, to request a preliminary reference from the Court. This is irrespective of whether the Member State erroneously applied the *acte clair* doctrine or overlooked a previous ruling of the Court on the matter. In the EU, a failure to comply with the obligation to make a reference for a preliminary ruling may result in infringement proceedings against the Member State under Article 260(2) TFEU. The Court may impose a lump sum or penalty payment in order to exert pressure on the Member State to comply with its obligations under the Treaties.[194] For an individual to receive compensation for damages, a separate claim must be filed with a national court. The SCA, however, features no provision equivalent to Article 260(2) TFEU, and thus no obligation on behalf of an EEA EFTA State to pay a financial penalty for a failure to comply with the rulings or advisory opinions of the EFTA Court.

The EEA EFTA States have an obligation deriving from the principle of state liability to compensate individuals for damage caused.[195] An EEA EFTA State's failure to perform its obligations under the EEA Agreement or the SCA may, furthermore, lead to infringement proceedings under Article 31 SCA but not on grounds of an EEA EFTA State's national court not requesting or not following an advisory opinion from the EFTA Court. Only indirectly, through the EFTA Court's interpretation of a provision of the EEA Agreement in infringement proceedings may an EEA EFTA national court, by virtue of its obligation to conform with the judgment of the EFTA Court, be persuaded to bring its interpretation of EEA law in conformity with the EFTA Court's rulings.

The general attitude among the supreme courts of the EEA EFTA States has been accommodating towards the EFTA Court's advisory opinions, notwithstanding some examples to the contrary. The Norwegian Supreme Court notably set aside an advisory opinion in *STX*[196] with a reference to the advisory nature of the procedure.[197] The EFTA Court subsequently imposed the duty of cooperation under Article 3 EEA Agreement directly on the national courts of last instance stating that the 'EFTA citizens and economic operators benefit from the obligation of courts of the EU Member States against whose decision there is no judicial remedy under national law to make a reference to the [Court

---

[194] Case C-304/02 *Commission v. France* EU:C:2005:444, para. 91.
[195] Case E-18/10 *EFTA Surveillance Authority v. Norway* [2011] EFTA Ct Rep 202, para. 28.
[196] Case E-2/11 *STX* [2012] EFTA Ct Rep 4.
[197] Case HR-2013–00496-A *STX* (Norges Høyesterett, 5 March 2013), para. 46.

of Justice]'.[198] In *Jonsson*, the EFTA Court recalled the importance of the advisory opinion procedure for safeguarding the effectiveness of the EEA Agreement by both avoiding errors in the interpretation of the EEA Agreement and ensuring the coherence and reciprocity of the rights of the EEA citizens deriving therefrom.[199] Notwithstanding the strength of the recommendation, it does not have the legal effect of amending Article 34 SCA. In practice, however, homogeneity is also advanced by the EEA EFTA States' national courts, following the case law of the Court of Justice directly and thereby surpassing the EFTA Court.[200]

8.2.2.3 Energy Community

The EnCT contains no provisions on judicial dialogue between the Court of Justice and the non-EU parties to the EnCT, nor even an obligation of the contracting parties to ensure an EU law conforming interpretation of the Energy Community acquis. The only means of upholding homogeneity in the interpretation and application of the internal market acquis in the Energy Community is, therefore, the non-judicial dispute settlement mechanism provided in Articles 90–93 EnCT in the framework of which the Energy Community institutions are obliged to interpret identical acquis in conformity with the Court's case law.[201]

8.2.2.4 European Common Aviation Area

The ECAA Agreement contains a hybrid system of referrals for authoritative interpretations of the ECAA Agreement combining elements of the EU and the EEA treaties. First, each state party to the ECAA Agreement must ensure that individuals can invoke their rights under the Agreement before national courts.[202] Second, an ECAA Partner's court or tribunal, which is tasked with interpreting a provision of the ECAA Agreement or of the acquis annexed to the Agreement which is identical in substance to EU acquis, must refer a question to the Court of Justice if it deems the latter's interpretation necessary to be able to give a judgment in the case.[203] Differently from the EEA, thus, the non-EU

---

[198] Case E-18/11 *Irish Bank* (n 180) para. 58.
[199] Case E-3/12 *Jonsson* [2013] EFTA Ct Rep 136, para. 60.
[200] H Haukeland Fredriksen, 'The EFTA Court' in R Howse and others (eds.), *The Legitimacy of International Trade Courts and Tribunals* (Cambridge University Press 2018) 138, 179–180.
[201] Article 94 EnCT.
[202] Article 15(1) ECAA Agreement.
[203] Article 16(2) ECAA Agreement.

/EEA national courts must ask the Court for a preliminary ruling. From the perspective of maintaining 'a degree of uniformity'[204] in the absence of a separate ECAA court, this can be considered the most homogeneity-advancing solution available. An ECAA Partner may determine the extent and modalities of the request for a preliminary ruling including, for example, a specification as to whether to allow any national court to submit the ruling or to reserve the possibility for courts adjudicating at last instance.[205] The requests for preliminary rulings may concern both the validity and the interpretation of the ECAA Agreement, including the annexed acquis. Pursuant to Article 1(1) of Annex IV to the ECAA Agreement, the preliminary rulings of the Court are binding, thus complying with the requirements established by the Court in Opinion 1/91.[206] The ECAA contracting parties may, moreover, participate in the proceedings before the Court by submitting observations on the same grounds as the EU Member States.[207]

If an ECAA Partner's national court of last instance is unable to make a referral to the Court of Justice, any judgment of that court must be passed on to the ECAA Joint Committee 'which shall act so as to preserve the homogeneous interpretation of [the ECAA] Agreement'.[208] The Joint Committee must act within two months from receiving a Partner state court's judgment, which conflicts with the case law of the Court of Justice.[209] Should the Joint Committee fail to act within the given timeframe, the dispute settlement procedure of Article 20 ECAA Agreement may be applied including the possibility of the parties to the dispute to bring the matter to the Court of Justice under Article 20(3) ECAA Agreement. The Court will, thus, decide on the interpretation of the internal market acquis exported by the ECAA Agreement as the final judicial authority.

8.2.2.5 Transport Community

The procedures set up by the TCT for ensuring the homogeneous interpretation of identical acquis bear liking to the ECAA Agreement. The TCT contracting parties must ensure that individuals can invoke their

---

[204] Opinion 1/00 *ECAA* (n 27) para. 7.
[205] Article 16(2) ECAA Agreement and Article 2(1) of Annex IV to the ECAA Agreement.
[206] Opinion 1/91 *EEA I* (n 132) para. 61. See further in Chapter 6, Section 6.2.2.
[207] Article 1(2) of Annex IV to the ECAA Agreement.
[208] Article 16(3) ECAA Agreement.
[209] Ibid.

rights deriving from the Treaty in national courts.[210] The TCT, further-more, provides for a similar dialogue as the ECAA Agreement on the interpretation of identical acquis between the Court of Justice and the national courts of the SEE Parties. A preliminary ruling procedure has been established whereby a national court, if necessary to be able to give a judgment in a pending case, may refer a question concerning the interpretation or validity of the TCT acquis to the Court of Justice. As a sovereignty-preserving measure, the extent and modalities of the courts' possibility to refer may be determined by the respective non-EU parties to the TCT,[211] without, however, challenging the binding force of the Court's rulings on the SEE Party's courts adjudicating upon the case that prompted the question.[212]

8.3 Conclusion

The dispute settlement procedures established by all of the multilateral agreements exporting the internal market acquis are political or hybrid. In the EEA, the ECAA and the Transport Community, they include a possibility to refer a question on the interpretation of the acquis subject to dispute to the Court of Justice. Moreover, the judicial systems of three out of the four agreements reflect the decentralising dynamics present in the EU. Only the EnCT stands out by precluding any judicial dialogue between the national courts of the contracting parties and either a common court established by the treaty or the Court of Justice.

In the case of the EEA, the tensions in the EEA Agreement between the ambitious objectives of an expanded EU internal market and the reality of the agreement functioning in a regular international law setting that safeguards the sovereignty of the EEA EFTA States as contracting parties are not easy to reconcile. A truly homogeneous outcome necessitates that the rights and remedies under the EEA Agreement be aligned with those set up by the EU Treaties. This requirement, however, clearly collides with the wish of the EEA EFTA States to retain their sovereignty to the fullest extent possible and not to become part of a supranational legal order such as the EU. But as critics say, one cannot have their cake and eat it, too.[213] In the end, the individuals of the EEA EFTA States may find

---

[210] Article 18(1) TCT.
[211] Identical to the grounds provided in Annex IV to the ECAA Agreement; see Annex IV to the TCT.
[212] Article 19(2) TCT.
[213] S Magnusson, 'On the Authority of Advisory Opinions' (n 162) 549–550.

themselves unable to assert the rights conferred upon them by the EEA Agreement. This applies equally to the multilateral sectoral agreements.

A tension is also written into the institutional and procedural provisions of the acquis-exporting agreements. When the EFTA Court rules on a provision of EU law that is replicated in the EEA Agreement without the Court of Justice previously having adjudicated on the matter, and the Court subsequently decides to go in another direction, the homogeneity band between the EU and the EFTA pillars is cut. This flaw is written into the original homogeneity code of the EEA Agreement that aims to maintain both the homogeneity of the whole and the sovereignty or autonomy of the constituent parts. However, since neither the Court of Justice nor the EFTA Court has an obligation to follow the precedents of the other court or even of their own, the EEA homogeneity concept cannot be perceived to include a requirement of absolute uniformity of case law. After all, as the concept of *stare decisis* does not apply to the Court of Justice, it may deviate from previous interpretations if necessitated by the circumstances of a new case before it. Since the principle of *stare decisis* neither applies in the legal orders of most of the EU Member States, a similar level of uniformity could apply in EU by virtue of the objective of the internal market to closely resemble that of a national market.

Insofar as the EU Member States have surrendered a part of their national sovereignty to accommodate the common framework of rights and remedies, however, the same must be expected from third countries wishing to participate in the EU internal market project to the same extent as the EU Member States. Otherwise, the outcome can merely resemble an extension of equal rights and obligations without reaching up to safeguarding their enjoyment in practice.

9 Conclusion

Internal Market – United in Everything but Membership?

The practice of expanding the EU internal market by exporting internal market acquis to non-EU Member States is no longer a novelty. The EEA Agreement has celebrated its 25 years' anniversary and the citizens of Europe take free movement between the EU and the EEA EFTA States for granted. The three multilateral sectoral agreements concluded or negotiated more recently in the fields of energy, aviation and transport cooperation cement the trend visible in both the EU's external relations and internal policies towards profound integration of neighbouring countries into the EU's internal market. New opportunities for expanding the internal market are anticipated in the conclusion of additional new generation AA/DCFTAs with the eastern neighbourhood countries, and the, from this perspective, peculiar case of negotiating a post-Brexit arrangement between the EU and the United Kingdom.

The objective of any exporting/expanding/extending/integrating exercise involving the EU internal market acquis and third countries – in practice countries in the EU's immediate neighbourhood – is to allow the latter to become full participants in the internal market or a sector thereof without joining the EU and, thereby, adhering to all EU policies. For the EU, in addition to the economic benefits of access to third countries' domestic markets, the expansion of the internal market entails political advantages in the form of enhanced prosperity in the neighbourhood and better preparation of the current or future candidate countries for membership in the Union. The multilateral sectoral agreements, in particular, have benefitted both the neighbourhood countries that would not be able to align their legal orders fully to the EU, and the EU in policy areas where cross-border cooperation is inevitable.

Full participation in the internal market or a sector thereof means that in the areas covered by the particular agreements the non-EU market actors are able to trade and move on equal footing with their EU counterparts. The non-EU Member States gain full participation rights in the internal market on the condition of adopting and implementing EU internal market acquis whereas market access applies equally to the EU actors in the respective third countries. The precondition of equal footing is the enjoyment of the same set of rights and obligations across the geographical borders of the Union. The rights and obligations are, first, derived from the substantive rules of the acquis. Second, the equivalence of rights and obligations across the internal market requires that the differences between the acquis as applicable across the internal market are minimal and remain within previously agreed limits. Third, equal rights and obligations necessarily call for a similar degree of effectiveness in the application of the identical set of rules in order to enable individuals to enjoy and effectively enforce their rights. The achievement of these three stages requires appropriate institutional and procedural structures. On the one hand, institutions and procedures are important for guaranteeing that the same rules are applicable in all states participating in the internal market, or a sector thereof, at any point in time. On the other hand, institutions and procedures help ensure that identical rules are given the same effect in the course of implementation, interpretation and application across the expanded internal market. Only if all of these elements are in place and function properly, it is possible to speak of a true extension of the internal market.

The analysis in this book has questioned the twofold boundaries of the internal market and sought to establish whether the ideal situation of an internal market, or a sector thereof, extended beyond the borders of the Union to encompass non-EU Member States could be attained in the framework of the EU Treaties and the case law of the Court of Justice. If this is the case, how does participation in the expanded internal market differ from membership in the EU or, if not, what are the main limitations? In order to establish the content of the same rights and obligations, recourse must be had to the concept of the internal market. While initially perceived as comprising the four fundamental freedoms and competition policy, the developments of the past few decades have seen a significant transformation of the concept. The four freedoms and competition policy are strongly influenced by a number of non-economic considerations both in the policy-making and implementation stages. The latter considerations notably include horizontal provisions, such as environmental protection, social policy, consumer protection and public health, as well as fundamental rights. Overall, they reflect the 'social function' of the internal market which is ancillary to its economic function. The variety of functions represented in the concept of the internal market also has an impact on its expansion to third countries. In order to ensure that the same rules, indeed, apply in the EU and in the respective third countries, the non-economic factors, insofar as they are embedded in and affect the scope of the fundamental freedoms and competition policy in the internal market, need to be included in the exported acquis. This is necessary for the economic core of the exported acquis to be interpreted and applied in a similar manner both inside and outside the EU.

The adoption and application of the same set of rules implies a certain level of coherence. Both the EU legal order and the concept of the internal market are characterised by unity. Unity does not require complete uniformity, but adherence to a minimum set of key elements – a 'core' – in order to retain the special characteristics of the internal market. The core elements, which comprise principles rather than concrete legal acts, may vary somewhat from one sector of the internal market to another insofar as all of the elements of the internal market are not equally relevant for each policy sector. The aviation and transport sectors, for example, are heavily service-dominated whereas emphasis in the agriculture and fisheries sectors is on the free movement of goods. Nevertheless, the full realisation of the objectives of the internal market, including in its individual sectors, precludes the exclusion of any of the fundamental freedoms and rules on competition policy in combination with the range of non-economic considerations that shape their application.

Maintaining the unity of the internal market is highly relevant in the case of expanding the internal market to third countries. The fact that exporting the acquis takes place via an international agreement means that unity must be guaranteed in two dimensions – within the international agreement, such as the EEA Agreement, and in the dimension of the international agreement vis-à-vis the EU. Unity in the latter sphere precludes the states parties to the exporting agreements from picking and choosing their preferred depth and breadth of integration – an entire sector of the internal market being an exception in the case of sectoral agreements. Otherwise, the expanded single market constellation will lose one of the inherent qualities of the EU internal market and, thus, defeat homogeneity.

A true extension of the internal market further requires that the same set of rules that is applied in the territory of the extended internal market at any time be given similar effect for the purposes of the effective protection of individual rights. Individuals enjoy a special status in the EU internal market, which must necessarily be upheld when extending the internal market to third countries. The quest for effectiveness in the internal market pertains to the direct effect of the provisions, the rank of the exported acquis in the hierarchy of norms, the interpretation of national law in conformity with the acquis and the liability of the state for breaches of the acquis – the doctrines of direct effect, primacy, consistent interpretation and state liability, respectively. The challenge of the international agreements seeking to expand the internal market is to ensure that comparable safeguards for maintaining the effectiveness of the exported acquis exist in the legal orders created by the agreements. In an international law setting, the principle of state sovereignty affects the effectiveness of the domestic application of the internal market acquis to a larger degree than in the supranational EU legal order. The EU has established the necessary legal means for ensuring the effective protection of individual rights whereas the effective application of the internal market rules in third countries depends primarily on the third countries' legal orders unless the agreements or the institutions they set up develop supranational principles analogous to the EU's foundational principles.

Two crucial elements in the project of expanding the internal market are the institutional and procedural arrangements that support the norms export and the uniform interpretation and application of the acquis in non-EU Member States. The greatest challenge to setting up appropriate institutions and procedures that would ensure that the same rules apply and enjoy the same effect across the extended market is posed by the EU legal order, especially the principle of autonomy vigorously enforced by the Court of Justice. Developed in the Court's case law, the principle prescribes that international agreements concluded by the Union may not alter the essential character of the EU's powers and institutions, and that the authoritative power of interpretation in the EU legal order rests with the institutions of the Union, especially the Court itself. The Court has deemed the institutional designs of several international agreements, including the first version of the EEA Agreement, incompatible with the principle of autonomy and thus prevented their conclusion. The stringent and frequently criticised case law of the Court clearly prioritises EU integration and the protection of the essential characteristics of the EU legal order over the achievement of external policy goals, including norms export. A more lenient approach towards autonomy would expectedly increase the Union's influence as a global and a regional actor, especially in its closest neighbourhood where the Union has a long-standing experience in using the internal market as a vehicle for integration. In the foreseeable future, however, it is unlikely that the EU and the Court would follow down this path with the risk of jeopardising the effectiveness of the legal order and a further fragmentation of EU policies. Owing, furthermore, to the political unfeasibility of treaty amendment to surpass the autonomy-protecting case law of the Court and to, thereby, enable the Union to export its acquis more efficiently, significant institutional craftsmanship is required from the treaty negotiators to establish homogeneity-supporting institutional and procedural safeguards. In the absence of the latter, the expansion of the internal market is not impossible, but the task of preserving homogeneity therein is largely shifted to the institutions of the third countries.

A complete and timely transfer of the relevant acquis to the third countries is a prerequisite for the expansion of the internal market in a homogeneous manner. First, the system must be sufficiently dynamic in order to ensure a swift process of updating the acquis in all parts of the extended market. Second, international agreements concluded by the EU operate under public international law. Their application is, thus, largely dependent on the third countries' national constitutional procedures and the approval of the acquis by the national legislatures. Strong emphasis must, therefore, be placed on the preliminary stages of law making in the EU in which the third countries' early acceptance of the new acquis can be promoted through information sharing and consultations. The new governance methods of decision-making in the EU, especially visible in the areas of social and environmental policy, can both promote and limit the participation of non-EU actors in the EU's policy and law making. Third country stakeholders may either be granted the possibility to participate in policymaking outside the 'classic Community method' or, conversely, their participation in the expert groups that prepare legislative proposals in the ordinary law-making procedures may be restricted or even excluded when alternative policy-making fora are used.

Finally, the enjoyment of the same rights and obligations by all market participants in and outside the EU depends heavily on the existence of appropriate surveillance and enforcement procedures and institutional safeguards as to the uniform interpretation and application of the acquis across the expanded market. Whereas the Union's institutional and procedural framework serves as a benchmark for evaluating the adequacy of corresponding frameworks set up by the international agreements, one cannot disregard the imperfections of the EU system of judicial protection, especially as concerns the uniform interpretation and application of EU law in all Member States. This owes to the fact that the EU, too, is an international organisation, albeit a supranational one, whose constitutive entities – the Member States – enjoy national procedural autonomy. The judicial dialogue between the EU judiciary and the Member States' courts both strengthens and obstructs uniformity in the EU legal order. In the name of fostering a cooperative relationship between itself and the Member States' courts, it is, for example, problematic for the Court of Justice to condemn the highest courts in the national legal systems, even when EU law is breached. Insofar as elements of ineffectiveness are embedded in the EU legal and judicial system, it cannot be maintained that the same faults must necessarily be remedied by an international agreement exporting the acquis for the sake of expanding the internal market. Rather, these constitute an intrinsic part of the institutional structures supporting the EU internal market as well as the multi-level character of the EU.

The book has scrutinised, in detail, four international agreements exporting internal market acquis to third countries with the objective of expanding the internal market – the comprehensive EEA Agreement and the sectoral agreements establishing the Energy Community, the ECAA and the Transport Community, respectively. The analysis has demonstrated that a genuine extension of a sector of the internal market to third countries is a more complicated task than the expansion of the internal market in its entirety. First, it is politically challenging to justify for the EU Member States and non-Member States alike a general extension of the fundamental freedoms and competition policy to the latter if the agreement at hand only covers a single policy sector. All of the fundamental freedoms must, therefore, be restricted to apply only to the relevant sector. The difficulty of extending to third countries all the relevant non-economic aspects that form part of the core of the internal market is, however, common to the sectoral as well as the comprehensive agreements. Second, all acquis-exporting agreements aiming to expand the internal market must feature a suitable institutional and procedural framework. The main factor affecting the elaborateness of the institutional and procedural structures of the multilateral agreements is their scope, whereas the number of non-EU contracting parties in the multilateral agreement has no particular effect on the intricacy of procedures and institutions.[1]

The EEA Agreement features the most elaborate institutions and procedures as well as the most explicit aim of homogeneity between EU and EEA law. The EEA's parallel institutional framework and the strong links between the EU and the EFTA pillars of the EEA in addition to the independent institutions help ensure that the EEA legal order closely mirrors that of the EU. A large part of the homogeneous result is attributable to the EFTA Court. The EFTA Court has, on the one hand, developed a set of principles analogous to the EU foundational principles to be applied in the EEA legal order. On the other hand, the EFTA Court has been promoting continuous dialogue with the Court of Justice on all, including post-signature case law of the Court of Justice, which the EFTA Court is legally obliged to merely take due account of. Not without importance in the success of the EEA system of expanding the internal market is the fact that the EEA EFTA States have, indeed, surrendered a part of their sovereignty, and thereby made the EEA legal order partly a supranational one; if not explicitly under the EEA Agreement then implicitly by means of the mechanisms of the EEA Agreement that render it politically challenging for the EEA EFTA States to refuse an update of the EEA Agreement.

Compared with their EEA counterparts, the institutions and procedures set up by the EnCT are of political nature and have limited contact with the parallel institutions of the EU. This is notwithstanding the European Commission that coordinates the activities of the Energy Community and participates in the Energy Community institutions. Among the multilateral sectoral agreements, the EnCT most closely resembles a traditional international agreement establishing an international organisation. The ECAA, on the other hand, features only one institution – the Joint Committee – but has also set up direct links with the EU institutions in the areas of, for example, dispute settlement, interpretation of the acquis and surveillance, which in some fields covered by the ECAA Agreement is conducted by the Commission. The most recently concluded TCT features several institutions and a procedural framework that in some parts

---

[1] The original membership of the EEA was much larger than the current, presumably justifying a large institutional apparatus.

replicates the ECAA Agreement. Overall, the administrative capacity of the sectoral agreements in terms of maintaining homogeneity in the expanded internal market is not comparable to the EEA Agreement. For this reason, the main burden of safeguarding homogeneity falls on the participating third countries' legislatures, courts and administrations.

The success of the project of expanding the internal market is in inevitable correlation with the loss of sovereignty on behalf of the third countries adopting EU acquis. On the one hand, the loss of sovereignty pertains to the effect of the EU acquis in the third countries' legal orders, the rank that the constitutional systems accord to rules of EU origin in the national hierarchy of norms, as well as to the teleological interpretation of those rules and the recognition of the liability of the state for damages incurred as a result of their breach. On the other hand, the processes of ensuring the dynamic updating of the agreements to reflect the changes in the EU acquis and the effective application of the exported acquis depend on appropriate institutional and procedural arrangements, such as a mandatory preliminary ruling procedure, that may impinge upon national sovereignty. The loss of sovereignty holds true for the EU Member States and demonstrates that exporting the internal market acquis to non-EU Member States may lead to a true extension of the internal market on the condition that the non-EU Member States surrender their independence to a similar degree as their EU counterparts. The EU Treaties impose certain limitations on homogeneity-advancing institutional and procedural solutions, but the latter serves as a guarantee for the proper functioning of the internal market rather than a precondition. The effectiveness of the internal market can be safeguarded to an equal degree if the institutions of the non-EU Member States instead assume the task of maintaining homogeneity with EU acquis in the absence of supranational principles and institutions. Without a (partial) loss of sovereignty, homogeneity can, nevertheless, not be guaranteed but only achieved.

The nature of the EU legal order does thus not preclude the possibility of expanding the internal market without enlarging the Union provided that there are third countries that wish to participate in the EU internal market sharing everything but membership.[2] The substantive boundaries of

---

[2] Cf 'sharing everything with the Union but institutions': R Prodi, 'A Wider Europe – A Proximity Policy as the key to stability', speech held at the Sixth ECSA-World Conference 'Peace, Security and Stability International Dialogue and the Role of the EU', Brussels, 5–6 December 2002, SPEECH/02/619.

the internal market may well exceed the geographical borders of the Union and in many respects do so today. This notwithstanding, the currently concluded agreements do not make full use of the potential of integration into the internal market without membership. The multilateral sectoral agreements, in particular, boast much more modest objectives and institutions than can be accommodated by the EU legal order. Practical considerations aside, the most profound form of integration – sharing everything but membership – may prove a meek motivator verging on unwanted result should it show signs of becoming an eternal antechamber for countries in the accession process.

Since the early days of the Union, the internal market acquis has been omnipresent in the EU's cooperation with the neighbourhood. It has fulfilled a variety of functions ranging from the establishment of initial partnerships to full-scale integration of third countries into the internal market. For Brexit, the success of the internal market project and its expansion may, however, have unexpected consequences. Practice has shown that the internal market is an expandable creature, albeit a bleaker copy of the original. Despite general acceptance for ample variation in the depth and breadth of third country cooperation with the Union and integration into its internal market, however, a different logic applies to a former Member State. Whereas sectoral integration in the example of the multilateral sectoral agreements is welcome, disintegration from the Union and downgrading to sectoral cooperation is perceived by the Union as cherry-picking detrimental to the integrity and the proper functioning of the internal market. Gradual access to the internal market is possible for countries whose legal and political systems need serious upgrading to match EU standards, whereas a withdrawing member may in a drastic scenario be left with a humble choice between all or (almost) nothing: a comprehensive internal market package or a meagre FTA. From the Union's perspective, expanding the internal market is thus not merely an altruistic project but – coupled with the Union's bargaining power – one pressing high demands on loyalty and obligation.

This notwithstanding, even less intensive cooperation in the internal market carries greater advantages for both the Union and a withdrawing state than no ties at all. From the Union's perspective, the extensive application of the EU acquis by the neighbourhood countries is key to securing long-term commitment to the European project both within the Union and in its neighbourhood and corroborates the Union's thrust as a regional normative superpower. A continued expansion of the borders of the internal market in breadth - geographical and substantive - and depth will not only strengthen regional cooperation but provides a wholly new dimension to the Union's commitment to create an ever closer union among the peoples of Europe.

Bibliography

Accetto M and Zleptnig S, 'The Principle of Effectiveness: Rethinking Its Role in Community Law' (2005) 11 *European Public Law* 375

Ago R, 'Binding Advisory Opinions of the International Court of Justice' (1991) 85 *American Journal of International Law* 439

Andersen S and Sitter N, 'Differentiated Integration: What Is It and How Much Can the EU Accommodate?' (2006) 28 *European Integration* 313

Aust A, *Modern Treaty Law and Practice* (Cambridge University Press 2013)

Azoulai L, 'The *Acquis* of the European Union and International Organisations' (2005) 11 *European Law Journal* 196

'The Court of Justice and the Social Market Economy: The Emergence of an Ideal and the Conditions for Its Realization' (2008) 45 *Common Market Law Review* 1335

Baetens F, '"No Deal Is Better Than a Bad Deal"? The Fallacy of the WTO Fall-Back Option as a Post-Brexit Safety Net' (2018) 55 *Common Market Law Review* 133

Balkin JM, 'Understanding Legal Understanding: The Legal Subject and the Problem of Legal Coherence' (1993) 103 *Yale Law Journal* 105

Baquero Cruz J, 'The Legacy of the Maastricht-Urteil and the Pluralist Movement' (2008) 14 *European Law Journal* 389

Barbé E and others, 'Drawing the Neighbours Closer . . . to What?' (2009) 44 *Cooperation and Conflict* 378

Barents R, 'The Internal Market Unlimited: Some Observations on the Legal Basis of Community Legislation' (1993) 30 *Common Market Law Review* 85

The Autonomy of Community Law (Kluwer Law International 2004)

Barnard C, 'Internal Market v. Labour Market: A Brief History' in M De Vos (ed.), *European Union Internal Market and Labour Law: Friends or Foes?* (Intersentia 2009) 19

EU Employment Law (Oxford University Press 2013)

The Substantive Law of the EU: The Four Freedoms (Oxford University Press 2013)

'The practicalities of leaving the EU' (2016) 41 *European Law Review* 484

Bates JDN, 'The Impact of Directives on Statutory Interpretation: Using the Euro-Meaning?' (1986) 7 *Statute Law Review* 174

Baudenbacher C, 'Between Homogeneity and Independence: The Legal Position of the EFTA Court in the European Economic Area' (1997) 3 *Columbia Journal of European Law* 169

'If Not EEA State Liability, Then What: Reflections Ten Years after the EFTA Court's Sveinbjornsdottir Ruling' (2009) 10 *Chicago Journal of International Law* 333

'The EFTA Court and the European Court' in P-C Müller-Graff and E Selvig (eds.), *EEA-EU Relations* (Berlin Verlag Arno Spitz 1999) 69

'The EFTA Court and Court of Justice of the European Union: Coming in Parts but Winning Together' in *The Court of Justice and the Construction of Europe: Analyses and Perspectives on Sixty Years of Case-law* (T.M.C. Asser Press 2013) 183

Baur G, 'From EU Law to EEA Law: the Decision-Making Process' (2015) EFTA Bulletin 18

Bebr G, 'The Relation of the European Coal and Steel Community Law to the Law of the Member States: A Peculiar Legal Symbiosis' (1958) 58 *Columbia Law Review* 767

Benöhr I, *EU Consumer Law and Human Rights* (Oxford University Press 2013)

Bercusson B, 'Democratic Legitimacy and European Labour Law' (1999) 28 *Industrial Law Journal* 153

European Labour Law (Cambridge University Press 2009)

Besselink LFM, *A Composite European Constitution* (Europa Law Publishing 2007)

Betlem G, 'The Doctrine of Consistent Interpretation—Managing Legal Uncertainty' (2002) 22 *Oxford Journal of Legal Studies* 397

Binder C, 'Does the Difference Make a Difference? A Comparison between the Mechanisms of the Law of Treaties and of State Responsibility as Means to Derogate from Treaty Obligations in Cases of Subsequent Changes of Circumstances' in M Szabó (ed.), *State Responsibility and the Law of Treaties* (Eleven International Publishing 2010) 1

Blockmans S and Van Vooren B, 'Revitalizing the European 'Neighbourhood Economic Community': The Case for Legally Binding Sectoral Multilateralism' (2012) 17 *European Foreign Affairs Review* 577

Boelaert-Suominen S, 'Non-EU Nationals and Council Directive 2003/109/EC on the Status of Third-Country Nationals Who Are Long-Term Residents: Five Paces Forward and Possibly Three Paces Back' (2005) 42 *Common Market Law Review* 1011

Bovenberg L, 'Unity Produces Diversity: The Economics of Europe's Social Capital' in W Arts and others (eds.), *The Cultural Diversity of European Identity* (Brill 2003) 403

Brand M, 'Divergence, Discretion, and Unity' in S Prechal and B van Roermund (eds.), *The Coherence of EU Law: The Search for Unity in Divergent Concepts* (Oxford University Press 2008) 217

Breidlid J and Vahl M, '20 Years on: Current and Future Challenges for the EEA' (2015) EFTA Bulletin 32

Breitenmoser S, 'Sectoral Agreements between the EC and Switzerland: Contents and Context' (2003) 40 *Common Market Law Review* 1137

Brinkhorst LJ, 'S.A.C.E. v. Ministry of Finance of the Italian Republic. Case 33/70.
Decision of December 17, 1970. Preliminary Ruling on Request of the
District Court of Brescia, Italy' (1971) 8 *Common Market Law Review* 384

Carrera S, 'What Does Free Movement Mean in Theory and Practice in an
Enlarged EU?' (2005) 11 *European Law Journal* 699

Chirico F and Larouche P, 'Conceptual Divergence, Functionalism, and the
Economics of Convergence' in S Prechal and B van Roermund (eds.), *The
Coherence of EU Law: The Search for Unity in Divergent Concepts* (Oxford University
Press 2008) 463

Christiansen T and Larsson T, 'Introduction: The Role of Committees in the
Policy-Process of the European Union' in T Christiansen and T Larsson (eds.),
The Role of Committees in the Policy-Process of the European Union (Edward Elgar
Publishing 2007) 1

Christodoulidis E and Dukes R, 'On the Unity of European Labour Law' in
S Prechal and B van Roermund (eds.), *The Coherence of EU Law: The Search for
Unity in Divergent Concepts* (Oxford University Press 2008) 397

Collins H, *Employment Law* (Oxford University Press 2010)

Contartese C, 'The Autonomy of the EU Legal Order in the ECJ's External
Relations Case Law: From the "Essential" to the "Specific Characteristics" of
the Union and Back Again' (2017) 54 *Common Market Law Review* 1627

Craig PP, 'Once More unto the Breach: The Community, the State and Damages
Liability' (1997) 113 *Law Quarterly Review* 67

'The Evolution of the Single Market' in C Barnard and J Scott (eds.), *The Law of
the Single European Market* (Hart Publishing 2002) 1

Crawford J, 'The System of International Responsibility' in J Crawford, A Pellet
and S Olleson (eds.), *The Law of International Responsibility* (Oxford University
Press 2010) 17

Brownlie's Principles of Public International Law (Oxford University Press 2012)

Cremona M, 'The "Dynamic and Homogeneous" EEA: Byzantine Structures and
Variable Geometry' (1994) 19 European Law Review 508

'The New Associations: Substantive Issues of the Europe Agreements with the
Central and Eastern European States' in SV Konstadinidis (ed.), *The Legal
Regulation of the European Community's External Relations after the Completion of
the Internal Market* (Dartmouth 1996) 141

'Enlargement: A Successful Instrument of Foreign Policy?' in T Tridimas and
P Nebbia (eds.), *European Union Law for the Twenty-First Century: Rethinking the
New Legal Order* (Hart Publishing 2004) 397

'The Union as a Global Actor: Roles, Models and Identity' (2004) 41 *Common
Market Law Review* 553

'Internal Differentiation and External Unity' in F Amtenbrink and others
(eds.), *The Internal Market and the Future of European Integration* (Cambridge
University Press 2019) 605

Cross R and Harris JW, *Precedent in English Law* (Oxford University Press 1991)

Curti Gialdino C, 'Some Reflections on the *Acquis Communautaire*' (1995) 32
Common Market Law Review 1089

Curtin D, 'Directives: The Effectiveness of Judicial Protection of Individual Rights' (1990) 27 *Common Market Law Review* 709

Damrosch LF, 'Role of the United States Senate Concerning Self-Executing and Non-Self-Executing Treaties' (1991) 67 *Chicago-Kent Law Review* 515

Dashwood A, 'The Principle of Direct Effect in European Community Law' (1977) 16 *Journal of Common Market Studies* 229

Davies G, *Nationality Discrimination in the European Internal Market* (Kluwer Law International 2003)

de Búrca G, 'Differentiation within the Core: The Case of the Common Market' in G de Búrca and J Scott (eds.), *Constitutional Change in the EU: From Uniformity to Flexibility?* (Hart Publishing 2000) 133

and Scott J, 'Introduction' in G De Búrca and J Scott (eds.), *Constitutional Change in the EU: From Uniformity to Flexibility?* (Hart Publishing 2000) 1

Delicostopoulos JS, 'Towards European Procedural Primacy in National Legal Systems' (2003) 9 *European Law Journal* 599

Denza E, 'The Relationship between International and National Law' in MD Evans (ed.), *International Law* (Oxford University Press 2006) 423

de Vries S, *Tensions within the Internal Market* (Europa Law Publishing 2006)

De Witte B, 'International Agreement or European Constitution?' in JA Winter and others (eds.), *Reforming the Treaty on European Union: The Legal Debate* (Kluwer Law International 1996) 3

'Non-market Values in Internal Market Legislation' in N Nic Shuibhne (ed.), *Regulating the Internal Market* (Edward Elgar Publishing 2006) 61

'A Selfish Court? The Court of Justice and the Design of International Dispute Settlement Beyond the European Union' in M Cremona and A Thies (eds.), *The European Court of Justice and External Relations Law: Constitutional Challenges* (Hart Publishing 2014) 33

Ott A and Vos E (eds.), *Between Flexibility and Disintegration: The Trajectory of Differentiation in EU Law* (Edward Elgar Publishing 2017)

Delcourt C, 'The Acquis Communautaire: Has the Concept Had Its Day?' (2001) 38 *Common Market Law Review* 829

Dewatripont M and others, *Flexible integration: Towards a More Effective and Democratic Europe* (Monitoring European Integration 1995)

Dhondt N, *Integration of Environmental Protection into Other EC Policies* (Europa Law Publishing 2003)

Dorssemont F, 'The Right to Take Collective Action *v.* Fundamental Economic Freedoms in the Aftermath of *Laval* and *Viking*' in M de Vos (ed.), *European Union Internal Market and Labour Law: Friends or Foes?* (Intersentia 2009) 45

Dougan M, 'The Treaty of Lisbon 2007: Winning minds, Not hearts' (2008) 45 *Common Market Law Review* 617

'An Airbag for the Crash Test Dummies? EU-UK Negotiations for a Post-Withdrawal "Status Quo" Transitional Regime under Article 50 TEU' (2018) 55 *Common Market Law Review* 57

Edwards G and Philippart E, *Flexibility and the Treaty of Amsterdam: Europe's New Byzantium?* (1997) CELS Occasional Paper No. 3

Eeckhout P, 'Opinion 2/13 on EU Accession to the ECHR and Judicial Dialogue: Autonomy or Autarky?' (2015) 38 *Fordham International Law Journal* 955

Egeberg M and Trondal J, 'Differentiated Integration in Europe: The Case of EEA Country, Norway' (1999) 37 *Journal of Common Market Studies* 133

Ehlermann CD, 'How Flexible is Community Law? An Unusual Approach to the Concept of "Two Speeds"' (1984) 82 *Michigan Law Review* 1274

Evans MD, *International Law* (Oxford University Press 2014)

Farnsworth EA, 'On Trying to Keep One's Promises: The Duty of Best Efforts in Contract Law' (1984) 46 *University of Pittsburgh Law Review* 1

Forwood G, 'The Road to Cotonou: Negotiating a Successor to Lomé' (2001) 39 *Journal of Common Market Studies* 423

Franssen E and Jacobs ATJM, 'The Question of Representativity in the European Social Dialogue' (1998) 35 *Common Market Law Review* 1295

Gaudissart MA and Sinnaeve A, 'The Role of the White Paper in the Preparation of the Eastern Enlargement' in M Maresceau (ed.), *Enlarging the European Union* (Longman 1997) 41

Gordon E, 'The World Court and the Interpretation of Constitutive Treaties: Some Observations on the Development of an International Constitutional Law' (1965) 59 *American Journal of International Law* 794

Govaere I, 'The Future Direction of the EU Internal Market: On Vested Values and Fashionable Modernism' (2009) 16 *Columbia Journal of European Law* 67

Grabitz B and Langeheine E, 'Legal Problems Related to a Proposed "Two-Tier System" of Integration within the European Community' (1981) 18 *Common Market Law Review* 33

Grant JAC, 'The Search for Uniformity of Law' (1938) 32 *The American Political Science Review* 1082

Graver HP, 'The Efta Court and the Court of Justice of the EC: Legal Homogeneity at Stake?' in P-C Müller-Graff and E Selvig (eds.), *EEA-EU Relations* (Berlin Verlag Arno Spitz 1999) 31

Halberstam D, '"It's the Autonomy, Stupid!" A Modest Defense of *Opinion 2/13* on EU Accession to the ECHR, and the Way Forward' (2015) 16 *German Law Journal* 105

Hanf D, 'Flexibility Clauses in the Founding Treaties, from Rome to Nice' in B De Witte, D Hanf and E Vos (eds.), *The Many Faces of Differentiation in EU Law* (Intersentia 2001) 3

   and Dengler P, 'Accords d'association' (2004) College of Europe Research Papers in Law 2004/1

   'The ENP in the Light of the New "Neighbourhood Clause" (Article 8 TEU)' (2011) College of Europe Research Papers in Law 2/2011

Hartley TC, 'The European Court and the EEA' (1992) 41 *International and Comparative Law Quarterly* 841

   The Foundations of European Union Law (Oxford University Press 2014)

Haukeland Fredriksen H, 'One Market, Two Courts: Legal Pluralism vs. Homogeneity in the European Economic Area' (2010) 79 *Nordic Journal of International Law* 481

'The EFTA Court 15 Years on' (2010) 59 *International and Comparative Law Quarterly* 731

'Bridging the Widening Gap between the EU Treaties and the Agreement on the European Economic Area' (2012) 18 *European Law Journal* 868

and Franklin CNK, 'Of Pragmatism and Principles: The EEA Agreement 20 Years On' (2015) 52 *Common Market Law Review* 629

'The EFTA Court' in R Howse and others (eds.), *The Legitimacy of International Trade Courts and Tribunals* (Cambridge University Press 2018) 138

Hession M and Macrory R, 'Balancing Trade Freedom with the Requirements of Sustainable Development' in N Emilou and D O'Keeffe (eds.), *The European Union and World Trade Law: After the GATT Uruguay Round* (John Wiley & Sons 1996) 181

Hillion C, 'Case C-265/03, *Igor Simutenkov v. Ministerio de Educación y Cultura, Real Federación Española de Fútbol*' (2008) 45 *Common Market Law Review* 815

'Anatomy of EU Norm Export towards the Neighbourhood: The Impact of Article 8 TEU', in P Van Elsuwege and R Petrov, *Legislative Approximation and Application of EU Law in the Eastern Neighbourhood of the European Union* (Routledge 2014) 13

Hofmann B, Jevnaker T and Thaler P, 'Following, Challenging, or Shaping: Can Third Countries Influence EU Energy Policy?' (2019) 7 *Politics and Governance* 152

Hofmann HCH and Türk AH, 'Policy implementation' in HCH Hofmann and AH Türk (eds.), *EU Administrative Governance* (Edward Elgar Publishing 2006) 74

Holzinger K, Knill C and Schäfer A, 'Rhetoric or Reality? 'New Governance' in EU Environmental Policy' (2006) 12 *European Law Journal* 403

Iwasawa Y, 'The Doctrine of Self-Executing Treaties in the United States: A Critical Analysis' (1985) 26 *Virginia Journal of International Law* 627

Jans JH, 'EU Environmental Policy and the Civil Society' in JH Jans (ed.), *The European Convention and the Future of European Environmental Law* (Europa Law Publishing 2003) 53

'Stop the Integration Principle?' (2009) 33 *Fordham International Law Journal* 1533

Jarrosson C, *La notion d'arbitrage* (Librairie Générale de Droit et de Jurisprudence 1987)

Jennings RY, 'Treaties' in M Bedjaoui (ed.), *International Law: Achievements and Prospects* (Martinus Nijhoff Publishers 1991) 135

Jordan A and others, 'European Governance and the Transfer of 'New' Environmental Policy Instruments (NEPIs) in the European Union' (2003) 81 *Public Administration* 555

Jørgensen KE, 'The Social Construction of the Acquis Communautaire: A Cornerstone of the European Edifice' (1999) 3 *European Integration online Papers* http://eiop.or.at/eiop/texte/1999-005a.htm accessed 10 February 2020

Kälin W, 'The EEA Agreement and the European Convention for the Protection of Human Rights' (1992) 3 *European Journal of International Law* 341

Kapteyn PJG and VerLoren van Themaat P, *The Law of the European Union and the European Communities* (Kluwer Law International 2008)

Keller B and Sörries B, 'The New European Social Dialogue: Old Wine in New Bottles?' (1999) 9 *Journal of European Social Policy* 111

Kilpatrick C, 'The Future of Remedies in Europe' in C Kilpatrick, T Novitz and P Skidmore (eds.), *The Future of Remedies in Europe* (Hart Publishing 2000) 1

Klamert M, 'The Autonomy of the EU (and of EU Law): Through the Kaleidoscope' (2017) 42 *European Law Review* 815

Komárek J, 'Federal Elements in the Community Judicial System: Building Coherence in the Community Legal Order' (2005) 42 *Common Market Law Review* 9

'Czech Constitutional Court Playing with Matches: the Czech Constitutional Court Declares a Judgment of the Court of Justice of the EU *Ultra Vires*; Judgment of 31 January 2012, Pl. ÚS 5/12, *Slovak Pensions XVII*' (2012) 8 *European Constitutional Law Review* 323

Koutrakos P, 'More on Autonomy – Opinion 1/17 (CETA)' (2019) 44 *European Law Review* 293

Krämer L, 'Giving a Voice to the Environment by Challenging the Practice of Integrating Environmental Requirements into Other EU policies' in S Kingston (ed.), *European Perspectives on Environmental Law and Governance* (Routledge 2013) 83

Kratochwil F and Ruggie JG, 'International Organization: A State of the Art on an Art of the State' (1986) 40 *International Organization* 753

Kristjánsson S and Kristjánsson R, 'Delegation and Accountability in an Ambiguous System: Iceland and the European Economic Area (EEA)' (2000) 6 *The Journal of Legislative Studies* 105

Kronenberger V, 'Does the EFTA Court Interpret the EEA Agreement as If It Were the EC Treaty? Some Questions Raised by the Restamark Judgment' (1996) 45 *International and Comparative Law Quarterly* 198

Kuijper PJ, 'Customary International Law, Decisions of International Organisations and Other Techniques for Ensuring Respect for International Legal Rules in European Community Law' in J Wouters, A Nollkaemper and E de Wet (ed.), *The Europeanisation of International Law* (T.M.C. Asser Press 2008) 87

Kux S and Sverdrup U, 'Fuzzy Borders and Adaptive Outsiders: Norway, Switzerland and the EU' (2000) 22 *Journal of European Integration* 237

Lane R, 'The Internal Market and the Individual' in N Nic Shuibhne (ed.), *Regulating the Internal Market* (Edward Elgar Publishing 2006) 245

Larsson T and Murk J, 'The Commission's relations with Expert Advisory Groups' in T Christiansen and T Larsson (eds.), *The Role of Committees in the Policy-Process of the European Union* (Edward Elgar Publishing 2007) 64

Lauterpacht H, 'Restrictive Interpretation and the Principle of Effectiveness in the Interpretation of Treaties' (1949) 26 *British Yearbook of International Law* 48

Lavenex S, 'EU External Governance in 'Wider Europe'' (2004) 11 *Journal of European Public Policy* 680

'Concentric Circles of Flexible 'EUropean' Integration: A Typology of EU External Governance Relations' (2011) 9 *Comparative European Politics* 372

Lehmkuhl D and Wichmann N, 'Modes of External Governance: A Cross-national and Cross-sectoral Comparison' (2009) 16 *Journal of European Public Policy* 813

Lazowski A, 'Box of Chocolates Integration: The European Economic Area and the Swiss Models Revisited' in S Blockmans and S Prechal (eds.), *Reconciling the Deepening and Widening of the European Union* (T.M.C. Asser Press 2007) 87

Lecomte F, 'Embedding Employment Rights in Europe' (2010) 17 *Columbia Journal of European Law* 1

Lenaerts K, 'The Rule of Law and the Coherence of the Judicial System of the European Union' (2007) 44 *Common Market Law Review* 1625

Lenski E, 'Turkey (including Northern Cyprus)' in S Blockmans and A Łazowski (eds.), *The European Union and Its Neighbours: A Legal Appraisal of the EU's Policies of Stabilisation, Partnership and Integration* (T.M.C. Asser Press 2006) 283

Levenbook BB, 'The Role of Coherence in Legal Reasoning' (1984) 3 *Law and Philosophy* 355

Levy MA, Young OR and Zürn M, 'The Study of International Regimes' (1995) 1 *European Journal of International Relations* 267

Leczykiewicz D, 'Effectiveness of EU Law before National Courts: Direct Effect, Effective Judicial Protection, and State Liability' in A Arnull and D Chalmers (eds.), *Oxford Handbook of European Union Law* (Oxford University Press 2015) 212

Lock T, 'Walking on a Tightrope: The Draft ECHR Accession Agreement and the Autonomy of the EU Legal Order' (2011) 48 *Common Market Law Review* 1025

Macrory R, *Regulation, Enforcement and Governance in Environmental Law* (Oxford University Press 2014)

Magen A, 'Transformative Engagement through Law: The Acquis Communautaire as an Instrument of EU External Influence' (2007) 9 *European Journal of Law Reform* 361

Magnusson S, 'On the Authority of Advisory Opinions' (2010) 13 *Europarättslig Tidskrift* 528

'Judicial Homogeneity in the European Economic Area and the Authority of the EFTA Court. Some Remarks on an Article by Halvard Haukeland Fredriksen' (2011) 80 *Nordic Journal of International Law* 507

'Procedural Homogeneity v. Inconsistency of European Courts - Comments on Order of the EFTA Court President of 15 June 2012 in Case E-16/11 EFTA Surveillance Authority V. Iceland' (2012) http://papers.ssrn.com/sol3/papers .cfm?abstract_id=2140717 accessed 10 February 2020

and Hannesson ÓÍ, 'State Liability in EEA Law: Towards Parallelism or Homogeneity?' (2013) 38 *European Law Review* 167

Majone G, 'The New European Agencies: Regulation by Information' (1997) 4 *Journal of European Public Policy* 262

Mangiameli S, 'The Union's Homogeneity and Its Common Values in the Treaty on European Union' in H-J Blanke and S Mangiameli (eds.), *The European Union after Lisbon* (Springer 2012) 21

Maresceau M, 'Pre-accession' in M Cremona (ed.), *The Enlargement of the European Union* (Oxford University Press 2003) 9

    and Montaguti E, 'The Relations between the European Union and Central and Eastern Europe: A Legal Appraisal' (1995) 32 *Common Market Law Review* 1327

Mather JD, 'The Court of Justice and the Union Citizen' (2005) 11 *European Law Journal* 722

Mayer FC, 'Supremacy - Lost? Comment on Roman Kwiecien' in P Dann and M Rynkowski (eds.), *The Unity of the European Constitution* (Springer 2006) 87

    'Van Gend en Loos: The Foundation of a Community of Law' in M Poiares Maduro and L Azoulai (eds.), *The Past and Future of EU Law* (Hart Publishing 2010) 16

McGee A and Weatherill S, 'The Evolution of the Single Market - Harmonisation or Liberalisation' (1990) 53 *The Modern Law Review* 578

McIntyre O, 'The Integration Challenge: Integrating Environmental Concerns into Other EU Policies' in S Kingston (ed.), *European Perspectives on Environmental Law and Governance* (Routledge 2013) 125

More G, 'The Principle of Equal Treatment: From Market Unifier to Fundamental Right?' in P Craig and G de Búrca (eds.), *The Evolution of EU Law* (Oxford University Press 1999) 517

Morgenstern F, 'Judicial Practice and the Supremacy of International Law' (1950) 27 *British Yearbook of International Law* 42

Mortelmans K, 'The Common Market, the Internal Market and the Single Market, What's in a Market?' (1998) 35 *Common Market Law Review* 101

Müller-Graff PC, 'Legal Framework for Relations between the European Union and Central and Eastern Europe: General aspects' in M Maresceau (ed.), *Enlarging the European Union* (Longman 1997) 27

Norberg S and others, *The European Economica Area: A Commentary on the EEA Agreement* (Fritzes 1993)

    'The European Economic Area' in PJ Oliver (ed.), *Oliver on Free Movement of Goods in the European Union* (Hart Publishing 2010) 487

Nugent N, *The European Commission* (Palgrave Macmillan 2001)

Nowag J, *Environmental Integration in Competition and Free-Movement Laws* (Oxford University Press 2016)

Öberg M-L, 'Third Countries in EU Agencies: Participation and Influence' in HCH Hofmann, E Vos and M Chamon (eds.), *The External Dimension of EU Agencies and Bodies* (Edward Elgar 2019) 204

O'Connell DP, *International Law* (Stevens & Sons 1970)

O'Leary S, 'Developing an Ever Closer Union between the Peoples of Europe? A Reappraisal of the Case Law of the Court of Justice on the Free Movement of Persons and EU Citizenship' (2008) 27 *Yearbook of European Law* 167

    'Free movement of persons and services' in P Craig and G de Búrca (eds.), *The Evolution of EU Law* (Oxford University Press 2011) 499

Oliver PJ (ed.), *Oliver on Free Movement of Goods in the European Union* (Hart Publishing 2010)

Opsahl T, 'An International Constitutional Law?' (1961) 10 *International and Comparative Law Quarterly* 760

Paasivirta E and Kuijper PJ, 'Does One Size Fit All?: The European Community and the Responsibility of International Organizations' (2005) 36 *Netherlands Yearbook of International Law* 169

Payandeh M, 'Constitutional Review of EU Law after *Honeywell*: Contextualizing the Relationship between the German Constitutional Court and the EU Court of Justice' (2011) 48 *Common Market Law Review* 9

Pelkmans J and Böhler P, 'The EEA Review and Liechtenstein's Integration Strategy' (2013) *Centre for European Policy Studies*

Pérez Crespo MJ, 'After Brexit . . . The Best of Both Worlds? Rebutting the Norwegian and Swiss Models as Long-Term Options for the UK' (2017) 36 *Yearbook of European Law* 94

Pernice I, 'Multilevel Constitutionalism and the Treaty of Amsterdam: European Constitution-Making Revisited' (1999) 36 *Common Market Law Review* 703

Pescatore P, *The Law of Integration* (Sijthoff 1974)
　'Aspects judiciaires de l'«acquis communautaire»' (1981) 20 Revue trimestrielle de droit européen 617
　'The Doctrine of "Direct Effect": An Infant Disease of Community Law' (1983) 8 *European Law Review* 155
　'Public and Private Aspects of European Community Competition Law' (1986) 10 *Fordham International Law Journal* 373

Petersmann E-U, 'Human Rights, International Economic Law and "Constitutional Justice"' (2008) 19 *European Journal of International Law* 769

Petrov R, *Exporting the Acquis Communautaire through European Union External Agreements* (Nomos 2011)

Prechal S, *Directives in EC law* (Oxford University Press 2006)

Reich N, 'The Constitutional Relevance of Citizenship and Free Movement in an Enlarged Union' (2005) 11 *European Law Journal* 675

Reymond C, 'Institutions, Decision-Making Procedure and Settlement of Disputes in the European Economic Area' (1993) 30 *Common Market Law Review* 449

Rhodes M, 'A Regulatory Conundrum: Industrial Relations and the Social Dimension' in S Leibfried and P Pierson (eds.), *European Social Policy: Between Fragmentation and Integration* (The Brookings Institution 1995) 78

Rognstad O-A, 'The Conflict between Internal Market and Third Country Policy Considerations in the EEA. Maglite Vs. Silhouette' in P-C Müller-Graff and E Selvig (eds.), *EEA-EU Relations* (Berlin Verlag Arno Spitz 1999) 131

Rogoff MA, 'Interpretation of International Agreements by Domestic Courts and the Politics of International Treaty Relations: Reflections on Some Recent Decisions of the United States Supreme Court' (1996) 11 *American University Journal of International Law and Policy* 559

Ruffert M, 'Rights and Remedies in European Community Law: A Comparative View' (1997) 34 *Common Market Law Review* 307

Sacco R, 'Diversity and Uniformity in the Law' (2001) 49 *American Journal of Comparative Law* 171

Sacerdoti G, 'The Prospects: The UK Trade Regime with the EU and the World' in F Fabbrini (ed.), *The Law & Politics of Brexit* (Oxford University Press 2017)

Sauter W, 'The Economic Constitution of the European Union' (1998) 4 *Columbia Journal of European Law* 27

Schaefer GF and Türk A, 'The Role of Implementing Committees' in T Christiansen and T Larsson (eds.), *The Role of Committees in the Policy-Process of the European Union* (Edward Elgar Publishing 2007) 182

Schilling T, 'The Autonomy of the Community Legal Order: An Analysis of Possible Foundations' (1996) 37 *Harvard International Law Journal* 389

Schimmelfennig F, 'Brexit: Differentiated Disintegration in the European Union' (2018) 25 *Journal of European Public Policy* 1154

Schweitzer H, 'Services of General Economic Interest: European Law's Impact on the Role of Markets and of the Member States' in M Cremona (ed.), *Market Integration and Public Services in the European Union* (Oxford University Press 2011) 11

Schwok R, *Switzerland–European Union: An Impossible Membership?* (P.I.E. Peter Lang 2009)

Scott J, *EC Environmental Law* (Longman 1998)

and Trubek DM, 'Mind the Gap: Law and New Approaches to Governance in the European Union' (2002) 8 *European Law Journal* 1

Senden L, 'Conceptual Convergence and Judicial Cooperation in Sex Equality Law' in S Prechal and G van Roermund (eds.), *The Coherence of EU Law: The Search for Unity in Divergent Concepts* (Oxford University Press 2008) 363

Shaw J, 'Relating Constitutionalism and Flexibility in the European Union' in G de Búrca and J Scott (eds.), *Constitutional Change in the EU: From Uniformity to Flexibility?* (Hart Publishing 2000) 337

Shaw MN, *International Law* (Cambridge University Press 2014)

Simma B and Tams CJ, 'Reacting against Treaty Breaches' in DB Hollis (ed.), *The Oxford Guide to Treaties* (Oxford University Press 2012) 576

Sloss D, 'Domestic Application of Treaties' in DB Hollis (ed.), *The Oxford Guide to Treaties* (Oxford University Press 2012) 367

Smismans S, 'EU Employment Policy: Decentralisation or Centralisation through the Open Method of Coordination?' (2004) *EUI Working Paper LAW* 2004/1 https://cadmus.eui.eu/bitstream/handle/1814/1881/law04-1.pdf?seq uence=1&isAllowed=y accessed 10 February 2020

Spiermann O, 'The Other Side of the Story: An Unpopular Essay on the Making of the European Community Legal Order' (1999) 10 *European Journal of International Law* 763

Stubb A, 'A Categorization of Differentiated Integration' (1996) 34 *Journal of Common Market Studies* 283

Sturley MF, 'International Uniform Laws in National Courts: The Influence of Domestic Laws in Conflicts of Interpretation' (1986) 27 *Virginia Journal of International Law* 729

Tovias A, 'Exploring the 'Pros' and 'Cons' of Swiss and Norwegian Models of Relations with the European Union - What Can Israel Learn from the Experiences of These Two Countries?' (2006) 41 *Cooperation and Conflict* 203

Toth AG, 'The Authority of Judgments of the European Court of Justice: Binding Force and Legal Effects' (1984) 4 *Yearbook of European Law* 1

Tridimas T, 'Horizontal Effect of Directives: A Missed Opportunity?' (1994) 19 *European Law Review* 621

The General Principles of EU Law (Oxford University Press 2006)

Trondal J, Murdoch Z and Geys B, 'On Trojan Horses and Revolving Doors: Assessing the Autonomy of National Officials in the European Commission' (2015) 54 *European Journal of Political Research* 249

Trubek DM and Trubek LG, 'Hard and Soft Law in the Construction of Social Europe: The Role of the Open Method of Co-ordination' (2005) 11 *European Law Journal* 343

Tuytschaever F, *Differentiation in European Union Law* (Hart Publishing 1999)

van Gerven W, 'The Genesis of EEA Law and the Principles of Primacy and Direct Effect' (1992) 16 *Fordham International Law Journal* 955

'Non-Contractual Liability of Member States, Community Institutions and Individuals for Breaches of Community Law with a View to a Common Law for Europe' (1994) 1 *Maastricht Journal of European and Comparative Law* 6

'Of Rights, Remedies and Procedures' (2000) 37 *Common Market Law Review* 501

Van der Loo G, Van Elsuwege P and Petrov R, 'The EU-Ukraine Association Agreement: Assessment of an Innovative Legal Instrument', *EUI Working Papers LAW* 2014/09 https://cadmus.eui.eu/bitstream/handle/1814/32031/LAW%20_WP_2014_9%20.pdf?sequence=1&isAllowed=y accessed 10 February 2020

The EU-Ukraine Association Agreement and Deep and Comprehensive Free Trade Area (Brill 2016)

'The EU's Association Agreements and DCFTAs with Ukraine, Moldova and Georgia: A Comparative Study' (2017) *CEPS Special Report* https://3dcftas.eu /publications/a-comparative-study-of-the-aa-and-dcftas-concluded-with-ua-mo-and-ge accessed 10 February 2020

Van Elsuwege P and Petrov R, 'Article 8 TEU: Towards a New Generation of Agreements with the Neighbouring Countries of the European Union?' (2011) 36 *European Law Review* 688

and Chamon M, 'The Meaning of 'Association' under EU Law' (2019) Study Commissioned by the European Parliament's Policy Department for Citizens' Rights and Constitutional Affairs www.europarl.europa.eu/think tank/en/document.html?reference=IPOL_STU%282019%29608861 accessed 10 February 2020

Van Harten G and Loughlin M, 'Investment Treaty Arbitration as a Species of Global Administrative Law' (2006) 17 *European Journal of International Law* 121

van Stiphout T, 'Homogeneity vs. Decision-Making Autonomy in the EEA
    Agreement' (2007) 9 *European Journal of Law Reform* 431
    'The L'Oréal Cases – Some Thoughts on the Role of the EFTA Court in the EEA
    Legal Framework: Because It Is Worth It!' (2009) 1 *Jus & News* 7
Verhoeven M, 'The 'Costanzo Obligation' of National Administrative Authorities
    in the Light of the Principle of Legality: Prodigy or Problem Child?' (2009) 5
    Croatian Yearbook of European Law and Policy 65
VerLoren van Themaat P, 'The Contributions to the Establishment of the
    Internal Market by the Case-Law of the Court of Justice of the European
    Communities' in R Bieber and others (eds.), 1992: *One European Market?*
    (Nomos 1988) 109
von Bogdandy A, 'The Legal Case for Unity: The European Union as a Single
    Organization with a Single Legal System' (1999) 36 *Common Market Law
    Review* 887
    'The European Union as a Human Rights Organization? Human Rights and the
    Core of the European Union' (2000) 37 *Common Market Law Review* 1307
    'Doctrine of Principles' (2003) Jean Monnet Working Paper 9/03
    'Founding Principles' in A von Bogdandy and J Bast (eds.), *Principles of European
    Constitutional Law* (Hart Publishing 2009) 11
    'Founding Principles of EU Law: A Theoretical and Doctrinal Sketch' (2010) 16
    European Law Journal 95
von Homeyer I, 'The Evolution of EU Environmental Governance' in J Scott (ed.),
    Environmental Protection (Oxford University Press 2009) 1
von Wogau K, 'Completing the European Home Market by 2009' (2003) 38
    Intereconomics 63
Walker N, 'Sovereignty and Differentiated Integration in the European Union'
    (1998) 4 *European Law Journal* 355
Waters MA, 'Creeping Monism: The Judicial Trend toward Interpretive
    Incorporation of Human Rights Treaties' (2007) 107 *Columbia Law Review* 628
Wattel PJ, '*Köbler, CILFIT* and *Welthgrove*: We Can't Go on Meeting Like This'
    (2004) 41 *Common Market Law Review* 177
Weatherill S, 'On the Depth and Breadth of European Integration' (1997) 17
    Oxford Journal of Legal Studies 537
    'Safeguarding the *Acquis Communautaire*' in T Heukels, N Blokker and M Brus
    (eds.), *The European Union after Amsterdam* (Kluwer Law International
    1998) 153
    'New Strategies for Managing the EC's Internal Market' (2000) 53 *Current Legal
    Problems* 595
    'Supply of and Demand for Internal Market Regulation: Strategies,
    Preferences and Interpretation' in N Nic Shuibhne (ed.), *Regulating the
    Internal Market* (Edward Elgar Publishing 2006) 29
    EU Consumer Law and Policy (Edward Elgar Publishing 2013)
    'The Several Internal Markets' (2017) 36 *Yearbook of European Law* 125
Weil P, 'Towards Relative Normativity in International Law' (1983) 77 *American
    Journal of International Law* 413

Weiler JHH, 'The Reformation of European Constitutionalism' (1997) 35 *Journal of Common Market Studies* 97

and Haltern UR, 'The Autonomy of the Community Legal Order—Through the Looking Glass' (1996) 37 *Harvard International Law Journal* 411

Weiss EB, 'Invoking State Responsibility in the Twenty-first Century' (2002) 96 *American Journal of International Law* 798

Westphal K, 'Energy Policy between Multilateral Governance and Geopolitics: Whither Europe?' (2006) 4 *Internationale Politik und Gesellschaft* 44

Wind M, 'Brexit and Euroskepticism' in F Fabbrini (ed.), *The Law & Politics of Brexit* (Oxford University Press 2017) 221

Winter JA, 'Direct Applicability and Direct Effect: Two Distinct and Different Concepts in Community Law' (1972) 9 *Common Market Law Review* 425

Wouters J, 'Constitutional Limits of Differentiation: The Principle of Equality' in B De Witte, D Hanf and E Vos (eds.), *The Many Faces of Differentiation in EU Law* (Intersentia 2001) 301

Wurzel RKW, Zito AR and Jordan AJ, *Environmental Governance in Europe* (Edward Elgar Publishing 2013)

Young OR, 'Regime Dynamics: The Rise and Fall of International Regimes' in SD Krasner (ed.), *International Regimes* (Cornell University Press 1983) 93

Index